The Politics of Big Data

Big Data, gathered together and reanalysed, can be used to form endless variations of our persons – so-called 'data doubles'. While never a precise portrayal of who we are, they unarguably contain glimpses of details about us that, when deployed into various routines (such as management, policing, and advertising) can affect us in many ways.

How are we to deal with Big Data? When is it beneficial to us? When is it harmful? How might we regulate it? Offering careful and critical analyses, this timely volume aims to broaden well-informed, unprejudiced discourse, focusing on: the tenets of Big Data; the politics of governance and regulation; and Big Data practices, performance, and resistance.

An interdisciplinary volume, *The Politics of Big Data* will appeal to undergraduate and postgraduate students, as well as post-doctoral and senior researchers interested in fields such as Technology, Politics, and Surveillance.

Ann Rudinow Sætnan is Professor of Sociology at the Norwegian University of Science and Technology, Trondheim, Norway.

Ingrid Schneider is Professor of Political Science in the Centre for Ethics in Information Technologies at the Department of Informatics at the University of Hamburg, Germany.

Nicola Green is a Research Fellow with the Openlab in the School of Computing, Newcastle University, UK.

Routledge Research in Information Technology and Society

www.routledge.com/Routledge-Research-in-Information-Technology-and-Society/book-series/SE0448

The Politics of Big Data

Big Data, Big Brother?

**Edited by Ann Rudinow Sætnan,
Ingrid Schneider, and Nicola Green**

Routledge
Taylor & Francis Group

LONDON AND NEW YORK

First published 2018
by Routledge
2 Park Square, Milton Park, Abingdon, Oxon OX14 4RN

and by Routledge
711 Third Avenue, New York, NY 10017

Routledge is an imprint of the Taylor & Francis Group, an informa business

British Library Cataloguing-in-Publication Data
A catalogue record for this book is available from the British Library

Library of Congress Cataloging-in-Publication Data
A catalog record for this book has been requested

ISBN: 978-1-138-29374-8 (hbk)
ISBN: 978-1-315-23193-8 (ebk)

Typeset in Times New Roman
by Wearset Ltd, Boldon, Tyne and Wear

Contents

PART IV
Postscript   319

Contributors

Rocco Bellanova is a Post-doctoral Researcher at the University of Amsterdam, The Netherlands. His research focuses on data-driven surveillance practices and their relation to data protection and privacy. His work sits at the intersection of politics, law and science and technology studies. He studies how data are discursively and materially transformed into building blocks of actionable knowledge, legal evidence, or statistical measurement. He has notably carried out research on border security and intelligence-led policing practices. Currently, he is testing the possibility of working with images, such as wildlife pictures, pop culture shows, or workflow representations, to better grasp surveillance politics.

Julia Fleischhack is a Post-doctoral Fellow in Cultural Anthropology at the Georg-August-University of Göttingen, Germany. She received her PhD in Anthropology from Zurich University in 2012 and held fellowships at Hamburg University and MIT. Her research areas cover computer- and Internet-related issues and ethnographic methods. Fleischhack's latest book was on *Eine Welt im Datenrausch. Computeranlagen und Datenmengen als gesellschaftliche Herausforderung (1965–1975)* (2016). Her recent ethnographic research explores the work of 'digital literacy initiatives' in Germany and how their members discuss and teach a safe and sovereign Internet use amongst young people and children.

Gloria González Fuster is a Research Professor at the Vrije Universiteit Brussel's Faculty of Law and Criminology. Member of the Law, Science, Technology and Society Research Group and of the Brussels Privacy Hub, she investigates legal issues related to privacy, personal data protection, and security, in addition to lecturing on European Union fundamental rights. She is currently contributing to several European research projects revolving around data and the rights of individuals, touching upon issues such as cybersecurity, access to data in cross-border criminal investigations, and research integrity and scientific misconduct. Her research addresses the many frictions between human rights and *datafication*, and encompasses a reflection about the multifaceted connections between music, sound, law, and surveillance. She has an academic background in Law, Communication Sciences, and Modern Languages and Literature.

Nicola Green is a Research Fellow with the Openlab in the School of Computing, Newcastle University. Her training is in interdisciplinary social sciences, being a sociologist by trade, and an interdisciplinary researcher by inclination. Her background has run the gamut of Social Sciences, HCI, Science and Technology Studies, Media and Cultural Studies, and Surveillance Studies; all intersecting via projects on digital media technologies and/or sustainabilities of various sorts. Her interest in Big Data is especially in terms of the normative generation and use of Big Data across devices and systems, including data sharing, and ethical informational ownership and control. Previous projects have explored: issues of embodiment, identity, organisation and discourse in virtual reality technologies; mobile technologies and everyday mobilities; the organisation and regulation of mobile data and dimensions of trust, risk and privacy; the social dimensions of lifestyles, values and environment; the water, energy and food nexus in domestic settings in respect of resource use and consumption; and the methodological dimensions of the study of digital technologies (particularly in respect of ethnographic, mixed, feminist, and participatory methods).

Nuno Amaral Jerónimo is Professor of Sociology of Culture and Communication, and Sociology of Consumption and Fashion at the University of Beira Interior, Covilhã, Portugal. He is a researcher at the institute LabCom.IFP-UBI. His PhD studied how comedians uncover reality through humorous discourses, and his research interests also cover the effects of digital exposure and transparency in people's daily life.

Tobias Matzner is Professor of Media Studies at Paderborn University, Germany. He has studied computer science and philosophy in Karlsruhe, Rome, and Berlin and holds a PhD in philosophy from the Karlsruhe Institute of Technology. His research interests lie at the intersections of theorising technology and politics. In particular, he deals with the interdependence of information technology and fundamental political concepts like subjectivity, agency, privacy, or autonomy.

Merel Noorman is a philosopher of technology at Maastricht University, The Netherlands. She has a background in artificial intelligence and science and technology studies. Her research interests centre on the ethics of complex computational technologies, and in particular on the distribution of responsibility around these technologies.

Carsten Ochs is a Post-doctoral Researcher at the Sociological Theory Department, University of Kassel, who studies digitisation processes from an STS perspective. His current focus is on privacy issues and data economies. He is author of *Digitale Glokalisierung* (2013) and numerous relevant papers.

Frank Pasquale is Professor of Law at the University of Maryland, USA. He researches the law and policy of Big Data, artificial intelligence, and algorithms. He is a co-founder of the Association for the Promotion of Political

Economy and Law (APPEAL). He is the author of *The Black Box Society* (Harvard University Press 2015). The book developed a social theory of reputation, search, and finance, which has recently been elaborated in articles including 'Two Narratives of Platform Capitalism'. He is now at work on a book tentatively titled *Laws of Robotics: Revitalizing Professions in an Era of Automation* (under contract to Harvard University Press).

Gernot Rieder is a PhD fellow at the IT University of Copenhagen, Denmark. His dissertation investigates the rise of Big Data in public policy and the social, ethical, and epistemological implications of data-driven decision-making. Gernot serves as an assistant editor for the journal *Big Data & Society*.

Ann Rudinow Sætnan is Professor of Sociology at the Norwegian University of Science and Technology, Trondheim, Norway. Her research has spanned over a number of empirical fields, primarily working conditions and organisation of work, gender, medical technologies, and surveillance. Earlier co-edited volumes are *Bodies of Technology – Women's Involvement with Reproductive Medicine* (together with Nellie Oudshoorn and Marta Kirejczyk, 2000) and *The Mutual Construction of Statistics and Society* (together with Heidi Mork Lomell and Svein Hammer, 2011).

Ingrid Schneider is Professor of Political Science and works in the Centre for Ethics in Information Technologies at the Department of Informatics at the University of Hamburg, Germany. She has worked on technology assessment and ELSI/STS studies for two decades, and advised various Parliaments and the European Commission on policy issues. She researches the relationship between Big Data, digitalisation and democracy, law, governance and regulation in the information age, and intellectual property rights on digital goods.

Maria João Simões is Professor of Sociology of Science and Technology, at the University of Beira Interior (UBI), Covilhã, Portugal, and Researcher at the Interdisciplinary Centre of Social Sciences (CICS.NOVA.UMinho) and LabCom.IFP. Her research interests embrace surveillance, political participation, gender and technology, and technological innovation and sustainable development.

Stefan Strauß is a Post-doctoral Researcher at the Institute of Technology Assessment (ITA) at the Austrian Academy of Sciences in Vienna, Austria, with a degree in business informatics/information systems. He explores the interplay between ICTs and society with particular focus on policy and governance issues, the implications of ICTs on political processes, identity construction, security, surveillance, and privacy. Further research interests include information- and computer ethics and the philosophy of information. Stefan has been involved in a number of European research projects, for example, on the nexus between privacy, security and surveillance, identity management, cloud computing and social networks, e-democracy, security, and vulnerability of critical infrastructures. He has authored a number of pub-lications, recently on e-democracy in Europe, the societal implications of big data, privacy impact assessment, and the trade-off between privacy and security.

Thordis Sveinsdottir is Senior Research Analyst at Trilateral Research Ltd, UK. Her areas of expertise and interest are broadly centred on the impacts of new ICT on contemporary culture and society, especially with regard to data technologies and practices, that is, Big Data, open access to research data and open eGovernment. She has co-authored papers on science policy and open access to research data and the book *Open Data and the Knowledge Society*, which was published by Amsterdam University Press in 2017. Prior to working at Trilateral, Thordis worked as a Research Associate at University of Sheffield, The Manchester Institute of Innovation Research, and lectured in Sociology and Media Studies at Sheffield Hallam University, UK. Thordis has a PhD in Sociology from the University of Surrey, UK.

Gunhild Tøndel is a Post-doctoral Researcher at the Norwegian University of Science and Technology (NTNU) in Trondheim, Norway and Researcher at the Unit for Diversity and Inclusion, NTNU Social Research. Her research interests include governance, organisation, quantification, measurement, tech-nology, surveillance, and the sociology of the invisible. She has published several articles about statistics as a tool of governance in healthcare, decision-making in welfare services and qualitative methodology.

Bridgette Wessels is Professor of Sociology in the School of Geography, Pol-itics and Sociology at Newcastle University, UK. She was part of the RECODE project and has undertaken a range of research projects that focus on the use of digital tools and services in social and cultural life. Her books include *Understanding the Internet* (2010), *Exploring Social Change* (2014) and *Inside the Digital Revolution* (2007, 2016).

Sally Wyatt is Professor of Digital Cultures at Maastricht University in the Netherlands. On behalf of the International Social Science Council, she parti-cipated in the preparation of the Science International Accord, *Open Data in a Big Data World*, published at the end of 2016, and since endorsed by more than 100 organisations, including regional and national academies as well as international scientific associations, universities, and research funding agencies.

Acknowledgements

We wish to thank all the whistle-blowers and critical thinkers who, over recent decades, kicked off conversations about Big Data, as well as all who have joined in those conversations and kept them alive. Thanks to William Binney, Ed Loomis, Diane Roark, J. Kirk Wiebe, Jesselyn Radack, Thomas Drake, Edward Snowden, Alan Rusbridger, Glenn Greenwald, Laura Poitras, many more who are cited in this volume, as well as others who remain unnamed. When it comes to our own participation in those conversations we thank the European Association for the Study of Science and Technology (EASST) for hosting the conference track that resulted in this book and for providing a congenial and inspiring collegial environment at the conference overall. We also thank all participants in the track for their contributions as presenters, discussants, and debaters. Thanks, too, to those who contributed their work to this volume, especially those who also did internal review work on chapters. Last but not least, thanks to our publishers, their editors, and anonymous reviewers whose comments have helped us immensely in improving and completing the text. Among these, special thanks to our copyeditor, Jen Hinchliffe, for her close attention to every detail – any errors or typos that remain are ours.

> 'Data is not information, information is not knowledge, knowledge is not understanding, understanding is not wisdom'.
>
> – Clifford Stoll

1 The politics of Big Data

Principles, policies, practices

Ann Rudinow Sætnan, Ingrid Schneider, and Nicola Green

Our focus and goal

Kranzberg's 'First Law of Technology' teaches us that '[t]echnology is neither good nor bad; nor is it neutral' (Kranzberg 1986: 547). By this, he means that technologies engage with complex social ecologies to produce social results, but that these results are not entirely controlled by the technologies' human interactors.[1] Having learned also from Barad (2007), we could state that technologies *intra-act* with human societies – both shaping and taking shape in each moment of entanglement. These mutual shaping moments occur whether we reflect on them or not; we can enter into them more or less watchfully, less or more carelessly. Furthermore, the mutual shaping happens continuously, throughout a technology's social history. As long as we engage with a technology, we continue to shape it and be shaped by it. By engaging reflexively in that reshaping process, we can also reshape the process itself.

Big Data is a case in point. Big Data is constituted by a nexus of technologies – data-processing hardware and software and a myriad of digitised apparatuses and processes networked through a constant data flow, each element embedded into the varied ecologies of current society.[2] This means we are constantly shaping and being shaped by Big Data. While this basic claim can be made of any technology, from the stone wheel to the atom bomb, it seems today that Big Data is taking form as a particularly powerful reshaping force. In this reshaping process, benefits and harms are unevenly distributed across social groups and across different aspects of social life. Forms and degrees of influence over the shaping processes also vary and are unevenly distributed. The more we learn about those distributions – both of benefits and harms being produced through the implementation of Big Data, and in what ways and how effectively individuals, groups and governments have so far been engaged in shaping Big Data – the more effectively we can engage in the shaping process and its outcomes in future.

This book focuses on the shaping of and by Big Data, approaching that theme from many angles. Here in Chapter 1 we will first describe what it is the contributors share in our conceptualisation of that theme. We will then describe a key element of what our various angles of approach have in common as well as how they differ in that regard. Finally, we will give readers a brief presentation of the structure of, and contributions to, the volume.

Our contributions to this book first came into conversation with one another when we all responded to a call for papers to form a conference track under the open and questioning title 'Big Data, Big Brother?' As those conversations proceeded, we saw that however varied our contributions were in some regards, they shared a sub-theme: they all addressed issues regarding the politics of Big Data. In other words, the very variety of our approaches served to tighten our shared focus on the political aspects of Big Data. At the same time, that variety of approaches demonstrated the breadth of the political focus, namely the breadth of what can be labelled as 'politics' and what as 'policies'. Accordingly, in this introductory chapter to the volume, we will discuss two concepts that define its scope:

1   What we mean by 'Big Data', and
2   What we mean by 'politics and policies'.

Big Data – does it exist, and if so, what is it?

In the discussion after the final session of our conference track, one member of the audience challenged us on the very concept of Big Data: 'Isn't Big Data all just hype?' he asked, 'Does it even actually exist?'[3] Our answer is that it both is and isn't 'all just hype', Big Data does and doesn't really exist; or rather, it certainly exists, but one might well ask in what sense and to what extent it exists.

At the very least, Big Data exists as a sociotechnical imaginary that serves as a meta-narrative to capture the present and future of digitisation, datafication, and globalised networks. For instance, boyd and Crawford (2012: 663) define Big Data as 'a cultural, technological, and scholarly phenomenon' that rests on the interplay of technology, analysis, and mythology, referring to the latter as the 'widespread *belief* that large data sets offer a higher form of intelligence and knowledge that can generate insights that were previously impossible, with the *aura of* [emphases added] truth, objectivity, and accuracy'. When that imaginary is expressed, for instance in the form of a definition, Big Data also takes on a semantic existence. From there, either as an imaginary or as a semantic reality, Big Data exists in a phenomenological sense, that is, as subjective perceptions that form an interpretive framework and a basis for action. And finally, Big Data exists because (as many of the empirical chapters will show) we can see those imaginaries and frameworks being acted upon. When Big Data imaginaries, semantics and interpretive frameworks are enacted and the actants (both human and non-human) of those frameworks engaged, Big Data takes on material form(s). Yet these forms do not always fully realise the shapes and traits imagined for them.

So what are these imaginaries and frameworks? A clear definition would make the phenomenon semantically more real while also bounding it in against conceptual drift, but definitions and undefined usages vary widely. It is perhaps unfortunate that there is no apparent consensus on a definition, however many definitions do seem to refer to some form of observable materiality.

Some definitions, as we shall see below, focus on size. Although hyped as revolutionary in that regard (see, for example, Mayer-Schönberger and Cukier's (2013) *Big data: A Revolution that will transform how we live, work, and think*), in a sense there is nothing new about Big Data. There is a long history of dealing with amounts of information that at some point seemed too vast to handle (see, for instance, Hacking 1982). Cynically speaking, the only thing 'new' about Big Data is the catchy name. Less cynically, what's new is its scale. Stipulating some minimum size that would deserve the name 'Big' might at first glance seem to set a precise boundary vis-à-vis older data practices. For instance, Intel defines Big Data organisations as those 'generating a median of 300 terabytes (TB) of data weekly' (Intel 2012). And, certainly there are such organisations.

However, size is a moving target. As data capacities rise and costs fall, 300 TB/week may soon seem not so big after all. Another dimension is relative size. Rather than a fixed number, the current Wikipedia (2017) article defines Big Data as 'data sets so large or complex that traditional data processing application software is inadequate to deal with them'.[4] Again, yes, certainly there are organisations that struggle to make sense of their data due to the sheer size of the databases they deal with.

For a company such as Intel, which sells data capacity, size – be it a fixed figure or a relative target – may be a useful definition criterion. For us as philosophers/historians/social scientists of technology, size, to be relevant, should preferably (at least also) relate to meanings, practices, and the social and ethical consequences thereof. Laney (2001) points to three purported traits of Big Data that may relate to meanings, practices, and consequences. While not presented as a definition of Big Data, the three traits – volume, velocity, and variety, also known as 'the three Vs' – have been much used as one (e.g. by UK POST 2014 and by Mayer-Schönberger and Cukier 2013).

For instance, it is used – and expanded upon – by one of the few book-size publications providing a critical analysis of Big Data. Based on literature reviews, Rob Kitchin (2014: 1–2) defines Big Data as:

- huge in volume, consisting of terabytes or petabytes of data;
- high in velocity, being created in or near real time;
- diverse in variety, being structured and unstructured in nature;
- exhaustive in scope, striving to capture entire populations or systems (n = all);
- fine-grained in resolution and uniquely indexical in identification;
- relational in nature, containing common fields that enable the conjoining of different data sets;
- flexible, holding the traits of extensionality (can add new fields easily) and scalability (can expand in size rapidly).

Discussing these traits one by one, Kitchin points out how each is not necessarily some sort of data-based 'superpower', but can also be problematic. Each strength can also be a weakness. For instance, volume challenges data storage and analysis capacity, although less so as capacities grow. Velocity challenges analysts' ability to define and capture relevant moments in ever-changing data flows and trends. Variety challenges the ability to curate – categorise, standardise, stabilise – data for collation, comparison, and analysis. The existence of whole conferences on the curation challenges of Big Data databases (e.g. IDCC 2017) points to the existence of such issues.

Some, for example, IBM (n.d.) add a fourth V for Veracity, but this is a misnomer. There is no evidence that massed data from multiple sources are 'truer' than data collected in traditional scientific endeavours. In fact, in their presentation of the fourth V, IBM subtitles 'veracity' as 'uncertainty of data'. Thus, veracity has to be questioned as data may be inaccurate or unreliable.

Other analysts have added Variability as a fifth V, where data qualities and results may change over time. Newly collected data may be added to existing datasets, for example. Furthermore, novel ways of using existing data may be developed by addressing previously unasked questions, by applying new methods of analysis, by correlating data formerly unrelated, or by creating alternative linkages to give a different picture (UK POST 2014).

Google has defined Big Data self-referentially by word-clouding search terms that co-occur with it (Ward and Barker 2013). That they managed to perform such an analysis is doubly self-referential evidence that the phenomenon exists, as a search term and as an approach to repurposing and analysing masses of stored data, in this case data from Google searches. We might even say the results were triply self-referential, as they pointed to other phenomena enmeshed with the concept and practices of Big Data: According to Ward and Barker (2013), Google users who seek information about Big Data often also seek information about Big Data analytics, in general or with specific reference to database technologies such as the data storage and retrieval architecture style known as NoSQL or data storage and analysis software programs such as Hadoop.

Big Data analytics, rather than database size alone, is also where the Big Data hype now focuses. This shift in hype focus may be similar to the focus shift from genomics to proteomics (see, for example, Fujimura 2005; Webster 2005). One way of interpreting such shifts is as Latour (1987: 114–121) describes the rhetorical mobilisation and hiding of barriers (moving attention from one problem to the next, and thus away from unachieved 'final' goals) as a strategy to maintain member loyalty in sociotechnical networks. In the case of Big Data we could paraphrase these as follows: 'You now have access to vast amounts of data and are only more confused? Don't abandon the bandwagon! We only need to develop a little more self-learning software; then we will reach your goals.' However, as we shall see, the problems may have stayed on the bandwagon too, especially if they were not merely about size, but also about analysis, ethics, legality, actionability, and so on.

Continuing from how big, via how difficult and how to do, many influential definitions (often implicit rather than explicit and, ironically, often anecdotal or casuistic rather than statistics-based) focus on what Big Data analytics have achieved. For instance, Mayer-Schönberger and Cukier (2013) define Big Data as 'The ability of society to harness information in novel ways to produce useful insights or goods and services of significant value' (ibid.: 2) and '... things one can do at a large scale that cannot be done at a smaller one, to extract new insights or create new forms of value' (ibid.: 6). Here we are getting to definitions we might challenge as pointing to a mythical object rather than a material one, to 'air ware' and hollow promises (or threats), or to boyd and Crawford's (2012: 663) aforementioned definition of Big Data as a belief system.

Although Mayer-Schönberger and Cukier (2013) temper their Big Data success tale with the caution that privacy may suffer, their emphasis is nevertheless on Big Data's purported advantages, summarising them as the very definition of Big Data. Others, for example Anderson (2008), mention no disadvantages whatsoever. While some (e.g. boyd and Crawford 2012; Kitchin 2014; Sætnan, Chapter 2 in this volume) go further in their critique of Big Data, examining even its success claims, most authors are less critical. And, judging by numbers of citations (according to both Google Scholar and ISI Web of Science), Big Data enthusiast texts clearly have greater traction than critiques. Through that traction, Big Data – however mythical its results may be – exists as a political, societal and commercial force, a force resulting in attempts to *perform* Big Data by (re-)collecting and attempting to (re-)use vast amounts of data.

We can readily find such arguments pitched towards businesses. Just do an Internet search for 'Big Data solutions' and there they are. One company, called Big Data Solutions, advertises that,

> We support our customers in capitalizing the data and combine it with other information in order to produce improved business insight. [...] Whether you are currently struggling with dirty, unorganized or unknown data assets looking to uncover opportunities and leveraging big data or embarking on your first master data management initiative, we can help you unlock the true value of your enterprise data.
>
> (Big Data Solutions n.d.)

Another company, SAP, advises potential client firms to, 'Discover the Big Data solutions that give you 360-degree insight into your business and help you find hidden growth opportunities within the digital noise' (SAP n.d.). And so the ads read, from company after company offering Big Data hardware, software, cloud storage and/or analytics services. Across all these ads, the message is clear: since you have all these data anyway, why not crunch their numbers and squeeze more profits from them? To put it even more succinctly – the data are yours; use them. From this, and playing as fast and loose with spelling as the age-old concept of 'Three R's' for Reading, wRiting, and aRithmetic, we could add yet another V to the description of Big Data: aVailability. A word of caution, however: this V does not necessarily mean that Big Data capitalises on data that are freely available. Data available to a given Big Data operator *may* be freely and openly available, but much is privately held, proprietary, confidential, even classified as secret. This, of course, entails that data now have commercial value, so Big Data operators may also be crunching numbers on data they have purchased. And, as with anything of commercial value, data are also tempting objects for crime: they may be hacked, stolen, forged, falsified ... and even when legally held, they may be illegally sold, shared, repurposed and/or combined (see Sætnan, Chapter 2 in this volume). So, aVailability highlights simply that Big Data capitalises on whatever data an operator has access to.

Summing up, we can now tentatively[5] define Big Data as *the collection and aggregation of large masses of (publicly, commercially, proprietarily, and/or illicitly) available data and its analysis,[6] largely in the form of correlation, pattern-recognition, and predictive analysis*. And by this definition again, yes, Big Data definitely exists. It exists in various sizes – some bigger, some smaller in terms of numbers of data points collected and numbers of persons covered by the data set, some simply stored unanalysed, some analysed through sophistic-ated algorithms including 'self-learning' artificial intelligence programmes. The data are collected by individuals, organisations, firms, states. Analysis is per-formed for commercial, medical, research, political, policiary, military, and criminal purposes. Sometimes the sole new purpose of a collection by one party is to sell the data on to yet other parties.

Much of this data is 'personal data'.[7] According to the 1995 EU Data Protec-tion Directive 95/46/EC (European Parliament 1995), 'personal data' is:

> Any information relating to an identified or identifiable natural person ('Data Subject'); an identifiable person is one who can be identified, directly or indirectly, in particular by reference to an identification number or to one or more factors specific to his physical, physiological, mental, economic, cultural or social identity.
>
> (95/46/EC article 2, §a)

This definition is similarly incorporated into the various national Data Protection Acts. For instance the Irish Data Protection Act of 1988, section 1, was amended in 2003 to state that:

> 'personal data' means data relating to a living individual who is or can be identified either from the data or from the data in conjunction with other information that is in, or is likely to come into, the possession of the data controller.
>
> (Irish Statute Book 2003)

The phrases 'or indirectly' and 'likely to come into the possession of' are key here. Perhaps at a given moment only a few factors that might identify you, the data subject, can be found within a given database, let's say your age and the purchases you made at the pharmacy yesterday. Suppose these two factors are in the database, but not your gender, your address, your hair colour, your name … nothing else that could identify you, and there are many people your age who were pharmacy customers that day, so your anonymity is safe. So far. But then, suppose it would be a simple matter for the controller of that database to find your address, or gender, or place of employment and link those together with your age and any other data recorded about you in the database. They might still not have your name, but they would have enough factors to render all the information about you in that database (including that which was previously considered safely anonymised) personally identifiable.

This is made even more explicit in the EU General Data Protection Regulation (GDPR 2016), which takes force in May 2018. Here an 'identifiable person' is defined not only by that person being linked to a name or number, but is any natural person 'who can be identified, directly or indirectly, in particular by reference to *an identifier*' with identifiers being not so much defined as exemplified through the list 'such as a name, an identification number, location data, online identifier or to one or more factors specific to the physical, physiological, genetic, mental, economic, cultural or social identity of that person' (GDPR 2016, Article 4(1), emphasis added).

Looking from these definitions of personal data back at Kitchin's (2014) definition of Big Data, and noting his points that such databases are 'fine-grained', 'indexical' and 'relational in nature', we can see how even the most innocuous and anonymous bits of data emanating from our daily activities quickly become personal, even intimately invasive, when linked together in Big Data collections. This concerns not only data we in some sense ourselves report. In the Internet of Things, sensors and smart devices may provide data and metadata that – even though not originally personalised – may be used for profiling and for re-identification of individuals and for classifying and predicting their behaviour. So even just our handling of daily objects can contribute to the masses of data that can potentially be traced back to us.

Historically, the most important large data sets (such as censuses or tax records) have been about persons as citizens, and have thereby contributed to constituting them (us) as such. Currently, and increasingly, Big Data will derive from our interactions with technical artefacts. The availability of sensors and our cultural fascination with things 'high-tech' and 'smart' may encourage manufacturers and platform providers to monitor use of their products by clients in ways that could create commercial value. Such sources and uses of data have hardly any historical precedent, and need to be scrutinised. For instance, how do they constitute us as users, as customers, as clients, as integrated aspects of technologies, etc. – and how might they change us as citizens?

So far we have concluded that yes, Big Data does exist. However, the caution remains that Big Data also in some sense does *not* exist. If we define Big Data according to what it is sometimes hyped up to be – that some shadowy 'They', through the vast collection and incredibly accurate analysis of secondary data, now know everything about everybody – then no. Big Data is not a collection and accurate analysis of everything about everybody, as will be discussed by Sætnan (Chapter 2) and by Matzner (Chapter 3) in this volume. Some might say 'not yet', but we would rather refrain from making alarmist, hyped-up predictions. We also believe that there can never be a collection of everything about everybody. Some persons, for at least some of their data, will always elude collection, and some aspects of our persons are not collectable in data form. And yet, dangerously, 'practically everything about everybody' does seem to be what some users and abusers, regulators and anti-regulatory activists, Big Data recorders and recorded, believe it to be (e.g. Whitaker 1999; Cole 2014) – and is certainly what some Big Data promoters would have them believe (e.g. Clarke 2013). Furthermore, some collections do come closer to 'everything about everybody' than many feel comfortable with: for instance the National Security Agency's data collections as revealed by Edgar Snowden (Greenwald 2014; Harding 2014), or Facebook's collection of not only our Facebook posts, searches, and 'likes', but also much of what we do online even when not logged on to Facebook (Gibbs 2015), or Google's collection of our entire Google search histories (Galperin 2012). Confronted with such vast and detailed collections of data, and with claimed capabilities and explicit aims of analysing these data, it is hardly surprising that social scientists would want to study Big Data. But what should we be asking and how should we go about seeking answers?

Politics as a perspective on Big Data

The researchers who presented at the 'Big Data, Big Brother?' track, most of whom have contributed to this volume, represent a variety of social science and humanities fields and disciplines: Anthropology, Cultural Studies, Gender Studies, Informatics, Law, Media Studies, Philosophy, Political Science, Science and Technology Studies, Sociology. When defining disciplines, there is a focus on how they differ in their core concerns. Here, we found that we shared an understanding of what we were (and still are) studying and why it was (still is) important to study it. We found that we were primarily studying Big Data in terms of how it serves to (re-)distribute power in social relationships. This means we shared a concern for the *politics* of Big Data, for instance as politics are defined in the Collins English Dictionary (2017):

> Politics (pɒlɪtɪks) 1. plural noun. Politics are the actions or activities concerned with achieving and using power in a country or society.

According to that definition, we share a general concern with politics. We deepen that perspective when, paper by paper, our respective political concerns focus on specific, more narrowly defined, aspects of the broad political field. Some focus on governmental policies seeking to promote, use, or regulate Big Data. These fit with the concept of politics according to the topmost – presumably most common – definitions in the Merriam-Webster Dictionary (2017):

1   a   the art or science of government
     b   the art or science concerned with guiding or influencing govern-
          mental policy
     c   the art or science concerned with winning and holding control over
          a government
2   political actions, practices, or policies

The Merriam-Webster definition of politics overlaps with what some would separate out as 'policies'. The divide between these two is contested, and since the
contest devolves into one of a semantic convention, only language history can
settle the question, and only the end of humanity can finalise language history.
For now, however, one fairly conventional way of separating between these concepts is to think of 'politics' as the matter of principles and priorities, the debate
or controversy side of the coin, and of 'policy' as the resulting pragmatic efforts
of governing bodies to regulate and order society. Some use the two terms the
other way around. There are, of course, many more ways of conceptualising the
divide. For instance, one might think of politics as the negotiative process of
overcoming conflicts and policies as a way to intervene and even exacerbate
conflicts.

Politics, whether viewed as debate and controversy or as negotiation, can be
studied from many angles. Political party programmes offer a view of their principles and goals, policy documents often begin with statements of overarching
aims, policies can be analysed to reveal the conflicting interests negotiated to
achieve them, media texts can be a window into, as well as a driving force for,
public opinion – just to mention a few such perspectives. All of these are represented in this volume. In Chapter 4, Strauß analyses the pressures of various
interests that have led to securitisation being a dominant theme in governance,
including Big Data policies. In Chapter 6, Rieder examines EU policy documents, focusing on their visionary side. In Chapter 10, Tøndel and Sætnan
follow public discourse on Big Data and surveillance through the window of
mass media texts.

The policy side of the politics/policy coin can itself include at least two coin
sides when it comes to Big Data. One side is efforts to regulate Big Data, as discussed by several chapters in this volume, most thoroughly by Schneider, who
takes us through national and supranational regulatory efforts and legal sanctions
in Chapter 8. The other side is governments' own usage(s) of Big Data as an
administrative tool, on which see Ochs (Chapter 13 in this volume), and also
Yeung (2017).

Of course, all the chapters in this volume address concerns of politics and/or
policies in one or more of these senses of the terms. Politics and policies as
matters concerning governments and electoral processes is the central theme of
Part II: Big Data policies: politics of governance and regulation, where it is
approached from a number of angles, ranging from overarching political imaginaries to undergirding public opinions. Policies are most directly discussed by
Pasquale in Chapter 7, where he discusses regulators' struggles to keep up with

the speed, spread and technological evolution of data-driven media when it comes to imposing editorial controls and citizen protections; and, by Schneider in Chapter 8, where she gives a detailed account of Big Data regulations and controls at both national and supranational levels and as practised by various branches of government. Both politics and policies also come up in the other sections. In Chapter 4, Strauß discusses why securitisation has such dominance amongst political goals and why Big Data is so often taken as a 'silver bullet' policy tool to achieve national security. In Chapter 12, Fleischhack gives an inside view of certain NGOs' attempts at 'taming' Big Data; then in Chapter 13, Ochs discusses why this 'self-protection' approach is both propounded and subverted by many governmental agencies, in part because Big Data is a tool governments themselves use in public administration. In Chapter 14, Noorman *et al.* discuss government policies aimed at promoting open access to research data, then follow up by discussing practical and ethical issues raised from Academe's 'grass roots' that have slowed the implementation of such policies. In other words, the book, examines multiple branches and levels of government in terms of their Big Data politics, policies and practices, be those aimed at promoting, using, and/or regulating Big Data.

Governmental agencies are not the only collective environment where technologies engage with social ecologies with results that affect social distributions. Humans act collectively in contexts outside of governments and electoral politics as well. Businesses and markets are one example, and several chapters deal with how businesses affect, and are affected by, Big Data. In fact, most chapters touch on this aspect, but some contain a specific focus on it, as when Ingrid Schneider (Chapter 8) discusses network effects in digital platforms and the forces of oligopolisation.

Another channel for collective human action (including intra-action with Big Data) is non-governmental organisations (NGOs). In Chapter 12, Fleischhack presents and analyses activities of several groups focused precisely on Big Data issues, in particular on individual citizens' data privacy. The NGO's 'digital literacy' and self-protection approach is not, of course, the only strategy with regard to privacy, a theme touched on by nearly all chapters in the volume.

But, much as governmental agencies are not the only channels for 'achieving and using power in a country or society' (i.e. not the only channels for politics as defined by Collins English Dictionary), neither are corporations or NGOs, however influential, the only alternative channels. Public discourse does not distribute power solely through its effects on electoral politics or legislative priorities. Discourse is a productive source of power in its own right through its regulation of what statements may be made, and by whom, regarding a given discourse topic (Foucault 1980). While it is primarily other concepts from Foucault that are used by authors in this volume, it is in keeping with this concept of discourse – as something that tentatively imposes an order and thus a worldview regarding what is shown, by whom, and by what means – that Big Data discourses are discussed in several chapters in the volume. Thus, discourses affect the mutual shaping of Big Data and society – not only through their influence on electoral outcomes or official policies, but also in terms of how they delineate the subjects and objects of Big Data, setting an agenda for what its issues are and who speaks authoritatively to those issues.

Of course, politics is not only about public office or public discourse. Politics, even when accessed through public office or public discourse is, in the final analysis, about power distributions in our everyday lives and relationships. The second-wave feminist slogan 'the personal is political' emphasised this fact on two counts: first, that power differentials in everyday lives and personal relationships are important, and second, that the responsibility for resolving them should not be relegated to individuals alone but is a legitimate matter for political organisation (Hanisch 2006). Thus, the everyday practices of Big Data systems – including not only how Big Data practices impact on ordinary, grass-roots citizens, but also how they are enacted and/or resisted individually and collectively – is an aspect of Big Data politics. We focus on this aspect in several chapters dealing with the everyday practices of Big Data, especially in Part III: Performance is political: Big Data practices, performance, and resistance. Aspects of everyday life discussed in this part include: how surveillance of our video watching preferences are recursively used to script videos we watch (Chapter 11), the online practices and competencies of children (Chapter 12), and the work practices and constraints of academics as these affect participation (or not) in open data schemes.

We also take heed that technologies are not merely passive mediators of their human designers' intentions. In his seminal article,[8] 'Do artefacts have politics?' (Winner 1980), Langdon Winner points out how redistribution of social goods and influence is sometimes designed into technologies intentionally. While such intentions may be inscribed into them, ascribed to them, de-inscribed from them and so on (Akrich 1992; Akrich and Latour 1992), social distribution outcomes are not a result of design alone. For one thing, designers' scripts will encounter 'user scripts' (Gjøen and Hård 2002; see also Oudshoorn and Pinch 2005) once a technology is implemented.[9] Furthermore, technologies' and other non-human actants' materiality may itself enable or resist humans' intentions (see, for example, Callon 1986). Looking at this from another angle: designers, users, technologies, and the objects they describe 'intra-act' with one another, all emerging reshaped from that intra-action (Barad 2007). Thus, the book also discusses technological aspects of Big Data, how these sometimes resist fulfilling Big Data designers' intentions, and how systems and citizens reshape one another when we are subjected to Big Data scrutiny. That, too, is an aspect of Big Data politics, an aspect dealt with especially in Part I: Principles and paradigms: questioning the tenets of Big Data, while the user side of the equation is highlighted most in Part III: Performance is political – Big Data practices, performance, and resistance. Intra-actions of users (a video streaming service), end users (video viewers), and non-human actants (Big Data and screenplay scripts) are the focus of Chapter 11, 'No (Big) Data no fiction?' by Rocco Bellanova and Gloria González Fuster.

Of course, any volume must find space between its covers. Therefore, there are inevitably topics within the theme of Big Data politics that we have covered only cursorily. One of these is how Big Data – or any data, large or small – influence not only data politics, but also politics overall. The theme is not entirely absent from the book, as the role of statistics in the practices of governance is touched on by Ochs in Chapter 13. For more thorough coverage of this theme, we can recommend a number of sources: see, for instance, Hacking (1990) and Desrosières (1998) on the history of statistics, Rose (1991) on the relation between democracy and practices of calculation, Barry (2002) about the 'political' and 'anti-political' use (and reappropriation) of quantification systems, Sætnan, Lomell and Hammer (2011) about intra-actions between statistics, policies, and practices, Bellanova (2017) about European data protection and the possibility to open a space of political critique with regard to data-driven governance, as well as Yeung (2017) mentioned above.

Finally, we regret that this volume on the politics of Big Data – a focus arising out of a shared interest in how Big Data discourses, policies, and practices reshape power relations – does not include chapters dedicated specifically to the analysis of Big Data in intra-action with major intersectional categories such as gender, race, or sexual orientation. These categories, too, refer to what are essentially power-distributive relations. Such categories are acknowledged in several chapters in the volume. We would have wished, however, to have found and included analyses focused specifically on intersectionalities. That we were unable to do so may reflect a gap in Big Data research as a whole, although we do know of research on intersectional aspects of surveillance more generally – for example, Browne (2015) on surveillance and race, van der Meulen and Heynen (2016) on surveillance and gender, and Lyon (2003) on surveillance as social sorting. Hopefully, our own 'missing' papers will soon be published elsewhere, extending the discourse on the politics of Big Data beyond the bindings of this book. But for now, let us return to what the book does contain.

The volume in brief

As has already been outlined, the main body of the volume is divided into three parts. Part I begins with a critical analysis of some of the key principles and epistemics of Big Data – that is, which knowledge is Big Data meant to generate and by what means? In Chapter 2, 'The haystack fallacy, or why Big Data provides little security', Sætnan evaluates the claims of central proponents of Big Data that the data in their sheer vastness and variety constitute nearly everything knowable, and that statistical principles developed for data samples are therefore obsolete. Sætnan also discusses problematic consequences of margins of error when Big Data are deployed into security contexts. Next, in Chapter 3, 'Grasping the ethics and politics of algorithms', Matzner presents a critical analysis of the next step in Big Data – algorithmic analytics – and finds that the problems remain. In Chapters 4 and 5 – 'Big Data – within the tides of securitisation?' (Strauß) and 'Surveillance as a critical paradigm for Big Data?' (Matzner) – we see the political forces driving the expansion and deployment of Big Data into national security measures, in spite of all the dangers such deployment carries with it. Matzner, however, also interrogates to what extent 'surveillance' as a critical paradigm, often expressed in the metaphors of the panopticon or the omniscient eye of Big Brother, is adequate to capture the challenges of Big Data. While critical of security applications of Big Data and of its potential for social and political harms, all four chapters point to potential benefits of Big Data, for instance as a market tool and for generating scientific hypotheses.

In Part II, the emphasis is on public policies more broadly and discourses potentially affecting these. In Chapter 6 ('Tracing Big Data imaginaries through public policy: The case of the European Commission'), Rieder analyses official documents of the European Commission to show what sociotechnical imaginaries underlie the Union's policy goals for a 'Big Data future'. Pasquale (Chapter 7, 'The automated public sphere') examines more specifically the policies relating to the algorithmic automation of the public sphere, and subsequent effects on opinion-building and political decision-making. Pasquale points out that consumer protection and media regulatory authorities must intervene and that new methods of monitoring and regulating Big Data will be needed in order to keep up with technological and economic developments. Schneider (Chapter 8, 'Bringing the state back in: Big Data-based capitalism, disruption, and novel regulatory approaches in Europe') explains the mechanisms behind the rise of digital platforms and the impacts of algorithmic ranking, rating and scoring on social sorting and the democratic social order. She also provides readers with a detailed, comprehensive, and critically analytical overview of EU and national regulatory policies relating to the political economy of Big Data. Schneider's overview demonstrates that many regulatory policies have been aimed at the protection of fundamental rights, including privacy. In Chapter 9, 'Rear window – transparent citizens versus political participation', Simões and Jerónimo argue that privacy is a mediating factor; the more important issue is citizens' autonomy, with loss of autonomy in the wake of Big Data posing a serious threat to democracy. Finally in this part, Tøndel and Sætnan (Chapter 10, 'Fading dots, disappearing lines – Surveillance and Big Data in news media after the Snowden revelations') examine the extent to which Edward Snowden achieved his stated goals for leaking National Security Agency (NSA) documents and the former editor-in-chief of the *Guardian*, Alan Rusbridger, his goals for agreeing to publish these highly critical revelations about bulk data surveillance. Did the Snowden leaks change public discourse on Big Data and surveillance, and if so, did that discourse lead to changes in public policy?

With a nod to Hanisch (2006), 'The Personal is Political', we have given Part III the title 'Performance is political: Big Data practices, performance, and resistance'. The four chapters in this section focus on three examples of everyday Big Data practices in different spheres of activity. In Chapter 11, 'No (Big) Data no fiction? Thinking surveillance with/against Netflix', Bellanova and González Fuster give an in-depth analysis of how the content streaming platform has used Big Data from its customers/viewers to tailor the content of a series on Big Data surveillance in politics. Netflix thus creates a recursive loop of watched → watching → watchers → debating watching and, potentially, of surveillance opinions → shaping surveillance presentations → shaping surveillance opinions. In Chapter 12, '"Data trainings" in German schools – Learning empowerment from hackers', Fleischhack reports from participant observation of grass-roots activist workshops aimed at motivating and enabling users of social media and other digital technologies to better protect their own and others' privacy. Fleischhack points to both resources for, and limitations of, such individual-based protections. In the next chapter (Chapter 13, 'Self-protection beyond the self: collective privacy practices in (Big) datascapes'), Ochs further analyses how individualised 'informational self-protection' strategies have come to dominate governmental policies, and how their logic is seriously flawed since self-protective tools and encryption practices are, of necessity, collective in nature. Turning to another inherently collective social endeavour, namely science, Noorman, Wessels, Sveinsdottir, and Wyatt (Chapter 14, 'Understanding the "open" in making research data open: policy rhetoric and research practice') examine the technological, organisational, and moral dimensions of the arguments for, arguments against, and pragmatic problems of, sharing research data. Of course, Big Data is deployed into and/or has repercussions within far more spheres of daily activity than these. Some, such as commercial applications, have been much discussed elsewhere. Others remain 'dark continents' on our virtual maps of the state of knowledge.

We could have no reasonable expectation of covering the whole terrain of Big Data practices. Our expectation is that this mix of fields and experiences – some eclectic and some almost universally relevant across applications – can inspire further reading and research. With this in mind, Green has written our concluding chapter as a methodological postscript: 'Big Data's methodological challenges'. The title could alternatively have been 'Big Data's reflexive methodological inspirations', or at least the reflexive inspirations from our own findings regarding Big Data. For instance, if we accept Ochs's findings (and we do accept them) that privacy protection must inherently be a collective enterprise, and reflect that the same is true of research, then we must ask ourselves how we might go about building a community effort to research Big Data. Might it involve learning from unexpected actors, such as the hackers in Fleischhack's chapter? How would we (as Noorman *et al.* point out that we must) make our data shareable within Big Data research as a community project? In Chapter 15, Green points to problems of in/visibilities, scale, location, and approach – problems that are perhaps universal in science, and that Big Data can help us resolve if we hold it up not only as an object of curiosity, but also as a research(ing) subject and a mirror.

Notes

1 Marvin Kranzberg, an historian, drew these 'laws' – which he says are not laws in a legal or moral sense so much as a 'series of truisms' (Kranzberg 1986: 544) – from a long career's experience researching technologies. The six laws are: (1) Technology is not good, or bad; nor is it neutral. (2) Invention is the mother of necessity. (3) Technology

comes in packages, big and small. (4) Although technology may be a prime element in many public issues, nontechnical factors take precedence in technology policy decisions. (5) All history is relevant, but the history of technology is most relevant. (6) Technology is a very human activity – and so is the history of technology (Kranzberg 1986). Similar points are made by the philosopher Andrew Feenberg, for instance, in his book *Questioning Technology* (1999) as well as in his article 'Ten paradoxes of Technology' (2010).

2 As we shall discuss in this chapter, we see Big Data as a nexus not only of technologies, but also of imaginaries, principles, policies, practices, and performances. When referring to this nexus, we will capitalise it and refer to it in the singular. Should we at some point speak of (lower case) big data, i.e. some collection of data points that happens to be big, we may then (depending on context) refer to data as plural (many data points) rather than as a singular set. Similarly, usage of the term 'data' as plural or singular will vary throughout the volume depending on contributing authors' preferences and feel for the specific contexts where the term occurs.

3 Not an actual quote, just our synopsis of his point.

4 One could also consider the issue of database size relative to data handling purpose, as when data protection authorities deny a data handling concession on the basis that the prospective data handler is requesting permission to gather and store more data than their stated purpose warrants. Data sets regarded as overlarge in such a context, however, are not used as defining cases for Big Data. Rather, promoters of Big Data tend to ignore this issue altogether, focusing on the opportunities large data sets provide rather than on the legality of vast data collections.

5 Authors may use other definitions in their respective chapters, but for now this one will serve to project an image of our object of study.

6 This is often secondary analysis (i.e. analysis for new purposes, other than those for which the data were originally produced and collected).

7 There are exceptions, such as data generated by sensors monitoring natural or atmospheric phenomena like the weather or pollution, or technical aspects of manufacturing processes.

8 The article sparked considerable debate and the theme of politics as an inherent aspect of technologies continues to this day. See, for instance, Joerges (1999).

9 Or, for that matter, non-user scripts, as resistance to implementation is also of consequence.

References

Akrich, M. (1992). The De-Scription of Technical Objects. In Bijker, W.E. and Law, J. (eds.) *Shaping Technology/Building Society*. Cambridge, MA: MIT Press: 205–224.

Akrich, M. and Latour, B. (1992). A Summary of a Convenient Vocabulary for the Semiotics of Human and Nonhuman Assemblies. In Bijker, W.E. and Law, J. (eds.) *Shaping Technology/Building Society*. Cambridge, MA: MIT Press: 259–264.

Anderson, C. (2008). The End of Theory: The Data Deluge Makes the Scientific Method Obsolete. *Wired Magazine*: 16.07. Available at: http://archive.wired.com/science/discoveries/magazine/16-07/pb_theory. [Accessed 31 October 2017].

Barad, K. (2007). *Meeting the Universe Halfway: Quantum Physics and the Entanglement of Matter and Meaning*. Durham, NC & London: Duke University Press.

Barry, A. (2002). The anti-political economy. *Economy and Society*, 31(2): 268–284.

Bellanova, R. (2017). Digital, politics, and algorithms: governing digital data through the lens of data protection. *European Journal of Social Theory*, 20(3): 329–347.

Big Data Solutions (n.d.). Big Data Solutions. Available at: www.bigdatasolutions.fi/. [Accessed 31 October 2017].

boyd, d. and Crawford K. (2012). Critical questions for Big Data. *Information, Communication & Society*, 15(5): 662–679.

Browne, S. (2015). *Dark Matters: On the Surveillance of Blackness*. Durham, NC & London: Duke University Press.

Callon, M. (1986). Some Elements of a Sociology of Translation: Domestication of the Scallops and the Fishermen of St Brieuc Bay. In Law, J. (ed.) Power, Action and Belief: A New Sociology of Knowledge? London: Routledge: 196–223. Available at: www.vub.ac.be/SOCO/tesa/RENCOM/Callon%20(1986)%20Some%20elements%20of%20a%20sociology%20of%20translation.pdf. [Accessed 31 October 2017].

Clarke, R.Y. (2013). Smart Cities and the Internet of Everything: The Foundation for Delivering Next-Generation Citizen Services. White paper sponsored by Cisco. *IDC Government Insights*. Available at: http://119.15.167.84:8080/share/proxy/alfresconoauth/api/internal/shared/node/q9Ij_C2XQhS0ElSMm-jJnA/content/GI243955.pdf. [Accessed 31 October 2017].

Cole, D. (2014). 'We kill people based on metadata'. *The New York Review of Books*, 10 May 2014. Available at: www.nybooks.com/blogs/nyrblog/2014/may/10/we-kill-people-based-metadata/. [Accessed 31 October 2017].

Collins English Dictionary (2017). Politics. Available at: www.collinsdictionary.com/dictionary/english/politics. [Accessed 31 October 2017].

Desrosières, A. (1998). *The Politics of Large Numbers. A History of Statistical Reasoning*. Cambridge, MA: Harvard University Press.

European Parliament (1995). Directive 95/46/EC of the European Parliament and of the Council of 24 October 1995 on the protection of individuals with regard to the processing of personal data and on the free movement of such data. Available at: http://ec.europa.eu/justice/policies/privacy/docs/95-46-ce/dir1995-46_part1_en.pdf. [Accessed 31 October 2017].

Feenberg, A. (1999). *Questioning Technology*. London: Routledge.

Feenberg, A. (2010). Ten paradoxes of technology. *Techné*, 14(1): 3–15. Originally presented as a keynote lecture in 2009. Available at: www.youtube.com/watch?v=-HzJ_Jkqa2Q. [Accessed 23 October 2017].

Foucault, M. (1980). *Power/Knowledge: Selected Interviews and Other Writings, 1972–1977*. New York: Pantheon Books. Available at: https://monoskop.org/images/5/5d/Foucault_Michel_Power_Knowledge_Selected_Interviews_and_Other_Writings_1972-1977.pdf. [Accessed 31 October 2017].

Fujimura, J.H. (2005). Postgenomic futures: translations across the machine-nature border in systems biology. *New Genetics and Society*, 24(2): 195–226.

Galperin, E. (2012). How to Remove Your Google Search History Before Google's New Privacy Policy Takes Effect. Entry on Webpages of Electronic Frontier Foundation. Available at: www.eff.org/deeplinks/2012/02/how-remove-your-google-search-history-googles-new-privacy-policy-takes-effect. [Accessed 31 October 2017].

GDPR (2016). Regulation on the protection of natural persons with regard to the processing of personal data and on the free movement of such data (Regulation (EU) 2016/679 of 27 April 2016). Available at: http://eur-lex.europa.eu/legal-content/EN/TXT/PDF/?uri=CELEX:32016R0679&from=EN. [Accessed 31 October 2017].

Gibbs, S. (2015). Facebook 'tracks all visitors, breaching EU law'. People without Facebook accounts, logged out users, and EU users who have explicitly opted out of tracking are all being tracked, report says. Available at: www.theguardian.com/technology/2015/mar/31/facebook-tracks-all-visitors-breaching-eu-law-report?CMP=share_btn_tw. [Accessed 31 October 2017].

Gjøen, H. and Hård, M. (2002). Cultural politics in action: developing user scripts in relation to the electric vehicle. *Science, Technology & Human Values*, 27(2): 262–281.

Greenwald, G. (2014). *No Place to Hide: Edward Snowden, the NSA, and the U.S. Surveillance State*. New York: Metropolitan Books.

Hacking, I. (1982). Biopower and the avalanche of printed numbers. *Humanities in Society*, 5(3–4): 279–295.

Hacking, I. (1990). *The Taming of Chance*. Cambridge: Cambridge University Press.

Hanisch, C. (2006). The Personal Is Political. The Women's Liberation Movement classic with a new explanatory introduction. Available at: www.carolhanisch.org/CHwritings/PIP.html. [Accessed 31 October 2017].

Harding, L. (2014). *The Snowden Files: The Inside Story of the World's Most Wanted Man*. New York: Vintage Books.

IBM (n.d.). The 4 Vs of big data. Available at: www.ibmbigdatahub.com/sites/default/files/infographic_file/4-Vs-of-big-data.jpg. [Accessed 31 October 2017].

IDCC (2017). International Digital Curation Conference (IDCC), Digital Curation Centre. Available at: www.dcc.ac.uk/events/internationa-digital-curation-conference-idcc. [Accessed 31 October 2017].

Intel (2012). Big Data Analytics. Intel's IT Manager Survey on how organizations are using Big Data. Available at: www.intel.com/content/dam/www/public/us/en/documents/reports/data-insights-peer-research-report.pdf. [Accessed 31 October 2017].

Irish Statute Book (2003). Data Protection (Amendment) Act 2003, Section 2. Available at: www.irishstatutebook.ie/eli/2003/act/6/section/2/enacted/en/html#sec2. [Accessed 31 October 2017].

Joerges, B. (1999). Do politics have artefacts? *Social Studies of Science*, 29(3): 411–431.

Kitchin, R. (2014). Big Data, new epistemologies and paradigm shifts. *Big Data & Society*, 1(1). Available at: http://journals.sagepub.com/doi/abs/10.1177/2053951714528481. [Accessed 31 October 2017].

Kranzberg, M. (1986). Technology and history: 'Kranzberg's laws'. *Technology and Culture*, 27(3): 554–560.

Laney, D. (2001). 3D Data Management: Controlling Data Volume, Velocity and Variety. Available at: http://blogs.gartner.com/doug-laney/files/2012/01/ad949-3D-Data-Management-Controlling-Data-Volume-Velocity-and-Variety.pdf. [Accessed 31 October 2017].

Latour, B. (1987). *Science in Action: How to Follow Scientists and Engineers through Society*. Cambridge, MA: Harvard University Press.

Lyon, D. (2003). *Surveillance as Social Sorting: Privacy, Risk and Digital Discrimination*. London and New York: Routledge.

Mayer-Schönberger, V. and Cukier, K. (2013). *Big Data: A Revolution That Will Transform How We Live, Work, and Think*. London: John Murray Publishers, Ltd.

Merriam-Webster (2017). Definition of Politics. Available at: www.merriam-webster.com/dictionary/politics. [Accessed 31 October 2017].

Oudshoorn, N. and Pinch, T. (eds.) (2005). *How Users Matter: The Co-Construction of Users and Technology*. Cambridge, MA: MIT Press.

Rose, N. (1991). Governing by numbers: figuring out democracy. *Accounting, Organizations and Society*, 16(7): 673–692.

Sætnan, A.R., Lomell, H.M. and Hammer, S. (eds.) (2011). *The Mutual Construction of Statistics and Society*. London: Routledge.

SAP (n.d.). Big Data Software Solutions SAP. Available at: www.sap.com/trends/big-data.html. [Accessed 31 October 2017].

UK POST (2014). Big Data: An Overview. UK Houses of Parliament, Parliamentary Office of Science and Technology (POST). July 2014.

van der Meulen, E. and Heynen, R. (2016). *Expanding the Gaze: Gender and the Politics of Surveillance*. Toronto: University of Toronto Press.

Ward, J.S. and Barker, A. (2013). Undefined by data: A survey of big data definitions. Available at: http://arxiv.org/abs/1309.5821. [Accessed 31 October 2017].

Webster, A. (2005). Social science and a post-genomic future: alternative readings of genomic agency. *New Genetics and Society*, 24(2): 227–238.

Whitaker, R. (1999). *The End of Privacy: How Total Surveillance is Becoming a Reality*. New York: The New Press.

Wikipedia (2017). Big data. Available at: https://en.wikipedia.org/wiki/Big_data. [Accessed 31 October 2017].

Winner, L. (1980). Do artifacts have politics? *Daedalus*, 109(1): 121–136.

Yeung, K. (2017). 'Hypernudge': Big Data as a mode of regulation by design. *Information, Communication & Society*, 20(1): 118–136.

Part I
Principles and paradigms

Questioning the tenets of Big Data

2 The haystack fallacy, or why Big Data provides little security

Ann Rudinow Sætnan

Introduction

Our increasingly digitised lives leave myriad electronic 'breadcrumbs' behind us, morsels of information about many of our activities and even thoughts.[1] Take, for example, the simple act of accessing the day's news. Only a few decades ago, media information streams were almost exclusively one way – from media to the public. Upstream traces left by media consumption were minimal and mostly voluntary. Newspapers were predominantly bought anonymously, for cash. Subscriptions left data links between media and address but said nothing about who in the household read what in the paper, listened to what on the radio, or watched what on the television (if indeed anything at all). Traces were left if you wrote a letter to the editor, but most readers never did. Broadcast audience numbers were estimated based on survey panels comprising minute fractions of the total audience – participation voluntary and responses self-registered. Advertisers had to base marketing decisions on media sales summaries, survey estimates of audience size, and whatever changes they could see in their own sales after a campaign. Certainly some subscriptions were tracked for political surveillance. Back in pre-Internet times, the detour certain checks took via the FBI was a large part of what constituted internal espionage overreach. All this is not so long ago, but for younger generations it is already buried in history.

Now media information streams are definitely two-way, and not narrow streams but broad, silt-laden rivers. Accessing an online 'newspaper' sends back traces not only of having logged onto a given front page, but also of which articles we opened, which advertisements we clicked to follow, which videos we watched and for how long, whether we 'skipped' the ads or not, whether we 'shared' or 'liked' any items, whether and what we commented. Some programmes track each keystroke, or tap into the resulting comment texts. Some even track eye movements, showing what catches viewers' attentions and how fast or slowly readers scan through an article. The volume and granularity of information flow from audience back to media has increased monumentally. We have become more than consumers of media content. Now we, or at least our 'data doubles' (Haggerty & Ericson 2000), are also its products.

Furthermore, media information streams are not merely two-way, but flared – frazzling out into multiple strands at either end that can then be braided together with other streams. At both ends of the stream, data are not simply used for one pre-defined purpose. They are recycled, repurposed, shared, modified, commodified, capitalised, requisitioned, appropriated, expropriated, stolen, and so on.

Of course, media usage is not the only example of this. More and more aspects of our lives are becoming digitised, with the resulting information crumbs being stored and made reusable in this way. I recently spent some weeks as a visiting scholar in Århus, Denmark. Early on, I tried to find a map of the bus routes around the city, but the bus company no longer makes them. Instead, passengers are told they must download the bus company's mobile app. With the app, you can find all you need to know about bus routes, and buy and download tickets. But of course, such a system is no longer anonymous. With a paper map, no one would know when I consulted it, what I looked for on it or whether I followed up my inquiry with a journey. A bus app records all these things: When did I look up a route on the map? Where was I when I did so? From where to where did I want to go? Did I download a ticket? How did I pay for it? Did I flash the electronic ticket on my screen to the reader instrument on the bus, and if so, when? In a city of some 300,000 inhabitants, that process rapidly builds a vast bank of travel information the bus company previously did not have and that now potentially offers them commercial value in its own right. My cell phone provider may also be collecting some or all of these data in parallel with the bus company, and both may be farming out data for analysis, selling it on for profit, storing it in ways not well secured against hacking.... In short, these data may be spread in ways I have little control over.

When the granular 'silt' of each such data stream is amassed over time and geo-social space, and especially if masses from various data streams (telecommunications data, GPS signals, library loans, credit card transactions, merchandise sales, acceleration and braking registered on your car's computer, RFID tags passing by recording portals, steps counted by your activity bracelet, etc. etc.) can then be combined and repurposed, analysed for commercial, medical, scientific, political, policiary, security ... well, whatever goals – then we are in the realm of the phenomenon now known as 'Big Data'.[2]

Big Data technophiles tell us that we are entering a marvellous new age of data-supported convenience with vast commercial and scientific opportunities; technophobes – that we are entering a 'Brave New World' of lost privacy and increased opportunities for oppression. Agnostically, we could ask these questions: *What purposes are well served by Big Data analyses and what goals might suffer? Can Big Data be used to make us safer, or does it inherently make us less safe?* This chapter addresses those questions by critically examining the claims made for Big Data accuracy and usefulness in general, and then taking a closer look at how these accuracy and usefulness issues might affect our security when Big Data are applied towards that particular goal.

Setting chapter parameters

What are data?

The empiricist view of data, and very likely the popular view amongst those of us not trained in science theory, is that data are simply the recorded, uncontestable, observed facts about things, people and events around us. For instance, one online dictionary defines data as:

1   *Facts* that can be analysed or used in an effort to gain knowledge or make decisions; information.
2   Statistics or other information represented in a form suitable for processing by computer.

(thefreedictionary.com n.d., emphasis added)

In our daily lives we, of necessity, act, at least for the most part, as if facts and data were such simple things. When we need to make snap decisions, however vital they may be, we, of necessity, take the same stance – a viewpoint called empiricism in science theory. Empiricism is a convenient simplification. To actively doubt and question each observation would be impractical, to say the least. But in a science context, or when we have time to take some care about vital decisions, we need to be aware that empiricism is flawed. Facts are not so obvious, observable, or uncontestable.

So, how do we turn our endless and boundless flow of observations/ sensations/emotions into discreet facts? The cosmos is a continuum without uncontestable boundaries. I may anthropocentrically think of myself as a neatly bounded body, separate from the air I breathe, the water I drink, the bacteria that form an essential part of my digestion and my skin … but I am not neatly bounded. I am porous. I-as-I-anthropocentrically-think-of-myself and my-surroundings-as-I-anthropocentrically-think-of-them emerge through intra-actions with one another (i.e. with our shared selves) and are thoroughly intra-dependent (Barad 2007). To consider conceptual units such as my-anthropocentric-self as one discreet unit about which discreet traits might be measured and recorded and the air as another such unit, or to similarly distinguish between 'different' species is to draw boundaries which, however conventional and/or well reasoned, are nevertheless, at some level, arbitrary. Such boundaries could always have been drawn differently, and sometimes *are* drawn differently. And this drawing of boundaries is just the first step of turning the cosmos into data.

Turning these constructed samenesses and differences into data involves further layers of constructed conventions and/or individual choices: what features of each category are worth recording (what counts?), and how they are to be counted (by what means and in what measurement units?). Each of these layers is equally arbitrary and changeable. The social processes of reaching a degree of consensus, layer by layer, are often fraught with contention (Bowker and Star 1999). It is only once a degree of consensus has been reached and/or enforced, once units and measurements have been conventionalised and stand-ardised, that the resulting data can be made to appear obvious, natural, observ-able, uncontestable – until, that is, someone again makes the effort to contest them (Latour 1987). Furthermore, explicit and implicit contestations, however marginal, are frequent. Therefore – as also discussed by Noorman *et al.* (Chapter 14 in this volume) – data require custodianship in order for standardisations to retain a degree of stability.

All this is not to say that data are useless or erroneous fictions. It only means that they could *always* have been otherwise and that it pays, especially in some contexts, to keep this in mind. The same goes for their (in)stability. It is not that data are too unstable, too fragile, to be of use. It is only that it pays to be aware of their potential instability and fragility and of the procedures being used to maintain and stabilise them.

What makes data 'big'?

Big Data is big along one or more of several dimensions that characterise data sets. First and foremost, it is big in terms of numbers of cases or instances recorded – numbers of persons, numbers of vehicles, numbers of transactions ... whatever the initial units triggering recording might be. Second, data sets referred to as Big Data often contain records of many variables about each case/instance/unit. Third, such sets often include linkage potentials to further data sets, big and/or small, thus allowing expansion of the original data set. Fourth, such data sets are usually big on speed – that is, the data they contain are often recorded automatically and more or less instantaneously as each unit occurs: as a person enters a shop through an RFID portal, as a credit card transaction occurs, as a vehicle passes an auto-pay toll station, as an email is sent, and so on. Fifth, such data sets are often structured and regulated to be big on flexibility, making the data available for a variety of analytical purposes. Separately and together, these features are generally thought to make Big Data big on power: statistical power, power to produce knowledge, power to influence events. However, as we shall see, each of these features also entails potential weaknesses.

When learning statistical research methods, one of the earliest lessons is that more data is better. More data (more cases) means more statistical power, more likelihood of statistically significant results, more widely generalisable results, less risk of findings being distorted by a handful of cases with entry errors or outlier values. But ... more data also means greater difficulty checking for errors.

It is similarly the case for more detailed data (more variables and more link-ages). Here, too, there are both advantages and risks. The more detail we have, the less likely we are to get stuck with an exciting finding, one that raises new hypotheses, and then not have relevant variables to explore that finding further. We're also less likely to get stuck with no variables that can explain whatever variations we see in outcomes. But ... more detailed data also means greater risk of finding spurious patterns.

Flexibility is also a source of both advantages and risks. The varied sources and types of data available in Big Data sets, the level of data detail and the potential for linkages all invite analysts to pose a wide variety of questions the data might perceivably offer answers to. This increases the practical, intellectual and market value of the data. But ... the repurposing of data to answer questions they were not initially collected to address carries a number of risks. Remember that data, however conventionalised and seemingly natural, are socio-material constructs. Their social and material construction histories leave an imprint on them. Data collected for one purpose are shaped by that purpose, which may render them misshapen in the context of some new purpose. While data expressions (a code or number) may well be both immutable and mobile (Latour 1987: 227), their meanings are not. At the very least, a process of reinterpretation must take place, if only an instantaneous (and mistaken) one of declaring the data to be pure and universal reflections of truths that travel effortlessly and unchangingly from one context to another.

Furthermore, in Europe at any rate, the repurposing of data may run afoul of privacy law. Privacy law in Norway (and Norwegian law is in this regard typical for European laws more widely) demands that any collection of personal data – that is, data that can be traced back to an identifiable person – must be mandated by either a specific law, a vital need, or the informed consent of each person concerned. Each of these sources for mandate requires an identified purpose for the data collection. When legitimately collected and stored data are moved to a new user and/or reused for some new purpose, the original mandate may not be presumed to follow. The law that mandated their collection and storage may not apply. The vital need may not be relevant. The informed consent cannot be presumed unless the new user and purpose were included in the original information given and consented to.[3]

In evaluating the claims of Big Data advocates, I will be considering both the advantages and risks of Big Data's characteristics. I will be asking how these advantages and risks seem likely to play out given what Big Data advocates claim regarding what Big Data can and should be used for and how.

What are Big Data good for, given how they are created, processed, and used?

Ideally, I should be answering this question by delving directly into Big Data collection processes and analysis algorithms. Those, however, are for the most part proprietary and/or confidential. It will take time to gain access, and then time to explore them deeply enough for interpretation – possibly more time than I, at 67, have remaining in my career. Algorithms are discussed by Matzner (Chapter 3 in this volume), but for my part I will now turn to the more general claims of Big Data advocates.

Authors such as Mayer-Schönberger and Cukier (2013) and Anderson (2008) make a number of claims as to why and how Big Data can 'extract new insights or create new forms of value' that cannot be achieved at a smaller scale

(Mayer-Schönberger and Cukier 2013: 242). Anderson's version is the most concise. His claims can be enumerated as follows:

1   The massive availability of data causes a new analytical approach.
2   Models, including causal models, are no longer relevant.
3   Theory is no longer relevant.
4   Data speak for themselves.
5   Correlation is enough.
6   Correlation results are correct to an unprecedented degree.

To this we can add a seventh point, not explicitly mentioned by Anderson, but implicit there and posited explicitly elsewhere (e.g. critically by Harford (2014)) as an argument for Big Data, namely that N (the number of instances included in the database for a given phenomenon) now equals very nearly all and that since N=all (or very nearly all) we are no longer dealing with samples nor, therefore, with sampling error. This is purported to explain why 'correlation is enough': it is enough because it is the whole.

So how do these seven arguments hold up to scrutiny? Not entirely well.

Because petabytes

Ignoring the irony that Anderson (2008) begins with a causal argument just before declaring causality moot, his causal argument is historically wrong. The availability of mass data is not the *cause* of Google's or others' inductivist/empiricist[4] approach to data analysis; it is a *result*. A substantial portion of those data were intentionally created by, for instance, Google and Facebook, whose business plans at the outset were to produce, harvest, analyse and market masses of data. Yes, there is also a vast amount of data that has been produced incidentally, as a by-product from other purposes – for instance communications traffic data initially produced for billing and/or for reconstituting data packets back into entire messages at the receiving end. However, the mere existence of that data does not force us to use it for other purposes than those for which it was created. In fact, as discussed above, such repurposing of data may be illegal.

Furthermore, even if legal, storing and using those data for new purposes implies both empiricism (as discussed above, the view that data are simply the registered 'mirror' images of observable and uncontestable truths, endlessly mobile and immutable) and inductivism (the view that knowledge is best built from data upwards by observing patterns in the data and then examining whether those same patterns hold for larger bodies of data).

Empiricism has already been discussed above as a useful, even necessary, but erroneous simplification. Inductivism is only 'wrong' if practised absolutely and exclusively. Many disciplines practice inductivism as their preferred style of research. However, inductivism practised thoroughly involves testing one's initial interpretations of patterns by looking at larger and larger data sets to see whether and under what circumstances the pattern still holds. In other words, good inductivism entails rather than precludes deductive steps, working one's way gradually upwards in data set size and/or outwards to data sets involving more and more categories of units. What Anderson and other Big Data advocates are claiming is that, given the vastness of the data sets available, one can skip those pesky, time-consuming deductive and/or iterative steps by going straight to the biggest data set and looking for patterns there inductively. But no, it is wrong to conclude that the ultimate data set in terms of size is the ultimate proof of any observed pattern and that work with smaller data sets is a waste of time. For instance, a pattern that holds true for a large data set viewed as a whole, might not hold true for some subset of that data set. Suffice it to say that iterative research, moving back and forth between data and tentative conclusions, is a form of 'due diligence', that jumping to conclusions in a single step is rarely wise, that inductive approaches are fine but best when combined with deductive ones as well, and that regardless of data availability we still have methodological choices to make. Soaring data handling capacities and falling data handling prices have created an *opportunity* (but not a requirement) which actors of an inductivist bent have seized upon. But, as I intend to show, even that opportunity has its limits.

[Causal] models are moot

Not so. Or at least, not entirely so. Yes, there are situations where we needn't care about causality, only about how acting on our predictions and understandings affects bottom line outcomes. One such situation is when gambling. In gambling, all we need is a marginal improvement in outcome probabilities, yielding us better odds than those taking our bets have calculated. We don't need to understand why, as long as we stop gambling before our predictions cease to produce that statistical advantage. Similarly with advertising: even a small margin saved on advertising costs or a small margin of increased sales will produce increased profits, without necessarily having to understand the reasons for customers' preferences. But, if we do happen to have a reliable causal understanding of why certain customers buy our product, we may be better able to anticipate shifts in the market and thus maintain our market advantage longer. Furthermore, there are other situations where an understanding of causality provides not just a statistical advantage, but precisely the sought-for outcome.

For instance, research is often directed towards offering policy advice, and policy is inherently a causality-motivated exercise. Policy is, ideally and practically, based on a balance between assessments of means and of desired outcomes. Each of these assessments is not only about pragmatics, but also about morality and politics as well. The question is not only what we can do, but also what we should do (or not do) and what it is socially acceptable that we do (or not do). Of course, pragmatics are also a part of the latter two questions, since what we should do and what it would be accepted that we do are to a significant extent matters of causal assessment: how effective are the means we are considering in terms of producing the outcomes we are aiming for? If we decline to discuss causality, we render ourselves irrelevant to policy discourse.

Security measures also build, implicitly or explicitly, on causal models. When various US authorities repeatedly threaten to bomb some enemy or terrorist threat 'back to the Stone Age',[5] this implies understandings (a.k.a. theories) about the causes of violent opposition, about what motivates or demotivates individuals to join in such opposition, and/or about what creates or destroys a group's capability to carry out such opposition. Acknowledging the theoretical implications and critically examining them might help to identify a (more) successful way forward.

Theory is irrelevant

Again, not so. Or at least, that depends on what we mean by 'theory' and 'relevant'. I would claim that theory is what invests observations with meaning, taking them from the realm of noise to the realm of data. Theory, in this sense, is our interpretive framework – however tentative, however much we treat that framework sceptically and are prepared to revise it. Of course, we may observe first and theorise later (the inductive path) or we may theorise first and observe on that basis (the deductive path). As discussed above, it is generally advisable to combine the two approaches in iterative alternations. Nevertheless, no matter which approach we have given to analysing numbers and other simplifications, sooner or later we must flesh out these numbers, skeletal simplifications that they necessarily are, with meanings. This brings us to the next point.

Numbers speak for themselves

Not so. Mathematics, I would argue, is an abstract language, a set of rules for thinking and communicating about anything socially deemed enumerable. Through those rules, numbers are positioned in relation to one another, but are left empty of otherwise meaningful content. X can stand for anything; so can 1; so can 5347–56 or any set of values or placeholders in any mathematical equation, however well their relationships to one another are defined by the equation. For a mathematical formula or any product of that formula to speak about anything beyond its own empty shells and grammatical rules, we have to fill those shells and relationships with meaning, we have to interpret, we have to add theory-relevant data.

Interpretation is a job numbers do not perform on their own. Indeed, it is a job that is never finally completed and settled. It is always possible to discuss the meanings of a set of data or the outcome of a data analysis. It is always possible to contest a meaning once agreed upon, or to add new layers of meaning to those already accepted, that is, data are always 'interpretatively flexible' (Collins 1981).

Sometimes interpretation is a purely personal matter (glass half full or half empty?). Often it is a social process. When researching with ready-produced data, it is important to know how each number/text string/classification/code was arrived at and what meaning(s!) it is understood to hold (for examples of this see Bowker and Star (1999); Sætnan *et al.* (2010)).

Correlation is enough

This goes against experience as taught in Probability 101. The more data you throw together into a database, the more likely it is that some of those data will fall into patterns, some of which will be entirely random and meaningless, also known as *spurious correlations*. For instance, did you know that over the 6-year period 2008–2013 the number of lawyers in West Virginia corresponds almost perfectly (correlation coefficient[6]: 0.987938) with overall US online revenue on Thanksgiving? Over the 12-year period 1999–2010, it correlates nearly as precisely with the number of suicides by hanging, strangulation and suffocation in all of the United States (correlation coefficient: 0.968413) (tylervigen.com n.d.).[7]

Advocates for Big Data claim that, for trend analysis, it doesn't matter if correlations make sense. You don't have to know why; correlation alone matters. If communities hit by flu coincidentally had surges of online dog biscuit orders, that too could have been included in the Google Flu Trends algorithm.[8] Doctors do use population-level correlations when diagnosing. It matters that you have symptoms x and y but not z. It may also matter that you live in region a (where one possible diagnosis explaining your symptoms is more common than another), have job b (which exposes you to certain disease vectors), gender c (which entails a different hormonal spectrum) and are d years old (and therefore more or less likely to get childhood diseases, more or less likely to show symptoms of degenerative diseases). But should I someday consult my doctor concerning suicidal thoughts, I hope s/he won't base her/his diagnosis on the number of lawyers in West Virginia, but only on factors that make logical sense to her/him and to me.

Results show unprecedented accuracy

Ironically, this is a claim supported by anecdotal rather than statistical evidence. We are told of instances where non-spurious correlations were found between variables and instances where inferences about individuals in the data set were drawn on the basis of such correlations and proved correct, but we are not told how many times similar inferences were drawn and proved incorrect.

There is the famous story about when Google, using search term statistics, spotted a flu epidemic, two weeks before the same wave of infection was spotted by the Centers for Disease Control, on the basis of physicians' reports. The story that Google Flu Trends later has *mis*-spotted flu epidemics (Harford 2014) is less referenced.

Equally famous is the story of how Target, tracking loyalty card links to sales of certain items, sent out baby product ads to a teenaged girl. Her father, outraged at first, apologised two weeks later when the girl admitted to him that she was in fact pregnant. This story is referenced in informatics textbooks as a triumph for Big Data (e.g. Siegel 2013; Bari, Chaouchi and Jung 2014; Sanders 2014). The story is not always accompanied by discussion of why Target and others, pursuing this form of advertising, have since changed strategy

(Greengard 2012), hiding such advertising by bundling it amongst numerous non-targeted ads and offers, thus protecting themselves against backlash should the targeted advertising prove hurtful because the algorithm's 'diagnosis' is wrong, or unethical even when it is right (see, for instance, Ebeling 2016).

N = *all*

N is never all. There are always some who are missing from (at least some parts of) the data set – for instance those too poor, too young, too old or too infirm to own smart phones, hold credit cards, purchase electronic travel cards, or access the Internet. There are also those who intentionally stay 'off the grid', be it for ideological, nefarious or other sorts of reasons. Furthermore, even if N=all at some given moment in time or space, that time–space is always a non-random sample from an infinite time–space continuum. A pattern may be real today, yet gone tomorrow.

For instance, consider Boston's experiment with using smartphones' GPS sensors and accelerometers to spot and report potholes in city streets. The algorithm 'works' to some extent, but must be corrected for the bias that neighbourhoods with predominantly poor and/or ageing populations – areas that often have the worst street conditions and/or greatest need for good conditions – have far fewer smart phones (Crawford 2013). The Boston pothole algorithm, then, is an example of the 'streetlight fallacy'. The streetlight fallacy gets its name from a joke:

> A man almost stumbles over another man on his hands and knees searching the ground under a streetlight. 'What are you looking for?' he asks. 'I'm looking for my wallet,' the searcher replies. 'Oh! Did you lose it near here?' 'No, I lost it over in that alley.' 'Then why aren't you searching in the alley?' 'Because the light's better over here!'

Similarly with Big Data: We are tempted to look for more or less everything in the vast databases that contain information about nearly everything, but the answers we need may require information that is *not* in those databases. That doesn't mean that it's wrong to look for answers through Big Data. It only means that it pays to think first what question you're asking and what data would best answer that question, then use Big Data databases only if the data you need is there (see a discussion of research questions by Green, Chapter 15 in this volume).

And then there's the old adage 'Garbage in, garbage out', which holds true also for enormous databases. One of the problems of large databases is that their very size makes it impractical, if not impossible, to proofread, fact-check and correct erroneous data. Even when data are automatically entered from digitised processes such as credit card transactions, there may be errors. If someone has hacked your credit card information, transactions attributed to you may not have been made by you at all, even if the data were correctly recorded as entered during the transaction itself. Such errors are non-random and will not cancel each other out in the vast mass of data; you have not accidentally charged other items to your hacker's account, nor have you sought symmetrical revenge by hacking the hacker's account. There will also, inevitably, be instances where data are wrongly entered more or less at random. A recent study of data quality in the Google Scholar, ISI Web of Science and Scopus databases (Franceschini *et al.* 2016) found that Google Scholar, though useful as a search engine, had far too many errors to be useful as a research tool. ISI and Scopus databases were perhaps useful, but results would have to be interpreted cautiously as they showed 6% and 4% errors respectively.[9] Tüür-Fröhlich (2016) found even worse results for the social science database ISCI. For one of the original articles he traced, only 1% of citations were registered without errors. Furthermore, the errors were not randomly distributed, but were systematically skewed by factors such as publication language.

So what?

What does it matter that Big Data as a source of knowledge is riddled with myths and errors? The answer depends on what it's used for. As a business model, it may or may not be a good gamble that increases its users' profit odds at least marginally. Economic risks do also get passed on to others (workers, suppliers, taxpayers, etc.) and those unchosen risks can be quite serious, but there are ways of ameliorating them. Who winds up carrying the risks is a political battle we may choose to engage in, but probably not to the point of proposing a ban on legitimate, consent-based data analysis. This does presume that the data are only used for the purposes to which we originally consented, which is far from always the case when it comes to our data being appropriated and repurposed by Big Data applications. But, what of security applications? What happens when Big Data are deployed as a key weapon in a strategy of what Strauß (Chapter 4 in this volume) calls 'securitisation'?

When it comes to using Big Data-based approaches to security issues, besides data collection being often involuntary and opaque and thus in itself a threat to democracy, the consequences risked by actions (and, for that matter, inactions) based on those data can be drastic and irrevocable. Four factors make security applications of Big Data particularly dangerous – the actions based on the data analyses, the frequency of errors in the analytical results, the mistaken faith put in those results' accuracy, and the overall social consequences of Big Data practices. Before discussing the actions and their consequences, let's take a closer look at the accuracy issues. What happens to needle-location accuracy when you build a bigger haystack? A simple percentage calculation can show how dramatically accuracy falls.

First we need to know the size of the haystack, then an estimate for the number of needles in it, and finally an estimate as to how accurately our search algorithm identifies needles and hay respectively. Let's suppose we are searching for terrorists. In 2014, *CNN* asked a number of security experts how many jihadi terrorist groups and group members they thought there were in the world (Bergen and Schneider 2014). Estimates varied from 85,000 to 106,000 members. Of course, not all terrorists are jihadists, not all consider jihadists to be terrorists, and numbers of members change over time,[10] but let's go with those figures for now, and for simplicity's sake let's call it a round 100,000. As for the size of the haystack, in an interview with Laura Poitras, William Binney (former NSA data analyst, now whistle-blower) states that the NSA's data storage facility in Bluffdale, Utah has the capacity to store 100 years' worth of all the world's electronic communications (Poitras 2012, minutes 2:35–2:53). The world population currently stands at over seven billion. Again for the sake of simplicity, let's stipulate that the world population is 7,000,100,000, of which 100,000 are jihadi terrorists. Of course, not all ordinary citizens are communicating electronically, but neither are all jihadi terrorists doing so. We could estimate some average number of electronic transactions per person per day, but if we estimated the same average for jihadi terrorists as for the population in general, then the two factors would cancel one another out. So, we may stipulate our haystack numbers as 7,000,000,000 'straws' and 100,000 'needles'.

Now let's give our hypothetical algorithm every benefit of the doubt. Let's stipulate that we have an algorithm that analyses all these electronic transactions – phone calls, purchases by credit card, loyalty card swipes, Internet searches, toll road passages, etc., etc. It is a complex and sophisticated algorithm. It analyses linkages amongst individuals and patterns of transactions. It is so incredibly precise that it correctly identifies 99% of the jihadi terrorist 'needles' and correctly exonerates 99% of the general populace 'straws'. Only 1% (1000) of the 'needles' are missed – that is, false negatives – correctly identifying the other 99,000 as true positives. Only 1% (70 million) of the 'straws' are drawn under suspicion (false positives), correctly exonerating the remaining six billion 930 million (true negatives).[11] How accurate, then, are the algorithm's positive 'hits' in the database?

As we can see in Table 2.1 below, the positive hits are far from 99% accurate. There are 70,099,000 (seventy million ninety-nine thousand) positive hits, of which only 99,000 are true positives. For this thought experiment, the rate of accuracy for each positive hit is 0.1412288335069% – *fourteen hundredths of one per cent*. Feel free to experiment by changing the numbers in the Table 2.1 spreadsheet. What happens when you increase the size of the haystack? What happens if you decrease it? What happens if the algorithm is less precise?

Usually there is a trade-off between false positives and false negatives. Suppose you agree with Blackstone that 'it is better that ten guilty persons escape, than that one innocent suffer' (Harvard Law Library n.d.). Then you would 'tune' your selection criteria to be as specific as possible, widening the openings in your search net so that only those highly likely to be guilty are marked for suspicion, even if that means that many others, equally guilty, go free. On the other hand, suppose you are seeking out asymptomatic sufferers of a deadly disease for which there are relatively painless and harmless tests and cures. Then you might tune your selection criteria to make the search net as tight

Table 2.1 Sample spreadsheet for estimating predictive values of search algorithm hits

Stipulated Algorithm Properties:

Sensitivity (percentage of true positives identified as positive):	99	% False negatives:	1
Specificity (percentage of true negatives identified as negative):	99	% False positives:	1

Results for 100,000 true positives among 7,000, 100,000 total in database

	Identified as positive	Identified as negative	
True positives	99,000	1,000	100,000
True negatives	70,000,000	6,930,000,000	7,000,000,000
Sum identified pos/neg	70,099,000	6,930,001,000	7,000,100,000
Predictive values (percentage true pos/neg among all so identified)	0.141228834	9.999998557	

as possible, even at the cost of frightening large numbers of healthy people and subjecting them to unnecessary further tests. Choosing a balance point between sensitivity (identifying as many 'needles' as possible) and specificity (exonerating as many 'straws' as possible) is a moral and practical call. Is it better that ten guilty go free? This may depend on context and the associated consequences of an initial positive. It may well be acceptable that ten (or more) healthy are put through further tests for each extra case of breast cancer caught in a mammography screening programme.[12] In a context of identifying presumed terrorists, however, the consequences would be far different. Being mistaken for a suicide bomber doesn't mean being subjected to further tests; it means being killed on the spot before you have a chance to set off a bomb … even if it turns out you weren't carrying one after all. What then if, out of fear of false negatives, you allow for more false positives – or vice versa? The answer to that question may depend on how much trust authorities place in each positive hit from the database.

The math here is simple: Crunching big numbers can lead you astray – further astray the higher the ratio of 'straw' to 'needles' in the database you search through and further astray the higher the mass of numbers you crunch. Recall too, that the size and data accumulation speed of Big Data databases almost of necessity will result in more data errors and inadequate time for data proofreading and correction.

Furthermore, history shows that it may not be lack of information but inadequate interpretation of available information that has hampered prevention of terrorist episodes. For instance: various authorities had been warned about the 9/11 suicide pilots' strange behaviour; one of the brothers allegedly responsible for the Boston Marathon bombing was known to the FBI through two prior investigations as well as warnings from Russia; and, French anti-terrorist police knew of the men alleged responsible for the Charlie Hebdo and subsequent attacks, but explained that 'there are far too many of them, and far too few of us' (*CNN* 2015). Under such circumstances, it is hard to see how increasing the information load and increasing the number of suspects, especially by adding thousands of false suspects, can help in preventing future terrorist attacks.

And yet security officials – for instance NSA top brass, in interviews and Congressional committee hearings – continue to claim that results from sifting through masses of electronic transaction records are exactingly precise, that more data is what they need, that limiting their data collection practices means taking responsibility for future tragedies. NSA General Counsel Stewart Baker is cited as having said, 'Metadata absolutely tells you everything about somebody's life. If you have enough metadata, you don't really need content.' Michael Hayden, former director (at different times) of both the NSA and the CIA, concurs, saying, 'Absolutely correct. We kill people based on metadata' (Cole 2014). An otherwise anonymous drone operator, apparently attempting to de-dramatise the picture, said, 'People get hung up that there's a targeted list of people. It's really like we're targeting a cell phone. We're not going after people – we're going after their phones, in the *hopes* that the person on the other end of that missile is the bad guy' (Scahill and Greenwald 2014, emphasis added). It's enough to give one pause any time you switch on your cell phone.

In conclusion

We have seen that in some ways Big Data simply doesn't work. These weaknesses can be dangerous when applied to critical social functions such as security. But what of the social consequences of Big Data analysis more generally, in the areas where it does work? When I buy a book at Amazon.com, I am immediately told what other books previous purchasers of that book bought or 'liked'. When I read certain articles online, or sign online petitions, newsfeeds and ad-feeds are adjusted, targeting me according to what the algorithm says are my interests and tastes. Sometimes the algorithm clearly gets it wrong. An accidental click on an advertisement now has me receiving endless tips on places to stay in Van Nuys, California. Irritating, but harmless. But let us assume for now that this 'works', that people have a better 'Facebook experience', more effective Google searches,[13] that Facebook and Google advertisers make more sales. Even if this doesn't work, but Facebook's and Google's paying customers *think* that it works, then it at least 'works' to produce profits for Facebook and Google. But what else might it produce? Does it contribute to a Balkanisation of society? Are we compartmentalised into ever-finer interest groups where we are increasingly exposed only to those who already agree with us? Does that create increasing polarisation of society, decreasing tolerance for ideas and values from outside our algorithm-defined groups (Tewksbury 2005; Schneider, Chapter 8 in this volume)? If so, then even when Big Data 'works', it may also work to make us less secure.

Recently we have also seen that Big Data may work in history-changing ways by marginally improving its users' odds in a variety of odds-based situations. For instance, the Trump campaign, possibly together with Russian hackers, used Big Data analytics to pull out a narrow win in critical states (Doward and Gibbs 2017). They only needed to improve their margin by a few percentage points in the right places. When the voting was so close, it didn't matter if their targeted ads missed the mark in many cases, as long as they did hit the mark in a few thousand more; it didn't matter if targeted voter registration purges also took out some Republican voters, as long as they took out a few thousand more Democrats. In that sort of situation, if you don't care about the consequences for democracy, then Big Data can work. But, as discussed above, when it comes to making security decisions, relying on Big Data can be disastrous.

Notes

1 But not *all* our thoughts and activities! We'll return to this point later.
2 I use quotation marks here to signify that I am introducing Big Data as a concept, as opposed to simply big (adjective) data. Hereafter, when referring to that concept as a fact or a set of practices, I will only capitalise it. If I do use quotation marks around the concept later, it will be to highlight irony in contexts where I and/or others I cite raise doubts as to Big Data's existence or capacities.
3 See Personopplysningsloven [Personal Data Law] pp. 8 and 9 (Lovdata.no 2000).
4 Inductivism is a variant of empiricism. Both share the notion that the cosmos is as we observe it and that observation is the route to knowledge, but where some branches of empiricism tout hypothesis-testing through experimentation, inductivism argues that knowledge is built through the accumulation of experience. For more on the history and variations on this position, see for instance: vetenskapsteori.se (2007–2017) or Philosophybasics.com (2008).
5 Amongst others, purportedly General LeMay re Vietnam in 1968 (Wikiquote.org n.d.); Secretary of State Richard Armitage in 2011 re Pakistan's resistance to joining the US in its 'war on terror' (Cullather 2006); and Senator Ted Cruz re ISIS (aka ISIL, IS, DAESH) in 2014 (Good 2014).
6 For those who have not taken Probability 101, the correlation coefficient is a measure of shared variability. Coefficients range from -1 to $+1$. A coefficient of -1 means that for every change in one variable, an equal and opposite change occurs in another. A coefficient of $+1$ means that an equal change occurs in the same direction for the second variable. A coefficient of 0 means that the two variables vary completely at random to one another.
7 The website is interactive in case you wish to explore further spurious correlations.
8 While that hypothetical correlation, which I initially made up out of thin air, was meant to seem silly, it later occurred to me that it could have generated some researchable and potentially non-trivial hypotheses. For instance, feverish dog owners, being less able to give their dogs enough exercise, might need more treats to control their dogs, and they might need to buy treats online if they're not up to going out to the store.
9 Others have reached opposite conclusions. For instance, Harzing and van der Wal (2008) find systematic errors in both Google Scholar and ISI but regard those in Google Scholar as less critical.
10 Here is another example of where causal models would be useful. Imagine if we knew what motivated people to seek political change through non-violent action and what motivated them to seek it through dramatic violence. Media reports indicate the

effectiveness of terrorist groups in using such knowledge to recruit members. Media reports also indicate that, by comparison, governments are less knowledgeable and/or less effective at using such knowledge to slow or reverse such recruitment. See for instance *NY Times* June 13 2015 'US sees failure in fighting ISIS on social media'.

11 Given the flaws of Big Data discussed above, this estimate is obviously a gross exaggeration of the imagined algorithm's accuracy.

12 Regarding actual false-positive rates of screening mammography, see for instance Elmore *et al.* (2002).

13 More 'effective' in the sense of finding what you already tended to look for more rapidly, but at the same time reducing your chances of serendipitous findings you didn't imagine might interest you.

References

Anderson, C. (2008). The end of theory: The data deluge makes the scientific method obsolete. *Wired Magazine*. Available at: http://archive.wired.com/science/discoveries/magazine/16-07/pb_theory. [Accessed 10 November 2017].

Barad, K. (2007). *Meeting the Universe Halfway: Quantum Physics and the Entanglement of Matter and Meaning*. Durham, NC: Duke University Press.

Bari, A., Chaouchi, M. and Jung, T. (2014). *Predictive Analytics for Dummies*. Hoboken, NJ: John Wiley & Sons.

Bergen, P. and Schneider, E. (2014). Jihadist threat not as big as you think. Available at: www.cnn.com/2014/09/26/opinion/bergen-schneider-how-many-jihadists/. [Accessed 10 November 2017].

Bowker, G. C. and Star, S. L. (1999). *Sorting Things Out. Classification and its Consequences*. Cambridge, MA: MIT Press.

CNN (2015). Terrorists slipping through serious security breaches in France. Available at: www.cnn.com/2015/01/11/world/terrorists-security-breaches-france/. [Accessed 10 November 2017].

Cole, D. (2014). 'We kill people based on metadata'. *The New York Review of Books*, 10 May 2014. Available at: www.nybooks.com/blogs/nyrblog/2014/may/10/we-kill-people-based-metadata/. [Accessed 10 November 2017].

Collins, H. M. (1981). Stages in the empirical programme of relativism. *Social Studies of Science*, 11(1), 3–10.

Crawford, K. (2013). The hidden biases in big data. *Harvard Business Review*. Available at: https://hbr.org/2013/04/the-hidden-biases-in-big-data. [Accessed 10 November 2017].

Cullather, N. (2006). Bomb the back to the Stone Age: An etymology. Available at: http://historynewsnetwork.org/article/30347. [Accessed 20 October 2017].

Doward, J. and Gibbs, A. (2017). Did Cambridge Analytica influence the Brexit vote and the US election? *Guardian*, 4 March 2017. Available at: www.theguardian.com/politics/2017/mar/04/nigel-oakes-cambridge-analytica-what-role-brexit-trump. [Accessed 14 August 2017].

Ebeling, M. F. E. (2016). *Healthcare and Big Data: Digital Specters and Phantom Objects*. New York: Palgrave Macmillan.

Elmore, J. G., Miglioretti, D. L., Reisch, L. M., Barton, M. B., Kreuter, W., Christiansen, C. L. and Fletcher, S. W. (2002). Screening mammograms by community radiologists: Variability in false-positive rates. *Journal of the National Cancer Institute*, 94(18), 1373–1380.

Franceschini, F., Maisano, D. A. and Mastrogiacomo, L. (2016). Empirical analysis and classification of database errors in Scopus and Web of Science. *Journal of Informetrics*, 10(4), 933–953.

Good, C. (2014). Cruz invites Obama to border, calls for bombing ISIS 'Back to the Stone Age'. Available at: http://abcnews.go.com/blogs/politics/2014/08/cruz-invites-obama-to-border-calls-for-bombing-isis-back-to-the-stone-age/. [Accessed 20 October 2017].

Greengard, S. (2012). Advertising gets personal. *Communications of the ACM*, 55(8), 18–20. Available at: http://cacm.acm.org/magazines/2012/8/153815-advertising-gets-personal/fulltext. [Accessed 10 November 2017].

Haggerty, K. D. and Ericson, R. V. (2000). The surveillant assemblage. *British Journal of Sociology*, 51(4), 605–622.

Harford, T. (2014, March 28). Big Data – Are we making a big mistake? *Financial Times*. Available at: www.ft.com/content/21a6e7d8-b479-11e3-a09a-00144feabdc0. [Accessed 10 November 2017].

Harvard Law Library (n.d.). 'It is better that ten guilty persons escape than that one innocent suffer'. Available at: http://library.law.harvard.edu/justicequotes/explore-the-room/south-4/. [Accessed 20 October 2017].

Harzing, A. W. and van der Wal, R. (2008). Google Scholar as a new data source for citation analysis? *Ethics in Science and Environmental Politics*, 8(1), 61–73.

Laney, D. (2001). 3D data management: Controlling data volume, velocity and variety. [pdf] Available at: http://blogs.gartner.com/doug-laney/files/2012/01/ad949-3D-Data-Management-Controlling-Data-Volume-Velocity-and-Variety.pdf. [Accessed 10 November 2017].

Latour, B. (1987). *Science in Action. How to Follow Scientists and Engineers Through Society*. Cambridge, MA: Harvard University Press.

Lovdata.no (2000). Personopplysningsloven. Available at: https://lovdata.no/dokument/NL/lov/2000-04-14-31?q=Personopplysningsloven. [Accessed 10 November 2017].

Mayer-Schönberger, V. and Cukier, K. (2013). *Big Data: A Revolution that will Transform How We Live, Work, and Think*. London: John Murray Publishers, Ltd.

New York Times (2015). ISIS is winning the social media war, U.S. concludes. 12 June 2015. Available online at www.nytimes.com/2015/06/13/world/middleeast/isis-is-winning-message-war-us-concludes.html. [Accessed 12 December 2017].

Philosophybasics.com (2008). British Empiricism. Available at: www.philosophybasics.com/movements_british_empiricism.html. [Accessed 10 November 2017].

Poitras, L. (2012). *The Program*. Documentary film. Available at: www.nytimes.com/video/opinion/100000001733041/the-program.html. [Accessed 10 November 2017].

Sætnan, A. R., Lomell, H. M. and Hammer, S., eds. (2010). *The Mutual Construction of Statistics and Society*. New York: Routledge.

Sanders, N. R. (2014). *Big Data Driven Supply Chain Management*. Upper Saddle River, NJ: Pearson Education.

Scahill, J. and Greenwald, G. (2014). The NSA's secret role in the U.S. assassination program, *The Intercept*, 2 October 2014. Available at: https://firstlook.org/theintercept/2014/02/10/the-nsas-secret-role/. [Accessed 10 November 2017].

Siegel, E. (2013). *Predictive Analytics: The Power to Predict who will Click, Buy, Lie, or Die*. Hoboken, NJ: John Wiley & Sons.

Tewksbury, D. (2005). The seeds of audience fragmentation: Specialization in the use of online news sites. *Journal of Broadcasting & Electronic Media*. Available at: www.researchgate.net/publication/238400693_The_Seeds_of_Audience_Fragmentation_Specialization_in_the_Use_of_Online_News_Sites. [Accessed 10 November 2017].

Thefreedictionary.com (n.d.). Data. Available at: www.thefreedictionary.com/data. [Accessed 10 November 2017].

Tüür-Fröhlich, T. (2016). *The Non-trivial Effects of Trivial Errors in Scientific Communication and Evaluation.* Glückstad: Verlag Werner Hülsbusch.

tylervigen.com (n.d.). Spurious correlations. Available at: www.tylervigen.com/. [Accessed 20 October 2017].

Vetenskapsteori.se (2007–2017). Theory of knowledge. Available at: www.vetenskapsteori. se/ENG/m1eepist.htm. [Accessed 10 November 2017].

Wikipedia.org (n.d.). Big data. Available at: http://en.wikipedia.org/wiki/Big_data. [Accessed 10 November 2017].

Wikiquote.org (n.d.). Curtis LeMay. Available at: http://en.wikiquote.org/wiki/Curtis LeMay. [Accessed 10 November 2017].

3 Grasping the ethics and politics of algorithms

Tobias Matzner

Introduction

Algorithms are used to choose the ads we see online, to determine who gets insurance, who can board planes, who gets parole, or even who is killed by a drone. This already broad scope of usage can be expected to expand in coming years – from algorithmic diagnosis of diseases to self-driving cars. The growing influence that algorithms and data-driven decisions have on our lives has summoned a wide spectrum of critical voices. Most of them conclude with the request for more transparency and accountability. But, this is at best a starting point for a political and ethical grasp on these technologies – and may even be counterproductive in some cases. This chapter will give an overview of these issues.[1]

Opening black boxes is not enough

Most of the algorithms used in Big Data applications are inaccessible even for those who use them, not to mention those who are affected by the results of algorithmic evaluations. Often the image of a black box is invoked to describe this situation (Pasquale 2015). This image comes with the hope that if we opened the black box, we could see what the algorithm does and check if it does what it is supposed to do, or if it does something wrong, for example, if it is biased (Zarsky 2013).

However, access to the algorithm can at best uncover deliberate tampering with the results or structural problems. For example, some early facial recognition algorithms were modelled on the typical contrasts of white faces – apparently due to ignorance rather than intent (Frankle and Garvie 2016). For many data-driven applications, however, it is very difficult to predict how the algorithm will react without knowing the data. Furthermore, sophisticated technologies in artificial intelligence and related fields do not just learn once how to classify data and thereafter apply these fixed categories (Kroll *et al.* 2016). Rather, they constantly evolve. Thus, checks that are done in advance before using an algorithm cannot rule out future failures. In these cases, a lot hinges on the data. The following sections show that it is impossible to ascertain the neutrality of an algorithm. But, even if we could, algorithms would still produce biased results on biased data.

Some methods, like neural networks, which are responsible for many of the impressive recent successes of 'deep learning', are notoriously difficult to scrutinise (Smolensky 1988; Bornstein 2016). Often, we only can ascertain what they have learned by watching how they react to data. But, we can never make sure if they would not go completely wrong on the next set of data they encounter.

This means that most checks are only possible in hindsight: We need to watch the system perform and we need a good base of data to compare the results with. If all these conditions are met, we can see inherent problems, for example, the recent uncovering of biased parole algorithms by ProPublica (Angwin *et al.* 2016).

Accountability must include defining who will be responsible for the failures and problems that no scrutiny can rule out in advance.

Some things cannot be done right

Demanding accountability, transparency, or scrutiny implies that we know a right way of doing things, that we have categories that tell us what is wrong or right. For example, asking for scrutiny of a biased algorithm implies that one could build an unbiased one. But often that is not the case (Conrad 2009; Harcourt 2007). Many algorithmic systems are meant to predict the future behaviour of people: who will buy this product (and thus should get the respective ads displayed); who will get seriously ill (and thus will be an expensive client for an insurer); who will commit a terrorist attack (and thus should be forbidden to board a plane or to enter the country). This means we use a person's features or behaviour to predict something the person is not (yet) or has not (yet) done. This implies that there are sure signs of that person committing a crime or buying a product – other than committing that crime or buying that product. This follows a simple logic: People who are X do Y. This is the same structure that bias has: people who are X steal, for example. Just that the X is mathematically more sophisticated in the case of algorithms. But still, in this sense:

Prediction is operationalised bias. It will always overgeneralise, that means there will always be people who fit the criterion X but are not what we are looking for. No process of scrutiny can avoid that. We have to ask ourselves if we should use such technologies if the consequences are as dire as not being allowed to fly, being denied access to countries, or even becoming the victim of a drone strike.

Some readers will now object: sure, ok, but that's not what happens. Algorithms just estimate risk factors. And then someone else uses them to decide with better information at hand. They are but one element of the decision. This leads to the next problem:

Risk does not work on individuals. Imagine a border control officer operating a sophisticated, Big Data-driven system. Upon scanning the passport of a citizen returning from abroad, the officer sees a flashing warning on the display in red letters: 80% likelihood of terror. What does that mean? What is the officer supposed to do? Deny a legal citizen entrance into his or her own country? Arrest?

Carry out further checks that infringe on fundamental rights like privacy and freedom of movement? All done on the pretext that the person concerned, who did nothing wrong in her or his entire life, maybe will?

This illustrates a fundamental problem of risk assessment: nobody is an 80% terrorist – 80% terrorists do not exist. There are just a few people who plan a terrorist attack and many, many more who don't. Risk is an invention from trade and insurance (Porter 1996). If I sell a million products and calculate the risk that 10% of them will fail, then I can use that estimate to calculate how much profit I have to make with the other 90% to pay the damage caused by such failures. Risk estimates make sense when concerning a population that is big enough that it does not matter if one is right or not when regarding a single instance. In such cases it does not matter if one predicts the failure of a particular unit of one's product correctly as long as the overall estimate is correct. Risk estimates make sense if one can weigh the part of the population that is risky against the part that is not risky. This is what actuarial thinking is about. Both conditions are not given when concerning individuals like the citizen at the border.

Risk estimates for individuals suggest a numerical objectivity that does not have much practical meaning.

Discrimination and bias are no accident

The experience of being judged, assessed, sorted, and controlled is not the same for all. White middle and upper-class persons living in Western countries experience such moments much more rarely than do their fellow citizens of colour, persons with a different citizenship than the country they live in, *sans papiers*, refugees, poor – and many more that fall on the weaker sides of the many intersecting axes of discrimination that structure our societies (Cheney-Lippold 2011; Gilliom 2001; Leese 2014; Lerman 2013; Matzner 2016a). Those who have to undergo such scrutiny rather infrequently and usually without problematic consequences can afford the view that a wrong result or a faulty categorisation might be an accident. But the fear of being 'accidentally' placed on a no-fly list is quite different from the factual routine exclusion of those who are migrants or refugees and fall under the pattern to assess terrorists. The fear of being 'accidentally' assigned a bad credit score is quite different from the structural discrimination of those who cannot even open a bank account.[2] If it were only a problem of such 'accidents', then transparency and scrutiny of algorithms could perhaps help. But such processes will never be able to bring into view the structural discrimination sustained by the exclusionary mode of operation of border controls, air traffic policing, credit scoring, healthcare benefits, and many other institutions that find algorithmic decision-making attractive. On the contrary:

The impression that these processes could be ameliorated by transparently controlled, accountable algorithms might increase the legitimacy of those unjust practices.

Human experts are not necessarily better

If we want transparency, accountability, and scrutiny, we need people who perform transparently and accountably, and people who scrutinise their work. But the entire idea of using algorithms, especially in the context of security and the legal system, for example, when evaluating CCTV footage or deciding on parole, was motivated by many cases in which humans have been biased. There is an entire corpus of results from the social sciences that shows how institutions like the DHS or Frontex, but also big banks or the insurance industry, have created their own logic, with its own necessities, dependencies, and aims which are often detrimental to the greater good of society (Bigo and Tsoukala 2008; Ewald 1986). Unfortunately, that is true for many supervisory bodies as well. But it is clear that only a body of experts could do the work. Transparency cannot be the burden of individuals, since it needs expertise, time, and structural independence. The security sector, in particular, has a horrible tradition of evading supervisory bodies – lying to parliaments and courts, working according to secret treaties, collecting data illegally – or installing rubberstamping authorities like the FISA court (Greenwald 2014). This does not mean that supervision cannot work. But it means that we have to take into account that humans will not necessarily be less biased than algorithms. That is why we have developed several important mechanisms that do not aim at neutrality but, rather, acknowledge that such neutrality is an unattainable aim and try to mitigate bias instead; for example, diversity rules for juries and boards, blind reviews and applications, etc.

Mechanisms to mitigate bias are not perfect but they are better than striving for an ideal of neutrality that in reality just conceals the bias at play.

The algorithm is just one part of the puzzle

Why is Google so successful? Is it because they have the best page rank algorithm? Or is it maybe because they have a clean and easy approach to interfaces that has rendered the Internet usable for millions of new users who have not bothered to learn technical details? Or is it because Samsung has managed to build their utterly successful smartphones piggy-backed on Google's Android? Or was that success rather due to advertising agencies than to engineers?

Why do we tend to believe that trending topics on Twitter or the stuff in our Facebook newsfeed are important? Because it is selected by a special algorithm? Or because it appears to be related to what our friends read and post? Or just because it is right there where we start our daily use of social media and we seldom find the time or motivation to look anywhere else?

The effects of an application of an algorithm cannot be derived from that algorithm itself (Dourish 2016; Gillespie 2014; Matzner 2017). It depends on the social setting, on user interfaces, on established practices, on highly emotional or affective decisions – or rather reactions (often carefully crafted and rehearsed with us by the best advertising agencies in the world). Opening black boxes and scrutinising algorithms is part of disentangling these complicated relations.

But that must not entice us to think that the algorithm – or the source code – is the definitive instance that gives us a lever to the important ethical and political issues (Chun 2008). On the contrary, what we can learn from profound scrutiny of technical systems is:

There is rarely a technical solution to social and political problems. Technology might be helpful in many ways, but only if its interrelations with social and material circumstances are part of the picture.

Superhuman artificial intelligence is not the main issue

With recent advances in artificial intelligence research, prominent persons have issued warnings that we must take precautions now – otherwise one day a superhuman artificial intelligence might just turn against its creators (Sainato 2015). But that issue is not the problem here. Many reputable artificial intelligence researchers admit that it may never be a problem since an intelligence that even comes vaguely close to humans is not on any realistic horizon (Dreyfus 1992; Floridi 2016). Furthermore, even if it were, discussions on superintelligent artificial intelligences easily distract from the real problems we already have.

The main issue is that we already have all kinds of systems coming out of artificial intelligence research that at best can solve a highly specialised task and have nothing to do with human intelligence. But we trust these 'dumb' systems to judge human beings, trade stock, and drive cars – amongst many other things. That is because in the cases in which such systems are applied, something human-like actually is not desired. We use such systems not in spite of their limited 'intelligence' but for that very reason (Matzner 2016b). We use them because they are seemingly different from humans in that they (seem to) solve the task they are made for without complaining about working conditions, without asking for more salary, without getting tired, with no moody days, and (seemingly) without bringing their prejudices to work. This apparent difference between humans and machines is deeply engrained in our worldview. Humans are seen as subjective, emotional, embodied beings, and often as prejudiced. On the contrary, machines are seen as neutral, rational, objective, functioning 24/7. This dichotomy is wrong on both sides. On the one hand, serious research has shown how much emotions, affects, and social structures are an inherent part of what we commonly call the rational faculties of human beings (see, for instance, Anderson 2003; Angerer 2014). On the other hand, machines are constructed by humans, with a certain social setting in mind and manifesting an objectivity and significance of numbers that often is not warranted, as has been discussed in the second section.

Rather than casting the machine as the effective – and ultimately fearful – opposite of humans we should enquire how this difference comes into being in the first place and what it does in our societies.

Conclusion

Opening black boxes is not enough because algorithmic scrutiny is difficult-to-impossible to achieve. Besides, even if we could do this we could not get it right, and humans are no better alternative either. This means that we have to drop the hope that transparency and accountability will make algorithmic systems the objective or neutral tools we always wanted them to be. We have to make explicit the inherent problems of such systems and either consciously accept and mitigate them – or give up algorithmic decision-making in areas where the consequences are just too far-reaching.

It is essential that we work with the overall technical and social picture (and in such a context, opening black boxes and transparency have their place). And we should focus on the current developments on algorithms and the problems they already present to our societies – rather than being distracted by the prospect of superhuman artificial intelligences.

Notes

1 This text was originally a blog post and thus is written in a more direct and compressed style than many academic texts. I want to thank the editors for inviting me to publish it in this volume nonetheless.
2 I am indebted to Michael Nagenborg for highlighting the importance of this issue.

References

Anderson, M.L. (2003). Embodied cognition: A field guide. *Artificial Intelligence* 149(1), pp. 91–130.

Angerer, M.-L. (2014). *Desire After Affect*. London and New York: Rowman & Littlefield International.

Angwin, J., Larson, J., Mattu, S. and Kirchner, L. (2016). Machine bias – ProPublica. *ProPublica*, 23 May. Available at: www.propublica.org/article/machine-bias-risk-assessments-in-criminal-sentencing. [Accessed 2 October 2017].

Bigo, D. and Tsoukala, A. eds. (2008). *Terror, Insecurity and Liberty: Illiberal Practices of Liberal Regimes after 9/11*. Routledge Studies in Liberty and Security. London and New York: Routledge.

Bornstein, A.M. (2016). Is Artificial Intelligence permanently inscrutable? Available at: http://prime.nautil.us/issue/40/learning/is-artificial-intelligence-permanently-inscrutable. [Accessed 2 October 2017].

Cheney-Lippold, J. (2011). A new algorithmic identity: Soft biopolitics and the modulation of control. *Theory, Culture & Society* 28(6), pp. 164–181.

Chun, W.H.K. (2008). On 'sourcery', or code as fetish. *Configurations* 16, pp. 299–324.

Conrad, K. (2009). Surveillance, gender, and the virtual body in the information age. *Surveillance & Society* 6(4), pp. 380–387.

Dourish, P. (2016). Algorithms and their others: Algorithmic culture in context. *Big Data & Society* 3(2), pp. 1–11.

Dreyfus, H.L. (1992). *What Computers Still Can't Do: A Critique of Artificial Reason*. Boston, MA: MIT Press.

Ewald, F. (1986). *L'état providence*. Paris: Grasset.

Floridi, L. (2016). True AI is both logically possible and utterly implausible – Luciano Floridi – Aeon Essays. Available at: https://aeon.co/essays/true-ai-is-both-logically-possible-and-utterly-implausible. [Accessed 19 September 2017].

Frankle, J. and Garvie, C. (2016). Facial-recognition software might have a racial bias problem. *The Atlantic.* Available at: www.theatlantic.com/technology/archive/2016/04/the-underlying-bias-of-facial-recognition-systems/476991/. [Accessed 2 October 2017].

Gillespie, T. (2014). The Relevance of Algorithms. In: T. Gillespie, P.J. Boczkowski and K.A. Foot, eds. *Media Technologies*. Cambridge, MA: MIT Press, pp. 167–194.

Gilliom, J. (2001). *Overseers of the Poor: Surveillance, Resistance, and the Limits of Privacy*. Chicago, IL: University of Chicago Press.

Greenwald, G. (2014). *No Place to Hide: Edward Snowden, the NSA, and the U.S. Surveillance State*. New York: Metropolitan Books.

Harcourt, B.E. (2007). *Against Prediction: Profiling, Policing, and Punishing in an Actuarial Age*. Chicago, IL: University of Chicago Press.

Kroll, J.A., Huey, J., Barocas, S., Felton, E.W., Reidenberg, J.R., Robinson, D.G. and Yu, H. (2016). Accountable algorithms. *University of Pennsylvania Law Review* 165, pp. 633–706.

Leese, M. (2014). The new profiling: Algorithms, black boxes, and the failure of anti-discriminatory safeguards in the European Union. *Security Dialogue* 45(5), pp. 494–511.

Lerman, J. (2013). Big Data and its exclusions. Available at: www.stanfordlawreview.org/online/privacy-and-big-data-big-data-and-its-exclusions/. [Accessed 19 September 2017].

Matzner, T. (2016a). Beyond data as representation: The performativity of Big Data in surveillance. *Surveillance & Society* 14(2), 197–210.

Matzner, T. (2016b). The model gap: Cognitive systems in security applications and their ethical implications. *AI & Society* 31(1), pp. 95–102.

Matzner, T. (2017). Opening black boxes is not enough – Data-based surveillance in 'discipline and punish' and today. *Foucault Studies* 23, pp. 27–45.

Pasquale, F. (2015). *The Black Box Society: The Secret Algorithms That Control Money and Information*. Cambridge, MA: Harvard University Press.

Porter, T.M. (1996). *Trust in Numbers: The Pursuit of Objectivity in Science and Public Life*. Princeton, NJ: Princeton University Press.

Sainato, M. (2015). Stephen Hawking, Elon Musk, and Bill Gates warn about Artificial Intelligence. *Observer.* Available at: http://observer.com/2015/08/stephen-hawking-elon-musk-and-bill-gates-warn-about-artificial-intelligence/. [Accessed 2 October 2017].

Smolensky, P. (1988). On the proper treatment of connectionism. *Behavioral and Brain Sciences* 11(1), pp. 1–23.

Zarsky, T. (2013). Transparent predictions. *University of Illinois Law Review* 4, pp. 1503–1570.

4 Big Data – within the tides of securitisation?

Stefan Strauß

Introduction[1]

During the last few years, the information society has become enriched with another technological trend: Big Data technology is hyped as the 'weapon of choice' to explore real-world phenomena by automatic analysis of large data sets. The success of Big Data is fostered not least by its nifty way of dealing with uncertainty and complexity. Implicitly presented as the means to reduce both, Big Data promises a variety of innovative forms of automated data analysis and visualisation to predict trends and enhance decision-making by employing algorithmic power (Strauß 2015). The scope of applications ranges from business intelligence, market- and trend forecasting, demand-oriented energy supply, medical research, health management, right up to predictive policing, security and (mass) surveillance utilisations. But, irrespective of specific application contexts, Big Data entails dynamics partially similar to the logic of securitisation. This chapter aims to shed light on these dynamics and explores potential interrelations between Big Data and securitisation.

Securitisation is a technique of governance that frames security as a permanent process linked to political objectives (cf. Buzan *et al.* 1998; Bigo 2000; Balzacq 2005; Watson 2011; Strauß 2017a). This framing is accompanied by a permanent strive for reducing uncertainty and insecurity which suggests gathering as much data as possible to, for example, calculate risks and develop preventive measures before risks become factual threats. Big Data is framed in a similar manner as a promising means to, for example, predict trends, events etc. and thus reduce uncertainty by preventive risk detection and support decision-making. To gain a bigger picture and better understanding of the implications of Big Data in relation to securitisation, this chapter critically discusses the general promises and perils of Big Data. This involves several examples from different domains to point out that various grey areas can emerge from Big Data, undermining its (promoted) objectives (enhancing decision-making, improving knowledge etc.). As will be shown, Big Data implicates complicated issues of uncertainty and insecurity, which are partially in opposition to its promises. There is thus a critical intersection given between the Big Data discourse and securitisation. This overlap is relatively explicit in surveillance contexts but implicitly given also in other contexts (in public as well as in private domains). Before elaborating on these issues, the chapter presents and discusses some basic aspects and claims of Big Data.

The general claim of Big Data – that massive amounts of data per se offer valuable information – follows a logic of 'the bigger the better' that, metaphorically speaking, suggests considering the whole haystack as a gold mine instead of just searching for a needle within it (see Sætnan, Chapter 2 in this volume). In line with this delusive view is the perception that data quality decreases in importance and instead finds that correlation is key to enhancing decision-making (cf. Bollier 2010; Mayer-Schönberger and Cukier 2013). In this regard, Big Data seems to be surrounded by a mystique of seemingly causal correlations, neglecting the fact that correlation is not causation. Consequently, boyd and Crawford (2012: 663) define it as 'a cultural, technological, and scholarly phenomenon' that rests on the interplay of technology, analysis and mythology. The latter addresses the 'widespread belief that large data sets offer a higher form of intelligence and knowledge to generate insights previously impossible with the aura of truth, objectivity and accuracy' (ibid.). This mystical dimension refers to a critical weakness of Big Data: there are limited options available for scrutinising the plausibility and validity of its functioning and of its analytical results. Revealing patterns and exploring correlations (as central concerns of Big Data analytics) can, of course, be very helpful in a number of contexts (as outlined above). However, this potential is not given per se, and, as will be shown, has a flipside that bears a number of risks and pitfalls. Thus, a critical reflection on the claims of Big Data seems to be important in order to come to a clearer understanding of its prospects and limits as well as its options for reducing its societal risks. The chapter therefore first outlines the role of Big Data and its pragmatic approach to exploiting digitised information. Thereafter, it critically discusses the issues of uncertainty, predictability and interpretation, and then presents and elaborates securitisation and its relation to surveillance technology. The overlaps between securitisation and Big Data are then discussed, as is the power of Big Data to reinforce technology dependencies, then on towards some concluding remarks.

A new data pragmatism?

A number of trends and drivers promoted the emergence of Big Data: technological developments such as social networks, mobile devices, cloud computing, apps, machine-to-machine communication and smart technologies all entail an increase in the processing and availability of digital information. In the economic and business sector, Big Data has already been known for some years under labels such as business intelligence or enterprise 2.0, aiming at taking strategic advantage of digital information for novel business models. In a societal context, the increase in social media, including informational self-exposure and trends such as the 'quantified self' also contribute to a further growth in digitally available personal data across many different domains. Put together, Big Data is closely linked to so-called datafication (Mayer-Schönberger and Cukier 2013; Lycett 2013) aiming at gathering large amounts of everyday life information to transform it into computerised, machine-readable data. Once digitised, the data can then be analysed by (semi-automated) algorithms to unleash the assumed enormous assets hidden in the large amounts of information. With this potential, Big Data is also linked to political trends of increasing emphasis on pre-emptive and preventive security measures, such as predictive policing. These developments are closely intertwined with securitisation (see further discussion below).

Behind the scenes of the Big Data mystique and related trends there might be a new paradigm of data pragmatism on the rise: 'Algorithmic living is displacing artificial intelligence as the modality by which computing is seen to shape society: a paradigm of semantics, of understanding, is becoming a paradigm of pragmatics, of search' (Boellstorff 2013). The rationale of this new data pragmatism is to gather and aggregate data from many different sources to search for hidden patterns with the aim to win new insights into whatever issue is of interest. Actually, Big Data is mainly based on algorithms that use so-called MapReduce programming models to analyse the basic structure of data and then aggregate parts of this structure. As the name suggests, the model uses two main functions termed *map* and *reduce*.[2] The former is used to specify and pre-structure the input information, the latter to specify how this information is aggregated to achieve a useful output. This allows for parallel computing and, thus, fast analysis of large data sets. For the implementation of MapReduce, the calculation of probabilities plays a crucial role (cf. Dyer *et al.* 2008; Fernández *et al.* 2014). This sophisticated programming approach fosters computing performance but it may also entail wider societal consequences due to its inherent reductionism.

In short: Big Data technology is mainly grounded in pattern-recognition and the calculation of probabilities. An important question related to that is therefore: What happens if there is a shift away from semantics, as Boellstorff (2013) assumes? Does syntax then become more meaningful, especially in Big Data analysis? Or, in other words: is there an incremental trend inherent to Big Data to quantify real-world phenomena to make them computable based on high-performance statistics? If yes, then there are risks that complex real-world phenomena become normalised because, obviously, not every phenomenon is sufficiently reducible to a set of computable numbers.

Referring to its aspirations to enhance decision-making and provide additional knowledge, Big Data enriches a quantity of syntax with meaning. To illustrate what Big Data is and what it is not, language translation is a useful example. Online translation tools (e.g. babelfish, google translate, deepl) search for patterns in large data sets about terms, phrases and syntax. They analyse the textual input information based on its structure and syntax to calculate the probabilities of the original text in a different language. Depending on the complexity of the text, the results do not ordinarily provide an exact translation, but can still give helpful hints. In many cases, this is sufficient to get a basic idea of a text, but without a solid interpretation and basic knowledge about the other language it is often only messy, complicated information. Thus, an essential challenge of Big Data (and particularly of its users) is the correct interpretation of the information it provides. Coping with this challenge can, however, be very complicated – as discussed in the following sections.

Uncertainty, predictability and interpretation

Big Data can be seen as a noble attempt to reduce uncertainty by employing complex data analysis, often cited as a means to predict future developments with predictive analytics. Indeed, exploring correlations and patterns with Big Data can be very helpful in many domains such as in the health sector, for example, by showing previously hidden interrelations between symptoms of different diseases, or exploring the side effects of drugs etc. This can, for instance, support tailored medical treatment and benefit preventive medicine by forecasting and early warning; or the analysis of anonymised health data about the population can contribute to exploring how diseases develop over time – such as the spread of cancer and so on. Similar potential can be found in other domains as well. However, it is important to consider that the capacity of Big Data to point out connections between items is mostly based on probabilities and not on causalities. If correlation and probability are confused with causation then, literally speaking, magic is traded for fact. This can lead to an increase in uncertainty, particularly in cases where Big Data results are difficult or impossible to verify or disprove. The subsequent paragraphs will present and discuss some examples in this regard.

Amongst the claims of Big Data enthusiasts is that inaccurate analytic results could be compensated by 'big enough data' (Mayer-Schönberger and Cukier 2013). However, this suggests that facts come with quantity, and consequently, Big Data risks not merely some inaccuracy but also taking the wrong decisions and distorting reality. Regardless of the enthusiasm it creates, Big Data is obviously not an oracle and thus not capable of predicting the future. The complications of common Big Data claims can be illustrated by the following simple example: The Google 'trends' service shows a significantly increasing interest in the search term 'Heisenberg' in autumn 2013 (see Figure 4.1).

What does this tell us? That people are suddenly astonished by the work of the great physicist? Or were people more interested in the last episode of the TV series 'Breaking Bad'[3] aired during this time? In 1927, the Nobel Prize winner Werner von Heisenberg formulated the uncertainty principle[4] – a cornerstone in quantum mechanics. The principle asserts that two complementary properties (such as position and momentum) of a particle cannot be exactly determined and thus cannot be completely *known* at the same time. The more accurately the position of a particle is determined, the less accurately its momentum can be ascertained – and vice versa (cf. Hilgevoord and Uffink 2014). In a Big Data context, the uncertainty principle could look as follows:[5] The position of a dataset is the information it represents at a specific moment in time. With particular usage (i.e. calculation), the dataset gains momentum. If the principle is

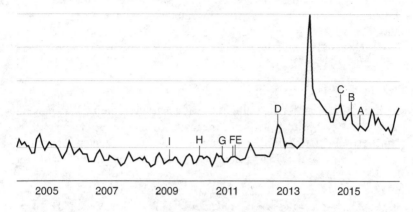

Figure 4.1 Google trend curve for the search term 'Heisenberg'.

valid also for data, one could argue that the more data is gathered and aggregated, the less can be known about its original contexts. In other words: there are
interpretational limits to Big Data that complicate its verifiability – and the
dimension of time plays a crucial role in this regard.

Boellstorff (2013) reminds us that '[d]ata is always a temporal formation'.
Thus no matter how big it is, data is always a construct emerging in the course
of time. Existing data in the present can only provide information about the past
until the present. It is therefore important to consider that predictive analytics of
whatever kind have a history that is also a natural limit to their effectiveness. In
other words: the future remains unpredictable with or without Big Data. This
rather simple fact seems to be neglected in the Big Data discourse.

Similarly, data seems to be misleadingly treated as equivalent to a valid fact.
Surely data can be valid facts, but not a priori. The term 'fact' is to be understood as something that is actually the case, or in the words of Ludwig Wittgenstein: 'The world is the totality of facts, not of things' (Wittgenstein, cited in
Casey 1992: 108). Above all, data are a set of numbers, characters, signs etc.
Without interpretation of the data, the only valid fact about data is its existence
– but the data itself does not reveal whether it is valid or true in a certain
context or not. Of course, there is already no doubt that information about the
existence of data and its correlations can be very supportive in developing
knowledge. Hence, the capacity of Big Data does not necessarily imply a predictive look towards the future. It bears potential to help to improve understandings of what has already happened and what is currently occurring. As
mentioned earlier, the health sector, for instance, can benefit from Big Data
analysis. However, in order to tap its potential, knowledge about its limits is
important. Otherwise, eventual misunderstandings of the nature of 'datafied'
knowledge might become reinforced as the following examples, related to the
health domain, illustrate. These examples reveal some of the limits and complications of Big Data results.

One of the seemingly 'big' success stories of Big Data, namely Google flu trends, was celebrated for its highly accurate detection of the prevalence of flu. However, as Lazer *et al.* (2014) pointed out, in the end the prevalence of flu was overestimated in the 2012/13 and 2011/12 seasons by more than 50%. The approach in total (using search terms for the analysis) is questionable – and this example already points to how misleading Big Data can be. The following two cases of health data analysis, though, raise much more serious concerns. Large data sets in general and medical data in the specific are complex things, and with an increase in automated data analysis as fostered by Big Data, it can become complicated to interpret the according results. A critical example is the faulty calculation of the US Big Data company 23andMe[6] that analyses the genetic data of their customers to check it against risks of diseases. In one case, the company informed a customer via email that the analysis revealed two mutations in his DNA that are typical for a genetic disease called limb-girdle muscular dystrophy. This disease leads to paralysis and is mostly lethal. After the first shock, the customer decided to find out whether this can actually be true. Being familiar with genetic engineering, he explored his genetic dataset on his own with expert software and learned that the analysis results provided to him were wrong – 23andMe made a mistake by not considering the double helix of his DNA (Hartmann 2013; Bernau 2014). It seemed to be true that his DNA had two mutations, but not in the same gene, which makes a significant difference. The Big Data analysis did not recognise this. The customer confronted the company with the error and all he received was a short confirmation about the error and an apology (Hartmann 2013; Bernau 2014; Williams 2014). This is not a single case; according to media reports, 23andMe made several mistakes such as sending 96 customers wrong DNA test results (Kincaid 2010). Similar issues exist with other companies providing personal DNA analysis as well (for a brief overview see, for example, Arthur 2016).

Genetic testing is basically limited in predicting health risks, as several studies argue, because diseases depend not merely on genetic factors but also on personal lifestyle and environmental factors (cf. Fleming 2014). Similar is the case for other domains as well and above all, predicting events is naturally tied to some uncertainty that is impossible to resolve completely. In another case in the US, where a young girl showed symptoms of kidney failure, Big Data was used on the fly to support the medical diagnosis. A treating physician assumed unusual lupus symptoms and an association with a certain propensity for blood clots. The doctor then decided to search a database for these issues and indeed found correlations with blood clots. Based on this, the patient was treated with anticoagulant medication.[7] As it turned out, the patient did not develop a blood clot (Greenwood 2014). However, this does not prove that there was even an association as assumed. It is simply impossible to find out whether the Big Data-supported diagnosis was a great success and the medication correct, or the diagnosis and the corresponding Big Data analysis wrong and ineffective for this patient (Bruce 2014). One may argue that this is less important as long as patients do not suffer from eventual mistreatment and wrong medication. There is also no doubt that, especially in the health sector, Big Data bears a lot of promising potential to support diagnosis and treatment. Nevertheless, it can be tempting to overestimate this potential and thus the significance of Big Data analysis. This can complicate the detection of mistreatment, which may cause serious problems such as additional health risks due to wrong medication.

The outlined cases teach some important lessons. The idea of Big Data is very seductive in supposing it as a novel tool to tackle complexity, predict future events and learn about yet unknown facts. Assuredly, it uses high-performance computing to exploit large amounts of data; and, statistical analysis can quickly provide information to interpret the data, which would not be possible by unaided humans in the same timescale. Furthermore, as shown in the second case, Big Data can reveal hidden information relevant for decision-making. However, the flip side of the coin is that complexity increases with the amount of data, and the increasing complexity of Big Data analysis, coupled with increasing automation, may trigger not merely uncertainties, but also unintended social consequences. With complexity, the propensity towards errors and a certain risk of false positives increases. The examples above demonstrate that Big Data bears enormous risks regarding proneness to errors or the detection thereof. The knowledge required to correctly interpret what such analyses present, and find out whether it is valid information or not, is far from being trivial. Besides the high mental stress caused by, for example, erroneous health information in the case of the individuals concerned, a pressing question remains: what if errors remain hidden? As outlined above, the predictive capacity of Big Data is naturally limited. If the results of predictive analytics are blindly trusted, then their verification or falsification can become further complicated. In particular, if a predicted event is taken for granted and actions are taken to prevent this event, then the prediction can hardly be verified or falsified. For instance: can a pre-crime be prevented? Or can a merely predicted disease be effectively treated?

Hence, Big Data entails high risks of failure and self-fulfilling prophecies, especially if correlation is confused with causation, as the Big Data discourse suggests (see Sætnan, Chapter 2 and Matzner, Chapter 5 in this volume). In combination with an increasing trend towards automated pattern-recognition and decision-making, this can even lead to situations where the social and economic costs for correcting errors become higher than the costs for simply taking Big Data results for granted. As a consequence, to some extent, Big Data even seduces us to ignore failure or hazard errors. This can be especially true in cases where it becomes too complex or hardly affordable to evaluate the validity of Big Data results. Finally, Big Data challenges the role and meaning of data quality and interpretation as the presented examples indicate. Data needs to be plausible and correct to reduce risks of false analysis. However, how can we verify whether the data and its interpretation are correct? This can be especially challenging as the aggregation of large data sets from various sources is a core feature of Big Data. A further increase in automated data analysis reinforces the demand to find appropriate answers to these questions and improve the accountability of Big Data. Furthermore, Big Data analysis is based on high-performance computing, which means that humans have a significant disadvantage: they need much more time for the same task as well as for scrutinising the results.

Securitisation and (surveillance) technology

As discussed in the previous sections, the innovative potential of Big Data is accompanied by increasing complexity of data analysis and uncertainty as regards its validity and its interpretation. As a consequence, there are a number of serious societal risks, such as hidden or unsolvable failure and self-fulfilling prophecies. In this respect, Big Data also bears the danger to normalise and disturb reality by implicitly reinforcing uncertainty and insecurity. The examples mentioned previously highlight this in a health context. But, the basic risks are given in any other context as well. This is particularly observable in the security and surveillance discourse, where securitisation and paradigm shifts in policy stimulate a perpetual strive for security. Entailed are reinforced threats to privacy and other fundamental rights. A closer look at the interrelations between datafication (inherent to Big Data) and securitisation reveals similar mechanisms in dealing with uncertainty on both counts, which triggers a sort of vicious self-dynamic. This dynamic can reinforce power asymmetries and technology dependencies. To better understand these issues, this section starts with a brief overview on securitisation.

Since the end of the Cold War, the role and meaning of security has significantly changed. During the 1990s, the traditional concept of state-centred security – with the main aim being to protect the integrity of the state from different kinds of threats – was gradually complemented by the concept of human security (cf. Owen 2004). The approach of human security put more emphasis on the individual than on the nation state. In 1994, the United Nations introduced the new concept of human security as an issue of international policy with two principal aspects: freedom from chronic threats such as hunger, disease and repression, coupled with protection from sudden calamities (UN 1994). While human security led to a general extension of the concept of security, its primary focus was on reducing insecurities so as to ensure human development in line with freedom and health. However, tendencies towards a comprehensive conceptualisation of security over the last two decades have also affected the original concept. Claims for a holistic security approach increased – an approach that used human security as 'an effort to re-conceptualise security in a fundamental manner', a framework where '(…) mitigating threats to the insecurity of individuals becomes a central goal of policy recommendations and actions' (Jolly and Ray 2006: 5).

This transformation had already occurred before the dramatic terrorist attacks on September 11, 2001, though 9/11 led to a further change in security policy on a global scale: the US and many other governments significantly reinforced security and surveillance measures (Ball and Webster 2003; Haggerty and Samatas 2010). To some extent, human security developed a life of its own: the intensified striving for a holistic security concept, spanning across many different domains, entails complications as regards the development of appropriate security measures. This is particularly the case if sectoral differences as regards the meaning of security are neglected (e.g. social security differs from national security etc.). As a consequence, security measures are at risk of being ineffective, inappropriate or even threatening in themselves, for example, when undermining fundamental rights.

From a theoretical stance, the paradigm shift in security policy is the effect of what many scholars termed 'securitisation', which conceptualises security as the indeterminate result of discursive and non-discursive security practices (cf. Buzan *et al.* 1998; Bigo 2000; Balzacq 2005; Watson 2011; Strauß 2017a). Securitisation entails a process view that is 'marked by the intersubjective establishment of an existential threat with sufficient saliency to have political effects' (Watson 2011: 3). In this process, security is not framed as an objective condition but is linked to political discourse (Balzacq 2005: 173). Thus a broad range of political issues becomes arbitrarily related to security. Moreover, security is presented as an issue superior to other state functions. Securitisation is observable, inter alia, in European security policy involving a broad spectrum of different security challenges and threats such as poverty, diseases, climate change, energy supply, terrorism and organised crime. While without any doubt each of these challenges needs to be addressed, a lacking distinction between different dimensions of security can complicate the task of developing appropriate measures, which may vary from domain to domain. This is especially true when the development of security measures mainly focuses on combatting crime and terrorism at the cost of other domains. A particular risk of securitisation lies in the fact that it can lead to a problematic 'security continuum' where the designation of 'certain persons and practices as "threats"' happens in a rather arbitrary manner (Guild, Carrera and Balzacq 2008: 2). In a Foucauldian sense, securitisation is a technique of government. In this regard, it is closely linked to 'a mode of governmentality, drawing the lines of fear and unease at both the individual and the collective level' (CASE 2006). Bigo (2000: 174) highlights the tendency of security discourses towards self-fulfilling prophecy, whereas securitisation is also 'a capacity to manage (and create) insecurity'. Hence, 'the processes of securitisation and of insecuritisation are inseparable' and can lead to a security dilemma where 'the more one tries to securitise social phenomena (…) to ensure "security" (…) the more one creates (intentionally or non-intentionally) a feeling of insecurity' (CASE 2006: 461). Such a framing carries the danger that security measures are weak in reducing realistic risks, but become introduced for self-serving purposes, or even misused to justify other political objectives. Consequently, security issues are then presented as existential threats that require particular 'measures and justifying actions outside the normal bounds of political procedure' (Buzan, Weaver and Wilde 1998: 28f.). An example is the conflation between internal and external security with increasing overlaps between the competences of police and military forces (cf. Bigo 2000; Guild *et al.* 2008).

Securitisation is intrinsically linked to the employment of security technology. Against the background of a growing and complex security landscape, security agencies and law enforcement increasingly rely upon the employment of technological means (Strauß 2017a). Security technology is frequently assumed to be the best means to tackle all kinds of risks and threats. A drastic example of the seductive power of technology linked to securitisation is provided by the Gulf War against Iraq by a U.S. led military coalition during the 1990s, which introduced a new era of warfare. 'Operation Desert Storm' became a blueprint of the so-called 'clean war' (at least in the media). Reports about military activity were widely reduced to presenting abstract images of 'smart' missiles and military drones precisely hitting their targets in Kuwait as well as in Iraq's capital Baghdad. Such images circulated around the globe conveying the subtle message of accurate attacks enabled by precision military technology such as laser-guided bombs (cf. Browne 1991; Sample 2003; Bourne 2014). However, it is clearly evident that many civilians were killed, and technology does not make wars cleaner, simply more abstract.

A further example for this is the increasing role of military drones in the war on terror and a variety of conflicts, which is linked to the securitisation mechanisms in the aftermath of the 9/11 terrorist attacks. In 2002, US forces conducted a so-called targeted killing by a drone for the first time (SPON 2010). Since then, drones have been and continue to be frequently used for military operations of various kinds, often with a rather unnoticed impact on civilians (see for example, CLS 2012). Drones are just one of many examples of a general trend to increasingly rely on technology to carry out, for example, complex or dangerous tasks. Entailed to this trend is an increasing abstraction of the tasks technology is employed for. Drone killings drastically exemplify this. Individuals being targeted by the technology are more or less reduced to data points. History bears a further drastic example, related to this: the so-called body count, that is, the number of people killed by military forces, mostly of the enemy. Body counts played an important role in the Vietnam War during the 1960s. Robert McNamara, the U.S. Defence Secretary during that time, was generally keen on statistics and used figures about killings by U.S. forces in Vietnam to demonstrate progress in the war. For this reason, the body count was frequently published in the newspaper (cf. Mayer-Schönberger and Cukier 2013). Although this example is from a period long before the age of Big Data, it bears serious issues important for today's developments. It points out where the reduction of individuals to statistical figures, driven by securitisation, can lead us. This reduction is not limited to the presented worst cases of military conflicts, drone killings and death statistics, but observable in other contexts as well.

Big Data as a tool of (in)securitisation

Basically, most forms of security and surveillance technology, such as automated CCTV, systems for mass surveillance of Internet communications or predictive policing, entail a certain mode of abstraction. Their employment involves the treatment of individuals as data points, which is a critical side effect of Big Data, exposed to securitisation. As a consequence, there is a risk of de-individuation which is a characteristic of panoptic power (in the sense of Foucault 1977). As mentioned earlier, there is a vicious self-dynamic as technology usage fosters Big Data and vice versa: in accordance with the logic of securitisation, the deployment of surveillance technology by (public or private) security authorities is showcased as an inevitable necessity to protect and improve security (which is assumed to be permanently threatened). Consequently, large amounts of data are gathered, serving extensive security and surveillance practices, presented as necessary security measures. As outlined in the previous section, securitisation frames security as an enduring process, conveying that these data collections would be essential to prepare for permanent threats. Or, in other words: securitisation constructs and reinforces the demand for perpetual security by generating an implicit state of permanent uncertainty and insecurity, which is then used to justify the continuous extension of surveillance technology. This can result in a vicious circle when surveillance technology is in operation without ex ante assessing the factual demand and purpose thereof. At the same time, complexity and uncertainty increase due to technology usages that remain widely unrecognised. The use of surveillance technology thus also 'extends the toolbox of securitization' (Strauß 2017a: 259).

In a security context, Big Data tempts its users with a seemingly predictive view of threats and improved effectivity of security measures (e.g. suggested by predictive policing). Security and surveillance practices are increasingly pre-emptive, aiming at eliminating potential threats before they become serious. Large-scale surveillance based on Big Data analysis fits perfectly in this mode of prevention and pre-emption based on the premise that maximum data collection per se benefits the development of new insights. In this logic, surveillance technologies that collect massive amounts of personal data are falsely framed as unavoidable to improve security. With these practices, the protection of fundamental rights such as the right to privacy are at a high risk of neglect. Furthermore, even their primary aim, that is, to strengthen security, can be undermined: as Bigo (2008: 13) points out, securitisation and the according technology usage can lead to a conceptual reduction of security. Hence, security is quasi-equated to

> technologies of surveillance, extraction of information, coercion acting against societal and state vulnerabilities, in brief to a kind of generalized 'survival' against threats coming from different sectors, but security is disconnected from human, legal and social guarantees and protection of individuals.
>
> (Bigo 2008: 13)

Entailed are serious risks that the opaque demand for surveillance technologies, deeply intruding into privacy, become reinforced and self-referential. Hence, the security continuum (induced by securitisation) can lead to a privacy vacuum where one's private sphere incrementally erodes as surveillance technology incrementally gains almost unlimited access to every personal detail of individuals (Strauß 2017a).

In the same way that securitisation is inevitably linked to insecurity, Big Data is ambiguously accompanied by uncertainty. To some extent, Big Data can even reinforce uncertainty and insecurity. The datafication of 'everything', conveyed as a purportedly desirable aim in the Big Data discourse, fits perfectly with the claim of securitisation towards an overarching framing of security, integrating multiple domains and contexts. The logic is then that uncertainty is only a matter of data quantity, resolvable by gathering more data from various domains of everyday life. On a general level, the rationale behind the strong belief in technology as 'weapon of choice' loaded with the mystical silver bullet is mostly an economic one. The assumption is that technology provides a simple, automated, cost-efficient and effective means to tackle security threats and challenges, free from human error. Gathering maximum data is seen as a desirable approach to reduce insecurity and prepare for all kinds of eventual risks. Big Data technology is presented as being equipped with these features, and thus is framed as a perfect tool in this regard. While Big Data does not generally represent a surveillance technology, its capacities and related claims fit quite well with a securitisation agenda. The employment and justification of mass surveillance is based on a similar logic to the promotion of Big Data: the claim is that the more data, the more precise the results. Massive amounts of personal information are gathered, purportedly in order to improve the level of security. The most prominent example of this is provided by the NSA, which collects about 20 billion communications events per day; far more, than a typical analyst can reasonably make use of (Greenwald 2014). That the growth of digital data is seen as a great asset for intelligence agencies is thus evident, prominently underlined by the recent announcement of James Clapper, the head of US intelligence: 'In the future, intelligence services might use the [Internet of things] for identification, surveillance, monitoring, location tracking, and targeting for recruitment, or to gain access to networks or user credentials' (quoted in Ackerman and Thielman 2016). Hence, also the Internet of things, as an emerging technological development, provides a further boost for the nexus between Big Data and surveillance. As extensive data collections mostly exceed human capacity to analyse them, automated algorithms are increasingly employed to seek out patterns and support decision-making. This entails increasing dependencies on these technologies and intensifying power asymmetries.

Increasing power asymmetries and technology dependencies

Lawrence Lessig (2006: 1) once proclaimed that 'code is law' meaning that software algorithms increasingly affect society. Similarly, Shirky (2009) used the term 'algorithmic authority' in this regard. The emergence and employment of Big Data underlines this critical assessment as technologies and their embedded algorithms steadily gain in authority.

A closely related side effect is that Big Data can reinforce the phenomenon of automation bias. Automation bias is the tendency of humans to uncritically accept computer-generated solutions. According studies can be found, for example, in the aviation sector (cf. Mosier *et al.* 1998/2009) or in the health sector where the use of clinical decision support systems can entail automation bias (cf. Goddard, Roudsari and Wyatt 2012). If Big Data is used for (semi-)automated decision-making, new forms of technology dependencies and automation bias occur that deeply affect the autonomy of the individual as well as of society. Autonomy basically means self-rule. In a Kantian sense (Kant 1785/1997), autonomy is the ability to freely and self-determinedly establish moral laws and act upon them. It implies the capacity to self-governance and self-determination so that the individual can (ideally) act free from external interference and take informed decisions. A precondition for taking informed decisions and actions is having information about the according context. As previously discussed, Big Data algorithms are typically applied for probability-calculating pattern-recognition techniques. These can be supportive for decision-making, not least because taking a decision also implies assessing options, excluding unrealistic or inappropriate ones, and thereafter selecting a suitable option. Thus there are, without any doubt, several useful applications in many domains where Big Data can present valuable information for decision support.

If Big Data provides information to reveal additional options to take informed decisions, it may also foster autonomy – for instance by improving the early recognition of health risks that may improve patients' quality of life, or new options for health governance, etc. This can strengthen autonomy for individuals and, from a wider perspective, also for society, for example, by the enhancing of healthcare systems. However, as shown with several examples in the previous sections, Big Data can cause several complications. A crucial issue in general is that Big Data bears the risk of overestimating the significance of quantities and probabilities in a sense that only the computable counts as a valid option, while others become sorted-out or even remain unrecognised. These risks can become reinforced by (semi-)automated decision-making which is amongst the aims of Big Data. In this regard, an important question is, therefore, what happens with rare, unlikely events? So-called black swans are exceptionally and highly improbable events, but they can have a particularly high impact (Taleb 2007). From a meta-perspective, Big Data might thus be understood as breaking ground towards a new techno-determinism that is capable of reshaping the future by transforming possibilities into probabilities. In this respect, there is also a certain threat that Big Data leads to an increase in power asymmetries, with intensifying conflicts between human autonomy and software- or algorithmic autonomy.

The mass surveillance activities revealed by Edward Snowden in 2013 alarmingly highlight the close and supportive relationship between Big Data, surveillance and control (Greenwald 2014; Lyon 2014; see also Tøndel and Sætnan, Chapter 10 in this volume). Together with its 'supportive relationship with surveillance', (Lyon 2014: 1) Big Data can reinforce a number of related threats, such as profiling, social sorting and digital discrimination (see Schneider, Chapter 8 in this volume). An example for automated discrimination is, for instance, the NSA software called 'XKeyscore' (Greenwald 2014; Zetter 2014). XKeyscore is a sophisticated search tool of the NSA, which allows exploring various information about particular individuals based on their Internet usage (including their online communications, social media activity etc.) (Greenwald 2014). Journalists and security researchers who analysed the tools' source code revealed that it categorises users of privacy-friendly software such as from 'The Tor Project' (2017) as 'extremists', thus rendering them potential targets of sur-veillance (Rötzer 2014; Doctrow 2014). The tool as such can be seen as a Big Data technology. The controversial Big Data company Palantir Technologies,[8] having a strategic partnership with the NSA, was involved in the development of XKeyscore (Biddle 2017). This tool is only one example of many others revealed by the Snowden files. The purposes for this form of mass surveillance are in many cases unclear. Evident, however, is that the metadata gathered by NSA surveillance is also used for so-called targeted killings in military operations conducted by the CIA, as announced in 2014 by the former NSA director Michael Hayden (Cole 2014). As outlined in previous sections, these killings are often conducted by drones. There is also evidence for false positives in drone warfare where civilians were killed (Ackerman 2011; CLS 2012). Hence, Big Data can literally also kill people.

Besides intelligence agencies, the use of Big Data technology is also spread-ing into law enforcement and police work. Together with developments towards predictive policing, aiming to identify 'likely targets for police intervention and prevent crime or solve past crimes by making statistical predictions' (Perry *et al.* 2013: 1f.), Big Data entails a number of serious challenges that can even strain cornerstones of democracy such as the presumption of innocence or the principle of proportionality. Predictive policing is already in use, for example, by the Memphis police, who employ IBM's software blue C.R.U.S.H.[9] (Hickman 2013). Another example is 'TrapWire', a system aimed at predicting terrorist attacks by gathering data from a large network of surveillance cameras linked to databases, inter alia used by several police departments in the U.S. but also in larger cities in the UK (Shachtman 2012). Similar approaches are spreading in other European countries as well, such as recent pilot tests of automated facial recognition systems in a train station in Berlin, Germany (Huggler 2017). These systems aim at automatically recognising suspects based on their facial images as stored in police records. Threat scenarios referring to the movie *Minority Report* (2017), based on Philipp K. Dicks' novel of the same title, may as yet be overestimated. However, automated predictive analytics may increase the pres-sure to act and even hamper a distinction between appropriate intervention and excessive pre-emption.

Another scenario dealing with threats of social sorting and discrimination is what can be called the '*Gattaca* scenario' where individuals become discrimi-nated because of their DNA. *Gattaca* (2017) is a movie from 1997 that draws a dystopia where people have pre-selected careers based on their genetic code.

People with higher risks for genetic diseases have lower chances for societal development and well-being. This scenario presents another red line that might be important to consider not to be crossed. These scenarios highlight that rampant approaches towards prediction, prevention and pre-emption can jeopardise cornerstones of democracy.

But also, dystopic examples from the surveillance discourse aside, there are several cases in everyday life where Big Data already reinforces power asymmetries. Examples such as correlations between beer and diaper sales seemingly detected by the U.S. company Wal-Mart (Whitehorn 2006) are weird but possibly harmless. In another strange case – less harmless – a teenage girl's pregnancy was predicted by analysing her consumer behaviour and disclosed to her father before she decided to tell him (Hill 2012; see also Chapter 2, this volume). These examples show how algorithms may strain human autonomy (see João Simões and Amarel Jerónimo, Chapter 9 in this volume) by secretly analysing behavioural patterns. The power of predictability is also exploited by some business models – for example the platform called 'The Numbers' (2017) aims to predict the revenues of a movie before it even appears on screen (calculating block buster probability). This prediction is based on factors such as how many famous actors are involved in a film. A consequence can be, for instance, that independent film-makers encounter additional problems in financing their projects, which often lack famous actors. In another example, a company called Marketpsych (2017) concentrates, inter alia, on exploiting information gathered from social media to learn about the impact of conflicts or wars, as well as emotional states such as fears, to identify investment and trading opportunities. Some recent business models are also grounded on algorithms that automatically generate news articles (cf. Rutkin 2014; Finley 2015). Furthermore, there were several rumours in the media about voter manipulation related to the Big Data company Cambridge Analytica during the U.S. presidential election in 2016, aimed at predicting and influencing the behaviour of voters to the benefit of then presidential candidate Donald Trump (Confessore and Hakim 2017; Beuth 2017).

From a wider view, Big Data can be seen as a new source of political, economic and military power (Zwitter and Hadfield 2014). Besides drastic examples of killed civilians, the power of Big Data can have severe implications for privacy as well as for the autonomy of the individual. Particularly, if the human factor becomes a subject of statistics, this raises a number of serious concerns in this regard. Hildebrandt (2006: 54) states that

> the most interesting thing about human nature is its indeterminacy and the vast possibilities this implies: our non-essentialist essence is that we are correlatable humans before being correlated data subjects. Whatever our profile predicts about our future, a radical unpredictability remains that constitutes the core of our identity.

There is thus a certain risk, that Big Data incrementally reduces individuals to data subjects based on statistical analysis of their behaviour, actions etc.

Amongst the consequences is that the results of such forms of analysis could even be used to influence and manipulate the behaviour of individuals (as outlined previously). Hence, with growing amounts of data, the concept of informational self-determination – which is a fundamental principle of privacy (cf. Rouvroy and Poullet 2009; Strauß 2017b) – becomes further strained. Large data sets facilitate techniques for de-anonymisation and re-identification – thus the boundaries between personal and non-personal information increasingly blur, as particularly observable in social media (Strauß and Nentwich 2013). Consequently, individuals are further hampered in protecting their privacy. The situation continues to deteriorate when privacy-aware people are treated as potential security threats (as by XKeyscore mentioned above). These practices reinforce the misleading trade-off between privacy and security inherent to securitisation: privacy is seen as a burden to security and in line with a 'nothing to hide' logic, mass surveillance is presented as desirable to improve security, and those who question this claim are then assumed to have something to hide and thus something to fear (Strauß 2017a).

Summary and conclusions

Big Data represents a new source of networking power in many different domains, which (as with every technology) can be a boost or a barrier to innovation. In general, a potential reason why society is prone to the belief in technology as a problem-solver is that technology provides an additional layer of abstraction that creates a certain distance from problems and conflicts, which then become less tangible and thus to some extent also less threatening. In a way, technology serves as a container for our fears, problems and insecurities, linked to the (unconscious) wish for their alleviation with the aid of technology. This wish for a reduction of insecurity and uncertainty becomes particularly visible in the context of Big Data. However, the claims to reduce uncertainty by predicting future events are widely misleading. Unsurprisingly, Big Data is definitely not a future-predicting oracle. A particular problem with this technology is its seductive power – the tendency to perceive it as a sort of crystal ball. Falling victim to this framing obscures a more realistic view of Big Data as a potentially useful tool for model-based learning on the basis of, as yet undiscovered, interrelations and correlations. Big Data technologies and applications present probabilities that can provide information useful for planning. This information is not predictive, but rather contributes to designing a framework that can be supportive in organising ways that deal with uncertainty – as it suggests possibilities by presenting probabilities. These possibilities are not factual, they do not in themselves present causal relations – and it should be kept in mind that the framings constructed, based on this information, can also themselves have impacts.

The shady side of winning new insights for decision-making is thus the potential emergence of new power asymmetries where a new data pragmatism celebrating quantity and probability curtails quality and innovation. In this regard, this data pragmatism risks becoming a new techno-determinism that increases propensity towards errors and false positives, and at the same time disguises failure. In a way, Big Data entails a threat of what could be called 'normalised uncertainty'. The algorithms are highly complex, and together with trends towards automated decision-making, it becomes increasingly tricky to scrutinise the results of Big Data analyses – particularly where these tools are used in domains that lack the capability and resources to critically assess their outcome. To reduce the risks associated with Big Data, it is reasonable to reconsider the thin line between overestimated expectations and underrepresented momentums of uncertainty that correlate with the Big Data discourse. Uncertainty and insecurity are essential components of the discursive power behind Big Data and securitisation. Both discourses follow a similar logic that is powerful in obscuring its transparency and impeding its scrutiny. Big Data can foster datafication of the individual and surveillance tendencies. Hence, there are big new challenges for effective concepts to effectively protect privacy, security, and increasingly also autonomy. Questions that are likely to become more pressing are, inter alia: how to avoid automation bias, how to use Big Data for enhanced anonymisation techniques, how to deal with automated decisions, and how to improve transparency and accountability.

Essential challenges ahead also include enhanced requirements for data quality and interpretation. In this regard, the human factor plays a crucial role, in as much as it is the human who is the one who has to interpret correctly, uncover failure and put results in applicable contexts. There is thus also a need for new analytical skills to handle predictive analytics with care, not least because of the increasing complexity that Big Data entails. As regards technology development, there are new challenges in the field of human–computer interaction with regard to designing interfaces that facilitate the handling of complex datasets (and their correct interpretation) without reducing too much information. This is crucial to allow for scrutiny of Big Data, which is amongst its major weaknesses. Thus, there is a high demand for transparency, replicability and verifiability of Big Data analytics, particularly as regards predicting events. This demand is somewhat pressing to reduce certain risks of autonomy loss inherent to Big Data as well as to its siblings in the field of machine learning and the recently revitalised domain of so-called 'artificial intelligence'.

To make use of Big Data and reduce risks of automated false positives, it might be essential to set the focus not merely on the myths and the magic of big numbers, but also on the exploration/information process and its components. This entails addressing questions such as: What information is used for Big Data? From which sources? For what purpose was it collected? What is the intention of the analysis (what should be explored)? Is the result plausible or not, and what are the reasons for its (im-)plausibility? What additional information did the analysis reveal? What are the limits of the results? These and similar questions, applied in a process-oriented view, could obtain useful information from Big Data without drastically increasing complexity. Of course, this is not a panacea for all of these risks, but it can at least contribute to revitalising Ernst

Friedrich Schumacher's 'small is beautiful' (Schumacher 2000) to allow for a sharpened focus on the essentials of large arrays of information.

Last but not least, there is need for governance and regulation to reduce the various societal risks Big Data entails. This involves scrutinising in what domains Big Data, and other forms of (semi-)automated technology, endanger rather than serve the well-being of society. The outlined examples, including the scenarios of *Minority Report and Gattaca*, indicate demand for better regulation to prevent social sorting, discrimination, as well as a reduction of privacy, self-determination and autonomy.

Acknowledgement

Parts of this chapter represent a condensed and modified version of Strauß (2015); licensed under Creative Commons Attribution licence (http://creative commons.org/licenses/by/4.0/).

Notes

1 Parts of this chapter represent a modified version of Strauß (2015).
2 For a brief overview on the basic functioning see, for example, IBM Analytics (2017).
3 The main protagonist of this TV series uses the pseudonym 'Heisenberg'.
4 In German called 'Heisenberg'sche Unschärferelation'.
5 An in-depth analysis of the role of the uncertainty principle for Big Data is beyond the scope of this chapter. But it is still used here to point out that the effectiveness of predictive Big Data analytics has natural limits.
6 Trivia: Anne Wojcicki, the founder of 23andMe, is the former wife of Sergey Brin, one of the founders of Google.
7 This dilutes the blood and reduces clots.
8 Co-founder of Palantir is the controversial entrepreneur Peter Thiel, who, inter alia, supported the current U.S. president Donald Trump.
9 Criminal reduction using statistical history.

References

All URLs in this chapter were last accessed on 10 September 2017.
Ackerman, S. (2011). CIA drones kill large groups without knowing who they are. *Wired Magazine*. 4 November. Available at: www.wired.com/2011/11/cia-drones-marked-for-death/.
Ackerman, S. and Thielman, S. (2016). US intelligence chief: We might use the internet of things to spy on you. *Guardian*. 9 February. Available at: www.theguardian.com/technology/2016/feb/09/internet-of-things-smart-home-devices-government-surveillance-james-clapper.
Arthur, R. (2016). What's in your genes? *Slate*. 20 January. Available at: www.slate.com/articles/health_and_science/medical_examiner/2016/01/some_personal_genetic_analysis_is_error_prone_and_dishonest.html.
Ball, K. and Webster, F. (2003). *The Intensification of Surveillance*. London: Pluto.
Balzacq, T. (2005). The three faces of securitization: Political agency, audience and context. *European Journal of International Relations*, 11(2), pp. 171–201.

Bernau, V. (2014). Sorry, Fehldiagnose. *Sueddeutsche Zeitung*. 6 July. Available at: www.sueddeutsche.de/digital/falsche-genanalyse-von-us-firma-sorry-fehldiagnose-1.2031046.

Beuth, P. (2017). Die Luftpumpen von Cambridge Analytica. *Die Zeit*. 7 March. Available at: www.zeit.de/digital/internet/2017-03/us-wahl-cambridge-analytica-donald-trump-widerspruch.

Biddle, S. (2017). How Peter Thiels Palantir helps the NSA to spy on the whole world. *The Intercept*. 22 February. Available at: https://theintercept.com/2017/02/22/how-peter-thiels-palantir-helped-the-nsa-spy-on-the-whole-world/.

Bigo, D. (2000). When two become one: Internal and external securitisations in Europe. In: M. Kelstrup and M. Williams, eds., *International Relations Theory and the Politics of European Integration – Power, Security and Community*. London: Routledge, pp. 171–204.

Bigo, D. (2008). Globalized (in)security: The field and the Ban-Opticon. In: D. Bigo and A. Tsoukala, eds., *Terror, Insecurity and Liberty. Illiberal Practices of Liberal Regimes after 9/11*. Oxon/New York: Routledge, pp. 10–48.

Boellstorff, T. (2013). Making big data, in theory. *First Monday*. 18(10). Available at: http://dx.doi.org/10.5210/fm.v18i10.4869.

Bollier, D. (2010). The promise and peril of big data. EMC analyst report. Washington DC: The Aspen Institute. [pdf] Available at: www.emc.com/collateral/analyst-reports/10334-ar-promise-peril-of-big-data.pdf.

Bourne, M. (2014). *Understanding Security*. Basingstoke: Palgrave Macmillan.

boyd, d. and Crawford, K. (2012). Critical questions for big data: Provocations for a cultural, technological, and scholarly phenomenon. *Information, Communication & Society*, 15(5), pp. 662–679.

Browne, M. W. (1991). Invention that shaped the Gulf War: The laser-guided bomb. *New York Times*. 26 February. Available at: www.nytimes.com/1991/02/26/science/invention-that-shaped-the-gulf-war-the-laser-guided-bomb.html.

Bruce, P. (2014). Big data accelerates medical research? Or not? Available at: www.kdnuggets.com/2014/10/big-data-accelerates-medical-research-or-not.html.

Buzan, B., Weaver, O. and de Wilde, J. (1998). *Security: A New Framework for Analysis*. Boulder, CO: Lynne Rienner.

CASE Collective (2006). Critical approaches to security in Europe: A networked manifesto. *Security Dialogue*, 37(4), pp. 443–487.

Casey, G. (1992). Wittgenstein: World, reality and states of affairs. *Philosophical Studies*, 33, pp. 107–111.

CLS – Columbia Law School (2012). *The civilian impact of drones: unexamined costs, unanswered questions*. Research report, Human Rights Clinic at Columbia Law School and Center for Civilians in Conflict. New York: Columbia Law School. [pdf] Available at: http://civiliansinconflict.org/uploads/files/publications/The_Civilian_Impact_of_Drones_w_cover.pdf.

Cole, D. (2014). We kill people based on meta data. *The New York Review of Books Daily*. 10 May. Available at: www.nybooks.com/blogs/nyrblog/2014/may/10/we-kill-people-based-metadata/.

Confessore, N. and Hakim, D. (2017). Data firm says 'secret sauce' aided Trump; Many scoff. *New York Times*. 6 March. Available at: www.nytimes.com/2017/03/06/us/politics/cambridge-analytica.html.

Doctrow, C. (2014). If you read Boing Boing, the NSA considers you as target for deep surveillance. *Boing Boing*. 3 July. Available at: http://boingboing.net/2014/07/03/if-you-read-boing-boing-the-n.html.

Dyer, C., Aaron, C., Mont, A. and Lin, J. (2008). Fast, easy, and cheap: Construction of statistical machine translation models with MapReduce. In: *Proceedings of the Third Workshop on Statistical Machine Translation*, Ohio State University, 19 June, pp. 199–207.

Fernández, A., del Río, S., López, V., Bawakid, A., del Jesus, M., Benítez, J. M. and Herrera, F. (2014). Big data with cloud computing: An insight on the computing environment, MapReduce, and programming frameworks. *WIREs Data Mining and Knowledge Discovery*, 4, pp. 380–409. DOI: 10.1002/widm.1134.

Finley, K. (2015). In the future, robots will write news that's all about you. *Wired Magazine*. 3 June. Available at: www.wired.com/2015/03/future-news-robots-writing-audiences-one/.

Fleming, N. (2014). Can we ever fully trust personal gene tests? *BBC Future*. 29 January. Available at: www.bbc.com/future/story/20140129-personal-gene-tests-what-next.

Foucault, M. (1977). *Discipline and Punish: The Birth of the Prison*. Translated from the French by A. Sheridan, 2nd edn 1995. New York: Vintage Books/Random House.

Gattaca (2017). *Wikipedia*. Available at: https://en.wikipedia.org/wiki/Gattaca.

Goddard, K., Roudsari, A. and Wyatt J. C. (2012). Automation bias: A systematic review of frequency, effect mediators, and mitigators. *Journal of the American Medical Informatics Association*, 19(1), pp. 121–127. Available at: https://dx.doi.org/10.1136/amiajnl-2011-000089.

Greenwald, G. (2014). *No Place to Hide – Edward Snowden, the NSA, and the U.S. Surveillance State*. London: Hamish Hamilton.

Greenwood, V. (2014). Can big data tell us what clinical trials don't? *New York Times*. 3 October. Available at: www.nytimes.com/2014/10/05/magazine/can-big-data-tell-us-what-clinical-trials-dont.html.

Guild, E., Carrera, S. and Balzacq, T. (2008). The changing dynamic of security in an enlarged European Union. Research paper No. 12, CEPS Programme Series. Brussels: Centre for European Studies. [pdf] Available at: www.ceps.eu/system/files/book/1746.pdf.

Haggerty, K. D. and Samatas, M. (2010). *Surveillance and Democracy*. Oxon: Routledge-Cavendish.

Hartmann, L. (2013). My deadly genetic disease was just a bug. *Gizmodo*. 24 November. Available at: http://io9.gizmodo.com/my-deadly-genetic-disease-was-just-a-bug-14714 47884.

Hickman, L. (2013). How algorithms rule the world. *Guardian*. 1 July. Available at: www.theguardian.com/science/2013/jul/01/how-algorithms-rule-world-nsa.

Hildebrandt, M. (2006). Privacy and identity. In: E. Claes, A. Duff and S. Gutwirth, eds., *Privacy and the Criminal Law*. Antwerpen/Oxford: Intersentia, pp. 43–57.

Hilgevoord, J. and Uffink, J. (2014). The uncertainty principle. In: E. N. Zalta, ed., *The Stanford Encyclopedia of Philosophy*. (Spring 2014 Edition). Available at: http://plato.stanford.edu/archives/spr2014/entries/qt-uncertainty/.

Hill, K. (2012). How Target figured out a teen girl was pregnant before her father did. *Forbes*. 16 February. Available at: www.forbes.com/sites/kashmirhill/2012/02/16/how-target-figured-out-a-teen-girl-was-pregnant-before-her-father-did/.

Huggler, J. (2017). Facial recognition software to catch terrorists being tested at Berlin station. *Telegraph*. August 2. Available at: www.telegraph.co.uk/news/2017/08/02/facial-recognition-software-catch-terrorists-tested-berlin-station/.

IBM Analytics (2017). What is MapReduce? – *IBM Analytics*. Available at: www.ibm.com/analytics/us/en/technology/hadoop/mapreduce/.

Jolly, R. and Ray, D. B. (2006). *The Human Security Framework and National Human Development Reports: A Review of Experiences and Current Debates.* United Nations Development Programme, National Human Development Report Unit. NHDR Occasional Paper 5. New York: United Nations Development Programme.

Kant, I. (1785/1997). *Grundlegung zur Metaphysik der Sitten.* Werkausgabe Band VIII (herausgegeben von Weischedel, W.) Erstmals erschienen 1785. Berlin: Suhrkamp Taschenbuch Wissenschaft.

Kincaid, J. (2010). 23andMe sends wrong DNA test results to 96 customers. *Techcrunch.* 7 June. Available at: https://techcrunch.com/2010/06/07/23andme-sends-wrong-dna-test-results-to-96-customers/.

Lazer, D., Kennedy, R., King, G. and Vespignani, A. (2014). The parable of Google Flu: Traps in big data analysis. *Science Magazine*, 343(6176), pp. 1203–1205. DOI: 10.1126/science.1248506.

Lessig, L. (2006). *Code Version 2.0.* New York: Basic Books.

Lycett, M. (2013). Datafication: Making sense of (big) data in a complex world. *European Journal of Information Systems*, 22(4), pp. 381–386.

Lyon, D. (2014). Surveillance, Snowden, and big data: Capacities, consequences, critique. *Big Data & Society*, July–December, pp. 1–13, DOI: 10.1177/2053951714541861.

Marketpsych (2017). Available at: www.marketpsych.com/.

Mayer-Schönberger, V. and Cukier, K. (2013). *Big Data: A Revolution That Will Transform How We Live, Work and Think.* Boston, MA/New York: Houghton Mifflin Harcourt.

Mosier, K. L., Skitka, L. J., Heers, S. and Burdick, M. (1998/2009). Automation bias: Decision making and performance in high-tech cockpits. *The International Journal of Aviation Psychology*, 8(1), pp. 47–63. Republished online 2009. Available at: http://dx.doi.org/10.1207/s15327108ijap0801_3.

Owen, T. (2004). Challenges and opportunities for defining and measuring human security. *Disarmament Forum*, 3, pp. 15–24.

Perry, W. L., McInnis, B., Price, C. C., Smith, S. and Hollywood, J. S. (2013). *Predictive Policing: The Role of Crime Forecasting in Law Enforcement Operations.* Santa Monica: RAND cooperation. [pdf] Available at: www.rand.org/pubs/research_reports/RR233.

Rötzer, F. (2014). Wer seine Privatsphäre schützt, ist für die NSA ein Extremist. *Telepolis.* 3 July. Available at: www.heise.de/tp/artikel/42/42165/1.html.

Rouvroy, A. and Poullet, Y. (2009). The right to informational self-determination and the value of self-development: Reassessing the importance of privacy for Democracy. In: S. Gutwirth, Y. Poullet, P. Hert, C. Terwangne and S. Nouwt, eds., *Reinventing Data Protection?* Dordrecht: Springer, pp. 45–76.

Rutkin, A. (2014). Rise of robot reporters: When software writes the news. *New Scientist.* 21 March. Available at: www.newscientist.com/article/dn25273-rise-of-robot-reporters-when-software-writes-the-news/.

Sample, I. (2003). US gambles on a 'smart' war in Iraq. *New Scientist.* 19 March. Available at: www.newscientist.com/article/dn3518-us-gambles-on-a-smart-war-in-iraq/.

Schumacher, E. F. (2000). *Small Is Beautiful: A Study of Economics As If People Mattered.* 25th Anniversary edition (first published 1973). Vancouver: Hartley and Marks Publishers.

Shachtman, N. (2012). Trapwire: It's not the surveillance, it's the sleaze. *Wired Magazine.* 14 August. Available at: www.wired.com/2012/08/trapwire-strafor-biz/.

Shirky, C. (2009). A speculative post on the idea of algorithmic authority, 15 November. Available at: www.shirky.com/weblog/2009/11/a-speculative-post-on-the-idea-of-algorithmic-authority/.

SPON (2010). Killer app – drones are lynchpin of Obama's war on terror. *Der Spiegel.* 12 March. Available at: www.spiegel.de/international/world/killer-app-drones-are-lynchpin-of-obama-s-war-on-terror-a-682612.html.

Strauß, S. (2015). Datafication and the seductive power of uncertainty – A critical exploration of big data enthusiasm. *Information*, 6(4), pp. 836–847. Available at: www.mdpi.com/2078-2489/6/4/836.

Strauß, S. (2017a). A game of hide and seek? – Unscrambling the trade-off between privacy and security. In: M. Friedewald, P. Burgess, J. Cas, R. Bellanova and W. Peissl, eds., *Surveillance, Privacy and Security – Citizens' Perspectives*. New York: Routledge, pp. 255–272.

Strauß, S. (2017b). Privacy analysis – Privacy impact assessment. In: S. O. Hansson, ed., *The Ethics of Technology – Methods and Approaches*. London and New York: Rowman and Littlefield International, pp. 143–156.

Strauß, S. and Nentwich, M. (2013). Social network sites, privacy and the blurring boundary between public and private spaces. *Science and Public Policy 2013*, 40(6), pp. 724–732.

Taleb, N. N. (2007). *The Black Swan: The Impact of the Highly Improbable*. New York: Random House.

The Minority Report (2017). *Wikipedia*. Available at: https://en.wikipedia.org/wiki/The_Minority_Report.

The Numbers (2017). Where data and the movie business meet. Available at: www.the-numbers.com.

The Tor Project (2017). Available at: www.torproject.org/.

United Nations – UN (1994). *New Dimensions of Human Security – Human Development Report*. New York: Oxford University Press, Available at: http://hdr.undp.org/sites/default/files/reports/255/hdr_1994_en_complete_nostats.pdf.

Watson, S. (2011). The 'human' as referent object? Humanitarianism as securitization. *Security Dialogue*, 42(1), pp. 3–20.

Whitehorn, M. (2006). The parable of the beer and diapers: Never let the facts get in the way of a good story. *The Register*. 15 August. Available at: www.theregister.co.uk/2006/08/15/beer_diapers/.

Williams, D. E. (2014). How 23andMe got in trouble. *MedCityNews*. February 10. Available at: http://medcitynews.com/2014/02/23andme-got-trouble/.

Zetter, K. (2014). The NSA is targeting users of privacy services, leaked code shows. *Wired Magazine*. 7 March. Available at: 2014 www.wired.com/2014/07/nsa-targets-users-of-privacy-services/.

Zwitter, A. J. and Hadfield, A. (2014). Governing big data. *Politics and Governance*, 2(1), pp. 1–2.

5 Surveillance as a critical paradigm for Big Data?

Tobias Matzner

Introduction

Bruce Schneier famously coined the phrase 'surveillance is the business model of the internet' (quoted in Rashid 2014). He alludes particularly to the monitoring of our activities when using digital media and the complex techniques of evaluating the data that this monitoring produces. The desired results are behavioural patterns, targeted advertising and other information that predicts our consumption – and which provides the main income of many large Internet companies. The technologies used for data processing in these cases are often considered as exemplary for Big Data. Big Data is thus the set of technologies that enables surveillance as the business model of the Internet.

At least since Edward Snowden's revelations (Greenwald 2014) we also know that the Internet is not only surveilled for business purposes. The NSA, GCHQ and also many other secret services (Lyon 2015) have installed very sophisticated mechanisms of capturing Internet data and analysing it for purposes of surveillance – again using technologies summarised as Big Data. Big Data thus seems to be the enabling technology for a broad range of surveillance activities, which gives reason to interrogate how closely Big Data is entangled with 'Big Brother' as the title of this volume suggests. It almost seems like every use of Big Data is somehow also surveillance – at least if we accept a broad definition of surveillance such as David Lyon's: the 'systematic, routine, and focused attention to personal details for a given purpose (such as management, influence, or entitlement [...])' (Lyon 2014: 2).

However, selling ads and holding persons in custody as terror suspects are quite different purposes of activities that are united by the term 'surveillance' in these discourses. They are performed by quite different actors, and persons might arguably have quite different intuitions concerning both. In fact, many seem to be quite at ease with being surveilled for business purposes while opposing surveillance by the state at the same time. Thus, in the following I ask, what does Big Data do when it is used for surveillance? Which concept of surveillance is suitable for grasping these problems and implications of Big Data?

To answer these questions I will first introduce some prominent concepts of surveillance and their application to Big Data. This discussion will be linked to important critiques of Big Data on epistemic grounds that challenge the kind of information or knowledge that can be derived from Big Data, its accuracy and validity. This is important in this context to clarify what the contested epistemic status of Big Data entails for the critique of surveillance. In order to approach this issue, I will show that the epistemic issues are often used for a critique of surveillance based on a representative model of data. Essentially it is shown that surveillance apparatuses do not say about the world what they purport to say. While this is a very important point, I will outline four problematic aspects of Big Data used for surveillance which need a critical engagement with surveillance beyond the question of what kind of knowledge such surveillance (using Big Data) generates about the world. Those four aspects are the decoupling of generation and analysis of data, and the explorative character of the analysis – which are characteristic features of Big Data. Furthermore, I discuss data-based analysis as an incentive to act in the context of surveillance, and its double relation to the future when data are used for prediction.

Big Data and dataveillance

When I started discussing surveillance it was based on David Lyon's (2014: 2) definition: 'systematic, routine, and focused attention to personal details for a given purpose (such as management, influence, or entitlement […]).' This is a rather recent formulation in a paper discussing the ramifications of Edward Snowden's revelations. It slightly reformulates his earlier conception, which has significantly informed the debate, framing surveillance as 'social sorting' (Lyon 2003). Thus, the purpose he talks about has been a little more narrowly defined as making discriminations amongst groups. But even that definition would still encompass all kinds of discriminations, from discerning probable customers to probable terrorists. Consequently, Degli Esposti uses Lyon's definition as starting ground for her update on Clarke's (1988) concept of data-based surveillance – dataveillance – for the age of Big Data. In a similar fashion to Lyon she defines 'mass dataveillance' as 'the systematic monitoring of people or groups, by means of digital information management systems, in order to regulate or govern their behavior'. She discerns four steps that comprise dataveillance: 'recorded observation', 'identification and tracking', 'analytical intervention', and 'behavioral manipulation' (Degli Esposti 2014: 211).

Big Data plays a particular role for the third step, analytical intervention: She describes this as the transformation of 'so-called "raw" data' into information, which then can orient intervention, or quoting Gandy (2012), to render data actionable. Degli Esposti warns her readers that such insights extracted from the data should not be seen as objective truth, because there they are influenced by the methods of analysis and the analyst (Degli Esposti 2014: 212). Yet, this underestimates the challenge Big Data poses to claims for knowledge. Even before the advent of Big Data, the critical distinction between raw data and the information extracted from it had already been made. While, in fact, data means 'given', it has always been given for a particular purpose, given in a particular way (Rosenberg 2013). It is thus no raw material, but itself the result of a complex sociotechnical arrangement (Bowker 2013). Therefore, the idea that something can be learned from data without taking into account the particular way the data has been created, is problematic. Big Data increases the gap between data creation and analysis. In fact, it is one of the alluring promises of Big Data, that of being able to tie in all kinds of sources for analysis. For example, several countries want to use social media data for border controls and visa applications, that is, data that was created in the context of work, family or friendships. This is to be combined with official records and additional sources like passenger records from airlines. Huge amounts of data are collected and stored, processed, transferred and sold, for later analysis. Thus Big Data deals with heterogeneous data sources, not just data collected for the specific purposes of surveillance. This is in contrast to established accounts of surveillance. Foucault, for example, described disciplinary institutions – like schools, prisons or hospitals – as having their own sophisticated processes of measurement and protocols, thus creating data particularly for the purpose of evaluating the subjects under surveillance (Foucault 1977). Both secret services and advertising agencies, however, use data created for all kinds of purposes. They 'listen in' on mails and chats, they scrutinise social media profiles, financial movements, travel arrangements and diets. A second way in which Big Data decouples data creation and analysis is temporal: huge troves of data are stored for future scrutiny. It is questionable whether such methods can adequately account for the particularities of the way the data have been produced. Before I continue to clarify the way Big Data is or can be surveillance, I thus want to clarify its status as data analytics.

Epistemic issues in Big Data

As boyd and Crawford have pointedly noted, Big Data is not just a technology or a process of analysis, it is also a mythology: 'the widespread belief that large data sets offer a higher form of intelligence and knowledge that can generate insights that were previously impossible, with the aura of truth, objectivity, and accuracy' (boyd and Crawford 2012: 663). In particular, many of the claims related to Big Data – and often at least implicitly accepted when discussing their potential for surveillance – are disputed. On a very general level they contend that Big Data, like all tools, is at the same time enabling and constraining in what one can do. Furthermore, a lot of the analysis happens automatically, which may introduce both data biases and algorithmic biases. Quite early on, Introna and Nissenbaum (2000) identified some of the internal biases and presuppositions of big Internet search engines such as Google – an exemplary use case of Big Data. For example, they found that search engines prefer bigger sites created by professionals, to smaller sites and those created by non-trained individuals. This is not a conscious choice of the search engine but rather due to certain technical choices how to crawl and rank pages. It is only reasonable to expect similar problems for other use cases.

However, even with very cautious programmers and analysts trying to address and consider these problems, Big Data remains problematic. This is tied to the very promise that Big Data is not just a search for something in a huge database. Big Data pertains to technologies that are meant to discover new insights from huge troves of data. So rather than looking for something in the data, the data itself should tell us what to look for. In particular, because we do not know how the potential buyers for a new product are discernible, Big Data lures us with the promise of uncovering new patterns that can identify such customers – or terrorists. The insights that can be derived from those patterns, however, are far from clear. This therefore depends on the particular technology used.

All statistical approaches have a similar problem in that, in the end, they can only discern correlations and not causal relations (see Sætnan, Chapter 2 in this volume). Often this is related to the quite hilarious correlations that can be found if enough data is put into the relationship.[1] Yet, there are many more sophisticated approaches in pattern-recognition, machine learning or knowledge discovery that use complex models to grasp the relations and dependencies amongst several dimensions of the input data. And indeed, new results about impressive and worrying insights that can be derived from data are published regularly – for example, Facebook data reveals sexual orientation (Jernigan and Mistree 2009), as well as other private traits (Kosinski *et al.* 2013). Horvát *et al.* (2012) even managed to predict relations amongst persons that are not on Facebook, but just know Facebook users. However, these are carefully crafted studies that show the kind of insights that can be derived from data. But at the same time, they underline the point that good analytics needs background knowledge about the context. Also on the issue of Facebook 'friends', boyd and Crawford (2012: 668) note all kinds of social relations can lead to 'friending' on Facebook, and only careful use of contextual knowledge can protect against drawing biased or inaccurate conclusions about what such a connection means.

Manovich (2012), focusing particularly on social data, cautions that even if Big Data allows us to access impressive amounts of data, this is still a sample. Most studies based on social media data represent a particular snapshot provided by the big Internet firms – often without information about how this sample was chosen (Kinsley 2015). We can assume that these limits do not hold for secret services, but even if we get data from all users of a website, and even if that is millions, this is still a particular sample. Social media, in particular, promise to provide 'authentic' knowledge about many persons, since they contain content that those persons have produced themselves. Manovich rightly points out, however, that such content is created in many social contexts, answering all kinds of pressures and expectations. But even if we can express ourselves freely, we express an image of ourselves that might differ from what a more objective referent would convey. Finally, Manovich illustrates that both methods in the digital humanities and established methods yield interesting results. However, the digital methods provide different insights than an experienced human researcher would derive from the same material. Big Data analysis thus is not 'better' or 'worse' but rather entails a complex shift in what becomes visible, what remains invisible, which contextual factors are part of the analysis and what kinds of presuppositions about the analysed matter are at work. Ribes and Jackson (2013) also illustrate how data are co-dependent with the institutions or organisations which produce them. This context, however important it is for producing and understanding data, is not firmly tied to the originally created data itself, and might get lost in sharing or moving data over time. 'Data,' the authors claim, 'are ephemeral creatures that threaten to become corrupted, lost, or meaningless if not properly cared for' (Ribes and Jackson 2013: 147).

Kitchin extends this critical discourse by focusing on the explorative character of Big Data. 'Big Data analytics enables an entirely new epistemological approach for making sense of the world; rather than testing a theory by analysing relevant data, new data analytics seek to gain insights "born from the data"' (Kitchin 2014: 2). We will cover this issue more comprehensively in the following discussion. Concerning the epistemic status of the data, Kitchin demonstrates the explorative use of a plethora of algorithms provided by artificial intelligence, machine learning etc. Abundant computing power allows us to explore which method of analysis brings interesting results (Kitchin 2014: 2). But it is also the case that the algorithms themselves are tailored to discover patterns, relations, regularities or rules hitherto unnoticed (Cios *et al.* 1998; Schmidhuber 2015). This evokes the image of information being somehow already hidden within the data, which then only needs to be extracted (and the metaphoric language of data 'mining', or data as 'raw material' or 'resource', underlines this). In this way, the insight derived from the data is implied as objectified, as something already present but so far unnoticed by human beings. By way of contrast, Kitchin holds that 'the inductive strategy of identifying patterns within data does not occur in a scientific vacuum and is discursively framed by previous findings, theories, and training' (Kitchin 2014: 5). A similar claim tied to Big Data is that the role of the analysts is diminishing, since theories and presuppositions play a smaller role, when the data simply produce 'effects and patterns' (Prensky 2009; Kitchin 2014: 4). Kitchin admits that, indeed, a good deal of science is conducted following this conceit. However, this assumption is characterised, its result 'is reductionist, functionalist and ignores the effects of culture, politics, policy, governance and capital (reproducing the same kinds of limitations generated by the quantitative/ positivist social sciences in the mid-20th century)' (Kitchin 2014: 5).

Amending the epistemic critique: critical issues of Big Data as surveillance

The epistemic reflections summarised in the last section amount to an important critique of surveillance. If the 'knowledge' derived from data is no knowledge at all, but rather the expression of dissimulated contexts and preconditions, then its legitimising force diminishes. Furthermore, such a critique can assist many individuals by demonstrating that they have been falsely suspected or accused of criminal or terrorist acts. However, in the following it will be shown that this perspective does not suffice to critically grasp the challenges that data-based technologies pose in surveillance and security applications. This is due to a premise I call 'representationalist' (Matzner 2016a). This is the perspective that data are the representation of something in the world. The epistemic criticism then amounts to the claim that data actually do not represent what they are purported to: rather they are biased, depend on dissimulated influences, and are created in particular organisations, which influence them. These are very important issues. Yet, the epistemic criticisms do not suffice to grasp the scope of critical issues brought about by using Big Data for surveillance. Often, this perspective implicitly accepts the claim that data should say something about the world. However, surveillance studies have – at least since Foucault – conceived of surveillance not just as producing knowledge about subjects, but doing something to subjects, or even creating the subjects under surveillance in the first place (Foucault 1977). Thus, the legitimising force of surveillance never has been exclusively based on the knowledge that surveillance produces, but rather on the same dissimulated contexts and preconditions which the critics of the epistemic status of data foreground. Thus, such an emphasis does not necessarily delegitimise the claims of surveillance apparatuses. Furthermore, Surveillance Studies have focused on the changes in societies and communities brought about by the introduction of surveillance apparatuses. The critical perspectives on Big Data have to engage with these issues, which go beyond the representationalist perspective on epistemic questions. In the following, I discuss four central features of Big Data and their implications for data-based surveillance that show why these issues gain particular importance for surveillance using Big Data. These four features are the decoupling of generation and analysis; the explorative character of analysis; analytics creating incentives to act, not (just) information; and finally its double relation to the future.

The decoupling of generation and analysis of data

Big Data promises to integrate all kinds of sources. One of the defining characteristics of Big Data is variety (Kitchin 2014: 1). For example, it has recently been suggested that IBM's i2 Enterprise Insight Analysis be used to assess all the refugees that try to enter Europe after the emerging crisis in the Middle East since 2011. The proposed scenario would integrate data from such different sources as lists of casualties in the war, assessments of illegal markets in the 'deep web', openly accessible social media, phone calls or parking tickets (Tucker 2016). The promise of tackling such a variety of sources has led to a rule of thumb to store all data that accrues in a particular application of information and communication technologies, since one can never know whether it might be useful in the future. Sometimes this is data that is necessary for the operation of the respective service, like the data used for billing telephone customers; sometimes it is data that is just generated for the possible future applications, like effectively mining transaction data. Concerning surveillance, this leads to a phenomenon which one could call 'prospective surveillance': huge databases that exist just because they may be used for purposes of surveillance in the future. These data often accrue in contexts that relate to activities and possibilities many people want to have, for example, social networking, cell phones (especially, but not only the 'smart' type), having electricity at home, driving cars, getting health services, working, and more. Surveillance is not a separate application of Big Data but a potential that emerges from all uses of data storage in the aforementioned domains. This fact, of course, has brought about the catchphrase of 'surveillance as the business model of the internet' (Rashid 2014). If, however, we consider the aforementioned issue, that the organisations and technologies used to produce data also shape its content, such general statements have to be taken with care. An organisation to rate prospective customers and distribute ads has quite different structures, aims and processes than a security agency. While both are doing surveillance somehow, we are now faced with data being created in one context and being evaluated in another. To stick with the example, a person's habits might be seen as one potential indicator for a security assessment. Thus, data created in a particular time and place for a particular purpose, for example, tracking website visits to enable targeted advertising, can be stored and analysed at a different time and place for a different purpose, for example, in a security screening. This means that the production and analysis of data are decoupled. Often, during analysis, the data is recontextualised with data from different sources, as the proposed system by IBM illustrates. This transfer and use of data is still tied to the view that data carries information that can be extracted regardless of external factors. Often, this presumption is voiced in the idea of 'raw data', which can be stored, copied, and moved until it is analysed. As the epistemic critique in the preceding section shows, however, data is always already 'cooked' (Bowker 2013). In addition to these issues that question what the data actually mean, the decoupling of creation and analysis raises another set of issues. In addition to asking what the data mean and what they do not mean, we have to ask what data can become. Through the integration of all kinds of sources, data is always at risk of becoming something else. What used to be passenger records can turn into a risk factor during a security screening. Only the moment of the query decides which data becomes data for that query, for the current purpose. This is particularly salient in the use of dynamic data sets like social media. Social networking sites or microblogging services with millions of users constantly change. Surveillance systems, which access this data in real time get a new database for every query. That state of the data, however, will already be lost when the next query takes place.

This fact in itself, however, changes the entire social and moral setting. Issues like consent or autonomy become shaky, when the perceived uses of data are never foreseeable: they never definitely are, but can always become, the basis for surveillance. But in even more complex terms, this ties in epistemology: for example, persons express themselves on social media with an audience in mind (Litt 2012). Boellstorff (2013) argues that large volumes of data are not created by a removed spectator as in the metaphorical case of the tower in the panopticon – rather, they are available due to incentives for 'confession'. Confession in this sense is a concept employed by Foucault in the *History of*

Sexuality and which Boellstorff juxtaposes to disciplinary surveillance: 'The confession is a modern mode of making data, an incitement to discourse we might now term an incitement to disclose. It is profoundly dialogical: one confesses to a powerful Other.' However, we confess not by reacting to force, but because this opens up a 'dialectic of surveillance and recognition' (Boellstorf 2013). Only by making ourselves perceptible to surveillance can we enter the relations of recognition that structure our social lives. Furthermore, persons provide data not only for their own, individual recognition. There are many uses of data that promise to be beneficial to society: from weather warnings (Mass 2012), to the organisation of efficient response in catastrophes, to scrutiny of government activities. In a sense, they are all based on surveillance, but for quite different purposes. And while many might endorse these uses of data, they might simultaneously oppose the use for the data for surveillance by security agencies or big commercial enterprises. This means that surveillance as a perspective must not override the critical distinction of the surveilling institutions, their epistemic regimes, their organisational structures and aims. Otherwise we risk not only an epistemic misattribution, but also a normative one.

The explorative character of analysis

A lot of work following Lyon's concept of surveillance as social sorting has demonstrated some of the implicit and explicit biases and problematic discriminations in data-based categorisation (see Sætnan, Chapter 2 and Schneider, Chapter 8 in this volume). As discussed above, this can also illuminate data-based surveillance. But in a sense, Big Data and related methods of analysis could be seen as an attempt to answer this criticism: instead of using problematic categories or theoretical presuppositions, they try to derive localised and temporally indexed criteria directly from the data. Thus, they could be seen as an acknowledgement of the contingency of the world that has often been cited by scholars in surveillance studies and STS against critical presuppositions hidden in technology. To avoid misunderstanding: I do not think such attempts are successful. But they open up new practices for surveillance, with a different self-understanding: Rather than checking whether a particular, pre-defined feature pertains to a person, these processes are interested in patterns, rules and associations.

For example, Louise Amoore describes the role of data mining in contemporary security procedures. She focuses on a technology called association mining (Amoore 2013: 39f.), which was originally developed for evaluating sales data (Agrawal *et al.* 1993). The basic presumption is that particular patterns can be observed in the data, which can be translated into rules that allow a generalisation. Those are rules in the form of 'if *** and ***, in association with ***, then ***' (Amoore 2013: 59). Originally, in the context of marketing, such rules have been derived based on the frequency of transactions and consequently rules have been discerned that are supported by a large enough number of transactions (Agrawal *et al.* 1993: 208). Yet, the abstraction of the association allowed the transfer of this approach to security – a transfer in which the developers of the original approach have been involved (Amoore 2013: 43). At first glance, that makes sense. If businesses have developed an efficient approach to surveil their customers and derive usable rules from it, why not use that for surveillance against potential terrorists as well. This intuition has, for example, been summarised in former assistant attorney general Viet Dinh's claim 'If Johnson & Johnson can use these technologies to sell soap, we should be able to use them to fight terrorism' (Rosen 2004: 98). Yet again, the circumspect use of the term surveillance might be misleading. The shift from marketing to fighting terrorism entails a quite important change: from observing rules based on a large empirical support to finding hints for rare, but possible events. Amoore expresses this in her concept of 'politics of possibility'. Rather than caring for probability, for what is normal, such data is discarded in search of grasping the possible (Amoore 2013: 67). This entails that data in data-based surveillance is not used to learn something about a particular person under surveillance. A lot of data is gathered as a resource to derive meaningful rules and patterns from it. Only much later are these rules and patterns used to judge particular subjects. Amoore calls this mode of analysis the creation of 'data derivatives', whereby such techniques are compared to derivatives in finance that abstract the risk from the underlying financial asset. 'Data derivatives' are created from data collected in surveillance, but have the 'capacity to move, to be shared, divided, traded, or exchanged indifferent to, and in isolation from, underlying probabilities' (Amoore 2013: 61).

Taking into account the decoupling of data production and analysis, as well as this particular derivative mode of analytics, we can see that the data which is collected from a particular set of persons can be engaged to judge a quite different set of persons later on (Matzner 2014). This is a very important insight, because many discussions of surveillance focus still on the persons who are 'watched' – or in this context, from whom data are gathered – often in conjunction with the claim that they do not or should not object to being watched if they have 'nothing to hide'. There is an important strand in surveillance studies that has criticised this focus on being watched. For example Haggerty and Ericson's concept of the 'surveillant assemblage' captures the decontextualising feature of data-based surveillance. They write:

> The 'surveillant assemblage' [...] operates by abstracting human bodies from their territorial settings and separating them into a series of discrete flows. These flows are then reassembled into distinct 'data doubles' which can be scrutinised and targeted for intervention.
>
> (Haggerty and Ericson 2000: 606)

The authors make clear that this transcends a 'purely representational idiom': 'Rather than being accurate or inaccurate portrayals of real individuals, they are a form of pragmatics' (Haggerty and Ericson 2000). So here, the 'data double' is not a representation of the world but rather something that is assembled and moveable, quite similar to Amoore's 'data derivative'. Again, surveillance studies provide important insights into the pragmatics of data-based surveillance that move beyond a critique of surveillance in epistemic terms. However, this descriptive accuracy is often left behind normatively. Many normative texts that employ Haggarty and Ericson's or Amoore's perspectives are based on a kind of normative representationalism. A unitary, given subject is then opposed to the data double or derivative – and implicitly, the normative force of this opposition is derived from the claim that this subject is not correctly represented, but has to yield to a construction. This mode of argument is, for example, used by David Lyon: Surveillance in the era of Big Data

> 'makes up' the data double, Deleuze's 'dividual' and that entity then acts back on those with whom the data are associated, informing us who we are, what we should desire or hope for, including who we should become.
>
> (Lyon 2014, 7)

Here a 'we' or 'us' is somehow presupposed as a given, and the construction of the data double, which has been 'made up' in surveillance, is then clearly an imposition – with the consequence that this construct could tell us who we should become. Thus, implicitly, 'we' or 'us' is a subject that is not done justice to. This however, does not grasp the way the judgements come to be. The data double or derivative does not aim at providing knowledge about 'us' in the first place. It tries to grasp patterns and association rules that can describe a certain risk, and only in particular moments of inquiry (e.g. when we try to pass a border) are these constructs related to individual subjects. Thus, the focus on the subjects from whom data are gathered therefore becomes problematic in the context of analytics that make data transient and models deduced form the data transferable. Protecting against surveillance can no longer mean protecting against being 'watched', against data being collected, but must also include protection against being judged by the data-based surveillance systems concerned. Especially speaking from a standpoint within Europe or the US we might otherwise miss those that suffer most from the real-life effects of data-based surveillance, which often live on the other side of the borders of these countries.

Amoore herself declares that she is 'not proposing some form of humanist project of proper ethical judgement' (Amoore 2011: 38). Thus, a direct reference to an originary (humanist) subject as a source for normativity is not her option. Rather, she claims that the 'derivative risk form acts through us and the prosaic, intimate, banal traces of our lives, but yet it forgets us. As necessarily incomplete, complex, undecided people, it forgets us'. What is forgotten here is a life that is the potential, indefinite life that is 'never amenable to calculation'. Thus she derives the normative source of ethics from the fact that life is 'difficult' beyond all that risk calculus could capture (Amoore 2011: 39). While she does not aim at the humanist subject – although some of her formulations like the 'digitized dissection of a person into degrees of risk' (Amoore 2013: 71) might suggest that – she still aims at an 'outside' that the security apparatus cannot do justice to, as a source of normative critique. Such an affirmation of different potentials is an important line of critique of surveillance. But I think that in addition to establishing differences or outsides to the work of surveillance, a critical stance is needed towards what surveillance based on data does – not only what it does not do, that is, what it omits or fails to represent, what it does not do justice to, what is not amenable to calculation. This is particularly important because such an 'outside' is increasingly hard to find.

This increasing impossibility of finding such an outside is the central problem that Antoinette Rouvroy identifies in data-based surveillance. For her, there are not even data doubles at play. What she calls

> [a]lgorithmic governmentality does not allow the process of subjectivation to happen, because it does not confront 'subjects' as moral agents (avoiding having to question them about their preferences and intentions, about the reasons and motivations of their actions) but attunes their future informational and physical environment according to the predictions contained in the statistical body.
>
> (Rouvroy 2013: 157)

Thus, the effects of data-based surveillance are even further removed from the creation of subjects, which has been at the centre of surveillance since Foucault. In terms of a governance that does not care for subjects, surveillance rather provides the input for the attunement of 'informational and physical' environments. For Rouvroy, surveillance and biometrics are just two of many inputs for this system of governmentality (Rouvroy 2013: 156).

This dismissal of the subject might, however, be premature. In the foregoing discussion I have criticised the fallback to representation as a normative force for doing an injustice to the subject. Data-based surveillance does, however, have subjectivising effects. These systems no longer focus on the coherent subject that Foucault's discussion of discipline talks about, but they continue to produce heterogeneous, distributed moments of subjectification, like being controlled at a border or being singled out for additional screenings at the airport. In a sense, that happens when the 'attunement of environments' that Rouvroy discusses take their effect: they inhibit or impede, require or enforce certain acts that have consequences for the forms of subjectivity that are possible in such an environment. Such differences on the 'inside' of surveillance should amend a possible 'outside' as a normative source. Again we have to be careful about the contexts in which such means are taken, because not all of these means can be just described as attuning an environment. Or at least they are environments that actively react, and very selectively so, engaging in particular ways with particular forms of subjectivity. This will be illustrated by the next feature of data-based surveillance: creating incentives to act.

Data-based analysis as incentive to act

Surveillance is a particular mode of knowledge but also a way of relating this knowledge to action. Almost all theories of surveillance discuss this relation.

So, for example, Degli Esposti emphasises the 'potential for change embedded in the knowledge created' (2014: 212), since this enables the next step in her theoretical formulation, behavioural manipulation, in the first place. Similarly, Gandy describes the aim of data-based analytics as creating 'actionable intelligence' (Gandy 2012: 125). However, the concrete implementations of data-based surveillance often do not aim at the production of knowledge at all. They are meant to produce activities themselves or at least direct incentives to act – which is an important difference. For example, most of the surveillance that drives 'the business model of the internet' is automated. Our behaviour online is judged by algorithmic systems, which then automatically serve ads, change the selection of products or prizes in online shopping, attune the layout of the website and many other examples (Cheney-Lippold 2011). In a similar fashion, the 'timelines' or 'feeds' on social media or social networking sites are automatically curated based on the surveillance of our inputs and that of our 'friends', 'followers' or other persons with which we have established a similar formalised relation (Pasquale 2015 and see Pasquale, Chapter 7 in this volume).[2] In security systems, human contributions still play an important role for the effects of surveillance. However, it is not the case that analysis simply provides knowledge, which humans then use as a basis for deciding how to act. For example, Peter Adey analyses how border control has become permeated by data-based surveillance on many levels. Both the US and the EU have installed complex data management systems, like ESTA in the US or the various instances of the SIS in Europe (Adey 2012: 197). These systems also follow the promise of Big Data that analytics can unite all kinds of heterogeneous sources. All kinds of data from all aspects of life are used to be able to discern 'suspects' at the border. This means that the physical border itself is no longer the locus of the decision. The border is decentralised, it is 'moved off-center and off-shore' (Adey 2012: 198). Consequently, the 'border agent-bureaucrat delegates the sovereign decision to allow one entrance to a state and to make the routine distinctions between citizen/foreign'. These 'decisional moments of sorting are becoming deferred onto code and software which has the capacity to 'decide' or discriminate automatically' (Adey 2012: 196). The border is no longer a geographic line but a data-based construct that judges everyone completely. The border guards themselves simply enact a decision based on data that tries to track persons long before they arrive at the border. In this sense, the border is not just there, but 'the sovereign decision is repeatedly performed and re-performed in the remaking of the border by distributed border agents' (Adey 2012: 196).

What Adey does not discuss, however, is the contention that these acts not only perform a border – they also turn the person appearing at this border into a particular subject: a suspect. As I have shown above, the patterns and rules used in these decisions can be derived from data that do not contain a single bit of information from the subject in person. So again, the 'correct' representation of the subject is not an issue – but at the same time, contrary to Rouvroy's analysis, such a verdict at the border ('you cannot enter') has subjectivising force. This is a form of governance that does not aim at the coherent subject that disciplinary power created. It is rather a heterogeneous moment of subjectification that comes unexpectedly, with no prior relation to the authority in question. But the problem in this case is not only that the 'real' subject is ignored (or rather its potential for a different life, an 'outside', is not considered); rather, critical inquiry also has to focus on who is allowed to produce such a subject and how such subjectification is legitimised.

The perceived knowledge to be had from analytics can only partially legitimise that moment of subjectification, because knowledge does not play the central role. In the context of security, debates on securitisation have always emphasised the affective character of security discourses (see Strauß, Chapter 4 in this volume). In one of the 'founding texts' of critical security studies, for example, which claims that security issues are not 'in the world' but brought about by speech acts, Buzan *et al.* (1998) show that security is tied to imminent danger. Thus it does not mean we need better knowledge, but that we need to *do* something. This plays an important role in the way data-based surveillance works. If we consider even rather simple cases of partially automated surveillance – such as smart CCTV, that has one defined source of data (a CCTV image) – the system creates a situation where any interpreting human is already part of a complex decision system and not an independent agent who judges based on knowledge provided by the automatic analysis of the image. In this case, the system is meant to ameliorate human shortcomings, that is, to detect something that humans could not detect. Thus humans have to react to the incentives of the system. Even if this reaction is just to perform further checks, this often already creates ethical problems, such as repeated exposition to searches and arrests for particular groups of society (Matzner 2016b).

This problem becomes even more complex when we address the complex interplay of humans and technology in the context of data-based surveillance. For example, Leese (2016) compares such diverse systems as risk flags in payment systems or body scanners at the airport. Both of these systems share the property that the users, or in the case of body scanners, the personnel, simply receive a very reduced visual cue that says nothing about the way this verdict came to be (Leese 2016: 148). It comes with a clear incentive to act: do not trust this customer, detain this passenger for further checks. There is no knowledge provided. At the same time, the signal is supplemented with affectivity – at least for security applications, not least because the signal to act comes with the subtext that the subject in question might be dangerous. This has to be seen against the general role which affectivity, and in particular fear, plays in politics after the 'war on terror' (Massumi 2007). Leese thus reads the visual signals as 'affective triggers' that 'have the potentiality to radicalise what was once elaborated probabilities and compress them into the urgent dichotomy of threat/no threat' (2016: 150). He thus connects the output of data-based surveillance technologies to the motive of urgency that permeates security discourses. This affectively laden incentive to act thus creates a particular site of subjectification. In particular, it produces a particular subject, a suspect, by subjecting them to security measures (Matzner 2016a).

But even the quiet, automatised attunement of digital environments has subjectivising effects – Cheney-Lippold, for example, describes a 'soft' biopower 'operating through conditional access to circuits of consumption and civility' (2011: 166). In particular, he analyses the data-processing technologies of a data broker, which promises to guess the gender of persons surfing the web and aims to provide different designs and buying incentives based on this assumption. This is not just marketing to a pre-existing target population. Gender studies have long established that buying incentives and the availability of commodities contribute to gender identity: starting from the pink and blue colour codes of children's toys, to the bodily practices of grown-ups enhanced by all kinds of products, to the gendered offerings of all kinds of technology to ameliorate the 'problems' of growing old (Cheney-Lippold 2011). The decision as to whom these offers and incentives are presented, and consequently who is thus gendered (and how), is therefore now the result of data analysis and automation. Data-based 'access to circuits of consumption and civility' becomes part of gender identity.

As we have seen then, the efficacy of data-based surveillance has subjectivising effects, without necessarily circumscribing those effects into a coherent subject. But again, we have to take care to continue to make critical distinctions. The production of suspects at the border is something quite different from the production of commercialised, objectified gender roles in marketing – seeing surveillance as subjectivising is therefore a very important point. At the same time, the general perspective on surveillance must not preclude important distinctions amongst the kinds of subjectivities that are produced. This is particularly important since many areas of surveillance become interrelated by the ability to unite many different data sources. So, the data collected to assess customers can in any instance become data used to produce suspects. The moments of suspecting derive their authority from the fact that they can access other ways in which we become subjects. And these modes of subjectivation – such as that of the gender example – are also based on data and thus easily appropriated for suspecting. Thus, surveillance in the area of security stands in a parasitical relation to many other modes of data-based subjectivity (Matzner 2016a).

The double relation to the future

We have already discussed the ways that the process of decoupling data production and analysis produces many datasets that are stored as a resource for future judgements. The generation of patterns, rules, and associations thus assembles the means from which the users hope that they will be able to assess all kinds of persons that may be future objects of inquiry. In the case of IBM's proposed refugee controls, for example, this entails the possibility of assessing millions of potential refugees in an efficient manner. But the verdicts created by data-based surveillance systems are also tied to the future: they are attempts at predicting future events. They are meant to single out future customers, potential clients, or suspects of criminal acts. This makes it even more difficult to understand the outcomes of data-based surveillance systems as a representation of a state of the world. They describe a probable or potential future event – but this very event will never take place and thus the accuracy of the description cannot be verified. The event will not take place because the outputs of data-based surveillance systems are immediately rendered into actions – as described in the previous section. Furthermore, these actions will be aimed at influencing whether and how the prescribed event happens. In the case of security, this is an exemplary instance of what Brian Massumi (2007) calls the 'politics of pre-emption'; this kind of politics is defined by the very relation to the future that is at play in data-based predictions. Pre-emptive politics, Massumi writes, 'must convert an effect that has yet to eventuate into a cause: a future cause'. This predicted future then is the incentive to take immediate pre-emptive actions. This will change the course of things, and this is the reason the predicted event never happens. 'Truth, in this new world order, is by nature retroactive. Fact grows conditionally in the affective soil of an indeterminately present futurity. It becomes objective as that present reflexively plays out, as an effect of the pre-emptive action taken' (Massumi 2007: section 20). What we can witness then are the effects of the measures spurred by the data-based surveillance. Thus, prediction is not about gaining knowledge but about producing a future. Rouvroy's (2013) notion of attunement of 'informational and physical' environments is a good way of describing forms of these productive activities. Others, as I have described above, have to be seen as heterogeneous moments of subjectification. But again, surveillance based on data can prompt all kinds of activities. While Massumi's focus is on pre-emptive security politics, the example from Cheney-Lippold regarding consumer surveillance points in another direction: rather than preventing particular events, the 'soft biopower' he talks about aims at producing the very potential customer that has been predicted by the software. So while there are structural similarities in that the logic of data-based surveillance aims to bring about the future it is meant to predict, the productive forces play out in different commercial, ethical and legal registers.

Conclusion

Summing up, is surveillance a suitable critical perspective on Big Data? We have seen that this depends on the concepts of surveillance involved. Beginning with the notion of surveillance as defined by gaining insights into a population and using the insights produced, we have seen that this opens up all kinds of critique on epistemic grounds. These critiques show that the insights purportedly gained from Big Data are quite uncertain. By pointing to four distinctive features of Big Data – the decoupling of generation and analysis; the explorative character of analysis; analytics creating incentives to act, not (just) information; and finally its double relation to the future – it has been shown that this perspective has to be amended to fully grasp the problematic aspects of Big Data.

Further theories and concepts from surveillance studies and related fields are more suitable to grasp the more productive or constructive effects of data-based surveillance. Haggerty and Ericson's (2000) 'data double', Amoore's (2013) 'data derivative' or my own account of data as performative (Matzner 2016a) are cases in point. In particular, it is important to include the subjectivising effects of surveillance in the picture. While theories of surveillance provide important insights in this regard, the often-implicit equation of surveillance with watching someone, or creating data about someone, can be misleading. The particular affordances of data-based analytics entail that those who are surveilled, and those who are influenced or are faced with actions based on the data, can be different groups of people at different points in time. Thus, concepts of surveillance have to be combined with political theories of governance, subjectivation, and control in order to assess the consequences of data-based surveillance.

These theories are also important to make essential distinctions about different use cases of Big Data. Concepts of surveillance are often very encompassing: they talk about 'behavioral manipulation' (Degli Esposti 2014) or 'targeted intervention' (Haggerty and Ericson 2000). Yet, in the two cases I have discussed, surveillance as the 'business model of the internet' and surveillance as key to pre-emptive security measures, important differences are at play. First of all, business aims at identifying the common and probable, security at finding the rare and possible. Second, surveillance on the Internet is tied to many services people actually endorse. That does not necessarily mean that they are ethically justified. But the sources of critique are quite different here – for example, their intricate relation in reproducing gender inequalities. In contrast, the actions spurred by pre-emptive security measures have a more direct impact on subjects and happen in a different register of political legitimisation. A similar third point can be made in terms of the relation to the future. Generally, data-based predictions create incentives to act and thus contribute in creating the future they are trying to predict. So they turn an uncertain future event into a present reality as the cause of activities. However, in the case of security they are affectively laden necessities to prevent imminent danger by attempting to identify every single suspect. The activities produced in marketing however are quite experimental, widespread disseminations of ads or buying incentives that are already successful if 1% of targeted clients react to it.

Most importantly, these distinctions have to be made since both areas of surveillance are related. It has been shown that the purported success of digital marketing bestows legitimacy on data-based surveillance in the area of security. This legitimising effect increases when surveillance technology in the field of security can access and cite other kinds of data about our daily lives, such as social networking or web searches which are also driven by Big Data. Conceptualising Big Data generically as surveillance supports these legitimising processes. At the same time such conceptualisation can create the impression of hopelessness: If surveillance drives the Internet, how can we still hope to evade it? Regarding the fact that surveillance itself often is seen as something negative, something to be evaded (Fuchs 2011), the beneficiary uses of Big Data cannot always be grasped as surveillance – although they enable potentials for surveillance. Thus the concept of surveillance has to be contextualised: surveillance by whom, for what purpose, with which legitimisation, in order to be a suitable conceptual tool for inquiries about Big Data. To that aim, theories of surveillance have to be united with accounts from political theory and social philosophy, to ask: what does Big Data do when used for surveillance?

Notes

1 See http://tylervigen.com/.
2 See, however, on the issue of misattributing agency to algorithms: Matzner (2017).

Bibliography

Adey, P. (2012). Borders, identification and surveillance. In: D. Lyon, K. Ball & K. D. Haggerty, ed., *Routledge Handbook of Surveillance Studies*, London: Routledge, pp. 193–201.

Agrawal, R., Imieliński, T. & Swami, A. (1993). Mining Association Rules Between Sets of Items in Large Databases, *Proceedings of the 1993 ACM SIGMOD International Conference on Management of Data*, ACM, New York, pp. 207–216.

Amoore, L. (2011). Data derivatives: on the emergence of a security risk calculus for our times. *Theory, Culture & Society* 28(6), pp. 24–43.

Amoore, L. (2013). *The Politics of Possibility: Risk and Security Beyond Probability*. Durham, NC: Duke University Press.

Boellstorff, T. (2013). Making big data, in theory. *First Monday* 18(10). Available at: http://firstmonday.org/article/view/4869/3750. [Accessed 22 July 2015].

Bowker, G. C. (2013). Data flakes. In: L. Gitelman, ed., *Raw Data is an Oxymoron*, Cambridge, MA: MIT Press, pp. 167–172.

boyd, d. & Crawford, K. (2012). Critical questions for Big Data. *Information, Communication and Society* 15(5), pp. 662–679.

Buzan, B., Wæver, O. & de Wilde, J. (1998). *Security: A New Framework for Analysis*. Boulder, CO: Lynne Rienner.

Cheney-Lippold, J. (2011). A new algorithmic identity: soft biopolitics and the modulation of control. *Theory, Culture & Society* 28(6), pp. 164–181.

Cios, K., Pedrycz, W. & Swiniarski, R. (1998). *Data Mining: Methods for Knowledge Discovery*. Dordrecht: Kluwer Academic Publishers.

Clarke, R. (1988). Information technology and dataveillance. *Communications of the ACM* 31(5), pp. 498–512.

Degli Esposti, S. (2014). When big data meets dataveillance: the hidden side of analytics. *Surveillance & Society* 12(2), pp. 209–225.

Foucault, M. (1977). *Discipline and punish: the birth of the prison*. New York: Vintage.

Fuchs, C. (2011). How can surveillance be defined? *MATRIZes* 5(1), pp. 109–133.

Gandy, O. H. (2012). Statistical surveillance: remote sensing in the digital age. In: K. Haggerty, K. Ball & D. Lyon, eds., *Handbook of Surveillance Studies*, New York: Routledge, pp. 125–132.

Greenwald, G. (2014). *No Place to Hide: Edward Snowden, the NSA, and the U.S. Surveillance State*. New York: Metropolitan Books.

Haggerty, K. D. & Ericson, R. V. (2000). The surveillant assemblage. *The British Journal of Sociology* 51(4), pp. 605–622.

Horvát, E.-Á., Hanselmann, M., Hamprecht, F. A. & Zweig, K. A. (2012). One plus one makes three (for social networks). *PLoS ONE* 7(4), p. e34740.

Introna, L. D. and Nissenbaum, H. (2000). Shaping the Web: why the politics of search engines matters. *The Information Society* 16(3), pp. 169–185.

Jernigan, C. & Mistree, B. (2009). Gaydar: Facebook friendships expose sexual orientation, *First Monday* 14(10). Available at: http://firstmonday.org/ojs/index.php/fm/article/view/2611. [Accessed 22 July 2015].

Kinsley, S. (2015). A political economy of Twitter data? Conducting research with proprietary data is neither easy nor free. Available at: http://blogs.lse.ac.uk/usappblog/2015/01/03/a-political-economy-of-twitter-data-conducting-research-with-proprietary-data-is-neither-easy-nor-free/. [Accessed 17 July 2017].

Kitchin, R. (2014), Big Data, new epistemologies and paradigm shifts. *Big Data & Society* 1(1), pp. 1–12.

Kosinski, M., Stillwell, D. & Græpel, T. (2013). Private traits and attributes are predictable from digital records of human behaviour. *Proceedings of the National Academy of Sciences* 110(15), pp. 5802–5805.

Leese, M. (2016). 'Seeing Futures' – Politics of visuality and affect. In: L. Amoore and V. Piotukh, ed., *Algorithmic Life: Calculative Devices in the Age of Big Data*. Milton Park/New York: Routledge, pp. 148–164.

Litt, E. (2012). Knock, knock. Who's there? The imagined audience. *Journal of Broadcasting & Electronic Media* 56(3), pp. 330–345.

Lyon, D. (2003). *Surveillance As Social Sorting: Privacy, Risk, and Digital Discrimination*. Milton Park: Taylor & Francis.

Lyon, D. (2014). Surveillance, Snowden, and big data: capacities, consequences, critique. *Big Data & Society* 1(2), pp. 1–13.

Lyon, D. (2015). *Surveillance After Snowden*. Cambridge: Polity.

Manovich, L. (2012). Trending: the promises and the challenges of big social data. Debates in the digital humanities. Available at: http://dhdebates.gc.cuny.edu/debates/text/15. [Accessed 22 July 2015].

Mass, C. (2012). Nowcasting: the promise of new technologies of communication, modeling, and observation. *Bulletin of the American Meteorological Society* 93, pp. 797–809.

Massumi, Brian (2007). Potential politics and the primacy of preemption. *Theory & Event*, 10(2). Available at: https://muse.jhu.edu/article/218091. [Accessed 22 July 2015].

Matzner, T. (2014). Why privacy is not enough privacy in the context of 'ubiquitous computing' and 'big data'. *Journal of Information, Communication and Ethics in Society* 12(2), pp. 93–106.

Matzner, T. (2016a). Beyond data as representation: the performativity of Big Data in surveillance. *Surveillance and Society* 14(2), pp. 197–210.

Matzner, T. (2016b). The model gap: cognitive systems in security applications and their ethical implications. *AI & Society* 31(1), pp. 95–102.

Matzner, T. (2017). The human is dead – long live the algorithm! *Theory, Culture and Society* (forthcoming).

Pasquale, F. (2015). *The Black Box Society: The Secret Algorithms that Control Money and Information*. Cambridge, MA: Harvard University Press.

Prensky, M. (2009). H. sapiens digital: From digital immigrants and digital natives to digital wisdom. Innovate 5(3). Available at: www.innovateonline.info/index.php?view=article&id=705. [Accessed 22 July 2015].

Rashid, F. Y. (2014). Surveillance is the Business Model of the Internet: Bruce Schneier. *Security Week.* Available at: www.securityweek.com/surveillance-business-model-internet-bruce-schneier. [Accessed 22 July 2015].

Ribes, D. & Jackson, S. J. (2013). Data Bite Man: the work of sustaining a long-term study. In: L. Gitelman, ed., *Raw Data is an Oxymoron*, Cambridge, MA: MIT Press.

Rosen, J. (2004). *The Naked Crowd: Reclaiming Security and Freedom in an Anxious Age*. New York: Random House Publishing Group.

Rosenberg, D. (2013). Data before the fact. In: L. Gitelman, ed., *Raw Data is an Oxymoron*. Cambridge, MA: MIT Press, 15–42.

Rouvroy, A. (2013). The end (s) of critique: data-behaviourism vs. due-process. In: K. de Vries & M. Hildebrandt, eds., *Privacy, Due Process and the Computational Turn – The Philosophy of Law Meets the Philosophy of Technology*. London: Routledge, pp. 143–167.

Schmidhuber, J. (2015). Deep learning in neural networks: An overview, *Neural Networks* 61, pp. 85–117.

Tucker, Patrick (2016). Refugee or Terrorist? IBM Thinks Its Software Has the Answer. Available at: www.defenseone.com/technology/2016/01/refugee-or-terrorist-ibm-thinks-its-software-has-answer/125484/. [Accessed 22 July 2015].

Part II
Big Data policies

Politics of governance and regulation

6 Tracing Big Data imaginaries through public policy

The case of the European Commission

Gernot Rieder

Introduction

In recent years, the term 'Big Data' has emerged as a major buzzword, widely used by both public and private actors. A precise definition, however, remains elusive, as various stakeholders have offered different views – pointing, for instance, to the volume, velocity, and variety of data produced (see Laney 2012), new and improved ways to collect, store, process, and analyse those data (see Ward and Barker 2013), or profound changes in how people think, work, and live (see Mayer-Schönberger and Cukier 2013).

Others have been more reluctant to buy into the hype, arguing that the current excitement is driven by inflated expectations rather than actual shifts in operational reality.[1] But, while claims that the 'Big Data bubble' is bound to burst sooner rather than later have been around for years (see Franks 2012), reports indicate that investments in Big Data solutions have only been increasing, with decision makers considering the ability to extract value from data as critical to future success (see Columbus 2015). Media and public interest, too, remains high, with the *New York Times* publishing 118 articles mentioning Big Data over the course of 2016[2] and a Google Trends analysis attesting to the continued popularity of the term in global search queries.[3] The reasons for the persistence of what has repeatedly been described as a 'fad' destined to fade (see Woody 2012) are arguably twofold: On the one hand, the ongoing computerisation of ever more areas of human life – from social interaction and commerce to health care, law enforcement, and education – has provided ample opportunity for Big Data small talk. The notion has therefore become a convenient umbrella term, broad enough to be applicable to almost anything technology-related, while imparting a sense of urgency and importance. Big Data's conceptual vagueness is thus very much part of the term's appeal, serving as a common point of reference in today's fast-changing digital environments. On the other hand, what may have started as a technical discussion[4] has since developed into a much more complex cultural phenomenon. Big Data is not just a fashionable catchphrase; it is a modern myth that has inspired an almost religious following (see boyd and Crawford 2012). This mythology, as will be shown below, is structured around a logic of promise and obligation that deals in metaphors and visions, hopes, dreams, and ambitions. As a result, Big Data no longer functions as a mere short-hand for a set of computational problems and methods, but acts as a powerful rhetorical device designed to boost support and ensure public consent.

Many of these narratives originated in the marketing departments of hard- and software vendors (e.g. see IBM 2012), only to be echoed in the reports of research and consultancy firms (e.g. see IDC *et al.* 2013). It was not long, however, until they found their way into political discourse: For several years now, policymakers on both sides of the Atlantic have stressed the great potential of Big Data, framing it as a potent antidote to a wide range of societal issues. The excitement and confidence expressed in numerous political speeches and communications is considerable, rivalling even the grand claims of industry stakeholders. Officials' widespread endorsement of Big Data has translated into concrete funding actions: In 2012, the Obama Administration announced a $200 million Big Data Research and Development Initiative to 'help solve some [of] the Nation's most pressing challenges' (OSTP 2012: 1). In 2014, the European Commission (EC) launched a €2.5 billion public–private partnership in an effort to 'master Big Data' and put the Union at the 'forefront of the global data race' (EC 2014b: 1). In view of such large-scale commitments, the (dis)qualification of Big Data as a short-lived buzz or fad seems both analytically wanting and conceptually inadequate, unable to account for the actual scale and longevity of the phenomenon.

Against this background, the chapter at hand aims to develop a better under-standing of the rise of Big Data in public policy. It will do so in two important ways: First, it will examine key *sociotechnical imaginaries* as they manifest in official policy documents, with recent publications of the European Commission serving as the main empirical material. Second, the chapter seeks to contextual-ise these narratives and visions by adopting a broader analytical perspective, pointing to a number of economic, institutional, and epistemic challenges that contribute to the production and perpetuation of the Big Data imaginary. Based on these observations, the chapter develops a pointed critique of the Commis-sion's Big Data rhetoric, arguing that it incorporates a set of values and beliefs that threaten to undermine key democratic principles as well as efforts towards responsible and sustainable ICT development.

Interlude: sociotechnical imaginaries

The concept of sociotechnical imaginaries, introduced in Jasanoff and Kim (2009) and further elaborated in Jasanoff and Kim (2015), has been influential within the field of Science and Technology Studies (STS). Loosely tied to earlier work on social imaginaries by Anderson (1983), Appadurai (1996), and Taylor (2004), but with particular emphasis on science and technology as key sites of modern imagination, it has inspired a growing number of case studies to look for and investigate 'collectively held, institutionally stabilised, and publicly performed visions of desirable futures' (Jasanoff 2015: 4). Crucially, such visions are considered to be both *situated* (meaning that they are culturally and temporally particular), embedded within specific socio-political environments, and *materially grounded* in the sense that they are co-produced within hetero-geneous networks of both human and non-human actors. The concept's focus, however, is not only on the *formation* of sociotechnical imaginaries but also on their *performative power*: Once imaginaries become widely accepted and used, they may shape trajectories of research and innovation, steering technological progress as well as public/private expenditure. Thus, while imaginative work can be understood as an important cultural practice that creates common narratives and enables shared interpretations of social reality, it can have serious *normative implications*: What starts as a description of potentially attainable futures may soon turn into a prescription of futures that ought to be attained (see Jasanoff and Kim 2009). Rather than mere fantasy, sociotechnical imaginaries thus constitute a 'crucial reservoir of power and action [that] lodges in the hearts and minds of human agents and institutions' (Jasanoff 2015: 17).

How then can the concept of sociotechnical imaginaries contribute to the kind of qualitative policy analysis proposed in this chapter? There are a couple of points to be made here. First and foremost, the very invocation of the imagina-tion as an object of study 'rejects the idea of politics as consisting simply of purposive, rational action' (ibid.: 7). Instead, it emphasises that political agendas are driven by culturally specific belief and value systems that produce different forms of techno-political order. The governance of nanotechnologies, for instance, has been shaped by contrasting visions and ideals in Germany and the United States (see Burri 2015), and narratives of national nuclear identity differ greatly between atom-free Austria (see Felt 2015) and radiating France (see Hecht 2009 [1998]). In this sense, the notion of sociotechnical imaginaries invites a close reading of the various expectations and concerns, the diverse norms, mores, and ideologies that guide and inform the articulation of national policies. Second, and equally important, the concept encourages a critical examination of dominant imaginaries in the sense that it takes into consideration the topographies of power that help these imaginaries to form, stabilise, prolifer-ate, and endure. Again, this is a hybrid process that involves not only humans and their respective aspirations, but also technical artefacts, institutions, indus-trial practices, and regulatory frameworks, to list but a few. Thus, in addition to its focus on values and beliefs, the concept calls for a broader assessment of techno-political regimes, their actors, structures, and embodiments, and how these participate in the cultivation and maintenance of specific collective imagi-nations. Third, and on a more methodological note, the concept explicitly refers to official documents – for example, policy texts, political speeches, press releases – as materials providing 'some of the most accessible and ubiquitous resources for analysing sociotechnical imaginaries' (STS-RPSI 2017). Studied carefully, such documents may reveal 'recurrent themes or tropes in references to national and cultural practices', including 'articulations of the public good, risk, and responsibility' (ibid.). This emphasis on language as a 'crucially important medium for the construction of imaginaries' (Jasanoff and Kim 2009: 122) makes the concept a suitable tool when seeking to identify and discuss prominent visions of techno-scientific futures in official policy discourse. Last but not least, the concept advocates comparative investigations as well as research on changes over time, suggesting that imaginations of particular socio-technical innovations can vary between different nations or stakeholders, and that shared visions may change with shifting circumstances. Diverging opinions, contrasting ideas, and signs of controversy should therefore be regarded as point-ers that may help to illuminate imaginaries together with their inscribed values, goals, and politics. Ultimately, it is through such comparisons that the distinctive features of prevalent imaginaries become apparent, while simultaneously provid-ing a clearer sense of possible alternatives.

Drawing on these insights, this chapter uses the notion of sociotechnical imaginaries as a sensitising concept to study visions of Big Data as they mani-fest in the official policy discourse of the European Commission. The aim is to gain a better understanding of the hopes and fears that drive these narratives, the ways in which they are related to particular constructions of the public good, and the broader historical and cultural contexts in which they are embedded. The European Commission presents a particularly interesting case as the institution has become an important regulator of digital services, its policies and directives not only affecting the national legislations of EU member states, but also impact-ing data-related laws, rights, and markets around the globe (see Buttarelli 2016). Tracing the Commission's Big Data imaginary through respective policy docu-ments[5] thus provides insight into the values and aspirations of a key political actor whose normative power can be expected to play a formative role in the cre-ation and design of our digital future.

Tracing Big Data imaginaries: the case of the European Commission

In early 2014, the then Vice-President of the European Commission responsible for the Digital Agenda, Neelie Kroes, declared at the European Data Forum in Athens that about 200 years after railways started to connect people and energise the economy, society now faces a new industrial revolution: a digital one, with Big Data as its fuel. Her dream, Kroes continued, was that Europe would take full part in this revolution, with 'European industry able to supply, European citizens and businesses able to benefit, [and] European governments able and willing to support' (Kroes 2014b: 1). A year later, in a speech at Hannover Messe, Kroes' successor in office, Guenther Oettinger, presented a similar vision. Europe's future is digital, he stated, with the availability and use of Big Data crucial for maintaining the Union's competitiveness. In order to not fall behind and realise the potential of digital technologies, Europe would need to act fast, becoming the avant-garde of digital manufacturing (see Oettinger 2015c).

Framings such as these, which emphasise Big Data's great economic poten-tial and the necessity to exploit it, have for years dominated the Commission's Big Data narrative. At its core, this narrative is characterised by a twofold dynamic: On the one hand, the frequent use of buzz-laden metaphors imparts a sense of novelty and excitement. Going through official EC publications, one can, for instance, find Big Data referred to as the 'new oil' (Kroes 2013c: 2); the 'motor and foundation of the future economy' (EC 2014b: 1); a 'key asset' (EC 2017a); a 'game-changer' (Šefčovič 2016); some 'magic material' (Kroes 2013a: 2); a 'goldmine' (EC 2015b: 1); the 'lifeblood of digital markets' (Oettinger 2015a). In such cases, the language of the Commission and its representatives resembles that of a marketing campaign, mystifying the product while stressing its value and functional benefits. On the other hand, there is also a sense of urgency to capitalise on what is seen as a great chance and opportunity. In order not to miss out, and to secure Europe's digital future, quick and decisive action is said to be required. Failing to act is considered a major concern (see Kroes 2013a), threatening to stifle innovation and the development of a flourishing EU data market (see EC 2014d). Accordingly, the main task would be to tackle any obstacles, create the right environment, and 'turn this asset into gold' (Kroes 2014b: 3).

What emerges most clearly from the documents is the conceptualisation of Big Data as an economic imperative, the key to unlocking a bright and prosperous future. Big Data's status is that of a raw material to be mined and exploited, a digital lubricant of growth and progress. While this master narrative already provides a rough account of the Commission's general position, a closer look reveals a somewhat more fine-grained pattern of claims and promises. More precisely, the EC's vision of Big Data appears to hinge upon three interrelated storylines: Big Data as the cornerstone of a thriving data-driven economy, Big Data as a way to transform and improve public services, and Big Data as a tool for evidence-informed policy and decision-making. We shall briefly examine each of these in more detail.

Big Data as the cornerstone of a thriving data-driven economy: This vision holds that Big Data is bound to play an integral role in the development of a strong European data industry, with Big Data technology and services expected to grow at a compound annual growth rate of 40% (see EC 2014d), saving manufacturers billions and boosting EU economic growth by an additional 1.9% by 2020 (see EC 2016g). What is more, by increasing productivity and accelerating innovation, Big Data is expected to stimulate an opportunity-rich market environment, creating 'hundreds of thousands of new jobs in the coming years' (EC 2014b: 2), gradually replacing lower-skilled work with new and higher-quality occupations (see Oettinger 2015c). From a global perspective, the availability and use of Big Data is said to be crucial for maintaining the EU's competitiveness (see ibid.); failure to harness this potential would mean becoming dependent on solutions from abroad (see Kroes 2013a). The creation of a thriving data market is thus presented as a simple binary choice: 'We can either be at the table – or on the menu' (Kroes 2013b: 3). And since the Commission is adamant to position the European Union (EU) as a 'digital world player' (Oettinger 2015d) that takes 'the global lead in data' (Kroes 2013c: 3), its strong support of Big Data as one of 'Europe's key economic assets' (EC 2014c: 1) appears a foregone conclusion.

Big Data as a way to transform and improve public services: On the public sector side, the use of Big Data technologies is seen as a way to increase both government efficiency and effectiveness, improving the quality of public services while reducing costs and administrative burden through new and optimised solutions (see EC 2017c). Example applications include the development of interoperable healthcare platforms, better management of traffic flows and energy consumption, or the design and implementation of automated translation systems (see EC 2017d).[6] In this narrative, public sector information is framed as a goldmine that must be unlocked (see Kroes 2013a), enabling a 'smarter use of public money' (Kroes 2014b: 1) together with more 'personalized, user-friendly and innovative services' (EC 2017c). In order to realise this vision, public data silos would have to be opened up, facilitating information-sharing, not only inside and between government agencies (improving efficiency) or between these agencies and ordinary citizens (improving transparency), but also between the public and the private sector. In the eyes of the Commission, the ability to reap Big Data benefits is thus tied to strong public–private partnerships (see EC 2014b) and the reuse of public sector information (see EC 2014a).

Big Data as a tool for evidence-informed policy and decision-making: With regard to public policy, there is the expectation that Big Data will enable 'policy-makers to make informed and evidence-based decisions' (EC 2017d), tackling societal challenges such as climate change (Vestager 2016), unemployment (Thyssen 2016), or migration (EC 2016c) with high precision and accuracy. In essence, Big Data technologies are supposed to provide timely, actionable insights, allowing administrations to make the 'right' choices more quickly. Techniques such as performance monitoring, opinion mining, or policy modelling are considered promising avenues to more targeted, data-driven policy designs (see EC 2015d). Rather than merely offering advice, however, Big Data technologies are meant to generate solutions (see EC 2014d), testing strategies and simulating outcomes at a systemic level (see EC 2016a). The need to predict and prevent figures prominently in this imaginary, marking a shift from reactive to more proactive modes of governance. From nowcasting[7] income distribution to forecasting crop yields, from 'predicting the traffic to predicting the economy' (Kroes 2013a: 2), there is hardly an area of public policy that is expected to remain untouched by advances in Big Data analytics.

Although clearly desired, according to the Commission, none of these outcomes are guaranteed. Instead, their realisation is said to depend upon certain prerequisites, including (i) a coherent data ecosystem that counters the paralysing fragmentation of the European market (see Kroes 2013a); (ii) a firm commitment to open data, facilitating the reuse of public sector information (see EC 2016d); (iii) significant investment in education and training to ensure Europe's workforce adapts to the new digital environment (see Oettinger 2015b); and (iv) the establishment of public–private partnerships that unite all relevant players and strengthen every part of the Big Data value chain (see EC 2017b). To 'get it right' would imply safeguarding a better economic future; to 'get it wrong' would mean losing out and risking European competitiveness on the international market (see Kroes 2013b: 2). With data governance believed to be at a crossroads, there is thus strong emphasis that the Union 'can't miss out on that kind of growth opportunity' (Kroes 2013c: 2). To turn away and 'not do' Big Data would constitute both a failure and a mistake since technology development is considered 'the only sustainable long term [sic] response to secure our digital future' (Oettinger 2015d). In the Commission's narrative, Big Data is thus viewed as a destiny without viable alternatives, a programmatic answer to the assumed truism that 'tomorrow's world will be digital' (Kroes 2013b: 3).

As might be expected, data-related worries and concerns only play a minor role in this imaginary. Rather, there appears to be agreement that one should not '[stop] the wonderful things, simply to prevent the not-so-wonderful' (ibid.: 2). If, however, potential risks and pitfalls are being addressed, these are, on the one hand, mostly thought to be limited to issues of privacy and security and, on the other hand, assumed to be amenable to technological fixes – that is, solutions that do not challenge the deployment of a technology or service as such, but only the particularities of its design, leaving little room for serious intervention. Legal regulation is also considered an option, but only to the extent that safeguards '[do] not come at the expense of innovation' (ibid.: 4). From the Commission's perspective, laws should be pragmatic and proportionate, with rules set up to 'maximize the value and minimise the cost of data' (Kroes 2013d: 2). Tools and laws together could then 'empower people' (Kroes 2014b: 2), giving users both control and responsibility over their data and making consent a 'cornerstone of data protection' (Kroes 2013b: 3). Ultimately, measures such as these are expected to boost public trust and confidence in digital services whose benefits are believed to outweigh any potential harms, with detrimental effects deemed the exception, not the rule (see Kroes 2012).

To sum up, while public debate about the impacts of Big Data is polarised and critical (see Cukier 2014), the European Commission upholds a decidedly positive vision, promoting the widespread use of modern data analytics as an opportunity not to be missed. In a digital future, Europe is seen as having the choice between leading or following, and the Commission is clear about its ambition to 'master Big Data' and put the Union 'at the forefront of the global data race' (EC 2014b: 1). Consequently, primary concerns include ways to strengthen the sector, accelerate innovation, and profit from an unleashed data-driven economy where 'data protection cannot mean data protectionism' (Kroes 2013b: 4). What emerges is an imaginary of Big Data for industrial growth and public sector transformation, spurred by aspirations of increased efficiency, reduced costs, and digitally aggregated value generation (see EC 2015c). With the continued fragmentation of the European market considered a threat to this vision, the Commission keenly stresses the need for an open and coherent data ecosystem, and 'every lawmaker, every public body, every vested interest who wants to push back [needs to be convinced] there's a better way of doing things' (Kroes 2014a: 3). What is initially presented as a choice thus quickly turns into a normative imperative and obligation. As former Commissioner Kroes maintained: ' "Data" isn't a four-letter word. […] It's something Europe needs to embrace' (ibid.: 3).

Discussion: data governance in times of crisis

The Commission's predominant focus on economic growth and organisational efficiency should not come as a surprise. Formally established in 1951 as the High Authority of the European Coal and Steel Community (ECSC) – and later joined by (in 1957) and merged (in 1965) with the executives of the European Economic Community (EEC) and the European Atomic Energy Community (EAEC) – the European Commission, throughout its institutional history, has sought to retain its legitimacy through policies aimed at contributing towards prosperity, competitiveness, and effective EU leadership (see Nugent and Rhinard 2015; Cini 1996). In times of social and economic unrest, pressures to strengthen the market and battle unemployment while cutting costs can be particularly pronounced, and there is no doubt that the Union has recently seen its fair share of turbulence, both financial (see EC 2009) and otherwise (see EC 2016e). Against such a troubled background, the promises of Big Data may seem particularly alluring: With average growth rates said to outpace not only the general economy but also the already healthy numbers of the traditional ICT market (see EC 2014d), the data sector presents itself as an opportunity 'Europe cannot afford to miss' (ibid.: 2). Moreover, by promising to disrupt other industries and change 'the way we do business' (Oettinger 2015c: 2) – with expected cost savings of as much as €426 billion and an additional GDP increase of €206 billion until 2020 (see EC 2016g) – the proclaimed data revolution may well appear as a panacea to an ailing European economy. It thus stands to reason that the Union's fragile economic situation has provided fertile ground for the promises of Big Data advocates, the current climate of excitement arguably a combined product of significant budgetary pressures and vested corporate interests.

However, it is not just about financials. As outlined in the previous section, there is considerable interest in data technologies for evidence-informed policy and decision-making,[8] stretching from policy modelling and simulation, to monitoring and analysis, and to enforcement and compliance, with the intention of improving 'the effectiveness, efficiency, and quality [of] decisions in the public sector' (see EC 2015d). But while the traditional view of the Commission as a technocratic body in constant need of expertise and information certainly holds some explanatory power (see Metz 2015), the recent rise of 'datatrust' (Rieder and Simon 2016) appears to be of a somewhat different nature. As Porter (1995: 146) argues, whereas technocracy presupposes relatively secure elites who would insist that 'cultivated judgment is required to solve social problems', attempts to mechanise decision-making usually occur under conditions of intense scrutiny, when pressured authorities seek to shield themselves against outside challenges by exchanging expert judgement for seemingly impersonal technical routines. Rather than the high point of technocratic ambition, the Commission's push for Big Data solutions is thus better understood as a contested political and administrative body's effort to maintain authority and legitimacy amidst strong opposition by both national political forces and a substantial proportion of the Union's population. With people's trust remaining low,[9] *trusted* analytical services are seen as a potential remedy, offering actionable insights surrounded by what boyd and Crawford (2012: 663) have referred to as an 'aura of truth, objectivity, and accuracy'. The 'promise of mechanical neutrality' (Gillespie 2014: 181) with its 'glow of veracity' (Daston and Galison 1992: 111) thus serves as a valuable tool and means to establish credibility and justify political action.

Finally, and on a related note, while the availability of ever more data and the ability to collect and analyse them contribute to governmental efforts to 'make society legible' (Scott 1998: 2), Big Data's focus on machine learning and pre- diction caters to – but also fuels – policymakers' 'craving for certainty' (Nowotny 2016: 1) and '*ex ante* assurances' (ibid.: 7). In light of the expressed need 'for organizing and managing […] increased complexity' (Šefčovič 2016), data-driven insights are seen as a way to battle volatility and regain control, sup- porting the governance of the present by turning *unmeasurable uncertainty* into *measurable risk* (see Knight 1921). Whereas the former threatens to grind the wheels of the political machinery to a halt, the latter provides a mandate for action based on probabilistic forecasts. Public officials' interest in Big Data is thus driven by a high demand for 'anticipatory intelligence' (EC 2015a: 18), which is thought to 'augment decision makers' (EC 2016b: 68) and 'reconfigur[e] the policy system in a way that makes it more apt to address long- term challenges' (EC 2015a: 19). In addition, the promise of universal applic- ability, most famously voiced by Anderson (2008), positions Big Data as a practical chance to expand the statistical colonisation of the future to an increas- ing number of governmental tasks and areas. To a bureaucratic institution that faces uncertainty but chases forward-looking policies, the prospect of 'knowing the odds' with unprecedented speed and accuracy may just constitute an offer too good to refuse. As a result, to date, the Commission's hopes are firmly pinned on Big Data.

In sum, the roots of the European Commission's Big Data imaginary can arguably be traced back to a specific amalgamation of economic, institutional, and epistemic factors and challenges: a Union in search of growth and prosperity amidst a severe financial crisis, a supranational authority experiencing a loss of trust and legitimacy, an agenda-setting political machinery in need of data and tools for probabilistic risk assessment. While a series of technological and meth- odological advancements have made Big Data possible, it is these contextual specificities that have elevated the term into a widespread sociotechnical phe- nomenon. The Commission's narrative, however, is not without its problems. In fact, it incorporates a number of claims and assumptions that warrant further critical examination. Even though a detailed discussion of the entrenched falla- cies is beyond the scope of this chapter, a few key points should briefly be addressed.

Datatrust: As Bowker (2005) points out, data are never raw, but always already cooked, a process that needs to be recognised and considered with care. In a similar vein, Rieder (2017) argues that the employment of algorithmic tech- niques may best be thought of as a situated epistemic practice that generates 'interested readings of empirical, "datafied" reality'. The insight that even highly formalised analytical methods produce interpretations from specific 'somewheres' rather than a 'view from nowhere' (Nagel 1986) gains significance in a world where numbers and their mathematical treatment are increasingly considered the unquestioned – and unquestionable – backbone of decision-making. Such *blind trust*, however, bears dangers of subverting the very foundations of deliberative democracy as well as key principles of the rule of law: With respect to the former, exaggerated faith in the neutrality and fairness of Big Data processes may undermine democratic deliberation by (a) deflecting from the goal-driven interests that shape and inform the design and implementation of analytical systems, (b) discouraging investigations into how Big Data practices can cause harm and unfair discrimination, and (c) rendering debates about alternative forms of business and governance both misguided and absurd. Regarding the latter, the sheer complexity of algorithmic operations can make the connection between input data and output decision-making murky (see Burrell 2016), yielding an inscrutable evidence base that jeopardises existing due process norms, and disrespecting individuals' rights to transparent and accountable adjudication (see Citron 2014, 2008). Given that Big Data's ultimate promise is not only to predict but to pre-empt, marking a fundamental shift from reactive to more 'aggressive', proactive measures (see Kerr and Earle 2013), blind trust in the veracity and social equity of mechanical reasoning appears a negative and irresponsible direction.

Trusted Technologies: Also related to the issue of trust, but approaching the topic from a different angle, are the Commission's attempts to strengthen individuals' trust and confidence in digital solutions, because '[w]ithout people's trust, a functioning [Digital Single Market] based on data will not work' (Ansip 2015b). In light of a perceived 'lack of trust in online services' (Ansip 2015a), the Commission thus aims to reduce fears, mitigate concerns, and create 'trusted' environments, encouraging citizens to 'embrace the digital revolution' (Bieńkowska 2016). What is problematic here is the rhetorical emphasis on *trust* rather than *trustworthiness*, on *trusted* rather than *trustworthy* computational systems. As Simon (2013) stresses, 'given the dangers of misplaced trust, [...] we should not simply trust, but trust those who are worthy of our trust'. From a governance perspective, attempts to 'build', 'boost', 'secure', 'restore', or 'maintain' trust should always be accompanied – and ultimately surpassed – by efforts to create trustworthy frameworks and environments that contribute to citizens' social, economic, and legal protection. Put differently, if the political goal is to create an *atmosphere of trust* that 'translate[s] into economic growth' and turns the Union into an 'economic powerhouse' (Jourová 2015: 5; see also Fukuyama 1995), the democratically preferable and presumably more sustainable way would not be to directly target people's confidence level – for example, through PR campaigns, shiny certificates, or repeated statements of intent – but to support and invest in systems that genuinely deserve such confidence. By strengthening citizens' digital rights, introducing new compliance obligations, and increasing monetary fines for violations, the EU's upcoming General Data

Protection Regulation (GDPR), which will take effect in May 2018, arguably presents an important step in this direction. Yet it will be the actual implementation and enforcement of the Regulation by EU member states that will decide whether the longing for trust will eventually lead to the development and deployment of truly trustworthy digital solutions (see Davies 2016).

Citizen Empowerment: One crucial way the Commission hopes to safeguard privacy and build trust in the digital economy is by giving people control over their data, conceptualising individuals as self-managing, entrepreneurial subjects who take charge and become makers of their own digital destiny (see Ochs, Chapter 13 and Fleischhack, Chapter 12 in this volume). As Commissioner Kroes declared at the European Data Forum, '[w]hat you need is to empower people, give them control, give them a fair share of that value. Give them rights over their data – and responsibilities too, and the tools to exercise them' (Kroes 2014b: 2). While such calls for the autonomous, self-reliant *homo datanomicus* may appeal to the ears of free-market liberals – and there are certainly good arguments for having users take part and profit from the monetisation of their personal data (e.g. see Rubinstein 2013) – the idea that individuals should act as tech-savvy guardians of their own privacy has several caveats: First, as critique of the informed consent model has highlighted time and again, users tend not to read terms of services and privacy policies, thus calling into question the image of the attentive, dutifully engaged data citizen that authorities seek to project (see Monteleone 2015). Second, even if users were to devote time and effort into data privacy self-management, chances are that long and rhetorically cloudy customer policies together with secretive corporate practices and opaque machine operations would render such attempts an almost impossible task, even for the digitally skilled (see Obar 2015). Considering that many EU citizens still have no or very low digital competences (see Eurostat 2013), the Commission's call for data privacy self-governance seems both unrealistic and, to a degree, insincere. Last but not least, the attribution of responsibility to the data subject involves a democratically dubious shifting of the burden to the individual who is (over)tasked with oversight in a context of high complexity and weak regulation. While the lengthy GDPR negotiations have shown how difficult it can be to strike a balance between industry and privacy interests,[10] a general redistribution of work and responsibility under the banner of citizen empowerment may prove incompatible with EU law, where the protection of personal data is recognised as a fundamental right (see European Communities 2000).

Open Data: A final concern pertains to the Commission's strong support of open data, that is, 'data made freely available for re-use to everyone for both commercial and non-commercial purposes' (EC 2014d: 5). While for the Commission, the free flow of data 'across sectors, languages, and borders' (ibid.: 6) constitutes a critical component in the establishment of a thriving, innovative digital economy, researchers have pointed to the dangers and limitations of this *sharing imperative*, arguing that the open distribution of public sector information may conflict with individuals' right to data privacy, underestimating the increasingly blurry lines between personal and non-personal data in the age of

Big Data analytics (Kulk and van Loenen 2012; see also Noorman *et al.*, Chapter 14 in this volume). As studies and real-world examples have shown, powerful computational models can now be used to infer highly sensitive personal information from seemingly innocuous data (see Kosinski *et al.* 2013; Duhigg 2012), and even when data have been anonymised, re-identification techniques may allow the linking of these data to specific individuals, undermining prior protection efforts (see Narayanan *et al.* 2008; Sweeney 2000). Given this, but also in light of concerns regarding increased data marketisation (see Bates 2012) and the establishment of open access research repositories (see Mauthner and Parry 2013), the Commission's push for liberal data-sharing policies in the name of transparency, efficiency, and growth should be viewed critically and with caution. Instead of an 'open by default' principle, as set out in the G8's Open Data Charter (see Group of Eight 2013) and repeatedly referred to in Commission documents (e.g. see EC 2014d), questions as to which data should be shared with whom, under what circumstances, and to what ends, ought to be properly discussed and addressed. In the UK, public resistance against the government's care.data programme has recently demonstrated that the distribution of personal-level information – even if anonymised – remains a highly controversial and divisive social issue (see Presser *et al.* 2015).

Though by no means comprehensive, the list above should provide a sense that the Commission's Big Data imaginary builds on a number of (epistemic) assumptions and (ideological) framings that, from an academic but also a purely democratic point of view, warrant critical scrutiny, if not outright rejection. To be sure, the problem is not so much that the Commission aims to create a strong and innovative digital market – after all, the fostering of trade and commerce has always been one of the institution's main responsibilities. Rather, it is that in this process, economic imperatives clearly outweigh wider social, ethical, and legal considerations, at times even to the detriment of fundamental rights and values. If the Commission truly wishes to (re)build trust as the basis of not only a thriving but a fair and sustainable digital economy, it should reconsider key elements of its Big Data narrative, sometimes even to the detriment of respective industry interests.

Conclusion

This chapter has sought to outline the European Commission's Big Data imaginary in some detail, reporting on the general thrust of the narrative, the claims and promises made, but also pointing to some of the major political challenges that have undoubtedly shaped the vision and its underlying values. What emerged from the assessed material was a strong free-market agenda in which trade barriers ought to be removed, regulatory burden ought to be reduced, and legislation ought to be tuned to industry requirements. In this normative framework, economic needs take precedence over questions of social desirability, and Big Data is mainly celebrated as the key to global competitiveness and a prosperous digital future.

But the strong economic imperative comes from a position of political weakness: Multiple crises and a deep sense of uncertainty have shaken the Union to its core, and the Commission has operated under conditions of high pressure and distrust in what has been appropriately labelled 'a challenging decade' (see EU 2017). Against this background, the hype around Big Data technologies, which are expected to reduce costs, increase efficiency, generate value, and improve decision-making, seems almost understandable. At the same time, however, the Commission's push for Big Data solutions involves certain concepts and convictions – from *blind trust* to *open by default* – that threaten to undermine basic democratic rights and principles. As an EU institution bound to uphold the Union's values and contribute to the protection of its citizens (see EU 2007), the Commission should re-evaluate both the quality and societal plausibility of its Big Data discourse, pondering, for instance, whether the current narrative lives up to the standards of responsible research and innovation (RRI) laid out in the Horizon 2020 Framework Program.

In order to situate the findings of this study, it is important to note that the Commission's vision of and for Big Data is only one part of European-level data and ICT governance. The EU's new General Data Protection Regulation, for example, does not explicitly refer to Big Data (see EU 2016b; Schneider, Chapter 8 in this volume), and neither does the equally new Directive, which lays down principles for the processing of personal data in the criminal justice system (see EU 2016a). What does this imply? In essence, it indicates that in current EU policymaking, the Big Data discourse runs separate from parallel discussions about data regulation, a peculiar *state of detachment* that allows for the continued use of Big Data as a generic marketing term, unburdened by the challenges of creating fair and sustainable data policies. On a positive note, this means that there is in fact political awareness of the problems and issues associated with rapidly progressing computerisation, even if such concerns are treated outside the Big Data rhetoric. In turn and somewhat less encouraging, however, this also entails that Big Data as an influential, value-laden catchphrase may remain politically unchallenged, fully co-opted by vendor interests and monetisation imperatives. Thus, while the Commission's Big Data narrative is heavily biased and skewed, its structural divorce from wider debates about the potential ramifications of large-scale datafication may allow this imbalance to persist.

From an academic and research perspective, the task is manifold: A first step would be to develop a better understanding of the Big Data imaginary itself, its origins, values, and inscribed politics. The present chapter has sought to contribute to this effort. A second step should then consider ways of improving the quality of the political discourse so that visions of an EU-wide Digital Single Market do not merely reflect industry and administrative needs, but also remain open to questions of social and cultural desirability, including the option to halt or reject particular technological applications. The call here is for critical participation rather than distant antagonism, for constructive reform rather than dogmatic opposition. Last but not least, there is a rising need for cross-disciplinary efforts: scholarship at the intersection of IT, on the one hand, and ethics/STS/ law, on the other, should be fostered to harness knowledge and expertise for sustainable development. European academia will have to rise to this challenge as high-quality interdisciplinary programmes remain rare. Yet with policymakers positively enthralled by the promises of Big Data advocates, further research on potential pitfalls and consequences as well as on socially responsible ways forward seems absolutely paramount.

Notes

1 This is perhaps best visualised in Gartner's (2013) Hype Cycle for Emerging Technologies, which shows Big Data right at the 'Peak of Inflated Expectations', gradually making its way towards the 'Trough of Disillusionment'.
2 Articles have been identified and counted using the *New York Times'* on-site search service.
3 Google's Trends graph measures interest over time by showing the number of searches for a particular term relative to the total number of searches performed on Google.
4 One of Big Data's origin stories leads to a series of presentations in the middle and late 1990s by John R. Mashey, a former chief scientist at Silicon Graphics who pointed to the challenge of increasing data traffic for IT infrastructures, for instance in his talk 'Big Data and the Next Wave of InfraStress' (Mashey 1999).
5 For this chapter's analysis, Google's Advanced Search feature was used to scrape the European Commission's official website, https://ec.europa.eu, for documents referring to Big Data. Using this term alone and in combination with other search queries (for example, names of commissioners, specific topics), roughly 120 publications (including communications, speeches, individual web pages) were collected and subjected to qualitative analysis, providing a decidedly partial but nevertheless rich picture of the Commission's Big Data imaginary.
6 For a more comprehensive overview of potential application areas, see 'Part III: Usage and Exploitation of Big Data' in Cavanillas *et al.* (2016).
7 In essence, the practice of nowcasting involves computational methods to 'predict the present' (Khan 2012) and provide near-term forecasts, for example regarding weather conditions, market movements, or influenza activity.
8 For some background on the 'ascendancy of evidence', see Solesbury (2002); for a recent state-of-the-art account of 'data for policy', see Poel *et al.* (2015).
9 According to the Standard Eurobarometer 86 survey of autumn 2016 (EC 2016f), only 36% of Europeans 'tend to trust' the European Union, with 54% saying that they 'tend not to trust'. Compared to pre-crisis levels, this is a low value. In spring 2007, for instance, trust in the Union was at 57% (ibid.: 14).
10 For a politically charged glimpse into the parliamentary negotiations around the EU data protection reform, see David Bernet's documentary *Democracy* (2015).

References

Anderson, B. (1983). *Imagined Communities: Reflections on the Origins and Spread of Nationalism*. London: Verso.
Anderson, C. (2008). The End of Theory: The Data Deluge Makes the Scientific Method Obsolete. *Wired Magazine*. Available at: www.wired.com/2008/06/pb-theory/. [Accessed 30 May 2017].

Ansip, A. (2015a). *Untitled Speech at the Digital Single Market Conference in Warsaw, Poland*. European Commission. Speech. Available at: https://ec.europa.eu/commission/commissioners/node/190797_fr. [Accessed 30 May 2017].

Ansip, A. (2015b). *Untitled Speech at the 3rd Annual Transatlantic Digital Economy Conference (AmCham EU)*. European Commission. Speech. Available at: https://ec.europa.eu/commission/commissioners/node/404234_et. [Accessed 30 May 2017].

Appadurai, A. (1996). *Modernity at Large*. Minneapolis, MN: University of Minnesota Press.

Bates, J. (2012). 'This Is What Modern Deregulation Looks Like': Co-optation and Contestation in the Shaping of the UK's Open Government Data Initiative. *The Journal of Community Informatics*, 8(2).

Bieńkowska, E. (2016). *Digital Transformation of the European Industries*. European Commission. Speech. Available at: https://ec.europa.eu/commission/commissioners/2014-2019/bienkowska/announcements/digital-transformation-european-industries_en. [Accessed 30 May 2017].

Bowker, G. C. (2005). *Memory Practices in the Sciences*. Cambridge, MA: MIT Press.

boyd, d. and Crawford, K. (2012). Critical Questions for Big Data. Provocations for a Cultural, Technological, and Scholarly Phenomenon. *Information, Communication, & Society*, 15(5), pp. 662–679.

Burrell, J. (2016). How the Machine 'Thinks': Understanding Opacity in Machine Learning Algorithms. *Big Data & Society*, 3(1), pp. 1–12.

Burri, R. V. (2015). Imaginaries of Science and Society: Framing Nanotechnology Governance in Germany and the United States. In: S. Jasanoff and S.-H. Kim, eds., *Dreamscapes of Modernity. Sociotechnical Imaginaries and the Fabrication of Power*. Chicago, IL: University of Chicago Press, pp. 233–253.

Buttarelli, G. (2016). The EU GDPR as a Clarion Call for a New Global Digital Gold Standard. *International Data Privacy Law*, 6(2), pp. 77–78.

Cavanillas, J. M., Curry, E. and Wahlster, W., eds., (2016). *New Horizons for a Data-Driven Economy. A Roadmap for Usage and Exploitation of Big Data in Europe*. Switzerland: Springer International Publishing.

Cini, M. (1996). *The European Commission. Leadership, Organisation and Culture in the EU Administration*. Manchester: Manchester University Press.

Citron, D. K. (2008). Technological Due Process. *Washington University Law Review*, 85(6), pp. 1249–1313.

Citron, D. K. (2014). *Big Data Should be Regulated by 'Technological Due Process'*. *New York Times*. Available at: www.nytimes.com/roomfordebate/2014/08/06/is-big-data-spreading-inequality/big-data-should-be-regulated-by-technological-due-process. [Accessed 30 April 2017].

Columbus, L. (2015). 56% of Enterprises will Increase their Investment in Big Data Over the Next Three Years. *Forbes*. Available at: www.forbes.com/sites/louiscolumbus/2015/03/22/56-of-enterprises-will-increase-their-investment-in-big-data-over-the-next-three-years/#178b120388b1. [Accessed 7 May 2016].

Cukier, K. N. (2014). The Backlash Against Big Data. *The Economist*. Available at: www.economist.com/blogs/economist-explains/2014/04/economist-explains-10. [Accessed 30 May 2017].

Daston, L. and Galison, P. (1992) The Image of Objectivity. *Representations*, 40, pp. 81–128.

Davies, S. (2016). The Data Protection Regulation: A Triumph of Pragmatism over Principle? *European Data Protection Law Review*, 2(3), pp. 290–296.

Democracy: Im Rausch der Daten. (2015). [film]. Germany: David Bernet.

Duhigg, C. (2012). How Companies Learn Your Secrets. *New York Times Magazine.* Available at: www.nytimes.com/2012/02/19/magazine/shopping-habits.html. [Accessed 30 May 2017].

EC (European Commission) (2009). *Economic Crisis in Europe: Causes, Consequences and Responses.* European Economy Series 7/2009. [pdf] Available at: http://ec.europa.eu/economy_finance/publications/pages/publication15887_en.pdf. [Accessed 30 May 2017].

EC (European Commission) (2014a). *Commission Encourages Re-Use of Public Sector Data.* Press Release. Available at: http://europa.eu/rapid/press-release_IP-14-840_en.htm. [Accessed 30 May 2017].

EC (European Commission) (2014b). *European Commission and Data Industry Launch €2.5 billion Partnership to Master Big Data.* Press Release. Available at: http://europa.eu/rapid/press-release_IP-14-1129_en.pdf. [Accessed 30 May 2017].

EC (European Commission) (2014c). *Frequently Asked Questions: Public-Private Partnership (PPP) for Big Data.* Memo. [pdf] Available at: http://europa.eu/rapid/press-release_MEMO-14-583_en.pdf. [Accessed 30 May 2017].

EC (European Commission) (2014d). *Towards a Thriving Data-Driven Economy.* Communication. [pdf] Available at: http://ec.europa.eu/newsroom/dae/document.cfm?action=display&doc_id=6210. [Accessed 30 May 2017].

EC (European Commission) (2015a). *Tool #4: Evidence-Based Better Regulation.* [pdf] Available at: https://ec.europa.eu/info/sites/info/files/file_import/better-regulation-toolbox-4_en_0.pdf. [Accessed 30 May 2017].

EC (European Commission) (2015b). *Digital Single Market Strategy: European Commission Agrees Areas for Action.* Press Release. [pdf] Available at: http://europa.eu/rapid/press-release_IP-15-4653_en.pdf. [Accessed 30 May 2017].

EC (European Commission) (2015c). *Making Big Data Work for Europe.* Website. Available at: https://ec.europa.eu/digital-single-market/en/making-big-data-work-europe. [Accessed 30 May 2017].

EC (European Commission) (2015d). *Policy-Development in the Age of Big Data: Data-Driven Policy-Making, Policy-Modelling, and Policy-Implementation.* Horizon 2020 Call. Available at: https://ec.europa.eu/research/participants/portal/desktop/en/opportunities/h2020/topics/co-creation-06-2017.html. [Accessed 30 May 2017].

EC (European Commission) (2016a). *Big Data Supporting Public Health Policies.* Horizon 2020 Call. Available at: http://ec.europa.eu/research/participants/portal/desktop/en/opportunities/h2020/topics/sc1-pm-18-2016.html. [Accessed 30 May 2017].

EC (European Commission) (2016b). *Digital Futures – Final Report. A Journey into 2050 Visions and Policy Challenges.* [pdf] Available at: https://ec.europa.eu/futurium/en/system/files/ged/futurium_scientific_report_v10revcl_v2_0.pdf. [Accessed 30 May 2017].

EC (European Commission) (2016c). *Migration Data Catalogue and Dynamic Data Hub – EU Migration Data at a Glance.* Website. Available at: https://ec.europa.eu/jrc/en/news/eu-migration-data-glance. [Accessed 30 May 2017].

EC (European Commission) (2016d). *Open Data.* Website. Available at: https://ec.europa.eu/digital-single-market/en/open-data. [Accessed 30 May 2017].

EC (European Commission) (2016e). *Refugee Crisis in Europe.* Website. Available at: http://ec.europa.eu/echo/refugee-crisis_en. [Accessed 30 May 2017].

EC (European Commission) (2016f). *Standard Eurobarometer 86. Autumn 2016.* Available at: https://ec.europa.eu/COMMFrontOffice/publicopinion/index.cfm/ResultDoc/download/DocumentKy/76422. [Accessed 30 May 2017].

EC (European Commission) (2016g). *The EU Data Protection Reform and Big Data Factsheet*. Website. Available at: http://ec.europa.eu/justice/data-protection/files/data-protection-big-data_factsheet_web_en.pdf. [Accessed 30 May 2017].

EC (European Commission) (2017a). *Big Data*. Website. Available at: https://ec.europa.eu/digital-single-market/en/big-data. [Accessed 30 May 2017].

EC (European Commission) (2017b). *Big Data Value Public-Private Partnership*. Website. Available at: https://ec.europa.eu/digital-single-market/en/big-data-value-public-private-partnership. [Accessed 30 May 2017].

EC (European Commission) (2017c). *Open Government*. Website. Available at: https://ec.europa.eu/digital-single-market/en/open-government. [Accessed 30 May 2017].

EC (European Commission) (2017d). *What Can Big Data Do for You?* Website. Available at: https://ec.europa.eu/digital-single-market/en/what-big-data-can-do-you. [Accessed 30 May 2017].

EU (European Union) (2007). *Treaty of Lisbon Amending the Treaty on European Union and the Treaty Establishing the European Community*. Official Journal of the European Union, C 306/1. Available at: http://eur-lex.europa.eu/legal-content/EN/TXT/HTML/?uri=CELEX:12007L/TXT&from=en. [Accessed 30 May 2017].

EU (European Union) (2016a). *Directive (EU) 2016/680 of the European Parliament and of the Council of 27 April 2016 on the Protection of Natural Persons with Regard to the Processing of Personal Data by Competent Authorities for the Purposes of the Prevention, Investigation, Detection or Prosecution of Criminal Offences or the Execution of Criminal Penalties, and on the Free Movement of Such Data, and Repealing Council Framework Decision 2008/977/JHA*. Official Journal of the European Union, L 119/89. Available at: http://eur-lex.europa.eu/legal-content/EN/TXT/HTML/?uri=CELEX:320 16L0680&from=EN. [Accessed 30 May 2017].

EU (European Union) (2016b). *Regulation (EU) 2016/679 of the European Parliament and of the Council of 27 April 2016 on the Protection of Natural Persons with Regard to the Processing of Personal Data and on the Free Movement of Such Data, and Repealing Directive 95/46/EC (General Data Protection Regulation)*. Official Journal of the European Union, L 119/1. Available at: http://eur-lex.europa.eu/legal-content/EN/TXT/HTML/?uri=CELEX:32016R0679&from=EN. [Accessed 30 May 2017].

EU (European Union) (2017). *The History of the European Union*. Website. Available at: https://europa.eu/european-union/about-eu/history_en. [Accessed 30 May 2017].

European Communities (2000). *Charter of Fundamental Rights of the European Union*. [pdf] Available at: www.europarl.europa.eu/charter/pdf/text_en.pdf. [Accessed 30 May 2017].

Eurostat (2013). *Quality of Life in Europe – Facts and Views – Education*. Website. Available at: http://ec.europa.eu/eurostat/statistics-explained/index.php?title=Quality_of_life_in_Europe_-_facts_and_views_-_education&oldid=238363. [Accessed 30 May 2017].

Felt, U. (2015). Keeping Technologies Out: Sociotechnical Imaginaries and the Formation of Austria's Technopolitical Identity. In: S. Jasanoff and S.-H. Kim, eds., *Dreamscapes of Modernity. Sociotechnical Imaginaries and the Fabrication of Power*. Chicago, IL: University of Chicago Press, pp. 103–125.

Franks, B. (2012). *Will the Big Data Bubble Burst in 2013?* International Institute for Analytics. Available at: http://iianalytics.com/research/will-the-big-data-bubble-burst-in-2013. [Accessed 7 May 2016].

Fukuyama, F. (1995). *Trust. The Social Virtues and the Creation of Prosperity*. New York: Free Press Paperbacks.

Gartner (2013). *Gartner's 2013 Hype Cycle for Emerging Technologies Maps Out Evolving Relationship Between Humans and Machines.* Available at: www.gartner.com/newsroom/id/2575515. [Accessed 7 May 2016].

Gillespie, T. (2014). The Relevance of Algorithms. In: T. Gillespie, P. J. Boczkowski and K. A. Foot, eds., *Media Technologies: Essays on Communication, Materiality, and Society.* Cambridge, MA: MIT Press, pp. 167–193.

Group of Eight (2013). *G8 Open Data Charter.* Available at: www.gov.uk/government/uploads/system/uploads/attachment_data/file/207772/Open_Data_Charter.pdf. [Accessed 30 May 2017].

Hecht, G. (2009 [1998]). *The Radiance of France: Nuclear Power and National Identity after World War II.* Cambridge, MA: MIT Press.

IBM (2012). *Business Value Accelerator for Big Data: Identify Opportunities for Enhanced Business Value from Big Data.* Available at: www.ibm.com/services/de/gbs/pdf/bao-bigdata-GBS03157-USEN-00.pdf. [Accessed 7 May 2016].

IDC, EY, Tech4i2 and Europe Unlimited (2013). *Business Opportunities: Big Data.* Available at: https://ec.europa.eu/growth/tools-databases/dem/sites/default/files/page-files/big_data_v1.1.pdf. [Accessed 7 May 2016].

Jasanoff, S. (2015). Future Imperfect: Science, Technology, and the Imaginations of Modernity. In: S. Jasanoff and S.-H. Kim, eds., *Dreamscapes of Modernity. Sociotechnical Imaginaries and the Fabrication of Power.* Chicago, IL: University of Chicago Press, pp. 1–33.

Jasanoff, S. and Kim, S.-H. (2009). Containing the Atom: Sociotechnical Imaginaries and Nuclear Power in the United States and South Korea. *Minerva,* 47, pp. 119–146.

Jasanoff, S. and Kim, S.-H., eds., (2015). *Dreamscapes of Modernity. Sociotechnical Imaginaries and the Fabrication of Power.* Chicago, IL: The University of Chicago Press.

Jourová, V. (2015). *EU Consumer Policy: Today's Challenges, Tomorrow's Solutions.* European Commission. Speech/XX. [pdf] Available at: http://ec.europa.eu/justice/events/european-consumer-summit/2015/files/speech_commissiner_jourova__consumer_summit_2015_en.pdf. [Accessed 30 May 2017].

Kerr, I. and Earle, J. (2013). Prediction, Preemption, Presumption. *Stanford Law Review Online,* 66, pp. 65–72. Available at: www.stanfordlawreview.org/online/privacy-and-big-data-prediction-preemption-presumption/. [Accessed 30 May 2017].

Khan, I. (2012). *Nowcasting: Big Data Predicts the Present.* ITworld. Available at: www.itworld.com/article/2719343/it-management/nowcasting-big-data-predicts-the-present.html. [Accessed 30 May 2017].

Knight, F. H. (1921). *Risk, Uncertainty and Profit.* Boston, MA: Houghton Mifflin.

Kosinski, M., Stillwell, D. and Græpel, T. (2013). Private Traits and Attributes Are Predictable from Digital Records of Human Behavior. *Proceedings of the National Academy of Sciences of the United States of America,* 110(15), pp. 5802–5805.

Kroes, N. (2012). *Opening Science through E-Infrastructures.* European Commission. Speech/12/258. Available at: http://europa.eu/rapid/press-release_SPEECH-12-258_en.pdf. [Accessed 30 May 2017].

Kroes, N. (2013a). *Big Data for Europe.* European Commission. Speech/13/893. [pdf] Available at: http://europa.eu/rapid/press-release_SPEECH-13-893_en.pdf. [Accessed 30 May 2017].

Kroes, N. (2013b). *Data Isn't a Four-Letter Word.* European Commission. Speech/13/1059. [pdf] Available at: http://europa.eu/rapid/press-release_SPEECH-13-1059_en.pdf. [Accessed 30 May 2017].

Kroes, N. (2013c). *The Big Data Revolution*. European Commission. Speech/13/261. [pdf] Available at: http://europa.eu/rapid/press-release_SPEECH-13-261_en.pdf. [Accessed 30 May 2017].

Kroes, N. (2013d). *The Economic and Social Benefits of Big Data*. European Commission. Speech/13/450. [pdf] Available at: http://europa.eu/rapid/press-release_SPEECH-13-450_en.pdf. [Accessed 30 May 2017].

Kroes, N. (2014a). *Embracing the Open Opportunity*. European Commission. Speech/14/556. [pdf] Available at: http://europa.eu/rapid/press-release_SPEECH-14-556_en.pdf. [Accessed 30 May 2017].

Kroes N. (2014b). *The Data Gold Rush*. European Commission. Speech/14/229. [pdf] Available at: http://europa.eu/rapid/press-release_SPEECH-14-229_en.pdf. [Accessed 30 May 2017].

Kulk, S. and van Loenen, B. (2012). Brave New Open Data World? *International Journal of Spatial Data Infrastructures Research*, 7, pp. 196–206.

Laney, D. (2012). *Deja VVVu: Others Claiming Gartner's Construct for Big Data*. Gartner Blog Network. Available at: http://blogs.gartner.com/doug-laney/deja-vvvue-others-claiming-gartners-volume-velocity-variety-construct-for-big-data/. [Accessed 7 May 2016].

Mashey, J. R. (1999). Big Data and the Next Wave of InfraStress. In: *1999 USENIX Annual Technical Conference*. Monterey, California. Available at: http://static.usenix.org/event/usenix99/invited_talks/mashey.pdf. [Accessed 30 May 2017].

Mauthner, N. S. and Parry, O. (2013). Open Access Digital Data Sharing: Principles, Policies, and Practices. *Social Epistemology: A Journal of Knowledge, Culture and Policy*, 27(1), pp. 47–67.

Mayer-Schönberger, V. and Cukier, K. (2013). *Big Data. A Revolution That Will Transform How We Live, Work, and Think*. New York: Houghton Mifflin Harcourt.

Metz, J. (2015). *The European Commission, Expert Groups, and the Policy Process. Demystifying Technocratic Governance*. European Administrative Governance Series. Basingstoke: Palgrave Macmillan.

Monteleone, S. (2015). Addressing the 'Failure' of Informed Consent in Online Data Protection: Learning the Lessons from Behaviour-Aware Regulation. *Syracuse Journal of International Law and Commerce*, 43(1), pp. 69–119.

Nagel, T. (1986). *The View from Nowhere*. New York: Oxford University Press.

Narayanan, A. and Shmatikov, V. (2008). Robust De-Anonymization of Large Sparse Datasets. In: *Proceedings of the 2008 IEEE Symposium on Security and Privacy*, pp. 111–125.

Nowotny, H. (2016). *The Cunning of Uncertainty*. Cambridge: Polity Press.

Nugent, N. and Rhinard, M. (2015 [2001]) *The European Commission*. London: Palgrave.

Obar, J. A. (2015). Big Data and The Phantom Public: Walter Lippmann and the Fallacy of Data Privacy Self-Management. *Big Data & Society*, 2(2), pp. 1–16.

Oettinger, G. (2015a). *A Digital Single Market: The Key to Europe's Industrial Leadership in the Digital Economy*. European Commission. Speech. Available at: https://ec.europa.eu/commission/commissioners/2014-2019/oettinger/announcements/speech-ict2015-digital-single-market-key-europes-industrial-leadership-digital-economy_en. [Accessed 30 May 2017].

Oettinger, G. (2015b). *CeBit & IT in Companies*. European Commission. Blog Post. Available at: https://ec.europa.eu/commission/commissioners/2014-2019/oettinger/blog/cebit-it-companies_en. [Accessed 30 May 2017].

Oettinger, G. (2015c). *Europe's Future is Digital*. European Commission. Speech. [pdf] Available at: http://europa.eu/rapid/press-release_SPEECH-15-4772_en.pdf. [Accessed 30 May 2017].

Oettinger, G. (2015d). *Innovation to Secure Digital Future*. European Commission. Blog Post. Available at: https://ec.europa.eu/commission/commissioners/2014-2019/oettinger/blog/innovation-secure-digital-future_en. [Accessed 30 May 2017].

OSTP (Office of Science and Technology Policy) (2012). *Obama Administration Unveils 'Big Data' Initiative: Announces $200 Million in New R&D Investments*. Press Release. Available at: www.whitehouse.gov/sites/default/files/microsites/ostp/big_data_press_release.pdf. [Accessed 7 May 2016].

Poel, M., Schroeder, R., Treperman, J., Rubinstein, M., Meyer, E., Mahieu, B., Scholten, C. and Svetachova, M. (2015). *Data for Policy: A Study of Big Data and Other Innovative Data-Driven Approaches for Evidence-Informed Policymaking*. Draft Report about the State-Of-The-Art: Invitation for Reflection. Available at: https://ofti.org/wp-content/uploads/2015/05/dataforpolicy.pdf. [Accessed 30 May 2017].

Porter, T. M. (1995). *Trust in Numbers. The Pursuit of Objectivity in Science and Public Life*. Princeton, NJ: Princeton University Press.

Presser, L., Hruskova, M., Rowbottom, H. and Kancir, J. (2015). *Care.data and Access to UK Health Records: Patient Privacy and Public Trust*. Technology Science. Available at: https://techscience.org/a/2015081103/. [Accessed 30 May 2017].

Rieder, B. (2017). Scrutinizing the Algorithmic Technique: The Bayes Classifier as Interested Reading of Reality. *Information, Communication & Society*, 20(1), pp. 100–117.

Rieder, G. and Simon, J. (2016). Datatrust: Or, the Political Quest for Numerical Evidence and the Epistemologies of Big Data. *Big Data & Society*, 3(1), pp. 1–6.

Rubinstein, I. S. (2013). Big Data: The End of Privacy or a New Beginning? *International Data Privacy Law*, 3(2), pp. 74–87.

Scott, J. C. (1998). *Seeing Like a State. How Certain Schemes to Improve the Human Condition Have Failed*. New Haven, CT: Yale University Press.

Šefčovič, M. (2016). Untitled Speech at the European Political Strategy Centre (EPSC) Seminar on 'The Energy Union and Climate Change Policy – A Transformative Agenda for the Modernisation of the Economy'. Available at: https://ec.europa.eu/commission/commissioners/2014-2019/sefcovic/announcements/speech-european-political-strategy-centre-epsc-seminar-energy-union-and-climate-change-policy_en. [Accessed 30 May 2017].

Simon, Judith (2013). Trust. In: D. Pritchard, ed., *Oxford Bibliographies in Philosophy*. New York: Oxford University Press.

Solesbury, W. (2002). The Ascendancy of Evidence. *Planning Theory & Practice*, 3(1), pp. 90–96.

STS-RPSI (STS Research Platform Sociotechnical Imaginaries) (2017). *Methodological Pointers*. Available at: http://sts.hks.harvard.edu/research/platforms/imaginaries/ii.methods/methodological-pointers/. [Accessed 7 May 2017].

Sweeney, L. (2000). *Simple Demographics Often Identify People Uniquely*. Carnegie Mellon University, Data Privacy Working Paper 3. Available at: https://dataprivacylab.org/projects/identifiability/paper1.pdf. [Accessed 30 May 2017].

Taylor, C. (2004). *Modern Social Imaginaries*. Durham, NC: Duke University Press.

Thyssen, M. (2016). *Speaking Points on Long-Term Unemployment and Four Dimensions of Work Quality at OECD Employment and Labour Ministerial Meeting*. European Commission. Speech. Available at: https://ec.europa.eu/commission/commissioners/

2014-2019/thyssen/announcements/speaking-points-commissioner-marianne-thyssen-long-term-unemployment-and-four-dimensions-work_en. [Accessed 30 May 2017].

Vestager, M. (2016). *Big Data and Competition.* European Commission. Speech. Available at: https://ec.europa.eu/commission/commissioners/2014-2019/vestager/announcements/big-data-and-competition_en. [Accessed 30 May 2017].

Ward, J. S. and Barker, A. (2013). Undefined by Data: A Survey of Big Data Definitions. *arXiv:1309.5821.* Available at: http://arxiv.org/abs/1309.5821. [Accessed 7 May 2016].

Woody, B. (2012). *Big Data is Just a Fad.* Simple Talk. Available at: www.simple-talk.com/sql/database-administration/big-data-is-just-a-fad/. [Accessed 7 May 2016].

7   The automated public sphere

Frank Pasquale

Introduction

As Internet usage grew in the 2000s, scholars promoted its emancipatory potential. Yochai Benkler praised not only the wealth that would be promoted by networks, but also its distribution – towards a platform of platforms that would enable millions of new voices to be heard online (Benkler 2007). This optimism also animated one of the United States's seminal cases on Internet regulation, *Reno* v. *ACLU* (1997), which presumed the openness of the Internet would redound to the benefit of all. The majority opinion in *ACLU* darkly cautioned the US government to avoid mucking about in many forms of Internet regulation, lest it infringe on free expression rights in an online environment that the justices, as well as later boosters, idealised. Large platforms themselves harbour utopian pretensions to this day; for example, Mark Zuckerberg has marketed Facebook as a nascent global community (even as social critics lament how time online diverts citizens from in-person engagement with friends and neighbours) (Rushkoff 2016).

Even in the 1990s, scholars warned about the implications of deregulating the Internet (Chin 1997). By the mid-2010s, it is hard to remain optimistic about the role of the Internet in organising a new, and critically important, digital public sphere. Wealth has emerged in online advertising, but it is largely claimed by two firms – Google and Facebook take about 75% of the US$73 billion digital advertising market in the US (Bond 2017). These information intermediaries are driven by profit, and their methods of selecting and arranging newsfeeds and search engine results pages are secret (Pasquale 2015b: 59–100). The promised *Wealth of Networks* has given way to a black box society – one where trolls, bots, and even foreign governments maraud to distort the information environment on Twitter, Facebook, Google News, Reddit, and other networks.

We now know that virtually every positive promise made about the Internet in the early 2000s, has a shadow side. While secrecy has empowered some voices who would otherwise be afraid to speak up, it has also protected trolls, doxers, and other bad actors online, who silence others' speech via intimidation. Moreover, online anonymity is of a piece with financial anonymity, which has empowered thousands of shell companies to obscure who is actually funding messages that could sway the public, legislators, and regulators. Everyone is invited to participate, but so, too, is 'everyone' capable of disrupting other communities of interest online, via hashtag spamming or trolling – whether by civil society groups, state actors, or miscreants pursuing disruption 'for the lulz'. First celebrated as a way to hold states accountable for illegal actions, Wikileaks has emerged as a witting agent of authoritarian state interference in elections with a troubling tendency to emit anti-Semitic messages. While major content owners have found their grip on public attention diminished, fragmentation of audiences has given megaplatforms unprecedented global power over attention-commanding interfaces.

That last reversal is the subject of this chapter. In a world of stable and dominant media firms, large social networks and search engines were in a rough equilibrium of power relative to the owners and creators of the content they selected and arranged (Pasquale 2010). However, a general trend towards media revenue decline (and platform revenue growth) makes a new endgame apparent: online intermediaries as digital bottlenecks or choke-points, with ever more power over the type and quality of media that reaches audiences (Bracha and Pasquale 2008; Pasquale 2008b).[1] The source of this power is, at bottom, Big Data – the ability of megaplatforms to accumulate ever more intimate profiles of users, which are then of enormous interest to commercial entities, political campaigns, governments – indeed, anyone aspiring to monitor, monetise, control, and predict human behaviour. Megaplatforms readily deploy Big Data to dividualise and demobilise voters, rather than to unify and motivate them.[2] Tailored manipulation disrupts already fragile processes of democratic will formation, undermining media pluralism and deliberative dialogue.

Large online intermediaries tend to reduce at least one good type of media pluralism, and tend to promote a very destructive type of diversity.[3] They make the metric of success online 'virality', promoting material that has received a good deal of attention or seems to match a sub-public's personalisation profile, regardless of whether it is true or even minimally decent (Pasquale 2006). That reduces pluralism by elevating profit considerations over the democratising functions of public discourse, and effectively automating the public sphere. Decisions that once were made by humans with plural aims and aspirations are now made by profit-maximising algorithms, all too prone to self-reinforcing logics of rapid, vapid, viral dissemination. Moreover, the same intermediaries also promote a very troubling diversity by permitting themselves to be manipulated by the most baseless and dangerous propagandists (Marwick and Lewis 2017).[4] Such media is particularly capable of influencing low-information, floating voters – exactly the persons all too likely to swing the results of elections.

This chapter first describes the documented, negative effects of online propagandists' interventions (and platforms' neglect) in both electoral politics and the broader public sphere (section one). It then proposes several legal and educational tactics to mitigate their power, or to encourage or require them to exercise it responsibly (section two). The penultimate section (section three) offers a concession to those suspicious of governmental intervention in the public sphere:

some regimes are already too authoritarian and generally unreliable to be trusted with extensive powers of regulation over media (whether old or new media), or intermediaries. However, I conclude that the inadvisability of extensive media regulation in disordered societies only makes this agenda more urgent in well-ordered societies, lest predictable pathologies of the automated public sphere accelerate the degradation of their democracies.

The long shadow of intermediary irresponsibility

As Jürgen Habermas observed in 1962, 'the process in which societal power is transformed into political power is as much in need of criticism and control as the legitimate exercise of political domination over society' (Habermas 1991: 210). As part of the Frankfurt school, Habermas was sensitive to the ways in which new media, manipulated by both corporate and state actors, had fundamentally altered processes of democratic will formation. He deemed such transitions a 'structural transformation' of the public sphere, since new forms of media both accelerated, altered, and reshaped the expression critical to opinion formation.

The basic contours of mass media-driven politics and culture evolved through much of the second half of the twentieth century. Since the mid-1990s, change has accelerated here, as it has in much of contemporary society (Rosa 2015). Megafirms like Facebook and Google have largely automated the types of decisions once made by managers and programmers at television networks, or editors at newspapers. Automated recommendations are often helpful, aiding audiences as they seek to sort out the blooming, buzzing confusion of topics online. But they are also destabilising traditional media institutions and circuits of knowledge.

For example, the US election featured deeply disturbing stories about manipulation of social media for political ends. Unreliable sources proliferated, particularly amongst right-wing echo chambers. In December 2016, a Facebook-fuelled fake news story about Hillary Clinton prompted a man to arrive in a pizza parlour in Washington DC with a gun (Abrams 2016). The fake story reportedly originated in a white supremacist's tweet. Politically motivated, profit-seeking and simply reckless purveyors of untruths all prospered. A Macedonian teen churned out stories with no basis, tarring Hillary Clinton with an endless series of lies, in order to score quick profits (Smith and Banic 2016). For profit-minded content generators, the only truth of Facebook is clicks and ad payments. Bence Kollanyi, Phil Howard, and Samuel Woolley estimated that tens of thousands of the tweets 'written' during the second US presidential debate were spewed by bots (Kollanyi *et al.* 2016). These bots serve multiple functions – they can promote fake news, and when enough of them retweet one another, they can occupy the top slots in response to tweets from candidates. They can also flood hashtags, making it very difficult for ad hoc publics to crystallise around an issue.

On Facebook, a metastatic array of fake content generators and hard-core partisan sites flooded news feeds with lies and propaganda. Facebook, as usual, disclaimed any responsibility for the spread of stories falsely claiming that the Pope had endorsed Donald Trump, or that Hillary Clinton is a Satanist (to give a mild pair of the lies that swarmed the platform) (Schaedel 2016; Evon 2016). But the Silicon Valley firm has several levels of responsibility.

Basic design choices mean that stories shared on Facebook (as well as presented by Google's AMP) have all looked very similar, for years (Chayka 2016). Thus a story from the fabricated 'Denver Guardian' can appear as authoritative as a Pulitzer Prize-winning *New York Times* investigation (Lubbers 2016). More directly, Facebook profits from fake news – the more a story is shared (whatever its merits), the more ad revenue it brings in (Molina 2016). Most disturbingly, we now know that Facebook directly helped the Trump campaign target its voter suppression efforts at African-Americans (Winston 2016).

Google has suffered from other racially tinged scandals (Noble 2018). Consider, for instance, recurrent problems with Google's 'autocompletes' – when Google anticipates the rest of a search query from its first word or two. Google autocompletes have often embodied racist and sexist stereotypes (Cadwalladr 2016). Google image search has also generated biased results, absurdly and insultingly tagging some photos of black people as 'gorillas' (Guarino 2016; Barr 2015).

If Google and Facebook had clear and publicly acknowledged ideological agendas, users could grasp them and 'inoculate' themselves accordingly, with scepticism towards self-serving views (Pasquale 2011). However, the platforms are better understood as tools rapidly manipulated to the advantage of search engine optimisers, well-organised extremists, and others at the fringes of political respectability or scientific validity. Thus a search for 'Hillary's Health' in October 2016 would have led to multiple misleading videos and articles groundlessly proclaiming that the US Democratic presidential candidate had Parkinson's disease. Google search results reportedly helped shape the racism of Dylann Roof, who murdered nine people in a historically black South Carolina church in the US in 2015. Roof said that when he Googled 'black on white crime, the first website I came to was the Council of Conservative Citizens', which is a white supremacist organisation. 'I have never been the same since that day,' he said (Hersher 2017). So, too, are sources of support for climate denialists, misogynists, ethnonationalists, and terrorists easily developed and cultivated in what has become an automated public sphere.

These terrifying acts of violence and hate are likely to continue if action is not taken. Nor is democracy safe in a carelessly automated public sphere. Without a transparent curation process, the public has a hard time judging the legitimacy of online sources. In response, a growing movement of academics, journalists and technologists is calling for more algorithmic accountability from Silicon Valley giants (Pasquale 2015a). As algorithms take on more importance in all walks of life, they are increasingly a concern of lawmakers. And there are many steps both Silicon Valley companies and legislators should take to move towards more transparency and accountability.

Towards a robust regime of intermediary responsibility

Activist and academic responses to these imbroglios have been multifaceted. Some communication scholars have rightly criticised Facebook for its apparent indifference to the problem of fake or misleading viral content (Tufekci 2016). Others have focused their ire on the mainstream media, claiming that it was the recklessness or lack of professional responsibility at right-wing news sources (and established media institutions like *CNN* and the *New York Times*), which accelerated the rise of authoritarian candidates like Trump (Kreiss 2016; Robinson 2016).

In truth, there is no contradiction between a critique of the new media and deep disappointment in old media. Moreover, any enduring solution to the problem will require cooperation between journalists and coders. Facebook can no longer credibly describe itself as merely a platform for others' content, especially when it is profiting from micro-targeted ads (Pasquale 2016a). It has to take editorial responsibility. So, too, should megaplatforms like Google take on some basic responsibilities for the content they distribute. This section describes several specific initiatives that would help counter the discrimination, bias, and propaganda now too often polluting (and even overwhelming) online spaces.

Label, monitor, and explain hate-driven search results

In 2004, anti-Semites boosted a Holocaust-denial site called 'Jewwatch' into the top ten results for the query 'Jew' (Pasquale 2006). Ironically, some of those horrified by the site may have helped by linking to it in order to criticise it. The more a site is linked to, the more prominence Google's algorithm gives it in search results. The Anti-Defamation League and other civil rights organisations complained to Google about its technology's gift of prominence to entities eminently unworthy of such attention.

Google responded to complaints by adding a headline at the top of the page entitled 'An explanation of our search results'. A web page linked to the headline explained why the offensive site appeared so high in the relevant rankings, thereby distancing Google from the results. The label, however, no longer appears. In Europe and many other countries, lawmakers should consider requiring such labelling in the case of obvious hate speech. To avoid mainstreaming extremism, labels may link to accounts of the history and purpose of groups with innocuous names like 'Council of Conservative Citizens' (Pasquale 2016a, 2008a).

Are there free expression concerns here? Not really. Better labelling practices for food and drugs have escaped First Amendment scrutiny in the US, and why should information itself be different? As law professor Mark Patterson has demonstrated, many of our most important sites of commerce are markets for information: search engines are not offering products and services themselves but information about products and services, which may well be decisive in determining which firms and groups fail and which succeed (Patterson 2016).

If they go unregulated, easily manipulated by whoever can afford the best search engine optimisation, people may be left at the mercy of unreliable and biased sources.

Audit logs of the data fed into algorithmic systems

We should expect any company aspiring to order vast amounts of information to try to keep its methods secret, if only to reduce controversy and foil copycat competitors. However wise this secrecy may be as a business strategy, it devastates our ability to truly understand the social world Silicon Valley is creating. Moreover, like a modern-day Ring of Gyges, opacity creates ample opportunities to hide anti-competitive, discriminatory, or simply careless conduct behind a veil of technical inscrutability.[5]

A recurring pattern has developed: some entity complains about a major Internet company's practices, the company claims that its critics don't understand how its algorithms sort and rank content, and befuddled onlookers are left to sift through rival stories in the press. Massive search operations are so complex, and so protected by real and legal secrecy, that it is almost always impossible for those outside a search engine or social network firm to identify all the signals that are driving a given set of results. Silicon Valley journalists tend to give their advertisers the benefit of the doubt; national media outlets find the mysteries of online content ordering perfectly fit into their own templates of balanced reporting. No one knows exactly what's going on when a dispute arises, so rival accounts balance into an 'objective' equipoise.

Regulators need to be able to understand how some racist or anti-Semitic groups and individuals are manipulating search and social media feeds (Pasquale 2010). We should require immutable audit logs of the data fed into algorithmic systems. Machine learning, predictive analytics or algorithms may be too complex for a person to understand, but the data records are not. They can be subject to algorithmic audits.

A relatively simple set of reforms could vastly increase the ability of entities outside Google and Facebook to determine whether and how the firms' results and news feeds are being manipulated. There is rarely adequate profit motive for firms themselves to do this – but motivated non-governmental organisations can help them be better guardians of the public sphere.

Ban certain content

In cases where computational reasoning behind search results really is too complex to be understood in conventional narratives or equations intelligible to humans, there is another regulatory approach available: to limit the types of information that can be provided.

Though such an approach would raise constitutional objections in the US, nations like France and Germany have outright banned certain Nazi sites and memorabilia. Policymakers should also closely study laws regarding 'incitement to genocide' to develop guidelines for censoring hate speech with a clear and present danger of causing systematic slaughter or violence against vulnerable groups. It is a small price to pay for a public sphere less warped by hatred. And unless something like it is done, expect social media-driven panics about minorities to have even more devastating impact.

To be sure, this approach would almost certainly draw immediate legal action in the United States, where a form of free expression fundamentalism has protected even the most reprehensible speech (Peters 2005). Cyberlibertarians tend to support further expanding First Amendment protections for algorithmic orderings of information. Relatedly, the same scholars and judges, eager to protect the 'speech' of computers, also promote the idea that massive corporations' 'expression' is deserving of exceptional protection from the very state so often suborned or co-opted by those same corporations. The science fictional appeal of Asimovian ideals of 'speaking robots' has fed into a romanticisation of corporate speech. The logical endpoint is a continual 'battle for mindshare' by various robot armies, with the likely winner being the firms with the funds to hire the top programmers and the network effect dynamics to gather the most data for the optimal crafting of messages for micro-targeted populations. It goes without saying that this type of decomposition of the public sphere does not represent a triumph of classic values of free expression (autonomy and democratic self-rule); indeed, it portends their evaporation into the manufactured consent of a phantom public.

Permit limited outside annotations to defamatory posts and hire more humans to judge complaints

Limited annotations – 'rights of reply' – could be permitted in certain instances of defamation of individuals or groups, or unfair or unbalanced depictions of them (Pasquale 2008a). Google continues to maintain that it doesn't want human judgement blurring the autonomy of its algorithms. But even spelling suggestions depend on human judgement, and in fact, Google developed that feature not only by means of algorithms but also through a painstaking, iterative interplay between computer science experts and human beta testers who report on their satisfaction with various results configurations. As Sarah Roberts, Lily Irani, and Paško Bilić have shown, supposedly digitised companies are constantly reliant on manual interventions by human beings (Bilić 2016; Irani 2013; Roberts 2016a, 2016b). Requiring a few more is not a major burden for these firms.

This step is important because we now know (if we ever doubted) that the hoary 'marketplace of ideas' metaphor is misleading. The best ideas are not necessarily the most highly valued; the most sensational or gratifying propaganda can beat out careful reporting. Highly motivated, well-resourced groups can easily manipulate newsfeeds or search engine result pages (SERPs). 'Dark ads' and sophisticated personalisation algorithms enable constant experimentation on unwitting human research subjects, so A/B testing (particularly when used to measure divergent responses amongst thousands of users) can reveal exactly what manipulation works best. Without conscientious and professional curation of such algorithmic orderings of information, the public sphere's automation is susceptible to distortion by the most well-resourced entities.[6]

Limit the predation possible by online intermediaries

Personalisation is leading advertisers to abandon traditional, and even not-so-traditional, publishers in favour of the huge Internet platforms. No other rival can approach either the granularity or the comprehensiveness of their data. The result is a revolution-in-process about who can afford to keep publishing, and concomitant alarm about the concentration of media clout into fewer and fewer hands. One platform owner, Jeff Bezos, accumulated wealth equivalent to 100 times the total value of the United States' second most important newspaper, the *Washington Post.* He bought the *Post*, with concomitant chilling effects on the paper's ability to criticise his own business empire-building, or similar strategies by platform capitalists. Given the leverage potential of their own ever-higher expected earnings, large platforms may soon be able to move to buy more content producers themselves, as cable networks and Internet service providers (ISPs) have done – or perhaps buy cable networks and ISPs. Further vertical integration would be a major threat to the autonomy of journalism.

Given all the negative externalities generated by online intermediaries, policymakers should limit the profits such intermediaries make relative to revenues of the content owners whose work they depend on. In the health care context in the US, private insurers can only keep a certain percentage of premiums (usually 15 to 20%) – the rest must go to health care providers, such as hospitals, doctors, and pharmaceutical firms. Such a rule keeps the intermediary from taking too much of the spending in a sector – a clear and present danger in monopolistic Internet contexts, as well. Governments could limit the amount of profits that search engines and social networks make as intermediaries, requiring them to pay some share of their revenues to content generators like newspapers and media firms (Lanier 2013; Lehdonvirta 2017). Alternatively, policymakers could simply force large platforms to pay a fair share of the tax they now avoid by shuttling income to tax havens (see Schneider, Chapter 8 in this volume), and use some of that revenue for public broadcasting alternatives.

Obscure content that is damaging and not of public interest

When it comes to search queries on an individual person's name, many countries have aggressively forced Google to be more careful in how it assembles data dossiers presented as search engine result pages. Thanks to the Court of Justice of the European Union, Europeans can now request the removal of certain search results revealing information that is 'inadequate, irrelevant, no longer relevant or excessive', unless there is a greater public interest in being able to find the information via a search on the name of the data subject (Pasquale 2016b).

Such removals are a middle ground between information anarchy and censorship. They neither disappear information from the Internet (it can be found at the original source, and in searches on terms other than the complaining party's name), nor allow it to dominate the impression of the aggrieved individual. They are a kind of obscurity that lets ordinary individuals avoid having a single incident indefinitely dominate search results on his or her name. For example, a woman whose husband was murdered 20 years ago successfully forced Google to take news of the murder off search results on her name. This type of public responsibility is a first step towards making search results and social network newsfeeds reflect public values and privacy rights.

Concerns and concessions

There will be fierce opposition to virtually all of the proposals I have listed above. Some will arise merely out of commercial motivations: policing hate speech and fake news is more expensive than letting it flourish. Platforms would rather just pile up advertising revenue. As Jodi Dean has demonstrated, outrageous content stokes at least as much engagement online as it has in the traditional media (Dean 2010). Indeed, the problem is easily intensified online, as personalisation allows platforms to deliver material precisely targeted to maximise clicks, likes, and shares (Citron 2014). Slowing down that accelerated engagement costs a platform potential advertising, and all-important data about its users (Srnicek 2017). It also impedes the platform's ability to shape its users into the kind of people who uncritically act in behaviouristically manipulable ways (Schüll 2012). Unless platforms can demonstrate that the intermediary responsibilities discussed above would compromise their ability to run the platform at a reasonable rate of return, such cost-based objections should be dismissed. Neither Mark Zuckerberg nor Facebook shareholders have any legitimate expectation of permanent, massive returns on their investment. Indeed, impeding their ability to accumulate the surplus they have used to buy rival and adjacent firms may well encourage innovation (Stucke and Grunes 2017).

Many apologists for big tech firms claim that this type of responsibility is impossible (or unwise) for a firm like Facebook to take on (Turton 2016; Lessin 2016). They argue that the volume of shared content is simply too high to be managed by any individual, or team of individuals. But this argument ignores the reality of continual algorithmic and manual manipulation of search results at Google. As technology writer Timothy Lee explains:

> During the 2000s, people got better and better at gaming Google's search algorithm. Some were running quasi-media companies whose writers churned out dozens of extremely short, poorly researched articles based on popular search terms. (…) In a January 2011 blog post, Google search quality czar Matt Cutts acknowledged that Google had a big problem with these 'content farms' (…). Later that year, Google brought down the

hammer, releasing changes to its search algorithm that caused traffic at major content farms to plummet. (…) [This] represented Google making a deliberate value judgment that some kinds of content were worse than other kinds. Early versions of Google took a naively data-driven approach, assuming that a link from one site to another was a sign of quality. [In later, more sophisticated iterations,] Google include[d] human reviewers in the mix because algorithms inevitably make mistakes and manual human review is needed to keep the algorithms on the right track. Previously reviewed pages can be fed back into Google's software, allowing the algorithms to learn from human judgment and get better over time. So Facebook doesn't have to choose between fighting fake news with algorithms or human editors. An effective fight against fake news is going to require heavy use of both approaches.

(Lee 2016)

There are powerful lessons in this passage. First, be wary of platforms' convenient self-reification. Facebook may aspire to be merely a technology company. Those aspirations may express themselves as a petulant insistence that unsupervised, rather than supervised, machine learning is the ideal way to solve problems on the platform. But that 'identity' is a constructed and convenient one, directly at odds with tech firms' repeated invocation of free expression protections to shield their actions from governmental scrutiny (Pasquale 2016c).

Beyond economic and technical objections, there is another, deeper objection to intermediary responsibility, focusing on the regulatory apparatus necessary to make it meaningful and robust. Authoritarian regimes have tried to stifle political dissent by regulating Facebook and Google. For example, the Thai, Russian, Chinese, and Turkish governments have aggressively policed criticism of national leaders, and have intimidated dissidents. Corrupt governments may be susceptible to excessive influence from well-organised lobbies. Fossil fuel lobbyists may influence regulators to force intermediaries to monitor and censor environmental activists committed to resistance against pipeline projects (Citron and Pasquale 2011: 1445; ACLU 2017). Overly onerous annotation requirements, or rights to be forgotten, may become a pretext for driving a popular platform out of a country. Governments may abuse taxation powers, too, in retaliation against a platform that enables stinging or politically effective criticism of them. Or platforms may successfully lobby to have their own personnel and allies appointed to the agencies and commissions set to regulate them. A search, or robotics, or social network commission, for example, might start out with a robust agenda, but over years or decades, may gradually find itself taken over by appointees closely aligned with dominant industry players.[7]

Still, there is little reason to assume that the actions of the worst governments are likely in other, more developed and democratic public spheres. Indeed, intervention in the public sphere while a polity is still well ordered may be the only way to keep it well ordered. Some of these concerns are variations on the classic problem of regulatory capture: the very institutions meant to regulate an industry may be taken over by that industry. Fortunately, the problem has now been so carefully studied that many prophylactic measures could be put in place to avoid it (Carpenter and Moss 2014). Revolving door rules could prevent officials and bureaucrats from working for the industry they are regulating for five or ten years after they depart their agency. Higher pay for regulators, coupled with long-term or even lifetime bars on revolving door employment, would also help assure more independence. So, too, would self-funding mechanisms limit certain forms of political interference (Kruly 2013). While serious, the problem of regulatory capture is not insurmountable.

More serious is a larger problem of circularity, well-identified by Charles Lindblom: the ability of powerful economic entities, to take over political institutions, and use that political power to enhance their economic power, which gives them resources necessary to further entrench political power (Lindblom 1977: 201–213). The rise of oligarchical power in nations around the world suggests how deep the problem of circularity can be (Winters 2011). The tendency of oligarchs to enact programmes that simultaneously harm the material conditions of their electoral base, while cultivating and consolidating its sense of political identity organised around common grievance, should also serve as a spur to reconsidering the foundations of the critiques that motivated the programme of reform developed above. In other words: in some societies, reform aimed at the public sphere is doomed to be counterproductive or worse, since governing institutions are hopelessly corrupt. This is the likely end-stage of what Jack Balkin has described as constitutional rot: the gradual corrosion of democratic institutions. Such a process may be incipient in many self-styled democracies today (Balkin 2017).

Well-intended reformers may also end up exacerbating the very dynamics they propose to ameliorate. For example, consider the classic problem of the filter bubble (Pariser 2011; Sunstein 2007), and its opponents' efforts to expose more persons to views they disagree with. Personalisation often enables Internet users to ignore points of view they disagree with, so the filter bubble model states, and therefore increases polarisation. Common solutions to the filter bubble dynamic presume, first, that 'all sides' or 'both sides' can be exposed to some critical mass of opposing or diverse viewpoints via, say, must-carry rules, or some privately implemented version of them (Pasquale 2016a: 499–500). To make that reform tractable, assume for now a binary society, divided between left and right voters. The great problem for advocates of 'filter bubble' reforms is that they cannot adequately model whether exposure of one side's adherents to the other side's version of facts, priorities, ideology, or values, will lead to understanding or revulsion, reconsideration, or recalcitrance.

To be sure, effects studies in media have been contested for decades. It may be impossible for today's digital deliberative democrats to demonstrate the empirical likelihood of open-mindedness amongst voters. But they should be open to understanding the danger of plausible models of asymmetrical openness to opposing views. A society may have a 'hard left' and a 'soft right', such that those on the right are quite willing to assess and even adopt some left proposals, while the vast majority of the left is unalterably opposed to accepting any right ideas. In such a scenario, all an assault on the filter bubble will likely do, is chip away at conservative self-identification amongst the 'soft right', and succour the hard left. A 'spiral of silence' may even develop (Noelle-Neumann 1977). Perhaps in intuiting that danger to its coherence and ability to project power, today's right in the United States may be inoculating itself against such ideological slippage. Very often, those in the centre right will defend or applaud those to their right, but the comity rarely goes the other way (Nagle 2017).

In a situation of asymmetrical persuadability, filter bubble inspired reforms will tend only to consolidate the power of the social group or political party most steadfastly committed to maintaining its own position. We can, of course, imagine *12 Angry Men*-type scenarios where a small remnant of deeply moral hold-outs uses its reform-granted exposure to others to gradually convince the rest of society of the wisdom of its position. However, just as likely is a splitting of society into the more contemplative and the more active, alas the famed quote on the 'reality-based community' from a member of the George W. Bush administration.[8]

This elementary challenge to filter bubble-driven reform suggests a larger problem with deliberativist political theory (Pasquale 2008c). How can democracy operate when large swathes of the population subscribe to diametrically opposed conceptions of the nature of politics? Consider the deliberativist approach as one end of a spectrum of theories of politics, with a Schmittian, decisionist approach on the opposite end. Deliberativists see politics as fundamentally a realm of reasoned disagreement, culminating in some form of agreement (or at least improved understanding) after debate (Parkinson and Mansbridge 2012; Gutmann and Thompson 2004). Jürgen Habermas detailed the 'ideal speech situation' as the regulative ideal of such political deliberation, where everyone would either be able to voice their own views, and learn from others, or at least count on their political representatives in a legislative body engaging in a similar process (Habermas 1991).

Habermas's conception of parliamentary democracy was part of a long scholarly campaign to lay to rest the type of post-rational, emotivist politics associated with Carl Schmitt (Müller-Doohm 2017). But Schmitt's critical ideas are finding more traction today, both in diagnoses of political polarisation, and in the actual attitudes and actions of many voters and politicians. For those committed to a Schmittian perspective, there are friends and enemies in politics, and almost no new information can dissuade them from their attachment to their party or leader. Donald J. Trump memorably bragged that he could 'shoot someone on Fifth Avenue', and his voters would still support him. That is a Schmittian devotion par excellence, increasingly reflected in polling data (Struyk 2017). More strategically, a political party may change voting rules to entrench its power, creating a self-reinforcing dynamic: the more the rules change in its favour, the more opportunities it has to entrench majorities and super-majorities that enable further rule changes (Daley 2015; Berman 2016). In such circumstances, some or all of the reforms mentioned above could backfire, simply adding to the power of a dominant party in a disordered polity, rather than preserving and promoting the type of pluralism that is a hallmark of a well-ordered democracy.

Conclusion: a return to professionalism

Given the potential pitfalls of regulating the automated public sphere, implementation of the reform ideas in the second section above should be undertaken with care in well-ordered polities, and may be impossible or counterproductive in disordered polities. But regardless of those difficult distinctions, those in media can do much to respond to the automated public sphere's infirmities.

Journalists should be more assertive about their own professional prerogatives and identity. In the aftermath of the fake news scandals, Tim O'Reilly asserted that decisions about the organisation of newsfeeds and presentation of information in them were inherently algorithmic functions, to be supervised by the engineers at Facebook (O'Reilly 2016). Certainly the alpha geeks whom O'Reilly describes as his subject share that view: the human editors of trending topics at Facebook were low status, contract workers, who were unceremoniously dumped when a thinly sourced news story asserted that conservative content was being suppressed (Ohlheiser 2016; CBS News 2016). Shortly thereafter, Facebook was swamped by the fake news that now is the topic of so much controversy. The real lesson here is that human editors at Facebook should be restored, and given more authority. Their deliberations should also be open to some forms of scrutiny and accountability; for example, an ombudsperson or public editor with staff should interface between such staff and members of the public aggrieved by their decisions.

Some communication scholars have resisted the idea of professionalisation of online content creation, curation, and delivery, in the name of citizen journalism, which would democratise the power of the press to anyone with a computer and an Internet connection. While a beautiful ideal in theory, in practice, a failure amongst the de facto sovereigns of the Internet to distinguish between stories on the real *Guardian* and the dubious *Denver Guardian* is not simply a neutral decision to level the informational playing field. Rather, it predictably accelerates propaganda tactics honed by millions of dollars of investment in both data brokerages and shadowy quasi-state actors now investigated by the CIA as sources of bias, disinformation, and illegal influence in the election (Revesz 2016; Feldman 2016). Freedom for the pike is death for the minnows.

In the 1980s, the chair of the US Federal Communications Commission, Mark Fowler, dismissed the bulk of regulation of broadcasters as irrelevant, since he viewed the television as nothing more than 'a toaster with pictures' (Boyer 1987). In the 2010s, for better or worse, vast conglomerates like Facebook and Google effectively take on the role of global communication regulators. Mark Zuckerberg's repeated insistence that Facebook is nothing more than a technology company is a sad reprise of Fowler's laissez-faire ideology. It is also deeply hypocritical, for the firm imposes all manner of rules and regulations on both users and advertisers when those norms generate profits (Pasquale 2015b).

The public sphere cannot be automated like an assembly line churning out toasters. As Will Oremus has explained, there are aspects of the journalistic endeavour that are inherently human; so, too, are editorial functions necessarily reflective of human values (Oremus 2014). Expect deep and persistent conflict over the proper balance between commercial interests and the public interest in assigning prominence to different sources and stories. These are matters of utmost importance to the future of democracy. They can no longer be swept under the rug by plutocrats more interested in stock returns and artificial intelligence advances than the basic democratic institutions and civil society that underpin each.

Notes

1 Note, too, that the filter bubble problem is not altogether plausibly one of left voters needing to be exposed to right voters' worldview, and vice versa (for who knows how far along the spectrum of ideology once should search for alternative views, or how rotten centrist consensus is). Rather, it is one of a lack of autonomy and understanding of how one's media environment is shaped.
2 As Deleuzian social theory teaches, the subjects of Big Data analysis

> are becoming less individuals than 'dividuals': entities ready to be divided into any number of pieces, with specific factors separated, scrutinized, and surveilled. What the person does becomes less important than the consequences calculated in response to emanated data streams.
>
> (Sadowski and Pasquale 2015)

3 Media pluralism is necessary for maintaining the integrity of the democratic process; reducing the impact of the misrepresentation and suppression of information; promoting access to diverse information and opinions; and protecting freedom of expression (Smith and Tambini 2012; Smith, Tambini, and Morisi 2012).
4 While the platforms will often insist that they are the true victims of propagandists, they somehow manage to seek out and stop a great deal of the web spam and manipulation that threatens their advertising business models.
5 The Ring of Gyges is a myth from Plato, which describes a ring that renders its wearer invisible. It is often framed as the prompt for moral reflection: would individuals act morally if no one knew what they were doing?
6 The European Union's commitments to rights to be forgotten, and rights of erasure, show that the algorithmic ordering of information can be a socially inflected process, with fairer modes of participation for citizens and civil society (Wagner 2016a, 2016b; Pasquale 2016b). To be sure, the right to be forgotten should not be a matter almost entirely decided by private firms with only cursory or very rare review by governmental authorities. Developing better-resourced management of difficult issues in data provision and management should be a key priority for authorities in this field. But the initial step towards algorithmic accountability is laudable.
7 Bracha and Pasquale (2008) included the first discussion in legal literature of a regulatory body targeted at search engines.
8 The journalist Ron Suskind authored an article that quoted a senior George W. Bush administration official as saying

> that guys like me were 'in what we call the reality-based community', which he defined as people who 'believe that solutions emerge from your judicious study of discernible reality.' (...) 'That's not the way the world really works anymore,' he continued. 'We're an empire now, and when we act, we create our own reality. And while you're studying that reality – judiciously, as you will – we'll act again, creating other new realities, which you can study too, and that's how things will sort out. We're history's actors (...) and you, all of you, will be left to just study what we do.'
>
> (Suskind 2004)

References

All URLs in this chapter were last accessed on 30 September 2017.

Abrams, A. (2016). Pizzagate gunman: 'I regret how I handled' Comet Ping Pong shooting. *Time*, 8 December Available at: http://time.com/4594988/pizzagate-gunman-comet-ping-pong-regret/.

ACLU. (2017). ACLU challenges warrant to search data of Facebook page for group protesting Dakota Access Pipeline [press release], 8 March. Available at: www.aclu.org/news/aclu-challenges-warrant-search-data-facebook-page-group-protesting-dakota-access-pipeline.

ACLU v. *Reno*, 521 U.S. 844 (1997).

Balkin, J. 2017. Constitutional Rot and Constitutional Crisis. *Maryland Law Review*. Available at: https://papers.ssrn.com/sol3/papers.cfm?abstract_id=2993320.

Barr, A. 2015. Google mistakenly tags black people as 'gorillas', showing limits of algorithms. *Wall Street Journal*, 1 July. Available at: https://blogs.wsj.com/digits/2015/07/01/google-mistakenly-tags-black-people-as-gorillas-showing-limits-of-algorithms/.

Benkler, Y. (2007). *The Wealth of Networks: How Social Production Transforms markets and freedom*. New Haven, CT: Yale University Press.

Berman, A. (2016). *Give Us the Ballot*. New York: Picador.

Bilić, P. (2016). Search algorithms, hidden labour and information control. *Big Data & Society*, 3(1). DOI: 10.1177/2053951716652159.

Bond, S. (2017). Google and Facebook build digital duopoly. *Financial Times*, 14 March. Available at: www.ft.com/content/30c81d12-08c8-11e7-97d1-5e720a26771b.

Boyer, P. J. (1987). Under Fowler, F.C.C. treated TV as commerce. *New York Times*, 19 January, p. C15.

Bracha, O. & Pasquale, F. (2008). Federal search commission? Access, fairness, and accountability in the law of search. *Cornell Law Review*, 93: 1149.

Cadwalladr, C. (2016). Google, democracy and the truth about internet search. *Guardian*, 4 December. Available at: www.theguardian.com/technology/2016/dec/04/google-democracy-truth-internet-search-facebook.

Carpenter, D. P. & Moss, D. A. (2014). *Preventing Regulatory Capture: Special Interest Influence and How to Limit It*. New York: Cambridge University Press.

CBS News. (2016). Facebook: 'No evidence' conservative stories were suppressed, 10 May. Available at: www.cbsnews.com/news/facebook-no-evidence-conservative-stories-trending-suppressed-gizmodo/.

Chayka, K. (2016). Facebook and Google make lies as pretty as truth. *The Verge*, 6 December. Available at: www.theverge.com/2016/12/6/13850230/fake-news-sites-google-search-facebook-instant-articles.

Chin, A. (1997). Making the World Wide Web safe for democracy: A medium-specific first amendment analysis. *Hastings Communications & Entertainment Law Journal*, 19: 309.

Citron, D. 2014. *Hate Crimes in Cyberspace*. Cambridge, MA: Harvard University Press.

Citron, D. K. & Pasquale, F. (2011). Network accountability for the domestic intelligence apparatus. *Hastings Law Journal*, 62: 1441–1494.

Daley, D. 2015. *RATF**KED: The True Story Behind the Secret Plan to Steal America's Democracy*. New York: Kirkus.

Dean, J. (2010). *Blog Theory: Feedback and Capture in the Circuits of Drive*. Malden, MA: Polity.

Evon, D. (2016). Spirit cooking. *Snopes*, 5 November. Available at: www.snopes.com/john-podesta-spirit-cooking/.

Feldman, J. (2016). CIA concluded Russia intervened in election to help Trump, WaPo reports. *Mediaite*, 9 December. Available at: www.mediaite.com/online/cia-concluded-russia-intervened-in-election-to-help-trump-wapo-reports/.

Guarino, B. (2016). Google faulted for racial bias in image search results for black teenagers. *Washington Post*, 10 June. Available at: www.washingtonpost.com/news/morning-mix/wp/2016/06/10/google-faulted-for-racial-bias-in-image-search-results-for-black-teenagers/?utm_term=.1a3595bb8624.

Gutmann, A. & Thompson, D. F. (2004). *Why Deliberative Democracy?* Princeton, NJ: Princeton University Press.

Habermas, J. (1991). *The Structural Transformation of the Public Sphere: An Inquiry into a Category of Bourgeois Society.* Burger, T. (Trans.). Cambridge, MA: MIT Press.

Hersher, R. (2017). What happened when Dylann Roof asked Google for information about race? *Houston Public Media*, 10 January. Available at: www.houstonpublic media.org/npr/2017/01/10/508363607/what-happened-when-dylann-roof-asked-google-for-information-about-race/.

Irani, L. (2013). The cultural work of microwork. *New Media and Society*, 17(5): 720–739.

Kollanyi, B., Howard, P. N. & Woolley, S. C. (2016). Bots and automation over Twitter during the second U.S. presidential debate. *COMPROP Data Memo*, 19 October. Available at: http://politicalbots.org/wp-content/uploads/2016/10/Data-Memo-Second-Presidential-Debate.pdf.

Kreiss, D. (2016). Social media did not give us Trump and it is not weakening democracy. *Culture Digitally*, 9 November. Available at: http://culturedigitally.org/2016/11/social_media_trump/.

Kruly, C. (2013). Self-funding and agency independence. *George Washington University Law Review*, 81: 1733.

Lanier, J. (2013). *Who Owns the Future?* New York: Simon & Schuster.

Lee, T. B. (2016). Facebook should crush fake news the way Google crushed spammy content farms. *Vox*, 8 December. Available at: www.vox.com/new-money/2016/12/8/13875960/facebook-fake-news-google.

Lehdonvirta, V. (2017). Could data pay for global development? Introducing data financing for global good. *Oxford Internet Institute* 3 January. [blog] Available at: www.oii.ox.ac.uk/blog/could-data-pay-for-global-development-introducing-data-financing-for-global-good/.

Lessin, J. (2016). Facebook shouldn't fact check. *New York Times*, 29 November. Available at: www.nytimes.com/2016/11/29/opinion/facebook-shouldnt-fact-check.html.

Lindblom, C. E. (1977). *Politics and Markets.* New York: Basic Books.

Lubbers, E. (2016). There is no such thing as the Denver Guardian. *Denver Post*, 5 November. Available at: www.denverpost.com/2016/11/05/there-is-no-such-thing-as-the-denver-guardian/.

Marwick, A. & Lewis, R. (2017). *Media Manipulation and Disinformation Online.* New York: Data & Society Research Institute.

Molina, B. (2016). Report: Fake election news performed better than real news on Facebook. *USA Today*, 17 November. Available at: www.usatoday.com/story/tech/news/2016/11/17/report-fake-election-news-performed-better-than-real-news-facebook/94028370/.

Müller-Doohm, S. (2017). *Habermas: A Biography.* D. Steuer (Trans.). Malden, MA: Polity Press.

Nagle, A. (2017). *Kill All Normies: The Online Culture Wars from Tumblr and 4chan to the Alt-right and Trump*. Washington, DC: Zero Books.

Noble, S. (2018). *Algorithms of Oppression: How Search Engines Reinforce Racism*. New York: New York University Press.

Noelle-Neumann, E. (1974). The spiral of silence: A theory of public opinion. *Journal of Communication*, 24(2): 43–51.

Ohlheiser, A. (2016). Three days after removing human editors, Facebook is already trending fake news. *Washington Post*, 29 August. Available at: www.washingtonpost. com/news/the-intersect/wp/2016/08/29/a-fake-headline-about-megyn-kelly-was-trending-on-facebook/?utm_term=.f857ac42b2e9.

O'Reilly, T. (2016). Media in the age of algorithms. *Medium*, 11 November. Available at: https://medium.com/the-wtf-economy/media-in-the-age-of-algorithms-63e80b9b0a 73#.9l86jw9r4.

Oremus, W. (2014). The prose of the machines. *Slate*, 14 July. Available at: www.slate. com/articles/technology/technology/2014/07/automated_insights_to_write_ap_ earnings_reports_why_robots_can_t_take_journalists.html.

Pariser, E. (2011). *The Filter Bubble: What the Internet is Hiding From You*. New York: Penguin Press.

Parkinson, J. & Mansbridge, J. J. (2012). *Deliberative Systems: Deliberative Democracy at the Large Scale*. New York: Cambridge University Press.

Pasquale, F. (2006). Rankings, reductionism, and responsibility. *Cleveland State Law Review*, 54: 115–139.

Pasquale, F. (2008a). Asterisk revisited: Debating a right of reply on search results. *Journal of Business and Technology Law*, 3: 61–86.

Pasquale, F. (2008b). Internet nondiscrimination principles: Commercial ethics for carriers and search engines. *University of Chicago Legal Forum*, 263–300.

Pasquale, F. (2008c). Reclaiming egalitarianism in the political theory of campaign finance reform. *University of Illinois Law Review*, 599–660.

Pasquale, F. (2010). Beyond competition and innovation: The need for qualified transparency in internet intermediaries. *Northwestern University Law Review*, 104: 105–174.

Pasquale, F. (2011). Restoring transparency to automated authority. *Journal Telecommunications and High Technology Law*, 9: 235.

Pasquale, F. (2015a). Digital star chamber: Algorithms are production profiles of you. What do they say? You probably don't have the right to know. *Aeon*, 18 August. Available at: https://aeon.co/essays/judge-jury-and-executioner-the-unaccountable-algorithm.

Pasquale, F. (2015b). *The Black Box Society: The Secret Algorithms Behind Money and Information*. Cambridge, MA: Harvard University Press.

Pasquale, F. (2016a). Platform neutrality: Enhancing freedom of expression in spheres of private power. *Theoretical Inquiries in Law*, 17: 487–514.

Pasquale, F. (2016b). Reforming the law of reputation. *Loyola Law Review*, 47: 515–540.

Pasquale, F. (2016c). Search, speech, and secrecy: Corporate strategies for inverting net neutrality debates. *Yale Law and Policy Review Inter Alia*, 15 May. Available at: http:// ylpr.yale.edu/inter_alia/search-speech-and-secrecy-corporate-strategies-inverting-net-neutrality-debates.

Patterson, M. R. (2016). *Antitrust Law in the New Economy*. Cambridge, MA: Harvard University Press.

Peters, J. D. (2005). *Courting the Abyss: Free Speech and the Liberal Tradition*. Chicago, IL: University of Chicago Press.

Revesz, R. (2016). Steve Bannon's data firm in talks for lucrative White House contracts. *Independent*, 23 November. Available at: www.independent.co.uk/news/world/americas/cambridge-analytica-steve-bannon-robert-rebekah-mercer-donald-trump-conflicts-of-interest-white-a7435536.html.

Roberts, S. T. (2016a). Commercial content moderation: Digital laborers' dirty work. In Noble, S. U. and Tynes, B. (Eds.), *The Intersectional Internet: Race, Sex, Class and Culture Online* (pp. 147–159). New York: Peter Lang.

Roberts, S. T. (2016b). Digital refuse: Canadian garbage, commercial content moderation and the global circulation of social media's waste. *Wi: Journal of Mobile Media*, 10(1): 1–18. Available at: http://wi.mobilities.ca/digitalrefuse/.

Robinson, N. J. (2016). The necessity of credibility. *Current Affairs*, 6 December. Available at: www.currentaffairs.org/2016/12/the-necessity-of-credibility.

Rosa, H. (2015). *Social Acceleration: A New Theory of Modernity*. New York: Columbia University Press.

Rushkoff, D. (2016). *Throwing Rocks at the Google Bus*. New York: Portfolio.

Sadowski, J. & Pasquale, F. (2015). The spectrum of control: A social theory of the smart city. *First Monday* 20: 7. Available at: http://firstmonday.org/article/view/5903/4660.

Schaedel, S. (2016). Did the Pope endorse Trump? *FactCheck.org*, 24 October. Available at: www.factcheck.org/2016/10/did-the-pope-endorse-trump/.

Schüll, N. D. (2012). *Addiction by Design: Machine Gambling in Las Vegas*. Princeton, NJ: Princeton University Press.

Smith, A. & Banic, V. (2016). Fake News: How a partying Macedonian teen earns thousands publishing lies. *NBC News*, 9 December. Available at: www.nbcnews.com/news/world/fake-news-how-partying-macedonian-teen-earns-thousands-publishing-lies-n692451.

Smith, R. C. & Tambini, D. (2012). Measuring media plurality in the United Kingdom: Policy choices and regulatory challenges. *Robert Schuman Centre for Advanced Studies*, Working Paper No. RSCAS 2012/36. Available at: http://cadmus.eui.eu/bitstream/handle/1814/23314/RSCAS_2012_36.pdf?sequence=1&isAllowed.

Smith, R. C., Tambini, D. & Morisi, D. (2012). Regulating media plurality and media power in the 21st century. *LSE Media Policy Project: Media Policy*, brief No. 7. Available at: http://eprints.lse.ac.uk/45041/1/LSEMPPBrief7.pdf.

Srnicek, N. (2017). *Platform Capitalism*. Malden, MA: Polity.

Struyk, R. (2017). 6 in 10 people who approve of Trump say they'll never, ever, ever stop approving. *CNN News*. Available at: www.cnn.com/2017/08/17/politics/trump-approvers-never-stop-approving-poll/index.html.

Stucke, M. E. & Grunes, A. P. (2017). Data-opolies. *University of Tennessee Legal Studies*, Research Paper No. 316. Available at: https://papers.ssrn.com/sol3/papers.cfm?abstract_id=2927018.

Sunstein, C. R. (2007). *Republic.com 2.0*. Princeton, NJ: Princeton University Press.

Suskind, R. (2004). Faith, certainty and the presidency of George W. Bush. *New York Times*, 17 October. Available at: www.nytimes.com/2004/10/17/magazine/faith-certainty-and-the-presidency-of-george-w-bush.html.

Tufekci, Z. (2016). Mark Zuckerberg is in denial. *New York Times*, 15 November. Available at: www.nytimes.com/2016/11/15/opinion/mark-zuckerberg-is-in-denial.html?_r=2.

Turton, W. (2016). *New York Times* Facebook Op-Ed is a joke, *Gizmodo*, 30 November. Available at: http://gizmodo.com/new-york-times-public-editor-slams-facebook-op-ed-1789511334.

Wagner, B. 2016a. Algorithmic regulation and the global default: Shifting norms in inter-net technology. *Etikk Praksis*, 10(1): 5–13.

Wagner, B. 2016b. Draft Report on the Human Rights Dimensions of Algorithms. Stras-bourg, France: Council of Europe.

Winston, J. 2016. How the Trump campaign built an identity database and used Facebook ads to win the election. *Medium*, 18 November. Available at: https://medium.com/ startup-grind/how-the-trump-campaign-built-an-identity-database-and-used-facebook-ads-to-win-the-election-4ff7d24269ac#.4oaz94q5a.

Winters, J. (2011). *Oligarchy*. New York: Cambridge University Press.

8 Bringing the state back in

Big Data-based capitalism, disruption, and novel regulatory approaches in Europe

Ingrid Schneider

> Some, in the 1990s, expected a collapse of nation-state sovereignty with respect to privacy. It hasn't happened. Instead, there's been a complicated shift, making the European Union the most influential voice in global privacy regulation, in part because it seems to care the most.
>
> (Wu 2008: 104)

In 1991, Marc Weiser, the 'father' of ubiquitous computing, wisely predicted 'The most profound technologies are those that disappear. They weave themselves into the fabric of everyday life until they are indistinguishable from it' (Weiser 1991: 94). In keeping with Weiser's point, this chapter argues that the most profound changes associated with Big Data and digitalisation are those which relate to the infrastructures behind and 'below' the surfaces of our daily digitised interactions. However, as these infrastructures and the (re-)distributive processes and larger transformations are invisible, they must be revealed and analysed to allow for assessment of their benefits, opportunities, costs, and risks.

Big Data is part and parcel of a broader process of digital transformation of the economy, state, politics, and the relationship of citizens towards themselves and to each other, to the state, and to private corporations. Hence, Big Data is to be understood as but one important facet of the digital metamorphosis of the world and its power relations. Will it bring about tectonic shifts? What is its impact on liberal democracy? Asking such 'big' questions, and asking them in such a way may already evoke a certain technological determinism, or may drive speculations difficult to prove. Nonetheless, such 'deeper' interrogation needs to be discussed to grasp the implications of Big Data for the future of market–state relationships, as well as for democratic societies. And such questions must be posed to enable a societal dialogue about the social shaping of technological progress, as technology and society have to be understood as co-produced (Jasanoff 2006), and in order to foster desirable decision-making and to try to avoid the undesirable impact of Big Data.

Big Data, as understood in this chapter, relies on (often automated) data collection, measurement, algorithmic analytics, mainly predicated on pattern-recognition and correlation, and on (assisted) decision-making based on scoring, ranking, and predictive analytics (Kitchin 2014; Lyon 2014). The volume and variety of data(bases) to be collected and analysed – at times in real time – continues to grow exponentially with the Internet of Things and other forms of 'smart' and networked technologies in traffic, energy, health, and other sectors. In this chapter, I will therefore use Big Data as often synonymous with larger processes of digitalisation, 'industry 4.0.' and 'work 4.0.', and emergent novel practices of machine learning and deep search. Special attention will be dedicated to platforms as recent expressions of digital Big Data-based capitalism.

In contrast to the innovation and digital opportunities semantics highlighted by corporations and political actors alike (see Rieder, Chapter 6 in this volume), this chapter aims at shedding light on the darker sides of Big Data-based digital capitalism. This is not to deny convenience, usefulness and efficiency enhancement of digital products and services. It also acknowledges positive potentials and potential positives of Big Data on energy, transport, health, and other areas of social life. Nonetheless, some of the predicaments associated with the disruptions Big Data is causing certainly deserve critical scrutiny.

The chapter proceeds as follows: The first section analyses some mechanisms of the transformations towards Big Data-based capitalism. Next, I investigate the impact in several areas of the democratic social order: first the area of media and the public sphere, second that of individual self-perception and subjectivation, and third that of social sorting and potentials for inclusion and exclusion. Finally, I present several measures by which European policymakers and courts try to counteract undesirable consequences and digital power asymmetries, specifically: (i) EU's General Data Protection Reform; (ii) Competition Law; (iii) Countermeasures to tax avoidance schemes; and (iv) the jurisdiction of the Court of Justice of the EU.

Digital platforms: network effects and oligopolisation

In terms of political economy, the rise of Big Data is accompanied by the rise of intermediaries, or so-called *platform industries*. According to Nick Srnicek (2017: 43–49), platforms rely on four characteristics:

1   Platforms are in the first instance digital infrastructures that enable two or more sides to interact, for example, customers, advertisers, and service providers.
2   Platforms produce network effects: The more users, the more valuable that platform becomes for everyone else.
3   Platforms often use cross-subsidisation: one arm of the company provides a service or good for free, another arm creates revenues to make up for these losses.
4   The rules of service and product development are set by the platform owner. In that respect, platforms 'embody a politics' as they not only gain access to data but also 'control and governance over the rules of the game' (Srnicek 2017: 47).

Platforms like Google Search enable search in the Internet in the first place, others like Facebook also allow for communication networks in social media, and a third form like Amazon allows for more direct retail and distribution chains. This has led to a situation that seems paradoxical at first glance: 'The world's largest taxi firm, Uber, owns no cars. The world's most popular media company, Facebook, creates no content. The world's most valuable retailer, Alibaba, carries no stock. And the world's largest accommodation provider, Airbnb, owns no property' (McRae 2015). Thus, it is these *interfaces* that nowadays allow for quick searching and finding of information, more efficient use of resources, and fast comparison and supply of consumer goods. Such intermediaries are fast-growing companies that 'sit on top of vast supply systems (where the costs are) and interface with a huge number of people (where the money is)' (Goodwin 2015). As a result, new value and profit chains have been created, disrupting other business models upon which traditional economy had been built. Some observers have hailed and welcomed these interfaces as building blocks of a new 'sharing economy' and even proclaimed the grand transition towards a 'Zero Marginal Cost Society' in which digitalisation would speed us ahead towards 'an era of nearly free goods and services, precipitating the meteoric rise of a global Collaborative Commons and the eclipse of capitalism' (Rifkin 2014: book cover). Others are far less enthusiastic, and point to the fact that, in some sense, these intermediaries are parasitic as they live off other people's work and investments. Newspapers, for instance, need to investigate, write, fact-check, buy paper, print, and distribute their newspapers to get their money from subscriptions and ads. In contrast, Google News, Facebook newsfeeds, and Youtube just live off content provided by the users and/or monetising content provided by others such as magazines, TV, film companies, etc. Another downside of the 'sharing economy' is the loss of tax revenue and of safety, as respective regulations for hotels and taxi drivers are often either bypassed or completely ignored (Baker 2014).

Certainly, large platforms have made the world of consumers more convenient and comfortable, as they provide apps that allow us to manage significant portions of our daily workload via smartphone. Nevertheless, people might be flummoxed about the broader disruption processes triggered by platform capitalism.

Large online platforms benefit from several effects, which economists have described and which, taken together, lead to oligopolistic structures. One of the most important mechanisms is *network effects*: While the fixed cost of building the platform in the first place may be large, the marginal cost of adding another user is tiny. After reaching a critical mass, positive network effects can create a positive feedback loop. The network becomes more valuable as more people join in and vice versa. This gives rise to increasing returns to scale. Over time, an ever-increasing number of subscribers will make the platform very powerful and marginalise other competitors or drive them out of the market (World Bank 2016: 11). It will also create *locked-in effects* and *high switching costs*. This has been the case for instance for Facebook or WhatsApp. When all your friends or classmates are on Facebook and use WhatsApp chat groups, it becomes difficult to stay connected if you are on Google+ or have decided to opt for Signal or Threema. Similarly, Apple's iTunes Store soon became the largest music vendor in the United States and in Europe. As the number of iPod and iTunes users grew, the number of available songs, cooperating music corporations, app developers, and equipment manufacturers increased as well. The iTunes ecosystem steadily grew in size and enabled Apple to capture a significant portion of the sales generated by songs from big music corporations. However, due to the new business model of music streaming services like Spotify, new entrants took some of Apple's market share and triggered Apple to introduce its own music streaming service, Apple Music. Here again, network effects play a crucial role. The success and value created by music streaming services strongly depends on playlist quality, which is created by recommendation systems themselves based on user preferences. Machine Learning and other Big Data analytics create better recommendations, but rely on a large number of users, whose preferences are analysed and combined with 'similar' users. Thus, with each additional user of the service, the value of the platform and the service provided to each individual user increases (David 2015).

Moreover, platform providers have tried to create *walled gardens* where the service provider, via his software system, has control over applications, content, and media, and restricts access to non-approved applications or content. Hence, closed platforms create closed ecosystems. Examples are Amazon's Kindle line of eReaders, Apple's iOS operating system or Google's Android, which are fairly restricted to running pre-approved applications from a digital distribution service.

Another economic mechanism is the *first-mover advantage*, which may reward huge profit margins and a monopoly-like status to the initial significant occupant of a market segment thanks to the competitive advantages of high numbers of users and control of resources. This is not to deny that the initial entry of Internet firms into certain sectors can disrupt traditional monopolies and promote competition. However, 'internet firms can be prone to anticompetitive behaviours by exploiting scale and network effects. So the regulators need to level the regulatory regime to guarantee free-market entry and prevent market shares from becoming too concentrated' (World Bank 2016: 51). In similar terms, the OECD, in a report on the Digital Economy, has pointed to the fact that

> (c)ompetition in major digital markets often takes on a rather distinctive form. First, competition between business models or platforms tends to be more important than competition within a business model because platform competition often leads to a winner takes all outcome. In other words, dominance – or even monopoly – can be the virtually inevitable outcome of success. Second, digital markets are often characterised by strong network effects and economies of scale, which reinforce this competition-to-dominance trait. Third, many digital markets are two-sided, so that two or more user groups benefit from use of the digital platform.
>
> (OECD 2013: 5–6)

Later in this chapter, some measures taken by the EU to curb anti-competitive effects will be described. It also is important to note that market dominance is not only due to brilliant design (Apple), or excellent search results and services (Google) but also due to the fact that many platform providers as yet outrightly ignore EU and national data protection laws and have built their empires upon such wilful ignorance (Zuboff 2015).

But first, the analysis aims at shedding some light on the shifts and transformations taking place through digital Big Data-based capitalism. The first focus is on the transformation of the public sphere and on the effects of quantification, metrification, ranking, and rating by Big Data techniques.

Big Data capitalism, platforms, and the public sphere

Only a few years ago, the Internet was celebrated as the force of and for democratisation. The move from 'one to many' communication in radio and TV towards 'many to many' communication by social media promised a broadening of the public sphere. Free speech, freedom of expression, attention, and resonance for everyone seemed to herald the move 'from the spectator to the participatory democracy' (Leggewie and Maar 1998). The Arab spring uprisings were titled 'Twitter and Facebook revolutions' and seemed to signal the advent of democracy from the bottom up. The euphoria, however, did not last for long. 'Filter bubbles' (Pariser 2012) indicated the fragmentation of the public sphere. Social media did not lead to everyone interacting with everybody else but to communities of people alike, more or less voluntarily locked in echo chambers.

Media are core elements for democratic systems, as they open up a public sphere of deliberation that is vital for democracy (Habermas 1991; see also Pasquale, Chapter 7 in this volume). Facebook, Google, and other platforms, however, have changed the rules of the game in the media market, as a new media economy in digital capitalism has been implemented.

The old business model of print media has been disrupted. Newspapers and magazines have lost their main sources of revenue as ads have moved to the Internet and print circulation has fallen. Readers, especially the younger generation, prefer free content on the Internet or do not read newspapers any more. Meanwhile, platforms create 'personalised' newsfeeds, which make use of content produced by others, ordered according to opaque algorithms, often focused on attention rather than on truthfulness or journalistic quality.

To give some numbers: Revenues in media businesses like newspaper publishing or the music business have, since 2001, fallen by 70%, while profits at Google, Facebook and Amazon have soared (Taplin 2017a). According to the US Bureau of Labor Statistics (2017), newspaper publishers lost over half their employees, shrinking from 412,000 to 174,000 between 2001 and 2016. In Europe as well, thousands of journalists have lost their jobs. From 1995 to 2012, German newspapers lost more than 30% of their circulation. The Spanish daily newspaper El País had to fire one-third of its employees in 2012. Other newspapers have closed altogether (Knüwer 2013). Billions of dollars have been reallocated from creators of content to owners of monopoly platforms. All content creators dependent on advertising must negotiate with Google or Facebook as aggregator, the sole lifeline between themselves and the vast Internet cloud (Taplin 2017b; Lanchester 2017; Wu 2017). In the first quarter of 2016, 89% of Google's and 96.6% of Facebook's revenues came from advertisers (Srnicek 2017: 53). In the US, Google and Facebook receive 76% of online advertising revenue and are taking 85% of every new advertising dollar (Srnicek 2017: 98).

These platforms do not consider themselves as media bound by editorial principles of quality and relevance, but are profit-driven. They have two priorities: growth and monetisation (García Martínez 2016; Wu 2017; Lanchester 2017). They primarily aim at keeping users as long as possible on their platform, and to incite them to click on ads. They measure success not in journalistic awards, but in visits, hits, and clicks. Platforms are indifferent to the truthfulness and originality of a certain news content, and distribute exclusive news created by investigative journalism very quickly, eliminating the premium on exclusivity as an incentive to buy newspapers. Loss of ads and circulation, together with a decline in willingness to pay, have almost destroyed the paid market for journalistic content. The unintended side effects are that quality journalism is more and more crowded out and replaced by 'content'. Thus, personalised or stratified Big Data-based 'individual' relevance replaces journalistic relevance: In our increasingly 'personalised' world, algorithms make guesses about what information users would like to see, based on what is known about him or her (e.g. location, past click behaviour, search and purchase history). Instead of seeking comprehensiveness in the reporting about the world, the optimisation of algorithms and scope of social media users is being sought for. Curating and staging of news 'events' is increasingly replacing investigative research. Content marketing and other pseudo-journalistic forms of influence-seeking content are marginalising real journalism more and more (Lobigs 2017). Thus, quality journalism as a form of democratic public sphere, which contributes to individual and social opinion-building and to influencing political will-building, is deteriorating. Public will-building is being replaced by the (automated) query of individual interests (Richter 2015: 54), which is quite different from democratic deliberation, built upon dialogue, argumentation, justification, reflection, persuasion, consensus-seeking, and/or compromise. Big Data does not aim at consensus but is based on correlation, behaviour analytics, and prognostics.

Big Data can create 'filter bubbles' or personal 'echo chambers' for individuals. Any information received is filtered in increasingly more complex and opaque ways. The danger is that people will less likely come across information that challenges their existing viewpoints. They will be increasingly effectively isolated in their own cultural and ideological bubbles and divided from the rest of society (EDPS 2015: footnote 12). Other forms of unpleasant and socially destructive effects of social media are shitstorms and cyberbullying. Hate speech and radical propaganda easily finds its way across digital channels. A turning point in the general assessment of the democratising force of the Internet has certainly been the year 2016, when the terms 'fake news' and 'post-truth' have also been coined. To name but a few incidents: the Brexit vote in the UK, Recep Erdogan's referendum in Turkey, and the victory of Donald Trump in the US elections – at least partly attributed to Russian propaganda influence, social bots, or untruthful and damaging news invented by Macedonian adolescents (Lanchester 2017). Since then, negative connotations of Internet media, platforms and their forms of news distribution abound. Without going into analytic details, a general feeling of disruption and confusion pervades. But, regulating platforms as well as social media, and reconstructing a lively and deliberative public sphere is far from straightforward. The European Parliament, in a Resolution in 2017, calls on the Commission and Member States

> to ensure that data-driven technologies do not limit or discriminate access to a pluralistic media environment, but rather foster media freedom and pluralism; emphasises that cooperation between governments, educational institutions and media organisations will play a pivotal role in ensuring that digital media literacy is supported in order to empower citizens and protect their rights to information and freedom of expression.

This call certainly addresses important topics, but in itself does not answer how to fix the problems raised (European Parliament 2017: 13).

Big Data, however, has more implications for democracy and the social order that need to be analysed. Therefore, the next step is devoted to the individual and social implications of metrics and rankings, as enabled by Big Data.

Big Data's impact on the social order: shifts in subjectivation and moral economy

Big Data is woven into broader trends of digitisation and datafication (Zuboff 2015). In Western and Asian societies, performance metrics are increasingly used in education and working life. So, too, are tracking and measuring in everyday consumption, social media interaction, health, housing, credit, employment, legal services, election campaigns, and even intimate relationships. Those data are transformed via opaque algorithms into ratings and rankings, scorings and screenings. As a result, perceptions of self and others are changing, as are schemes of cognition and valorisation. Social values and what counts as relevant are changing as well. According to sociologist Steffen Mau, the effects are threefold: (i) everyday life practices of value and social status are shifting; (ii) competition is universalised and competitive races via numbers and digits are staged; (iii) qualitative differences are transformed into quantitative inequalities. Altogether, these processes produce shifts in the social order because what was hitherto incomparable is being made comparable and brought into a hierarchical order (Mau 2017: 17).

The promise of Big Data lies in making sense of large amounts of various types of data, possibly in real time, to reveal new insights, analyses, and predictive outcomes. Big Data analytics carries the 'aura of truth, objectivity, and accuracy' (boyd and Crawford 2012: 663). In a society of 'omnimetrics' (Dueck 2013: 37), there is the appearance that everything is measured. Quantitative measurements create supposed *equivalences* and thus make comparable what had been formerly incommensurate. At the same time, they create *differences*: starting from numeric difference towards categorical differences. In order to create order and meaning, groups, systems of classification, taxonomies, and hierarchical forms of ordering are created. Hence, indicators and data are transformed into lists, ratings, and rankings – starting from Google Search Ranks up to school and university rankings, towards global lists of states in transparency and corruption rankings. Scores and rank orders both *de-contextualise* social practices and processes, and *re-contextualise*, as they put data into new forms of seemingly comparable or connectible relationships. Such forms of description of reality act as 'technologies of distance' (Porter 1996: ix), as they allow forms of non-hierarchical governance and steering from 'far away', without open and clear criteria, goals, or norms. In an ever-expanding 'audit society' (Power 2010), more and more social organisations and sectors are put under pressures of performance control and a culture of optimisation. Together with the progressive economisation of social sectors, an orientation towards efficiency and output, and neoliberal ideologies as additional driving factors (Mau 2017: 42), Big Data seems to announce the advent of another stage of capitalism. The capacity to collect, connect, and analyse digitised data may first and foremost marginalise or even crowd out other forms of describing and evaluating social realities which are not based on datafication practices. However, the consequences may go far beyond that.

As competition and social comparison become ubiquitous, new forms of social difference and inequality are created (Mau 2017: 257–277). According to Fourcade and Healy (2017: 9), Big Data equips both organisations and selves with lenses that force them into '*seeing like a market*', thus addressing social practices of calculative comparison, in which worth is not expressed in prices but in valorisations. Thus, more and more social systems – for example, health, education, universities – which had followed different logics of appropriateness, are being converted into quasi-markets by following an institutional 'data imperative'. Notably, not only consumers in traditional market-transactions but also people in different social spheres in conscious and unconscious behaviour can be 'seen', their individual data yielded and tracked, to become analysed and sorted into ever-finer-grained categories of interests, preferences, tastes, riskiness, performance and worth. 'Information dragnets [...] deepen the reach of the market and define new strategies of profit-making' in which 'individuals accrue a form of capital flowing from their positions as measured by various digital scoring and ranking [...] with potentially *stratifying* effects' (Fourcade and Healy 2017: 9). Such stratifications enable firms to 'personalise' and target their services and offers, as well as, for instance, to establish dynamic pricing systems, in which the same products are offered at various price levels, according to customers' purchasing power and with their urgency of need of the product. Vice versa, for the individuals classified, it means that they not only share a certain range of consumer opportunities but also experience 'reactive or performative effects on individual behavior [...] and on people's life-chances' (Fourcade and Healy 2017: 22). The latter – opportunities in life and options to act in society – is an aspect to which I will return later.

Fourcade and Healy's assertion about the implications of digital scoring is that these tend to establish a 'new economy of moral judgment' (2017: 24). Metrics thus become social attributions and assignments. These are actively appropriated and reified, when 'outcomes are experienced as morally deserved positions based on prior good actions and good tastes' (2017: 9). In other words, Big Data may establish a *moral economy*, in which people accept their social score as a fair and just assignment of societal place, as measured and classified by new infrastructures of data collection and analysis.

However, this assignment of place by digital traces is not a static exercise. Quite the contrary. Datafication and stratification put people into a steady treadmill of self-observation and outside observation, digital tracking, performance-measuring, and competitive practices of improving and outperforming. To put it differently, algorithmic authority is reformatting life. Such kinds of analyses stress the interrelationship between active participation in scoring and valorisation activities by users, and the development and application of such Big Data instruments by companies and social institutions. Thus, such sociological analyses focus primarily on new forms of *subjectification*, with the effect of creating a metric self (Mau 2017) or a quantified self (Swan 2013).

Commodification of social reality

Other scholarly approaches centre on *actors* in technology, pointing to the role of software development and data scientists: As Cathy O'Neil explains in her book *Weapons of math destruction* (2016), contrary to public opinion, algorithms are neither neutral nor objective. She claims that 'models are opinions embedded in mathematics', as they may encode human prejudice, misunderstanding, and bias into the software systems. Many programmers use proxies that are poor substitutes for data they really want but cannot measure directly. Referring to algorithmic selection and sorting processes, O'Neil (2016) argues that models define their own reality and use it to justify their results. They may use sloppy statistics and biased models that create their own 'toxic' feedback loops (O'Neil 2016: 11). Some of her examples relate to crime prediction software, others are e-scores computed online to evaluate potential customers by taking into account web browsing history, purchasing patterns, and location. At call centres, such e-scores are used to identify more profitable prospects. Henceforth, people from poor neighbourhoods get lower scores, less credit, and higher interest rates. Because algorithms intervene in social realities, it becomes unclear to which extent they *analyse* or *produce* a certain reality. As the underlying models are often opaque or even invisible to those affected by them, people cannot correct false assumptions. O'Neil further argues that algorithms tend to punish the poor and ethnic minorities, and are unfair in that they may damage or even destroy life prospects. Problems and adverse effects can arise from the choice of goals, such as, for example, desire for profit, which may far outweigh fairness considerations.

Some readers may contradict or even reject this as a too one-sided perspective. Worth noting, however, are at least some epistemic aspects of her analysis: data tracking, ratings, screenings and scores increasingly tend to *spill over* from one area of life where they have been collected to another, and are used to predict future behaviour. Ranks and scores do not just 'represent' hierarchical orders but *co-produce* them. At the same time, they are classifications that determine access to resources, life chances, and benefits. Digitisation, datafication and valorisation also have assignative functions: they display and assign (social) value. In effect, incentives are created to behave according to whichever (easily) quantified parameters are accorded value and weight. Thus, intrinsic motivation tends to be displaced by extrinsic motives, and people are guided towards subsequent forms of self-accounting and 'investments' into their selves. The datafication of social life hence boosts processes of commodification of selves and of personal data.

Power inequalities, discrimination, and socio-political implications of commercial data collections

While some sociologists mainly point to micro-sociological shifts in self-perception and behaviour, others focus on power inequalities and discrimination created or exacerbated by commercial entities using Big Data analytics. While search engines and social media platforms are well known, many commercial data brokers operate in the shadows. However, online platforms, data brokers, advertisers and other actors are increasingly connected, forming networks, and thus creating and interfering in personal data ecosystems, as Wolfie Christl (2017) who has performed extensive empirical research on such entities, explains. To extract from Christl's research: *Acxiom*, for instance, a large but little-known US data broker, collects, analyses and trades vast amounts of consumer information, and combines their client's customer data with data of other sources. Acxiom claims to provide access to up to 5,000 data elements on 700 million people worldwide, including customers in the US, the UK and Germany. Every person, household, and building in Acxiom's database gets assigned a globally unique identifier. The company provides not only data and marketing services, but also risk mitigation, identity verification, and fraud detection. Its identity verification services use data records about individual demographics, personal assets, education, licences, filings, business, bankruptcies, judgments, liens, and other so-called risk flags. In addition to classic information on housing and education, occupation, children, income and credit card use, Acxiom categorises its subjects according to detailed 'race codes' and 'health needs'. Available are also data on criminal records, voting behaviour, tendency to gamble, diet or smoking habits as well as information on allergies and chronic diseases. According to their data catalogue, Acxiom offers several scores to categorise people and predict their future behaviour. Corporate clients can obtain detailed information about individuals or households. Recently, Acxiom has started to cooperate with Google, Facebook and Twitter on targeting ads to their users and for other purposes, based on scoring and segmenting individuals' purchases in stores, online and offline activities (Christl 2017: 54–59). Mau reports that *Acxiom* segregates individuals into 70 socio-economic clusters, ordered hierarchically. The bottom 10% are internally coined as 'waste' – which implies that persons thus categorised will never get a good mobile phone contract, private health insurance, or housing credit (Mau 2017: 268).

Another data giant is the German marketing data broker *Arvato AZ Direct*, a subsidiary of the media titan Bertelsmann. It claims to maintain relationships with over 600 million consumers and business clients. Arvato has 70,000 employees in 40 countries and provides information about creditworthiness, claiming to perform 100 million credit checks per year. In its marketing data catalogue, those with the best credit rating are labelled 'A' and 'VIP clients', the worst are 'G' and 'postpone processing'. Information about people's creditworthiness has spilled over into online advertising. Thanks to data provided by Oracle's Datalogix, ads on Twitter, for example, can now be targeted according to users' predicted creditworthiness (Christl 2017: 42–44).

ChoicePoint, another controversial Big Data broker, acquired a decade ago by LexisNexis and now in the risk management division of RELX Group, has data records of over 500 million consumers. It offers services such as creditworthiness, background checks on employees and residents, and insurance scores. Their identity and authentication system TrueID offers Big Data linkages of biometric data from photos and fingerprints, voice recognition, and social media monitoring, with payment, customer cards, and other user data, promising 'to track transactional behavior throughout the customer lifecycle' (Christl and Spiekermann 2016: 106).

Personal characteristics on lifestyle, ethnicity, and creditworthiness can be inferred from data on purchasing behaviour, Facebook likes, and surfing and search behaviour. Such data are used not only for targeted marketing; personal data are now also used in almost all economic areas for customer-specific forecasting of risks, revenue opportunities or loyalty by so-called 'Business Intelligence'. Data brokers provide risk management solutions for companies in insurance, finance, retail, travel, gaming, the healthcare sector, and sometimes also local and federal agencies (Christl 2017).

Companies have started to predict consumers' creditworthiness based on data tracked in everyday life activities, such as the timing and frequency of phone calls, GPS location, customer support data, online purchases, web searches, and data from social networks. Large insurers in Europe and the US have introduced significant discount programmes if consumers agree to provide real-time data about driving behaviour and activities such as steps, grocery purchases, or fitness studio visits. Data brokers offer health-scoring products that predict individual health risks based on vast amounts of consumer data, including purchase activities (Christl 2017: 79–80). Thus, low and high-risk groups can be discerned, as well as highly profitable and less profitable customers. The new quality of these developments is expressed in 'the rise of social media and net-worked devices, the real-time tracking and linking of behavioral data streams, the merging of online and offline data, and the dissolution of the distinction between marketing and risk management data'. As a consequence, Christl sums up, 'individuals are constantly surveyed and evaluated, investigated and examined, categorised and grouped, rated and ranked, numbered and quantified, included or excluded, and, as a result, treated differently' (2017: 84).

Little is known about how user profiles are employed by platform giants in successive value chains. Anecdotal incidences such as Facebook's mood modification study (Kramer *et al.* 2014) or Uber's map of 'one-night stands' (Perry 2014) may suggest that companies extract and hold detailed knowledge about human weaknesses and vulnerabilities.[1] Unless they are forced to disclose what inferences they draw from aggregated and correlated datasets and account for their usage, the state and the general public will stay blind. And it is not only customer behaviour that is being addressed. Voters have also been micro-targeted in election campaigns, where more or intimate data about citizen's preferences is used to influence voting behaviour. We do not know whether and to what extent Donald Trump's presidency (or Brexit) was brought about by Cambridge Analytica (Grasegger and Krogerius 2017), combined with fake news manufactured by Macedonian adolescents eager for quick money, and a Russian government willing to influence the US election process. For now, that nexus remains a hypothesis, although the FBI investigation may yet turn up reliable evidence (Becker 2017; Kiely 2017; Elgin and Silver 2017).

These and other examples point to how Big Data may potentially cause distortions not only in economic life but also in the functioning of liberal democracy itself.

The social implications, risks, and threats are manifold. Due to the lack of transparency, users lose control, and cannot verify whether data are correct or false. Gaping power asymmetries between companies and users carry the risk of discrimination, exclusion and the individualisation of risks. This can be due to incorrect data and false forecasts, and/or spurious correlations, but also to 'correct' risk assessments. It might certainly be appropriate to match credit lending with predictions about whether a person will be able to repay the loan. However, for the lower strata, classification and categorisation implies stigmatisation and possibly exclusion. Descriptions of low economic and social status become ascriptions and prescriptions of (lack of) social and economic usefulness; creditworthiness becomes socialworthiness, especially when data are decontextualised and/or repurposed. Disregard of data protection laws by companies is hard to prosecute, as many aspects of data collection and processing are kept secret. Moreover, there is the danger of data misuse and theft, even if data were correctly and legally assembled. State access to the data collected by companies is a danger disclosed prominently by Edward Snowden (Greenwald 2014; Rosenbach and Stark 2014; GitHub 2017; Bauman *et al.* 2014; see also Tøndel and Sætnan, Chapter 10 in this volume). All this may lead to a loss of trust in communication technologies, arising from the very real threats to democracy as well as to individuals' freedom and autonomy.

Democratic societies – as yet – do not have plans and structures to establish a generalised and centralised 'Social Score', as envisioned and planned by the Chinese government. Most governments have not (yet) used such masses of data for control of the populace. If we do not act to prevent it, however, not only governments but also even commercial companies may attempt to do so. Google, Facebook, Amazon and Apple do have billions of users – more than any nation state. And they possess intimate data about search histories, personal interests and aversions, strengths and weaknesses. These platforms may soon become another powerful player in the commercial sector. If people and governments do not take preventive actions, those in possession of such data troves may eventually turn them into new sources of revenue and value chains (Morozov 2017), used in sub-companies in the health, traffic, and other sectors or for surveillance and behaviour manipulation (Zuboff 2015). Therefore, it is necessary to impose the rule of law before further harms are inflicted.

Big Data and the workplace

In Europe, the development of digital profiles and Big Data-based findings on sensitive personal information have so far been discussed mainly as topics of privacy, data protection or surveillance. Meanwhile, in the US, the debate has become more focused on questions of social inclusion and exclusion via Big Data analytics. This was extensively discussed in two reports from the Obama White House – the Podesta reports (White House 2014 and 2016) – as well as in a report by the US Federal Trade Commission (2016). The introductory statement used strong wording: 'Big data analytics have the potential to eclipse longstanding civil rights protections in how personal information is used in housing, credit, employment, health, education, and the marketplace' (White House 2014: i).

Many of these aspects have already been tackled in the previous sections. I will here focus on Big Data and the workplace. Digitisation and Big Data are changing not only the content and organisation forms of work, but also how workers are recruited and evaluated. Algorithmic estimates of qualifications and predictive analyses of performance are already used in job assessment centres and the selection of job applicants.

In theory, Big Data could serve to disclose existing discrimination, making access to jobs more egalitarian. However, Big Data also has the potential to exacerbate discrimination by introducing inequality into more and more social areas and pretending to make personality assessments computable. Furthermore, the pursuit of efficiency and effectiveness in decision-making encourages expansion of Big Data beyond recruitment and into work performance evaluation.

Personality profiles can rather easily be created on the basis of social media data. One influential study by Michal Kosinski combined easily accessible digital records of behaviour, Facebook likes – with demographic profiles and some psychometric tests. In 82% of the cases, the model correctly discerned their religious affiliation (Christian or Muslim), their skin colour ('Caucasian' or African-American, 95%), their political orientation (Democrat or Republican, 85%), the sexual orientation of men (88% of the cases), and alcohol and cigarette use (between 65% and 75% of the cases). The study showed that Facebook likes, 'can be used to automatically and accurately predict a range of highly sensitive personal attributes including: sexual orientation, ethnicity, religious and political views, personality traits, intelligence, happiness, use of addictive substances, parental separation, age, and gender' (Kosinski *et al.* 2013: 5802).[2]

Nowadays, job applicants are being profiled using references, prior employment, credit rating, driving record, criminal record, credit history, Facebook pages, and other sources that can impact hiring decisions. Human Resources departments use computer games and tests to measure memory, creativity, knowledge and cognition, emotional intelligence, and employees' willingness to take risks (Gumbus and Grodzinsky 2015). In assessment centres, sentiment analyses (tone, mood, vocabulary, emotions) are also applied, and probabilities for depression and other physical disorders are calculated. Such personality tests in hiring processes predate Big Data by decades but are now being refined in granularity and expanded by Big Data analytics (White House 2016).

Do these instruments lead to 'more objective' selection processes, or do they merely 'rationalise' (in both senses of the word) discrimination? A number of studies have shown that Big Data applications can reinforce bias, and distortions in data sets can exacerbate it. Historical prejudices set implicit but unrecognised and unconfronted marks on data used for training and machine learning. Thus inputs or results from the past are reproduced in the outputs of an algorithmic system. For example, patterns in which mothers were excluded from jobs or only given part-time jobs can be prolonged through algorithms that make career predictions based on number of children, employee's gender, and previous employment (Barocas and Selbst 2016: 689). People who identify themselves as female in their Google advertising settings and then search for jobs through Google receive fewer adverts for high paying, career advancement jobs than male users (Datta *et al.* 2015: 92).

According to anti-discrimination laws in place in many Western countries, age or gender discrimination is prohibited in the selection of personnel. However, indicators that allow inferences about gender and age can be used as proxies, and thus discriminatory preferences with respect to ethnicity, sex, age, or sexual orientation (Barocas and Selbst 2016: 692f) can be masked in the choice of job applicants (Hofstetter 2016: 380).

These analyses and results point to huge discrimination potentials in the working world. However, it is necessary to ask whether and to what extent analyses derived from the US apply to Europe. There is also the question of whether and how possible violations of anti-discrimination laws can be assessed and proven. In normative terms, Big Data-based discrimination in the labour market is countered by ethical demands for the preservation of human autonomy (Zuboff 2015), social solidarity (Rouvroy 2016), and fairness (Schneider and Ulbricht 2017), but Big Data algorithms remain business secrets and thus opaque.

Big Data has already entered the workplace and will in the future have further transformative effects that are difficult to anticipate. In general, some scholars have predicted a massive loss of jobs due to digitisation and Big Data analytics. Even though some of these extrapolations will probably prove overly pessimistic, we should also not underestimate the implications of digital transformation. Of course, automation is an opportunity to get rid of tedious, monotonous jobs, replacing human labour with digital production processes. In theory, people then might dedicate themselves to more important and creative matters. However, there is also the threat that humans will be devalued, marginalised, and that an ever stronger social division will occur between highly qualified people occupying high-pay jobs and people living in increasingly precarious terms of employment. If unemployment rises substantially, there is also a risk of social destabilisation, a rise of populist movements, political polarisation, pressure on welfare systems and a growing social divide. If automated jobs are not replaced by new ones, inequality and social gaps will increase. However, discussing the implications of digitisation on the labour market must be left to further analysis, as it goes beyond the scope of this book.

Fragmentation and polarisation of society

Online analytical processing, profiling, and data mining focus on past performance; predictive analytics forecasts future behaviour in order to inform and guide decisions. Data mining and correlation studies claim to tell what happened while predictive analytics claims to give advice on appropriate responses and actions. Key results such as trends, metrics, and performance indices are portrayed in scorecards and dashboards. Thus, Big Data develops a temporality of its own. Here, it must be stated that recorded data analysed by Big Data analytics behave differently than human memory, which fades and dynamically restructures events and information. As stored digital data biographies barely age, life plans and future options, opportunities and perspectives may become increasingly determined by data shadows and digital doppelgangers. Digital echo chambers exist not only with respect to attitudes and opinions. They may also be produced by fine-grained classifications converted into social capsules. Paradoxically, options are both augmented and narrowed down by digital means of Big Data analytics, possibly leading to the 'fragmentation and tribalisation' (Mau 2017: 278) of modern societies in the formerly so much hailed 'global village', as created by the Internet. Whether Big Data analytics actually allows for more personal freedom and self-expression needs to be questioned. It may also create ever-smaller segments of life worlds, micro-environments and social enclaves. Social status acquired by scores, ratings and ranks, as dynamic and unstable they seem to be, may also result in inescapably captivating fixations (Mau 2017: 279).

For those on the upper and lower end of rankings and reputation hierarchies, it is not unreasonable to assume that self-enforcing effects and vicious circles take effect: The age-old adage that 'success breeds success' was recently tested in a study using website-based experiments. Researchers found that early success bestowed on individuals produced significant increases in subsequent rates of success, in comparison to non-recipients of success (van de Rijt *et al.* 2014). For sociologists, the Matthew effect of accumulated advantage[3] as coined by Robert Merton (1968) and Harriet Zuckerman, is an effect often studied, described and confirmed. It will likely also be operant in social stratifications based on Big Data analytics. High reputation scores breed gratification revenues and tend to influence the wider communication system, playing a part in social selection processes and resulting in a concentration of resources. Vice versa, low scores lead to systematic disadvantage and downward spirals. Inequality regimes thus tend towards solidification (Mau 2017: 284). In effect, unless counteracting social measures are taken, social inequality gaps may widen.

Summing up: Big Data and social sorting reconsidered

David Lyon has long warned about 'social sorting' processes as powerful 'means of creating and reinforcing long-term social differences' and 'means of verifying identities but also of assessing risks and assigning worth'. He has rightly emphasised that questions of 'how categories are constructed therefore become significant ethical and political questions' (Lyon 2003: i). However, it is not only classification schemes themselves that should be critically questioned. The *effects* of classification and subsequent grading must also be revealed and assessed by social science scholars. Employers and private insurances will be inclined to use data made available to them. When Big Data reveals information about health status and disease predisposition, this can expose individuals and even their families to workplace or health discrimination. Creating 'at risk' categories for health will only be useful for individuals if adequate measures of prevention or therapy are available. Some such 'at risk' categories may reinforce racial and ethnic stereotypes (Lyon 2003: 4). Granular resolution of risk collectives in ever-smaller segments and sub-populations erodes collectives of solidarity (Mau 2017: 248) and may thus diminish social and institutionalised social solidarity, as inherent in the European social model.

Many scholars have pointed to these implications of algorithms and the choices made through them. What has been emphasised is the embedded values and biases inherent not only in algorithmic decision-making but also in novel forms of data processing, semantic analysis and so-called artificial intelligence and deep learning. Bolukbasi *et al.* (2016), for instance, revealed the hidden gender stereotypes in machine learning and word embedding, and the risk of amplifying biases present in data. Applying machine learning to ordinary human language already results in 'human-like semantic biases', as has also been shown by Caliskan *et al.* (2017).

Another point worth mentioning is how rationalisation and quantification processes tend to erase human judgement, ignoring the complexity of situations, events, or specific contexts. This raises complex questions of accountability and adequate policy responses (Lane *et al.* 2014; Amoore 2013; Pasquale 2015).

To conclude, Big Data analytics, if applied broadly and without thoughtful reflection, has the potential to perpetuate, reinforce and exacerbate social divides and inequalities. Increased social inequality has been known to negatively affect democratic societies, becoming a source of social unrest, nourishing populism, discouraging trust in fairness and opportunities for upwards social mobility, and eroding social solidarity, support, and the quest for the common good.

However, it is also important to stress that algorithms are neither fully automated nor omnipotent. Even though social sorting is often 'accomplished by means of remote networked databases', such categorisation and classification takes place

> in socio-technical systems by human agents and software protocols and are subject to revision, or even removal. And their operation depends in part on the ways that surveillance is accepted, negotiated, or resisted by those whose data is being processed.
>
> (Lyon 2003: 8)

Therefore, social analyses must not fall prey to assumptions of irreversibility or unchangeability of the current Big Data-based capitalist model, but stress varieties of social forms and political interventions into the processes of data accumulation and platform business. It would be outright wrong to conceive of current business models as immutable. Here is the right place to discuss regulation.

Regulation – efforts and approaches in the European Union

Some observers blame the enormous power asymmetries between Internet platform industries, users, and the state for insufficient regulation of Big Data capitalism (Zuboff 2015). Others suspect that there is not enough political willingness to regulate Internet giants because politicians are trapped into the belief that Big Data creates jobs and economic growth ('the new oil' – see Rieder Chapter 6 in this volume). Expected benefits of Big Data analytics for security policy are another reason for low regulation.

Massive lobbying efforts of Internet and telecommunication firms are also often referred to for gaps in regulation (Albrecht 2015; Pasquale 2015; Wever 2014). In the second quarter of 2017, Google spent more than US$6 million, more than any other company in the US, on lobbying (Taplin 2017a). The five major US technology firms – Facebook, Apple, Microsoft, Amazon, and Google – had spent US$49 million on lobbying by 2015, more than twice as much as the top five banks (Mohsin 2017). The Campaign for Accountability, a US non-profit group, found that under President Obama's administration, Google employees had 427 visits to the White House (Felschen 2017). In Europe, lobbying by Silicon Valley firms is also very much on the rise. According to a report by Transparency International EU, Google and Facebook are the two companies spending the most on lobbying the European Union in 2017, at

€4.25 million and €1 million respectively. Google's lobby spending has increased 240% since 2014. Disclosures indicate that Google has met with Commissioners and their closest advisors 142 times between 2014 and 2017. Four out of seven lobbyists currently accredited with the European Parliament have been hired directly from the Parliament to lobby their former colleagues (Kergueno 2017). Nonetheless, there is growing social pressure for better regulation.

While the first part of this chapter has demonstrated some impacts of Big Data-based digital capitalism, the second part is dedicated to efforts to regain some control, to counteract undesirable effects and to preserve central pillars of democratic liberty and fair societal structures.

To date, there is a widespread uneasiness about problematic aspects of Big Data, ranging from concerns about the opacity of analytics and prediction and the power of large platforms to the unknown effects on the social fabric. Many of these concerns are expressed in a 2017 Resolution of the European Parliament on Big Data. The MEPs stated that,

> the big data sector is growing by 40% per year, seven times faster than the IT market (...) triggering unprecedented shifts in the balance of power between citizens, governments and private actors; whereas such concentration of power in the hands of corporations might consolidate monopolies and abusive practices and have a detrimental effect on consumers' rights and fair market competition (...) interests of the individual and the protection of fundamental rights should be further scrutinized in the context of big data mergers.
>
> (European Parliament 2017: K–L)

While the Parliament stresses that Big Data

> has huge untapped potential as a driver of productivity and a means of offering better products and services to citizens; [it] underlines, however, that the generalised use of smart devices, networks and web applications by citizens, businesses and organisations does not necessarily indicate satisfaction with the products offered, but rather a broader understanding that these services have become indispensable to live, communicate and work, despite a lack of understanding about the risks that they might pose to our well-being, security and rights.
>
> (European Parliament 2017: K–L)

In addition, the Parliament underlines 'that compliance with the existing data protection legislation, together with strong scientific and ethical standards, are key to establishing trust in and the reliability of big data solutions' (European Parliament 2017: 2).

Loss of trust in digital environments and online platforms

As a result of such concerns, according to a 2015 study from the Pew Research Center, 91% of US adults believe they've lost control over how their personal information is collected and used. Sixty-four per cent believe the government should do more to regulate advertisers, compared with 34% who think the government should not get more involved (Gao and Madden 2017).

European citizens' trust in digital environments also seems to be very low – at least according to the results of a Eurobarometer study on data protection in 2015. According to this survey, conducted in March 2015 with almost 28,000 face-to-face interviews across the European Union, two-thirds of the respondents (67%) are worried about having no control over the information they provide online, while only 15% feel they have complete control. Six out of ten respondents do not trust online businesses, and seven out of ten people are concerned about their information being used for a different purpose from the one collected for. Six out of ten respondents say that they do not trust online businesses (63%), or phone companies and Internet service providers (62%). Respondents also have serious questions about the consequences of their data being collected, processed and used. Seven out of ten people are concerned about their information being used for a different purpose from the one it was collected for. Furthermore, citizens overwhelmingly believe that the protection of personal data should not be confined by national borders. Nine out of ten Europeans (89%) believe that they should have the same level of protection over their personal information, regardless of the country in which the authority or private company processing their data is based (Eurobarometer 2015).

Another Eurobarometer on online platforms was carried out in the 28 EU Member States in April 2016. The nearly 28,000 respondents revealed interesting results in digital literacy as well as attitudes towards those platforms. Nearly nine in ten Internet users use search engine websites at least once a week, and six in ten Internet users use an online social network on a weekly basis. In general, attitudes to search engines are positive: at least seven in ten respondents usually find what they are looking for when searching online (71%), while close to six in ten (59%) trust that the search results provided are the most relevant. However, only little more than half (53%) can clearly distinguish between sponsored and non-sponsored results. Opinion is also divided on the reliability of review rankings or online rating systems: 43% think they are reliable while 33% consider them unreliable.

Considering the extraction of personal data, almost two-thirds of respondents (64%) are aware that the Internet experience can be different for each user based on their prior online activities. At least half are concerned about the data collected on them when they are online. Therefore, there is a growing demand for regulation. Over half of all respondents (55%) agree that online platforms should be regulated by public authorities to limit the extent to which they display different search results to users based on the data collected about them. Only a minority (30%) are comfortable that search engines use information about their online activity and personal data to tailor advertisements or content to their interests. Just over one-quarter are comfortable with this fact when it comes to online marketplaces (27%) or social networks (26%) (Eurobarometer 2016).

These opinions have to be addressed by policymakers if they want to maintain credibility, ensure continued trust in online activities, and provide for the accountability of platform industries.

There are a number of political initiatives attempting to re-regulate what seems to have got out of control. In the following, I will address some actors and initiatives, which may gain influence in coming years, thereby potentially having an impact on the behaviour of important players in Big Data economics. I will start with some national activities of data protection agencies.

Coordinated action of national data protection authorities vis-à-vis Facebook

In reaction to Facebook's global revision of its data policy, cookie policy and terms, on 13 November 2014, the Data Protection Authorities of the Netherlands, France, Spain, Hamburg (Germany), and Belgium created a contact group. The members of the group have initiated national investigations on the quality of the information provided to users, the validity of consent and the processing of personal data for advertising purposes (CNIL 2017a).

In September 2017, the Spanish Data Protection Agency (AEPD) imposed on Facebook a penalty of €1.2 million. AEPD said it found three cases in which Facebook had collected data on ideology, sex, religious beliefs, personal preferences, and/or browsing activity of its millions of Spanish users without clearly informing them how and for what purpose such information would be used. According to the AEPD, Facebook did not sufficiently inform users about how it would use data collected on third-party websites, and did not obtain unambiguous, specific, and informed consent to use it. The AEPD also confirmed that users are not informed that their information will be processed through the use of cookies when browsing non-Facebook pages containing the 'like' button, a situation which also occurs when users are not members of the social network. Finally, the agency verified that Facebook does not delete the browsing information that it collects, but retains and reuses it later (AEPD 2017).

In May 2017, the French Privacy Authority, CNIL, imposed a sanction of €150,000 against Facebook. These fines were an outcome of coordinated action by the authorities of the above-mentioned contact group, that also initiated their respective investigation procedures to the company (CNIL 2017b).

In Germany in September 2016, Hamburg's Commissioner for Data Protection and Freedom of Information, Johannes Caspar, in order to protect the privacy of Germany's 35 million WhatsApp users and that of people saved in each user's address books, stopped Facebook from collecting user data from its WhatsApp messenger app and ordered the company to delete any data it had already received. Caspar stressed that Facebook had neither obtained an effective ex ante approval from the WhatsApp users, nor did any other legal basis for the data reception exist. He also recalled that at Facebook's 2014 acquisition of WhatsApp, it had promised that they would not share user data. In April 2017, the Hamburg Administrative Court confirmed the decision; Facebook appealed. (Gibbs 2017).

The fines imposed by the data protection authorities will not hurt Facebook profoundly; it had a turnover of more than US$25 billion and profits of US$10 billion in 2016. Whether the privacy authorities will ultimately succeed before the courts is also uncertain, as Facebook points to its main company seat in Ireland, claiming that other national authorities have no legal competence. Nevertheless, the fines have a decisive symbolic value. They disclose that Facebook's business model is still acting in a legal limbo. Various court proceedings are pending. As of May 2018, European supervisory authorities will also have the opportunity of stronger enforcement as they then can impose much higher penalties. We now, therefore, move on to the new regulation.

The EU General Data Protection Regulation

An important response to the challenges posed by digitalisation and Big Data is the EU data protection reform, which tries to allow innovation and protect fundamental rights at the same time. To achieve this, the established principles of European data protection law are to be preserved but applied in new ways (EDPS 2015: 16). The new Regulation will become effective from 25 May 2018.

Content of the data protection reform

The General Data Protection Regulation (Regulation (EU) 2016/679, hereafter GDPR), as is its official name, is a regulation by which the European Union intends to strengthen and unify data protection (EU 2016). The GDPR is seen as an essential step to (i) strengthen and enforce citizens' fundamental rights and control over personal data in the digital age, (ii) harmonise laws within the EU, and (iii) allow innovation and facilitate compliance by simplifying the regulatory environment for international business, thus allowing for the free movement of personal data in the EU's Digital Single Market. The reform is the preliminary end of a long negotiation process starting in January 2012, when EU Justice Commissioner Viviane Reding presented her first legislative proposal. For four years – accompanied by strong lobbying efforts, and more than 4,000 controversial text amendments – the GDPR took its course through the European Parliament guided by the rapporteur Jan Philipp Albrecht, then via the Council of the European Union and the European Commission, before being finally adopted on 27 April 2016 (European Commission 2017a). Unlike an EU directive, the GDPR does not require any enabling legislation to be passed by national governments and is thus directly binding and applicable. As a single law, the GDPR promises also to do away with the current fragmentation and some costly administrative burdens within the EU. The GDPR is complex and extensive, comprising 173 Recitals and 99 Articles.[4] Despite its length and comprehensiveness, it contains 70 so-called 'opening clauses', which allow further interpretation by national legislation.

The main points of the GDPR, as concerns the focus of this chapter, are those defining the digital rights and freedoms of citizens vis-à-vis large platform industries, and aimed at protecting and enforcing those rights. The GDPR in itself replaces the former 1995 EU Data Protection Directive. It preserves and updates the principles set up in previous European data protection legislation and jurisdiction. It sets out the rights of the individual and establishes the obligations of those processing the data, and those responsible for the processing of the data. It also establishes the methods for ensuring compliance as well as the scope of sanctions for those in breach of the rules.

The fundamental principles of established EU data protection law have not been altered but have been refined (EU 2016). Amongst those are:

1   the principle of informed consent, that is, that collection and processing of personal data is only lawful when those affected provide a 'freely given, specific, informed and unambiguous indication of the data subject's wishes by which he or she, by a statement or by a clear affirmative action, signifies agreement to the processing of personal data relating to him or her' (Article 4(11));
2   the right to disclosure, correction and erasure of collected personal data;
3   the requirement that data must be collected for a specified, explicit and legitimate purpose ('purpose limitation');
4   'data minimisation', which means that further processing of data must be adequate, relevant and limited to what is necessary in relation to the purposes for which they are processed (Articles 5 and 6).

With those stipulations, the rights of the data subject, that is, the individual whose personal data is being processed, have been modernised and strengthened – at least on paper. The aim of these rights is to give individuals more control over their personal data, including easier access by the subject to his or her personal data, the rights to rectification, to erasure and 'to be forgotten' (Articles 16–19), the right to object, including to the use of personal data for the purposes of 'profiling' (Article 21), and the right to 'data portability' from one service provider to another (Article 20). The Regulation also lays down the obligation for controllers (those responsible for the processing of data) to provide transparent and easily accessible information to data subjects on the processing of their data (Council of the EU 2016).

In order to enforce these rights and to ensure compliance, the Regulation details the general obligations of the controllers and of those processing the personal data on their behalf ('processors'). These include the obligation to implement appropriate security measures, according to the risk involved in the data-processing operations they perform ('risk-based approach'). Controllers are also required in certain cases to provide notification of personal data breaches.

All public authorities and those companies that perform certain risky data-processing operations will also need to appoint a data protection officer.

With respect to monitoring and compensation, the Regulation confirms the existing obligation for each EU member state to establish an independent supervisory authority at national level. Furthermore, it aims at establishing mechanisms to create consistency in the application of data protection law across the EU. In particular, in important cross-border cases where several national supervisory authorities are involved, a single supervisory decision is taken. This principle, known as a 'one-stop-shop mechanism', means that a company with subsidiaries in several member states will only have to deal with the 'lead supervisory authority', in most cases the data protection authority in the member state of its main establishment as single agency, and must not also negotiate with those in other countries. The GDPR includes the establishment of a European Data Protection Board consisting of representatives of all 28 (after Brexit: 27) independent supervisory authorities. In any given case, the Board should, within a determined period of time, issue an opinion. It is also empowered to adopt legally binding decisions.

The GDPR also recognises the right of data subjects to have recourse to a supervisory authority, as well as their right to judicial remedy, compensation, and in liability issues. To ensure proximity for individuals in the decisions that affect them, data subjects will have the right to have a decision of their data protection authority reviewed by their national court. This is irrespective of the member state in which the data controller concerned is established (Council of the EU 2016).

The GDPR also implements requirements for privacy by design and privacy by default. According to these, data processors and IT systems developers must take

> appropriate technical and organisational measures for ensuring that, by default, only personal data which are necessary for each specific purpose of the processing are processed. That obligation applies to the amount of personal data collected, the extent of their processing, the period of their storage and their accessibility. In particular, such measures shall ensure that by default personal data are not made accessible without the individual's intervention to an indefinite number of natural persons.
>
> (Article 25)

The aim here is to ensure that a strict principle of purpose limitation applies, and that only data genuinely required to provide the service are collected. This is intended to prevent services being used for excessive data collection on the basis of a single request for consent. It also aims to allow anonymous or pseudonymous use of services (Albrecht 2015: 11).

Amongst the major innovations in the GDPR are severe sanctions against controllers or processors who violate data protection rules. Companies can face fines of up to €20 million or 4% of their total worldwide annual turnover of the preceding financial year, whichever is higher (Article 83). These administrative sanctions are to be imposed by the national data protection authorities. The threat of such high sanctions is considered a very sharp sword and is expected to serve as a means to make companies, especially large platforms, comply with the rules.

Finally, the GDPR also covers the transfer of personal data to third countries and international organisations. To this end, it puts the European Commission in charge of assessing the level of protection given by a territory or processing sector in a third country and of ensuring that EU privacy laws are respected. Where the European Commission has not taken an adequacy decision on a territory or sector, transfer of personal data may still take place in particular cases or when there are appropriate safeguards (standard data protection clauses, binding corporate rules, contractual clauses). In addition, and complementary to the GDPR, the transfer of data between the European Union and the United States is regulated in agreements, in particular by the EU–US 'Privacy Shield' framework, which has replaced the International Safe Harbor Privacy Principles, which were declared invalid by the European Court of Justice in October 2015.

Other important innovations are the statutory provisions on the territorial scope of the GDPR, especially for companies located outside of the EU, as laid down in Article 3(2). The GDPR applies to any company located anywhere in the world that offers goods or services in the EU or monitors the behaviour of EU citizens, regardless of whether or not it has a presence in Europe or whether or not processing of personal data takes place in the EU. In other words, the GDPR stipulates, following the principle of *lex loci solutionis*, that all companies in the world must comply with the uniform rules set out in the GDPR when processing personal data, while offering their goods and services on the European common market. These stipulations on the territorial scope, if adequately enforced, may have a strong leverage effect on the activities of large Internet platforms. They were taken because data, unlike the traditional circulation of goods, crosses borders in milliseconds and is stored in 'clouds', making it increasingly difficult to tell where exactly personal data are saved. Moreover, in the past, companies whose business is based on data aggregation found it very easy to say that (strict) national data protection laws had no bearing on them because the data are being processed in Ireland or in the US (Albrecht 2015: 17). With the GDPR taking effect, if companies do not comply, they are liable for penalties that are uniformly high across the whole of the EU and can be enforced worldwide.

To sum up, the GDPR takes a carrot-and-stick approach: It offers companies uniform and clarified legal rules for their actions, gives incentives for high data protection standards, and provides for high sanctions to make them comply with the rules. As it covers all companies offering products and services in the European Union, regardless of whether they are located within or outside of Europe, it provides for a level playing field. One of the guiding ideas of the GDPR has been to encourage companies to set high data protection standards, and to initiate a race to the top in this regard. As the EU is a large market with more than 500 million citizens – possible customers – the GDPR aims at creating conditions which make progressive data protection a competitive advantage. Furthermore, the GDPR may serve as a reference model for other countries.

Assessment of the data protection reform

In conclusion, it can be stated that the GDPR unifies data protection law in the European Union. At least for some countries, the level of data protection is raised. However, the GDPR is complex and contains many political compromises between the European Parliament and the Council. As a consequence, there are many general clauses that need further interpretation. The GDPR comprises 70 so-called 'opening clauses' which need further determination by the national legislators, data protection authorities and courts. Therefore, as so much discretionary power has been left to national authorities, it is questionable whether the goal of legal harmonisation and unification has indeed been achieved.

To what extent the freedom, fundamental rights, and informational self-determination of citizens in the digital age will actually be strengthened, will very much depend on the future implementation of the GDPR. As yet, it is still 'dead-letter law'. It needs to become 'law in practice'.

Particularly as concerns Big Data analyses, the GDPR does not contain any definition or special wording. The term Big Data does not even appear in the legal text. Profiling, however, is defined in Article 4 (4) and rather extensively addressed in several Recitals and other Articles.[5] Article 22 relatively strictly regulates automated individual decision-making, including profiling. Moreover, profiling practices are subject to data protection impact assessment requirements according to Articles 35 (3) a, and 47 (2) e and f. Such clauses, if interpreted broadly, may provide more protection to citizens, and even be used against unfair discriminatory practices.

In addition, Recital 32 may be read as a prohibition on current practices of terms and conditions for apps and services that, in practice, imply a waiver of rights. Here, the regulation says: 'Silence, pre-ticked boxes or inactivity should not therefore constitute consent. Consent should cover all processing activities carried out for the same purpose or purposes' (Recital 32). Contrary to the strong wording on individual, and purpose-bound consent, however, Article 6 (4) in combination with Recital 50 might be used as a blanket clause for third-party uses of personal data without explicit consent. Recital 50 states, 'The processing of personal data for purposes other than those for which the personal data were initially collected should be allowed only where the processing is compatible with the purposes for which the personal data were initially collected.' Article 6 (4) specifies that the link, the context, the nature, and possible consequences of the intended further processing for data subjects as well as appropriate safeguards like encryption or pseudonymisation should be taken into account. It is questionable, however, whether this constitutes indeed an adequate, 'necessary and proportionate measure in a democratic society' (Article 6(4)) if such decision-making is left to large platform companies. Also the exemption from consent if 'processing is necessary for the purposes of the legitimate interests pursued by the controller or by a third party' (Article 6 (1) f) leaves the door wide open for a broad reading of 'legitimate interests' by the state and economic corporations (EU 2016).

In their appraisal, some observers have criticised the general focus on individual consent which forms the cornerstone of the GDPR, as individuals may be overstrained by this task – in particular, as the chains of processing and future analysing of data cannot be foreseen and algorithmic evidence-seeking cannot be observed. In their view, the GDPR should have taken more procedural measures to safeguard privacy and democratic values (Hofmann and Bergemann 2016). Such alternatives, however, would have to be spelled out more specifically.

Most notable is the extra-territorial scope of the GDPR, which obliges businesses and platform industries outside of the EU to obey EU rules, thus closing off corporate 'escape' strategies. Whether the cooperation and coherence mechanism of the supervisory data protection authorities (Articles 60 to 67) and the establishment of a European Data Protection Board (Articles 68 to 76) will be effective and lead to uniform and consistent application of the law, will need evaluation in due time. The new specifications on privacy by design and privacy by default, if implemented in practice, will also provide new opportunities to shift data protection upwards, potentially changing software programming practices for the benefit of the users.

To sum up, despite a number of shortcomings, the efforts taken, especially by the European Parliament, to pass a novel data protection law for Europe which keeps up with constant technical changes and with the dynamics of the Internet, and which affirms the digital rights of citizens, should be positively acknowledged. Many clauses may open litigation strategies for civil digital rights organisations and consumer protection agencies to combat adverse effects. All in all, the GDPR is certainly not the end but just the beginning of the ongoing project of 'civilising' Big Data capitalism.

Although the European regulatory debate has a clear focus on data protection, there are further regulatory deficits that cannot be regulated primarily by data protection. These include the aforementioned risk that Big Data can be used to discriminate groups or to manipulate individuals. Other potential negative societal consequences of Big Data include the shrinking and deteriorating public sphere and its fragmentation into ever-smaller filter bubbles (Zuiderveen Borgesius *et al.* 2016) as well as surveillance and intimidation with possible chilling effects on public speech and open deliberation (Lyon 2014; Yeung 2016).

Regulation by antitrust/competition law

Data protection is not the only form of regulation nor can it answer all forms of challenges posed by Big Data. Another type of regulation has thus started to address the power asymmetries between citizens, Internet platform corporations, and the state. Power gaps are due to many factors. One is lack of transparency when neither users nor supervisory authorities can know whether data on users are collected, managed, and used in accordance with the law. Another is the large resources corporations can use to defend their position in litigation. In terms of market capitalisation, Apple, Alphabet, Amazon, and Facebook occupy top ranks and today are the world's most valuable firms (Dolata 2017).

Market domination and numbers of users can be factors of power. Some market penetration shares are even more pronounced in Europe than in the US: In 2015, Google/Alphabet held 90% of the search market in the EU versus 76% in the US; Google's Android operating system had a 64% share in the EU as compared to 47% in the US. In the meantime, the numbers of users are rising: Each of Google's core services (Search, Chrome, Android, YouTube) now has more than a billion users; Gmail is only a hair's breadth away, with a total of 900 million active users each month (Anon 2015). In the United States, 71% of adults who use the Internet have a Facebook profile. Two billion monthly users make Facebook the largest social app in terms of logged-in users, above YouTube's 1.5 billion, WeChat's 889 million, Twitter's 328 million and Snapchat's estimated 255 million. Beyond YouTube (owned by Google/Alphabet), only Facebook's other apps have more than 1 billion users, including WhatsApp and Facebook Messenger, with 1.2 billion each. Instagram might soon also reach the billion as it recently rocketed past 700 million monthly users (Constine 2017).

Amazon's market penetration in the US is stronger than in Europe: In the United States, half of all online shopping searches start on Amazon. In 2016, it had over $63 billion in revenue from online sales in the US – more than the next 10 top online retailers combined. Amazon controls 74% of e-book sales and is the largest seller of clothes online in the US. Forty-three per cent of all online retail sales in the US went through Amazon in 2016 (Business Insider 2017). Amazon is also the most-visited online retailer in Europe (Ecommerce News 2017). Hardly known by a broader public, today Amazon is also one of the world's largest logistics networks and marketing platforms, as well as the dominant provider of cloud computing. Amazon not only hosts and transports goods but also directly makes and sells them. By integrating across business lines, Amazon now competes with the companies that rely on its platform. This has given rise to conflicts of interest, as it positions Amazon to give preferential treatment to itself. Amazon exploits data collected on the businesses using its platform to go head-to-head with them. Amazon dictates terms and prices to those dependent on its platform. Amazon's recommendation formulas determine whether customers see certain goods, and Amazon is capable of changing algorithms so that external retailers' sales can flow or dry up (Khan 2017).

These and other figures have alerted EU policymakers and company leaders. 'We don't want to be a digital colony of the U.S. Internet giants,' said former French Economy Minister Arnaud Montebourg in 2014. 'What's at stake is our sovereignty itself' (Stone and Silver 2017). And Mathias Döpfner, CEO of Axel Springer media company, wrote an open letter to Eric Schmidt titled 'Why We Fear Google'. He issued concerns regarding how Google will become a 'digital supra-state' and about the long-term integrity of the digital economy's ecosystem. This applies to competition, not only economic, but also political. It concerns our values, our understanding of the nature of humanity, our worldwide social order and, from our own perspective, the future of Europe.

He pronouncedly added, 'The question of who this data belongs to will be one of the key policy issues of the future' (Döpfner 2014).

It would be wrong to interpret these statements as simply a disguised form of protectionism. Often cast as a battle between a protectionist Europe and an innovative Silicon Valley, such Big Data struggles are better seen as a debate on which type of society we want to live in, and how to embed new digital technologies in social welfare types of market capitalism. Not least, it is also

a debate on what type of internet the world will end up with. A libertarian internet, where innovators break things first, and worry about the mess later? Or an internet that is mostly open, yet also managed with enforcement from regulators and self-regulatory action by companies?

(Heath 2017)

A regulatory approach taken by the European Commission and some national EU member states subsequent to such concerns is the antitrust law. Competition law promotes or seeks to maintain market competition by regulating anti-competitive conduct by companies. Market dominance and preventing the abuse of firms' dominant market positions are regulated under Article 102 of the EU Treaty (TFEU). Market dominance, as such, is not illegal under EU antitrust rules. Dominant companies, however, have a special responsibility not to abuse their powerful market position by restricting competition, either in the market where they are dominant or in separate markets. Otherwise, there would be a risk that a company once dominant in one market – even if this resulted from competition on the merits – would be able to use this market power to cement or even further expand its dominance, or to leverage it into separate markets. I now turn to several cases investigated under antitrust laws.

EU antitrust cases on Google

The European Commission has opened several proceedings against large platform companies like Google and Facebook. As yet, three cases against Google have been investigated (Stone and Silver 2017). Proceedings on the first one were opened in November 2010, following a number of complaints by European and US competitors. It related to the Google Search rankings in comparison shopping markets. The Commission investigated Google's market position in general Internet search in the EU since 2008, and found Google to be dominant in each country since 2008, except in the Czech Republic. Google's search engine has held consistently very high market shares in all European countries, exceeding 90% in most. Due to network effects, there are also high barriers to entry in these markets: the more consumers use a search engine, the more attractive it becomes to advertisers. Profits generated through ads can then be used to attract even more consumers. In addition, the user data a search engine gathers and analyses via Big Data tools can be used to improve algorithms and personalised search results.

The Commission found Google to have abused its market dominance in general Internet search by giving a separate Google product, namely 'Google Shopping' an illegal advantage in the separate comparison shopping market. According to the investigations, Google has systematically given prominent placement to its own comparison shopping service, while rival comparison shopping services have been subjected to demotions by at least two different algorithms. Evidence showed that even the most highly ranked rival comparison shopping service appeared on average only on page four of Google's search results, and others even further down. As a consequence, consumers very rarely saw rival comparison shopping services in Google's search results.

According to the Commission, this has had a significant impact on competition because of its impacts on user clicks and thus traffic: As studies have demonstrated, even on desktops, the ten highest-ranking generic search results on page one together generally receive approximately 95% of all clicks on generic search results, with the top search result actually receiving about 35% of all the clicks. The first result on page 2 of Google's search results receives only about 1% of all clicks. Given the much smaller screen size, the effects on mobile devices are even more pronounced.

As a result of Google's practices, Google's comparison shopping service made significant market share gains at the expense of rivals: It increased its traffic 45-fold in the United Kingdom and 35-fold in Germany. In contrast, traffic to certain rival websites decreased, following demotions applied in Google's generic search algorithms; evidence of sudden drops of 85% in the United Kingdom, 92% in Germany and 80% in France were given. All things considered, the Commission found that Google's practices deprived European consumers of the benefits of competition, namely genuine choice and innovation. Therefore, on 27 June 2017, the Commission fined Google €2.42 billion for breaching EU antitrust rules by abusing its dominant position in general Internet search, thereby stifling competition in comparison shopping markets. The fine was calculated on the basis of the value of Google's revenue from its comparison shopping service in the 13 European countries concerned. Google was ordered to stop its illegal practices within 90 days, and refrain from any measure that has the same or an equivalent object or effect. In particular, Google has to respect the principle of equal treatment (European Commission 2017b). Even more than the multibillion-euro fine, the Commission's instruction that Google change its algorithm matters, as it will cost it a lot more in the long term, and help its competitors.

On 11 September 2017, Google filed an appeal against the fine before the Court of Justice of the EU. The Luxembourg-based court is expected to take several years before ruling on Google's appeal. Google may be optimistic of a reversal since, in early September 2017, the European Court of Justice ordered a lower tribunal to re-examine Intel's appeal against a €1.06 billion fine, the previous record for an antitrust case (Boffey 2017).

Two other antitrust Google cases are under investigation by the Commission. These concern:

1   Google's Android operating system, which has a 64% share on smartphones in European countries. In April 2016, the Commission charged Google with abusing its dominant Android mobile operating system to shut out rivals. Google has been accused of limiting access to the Google Play Store unless phone makers also bundle Google search and Chrome apps. Google may be pursuing an overall strategy on mobile devices to protect and expand its dominant position in general Internet search (*The Verge* 2017; European Commission 2015b and 2016).
2   Google's 'AdSense for Search' platform, in which Google acts as an intermediary for websites such as online retailers, telecoms operators or newspapers. These searches produce results that include search ads. Here, the Commission is concerned that Google has reduced choice by preventing third-party websites from sourcing search ads from Google's competitors (Reuters 2017).

The Commission also continues to examine Google's treatment in its search results of other specialised Google search services. The high penalty in the first case (Google Shopping) is seen as a precedent that establishes a framework for the assessment of the legality of this type of conduct, which, however, does not replace case-specific analyses. Google has already been warned by the Commission that if found guilty of breaching EU antitrust rules, sanctions could reach 10% of the annual global turnover for each case. This could possibly hit hard: Alphabet made consolidated revenues of around US$90 billion in 2016 (Reuters 2017). Beyond the specifics of each case, these incidents could be a warning shot for other large platform industries not to abuse their dominant market position, which has largely been achieved due to network effects. It may thus trigger general deterring effects.

EU and national cases against Facebook

The European Commission has also flexed its muscle against Facebook. In this case, what is targeted is not abuse of dominant market share but acquisition strategy.

In 2014, Facebook bought the Internet messaging service WhatsApp for the record sum of US$19 billion (€13.8 billion). This extraordinary high sum was paid despite the fact that WhatsApp had only a low turnover of about US$10 million. The takeover itself was approved by the European Commission in 2014, despite strong criticism from consumer protection organisations. However, in May 2017, the social network was fined €110 million for giving misleading statements during the company's acquisition of WhatsApp (Scott 2017). When Facebook took over WhatsApp, it told the Commission it would not be able to match user accounts on both platforms, but went on to do exactly that. The Commission found that Facebook staff knew in 2014 that it was technically possible to link WhatsApp phone numbers with Facebook users' identities, contrary to their public statements about the merger (Rankin 2017).

The penalty is also meant to act as a warning for other companies, demonstrating that competition law is progressively used to enforce national and EU laws.

National antitrust cases in Europe and new regulatory approaches

Apart from the European Commission's cases, national antitrust inquiries are also underway. The German Federal Cartel Office (*Bundeskartellamt*) is investigating whether Facebook is abusing its dominant position by failing to inform people about how their personal data is being used. Similar investigations are also underway in Belgium, the Netherlands, and Spain (Rankin 2017). While the Commission is still pursuing a traditional investigation of abuse of market dominance, French and German antitrust authorities are trying to take this a step further. Their idea is to assess whether competition rules need to be updated to reflect the actual power of data-collecting companies. In particular, they ask whether privacy considerations should enter competition law, and whether another metric for fines should be applied. To this end, in May 2016, the French *Autorité de la concurrence* and the German *Bundeskartellamt* (2016b) published a joint paper on data collection in the digital economy and its implications for competition law. The paper discusses the various interfaces between Big Data and established concepts of competition law enforcement, and identifies key issues and parameters that may need to be considered when assessing the relevance of data for competition law enforcement. According to this paper, assessing why, how and to what extent the collection of (personal) data may become an instrument of market power needs to be determined to take into account the economic role of digital platforms and to foster a constructive policy debate. The challenge can be described as follows: Digital platforms and social media providers often offer their services free of charge. 'For consumers, therefore, personal information operates as a currency, and sometimes the sole currency, in the exchange of online services' (EDPS 2014: 10; see also Patterson 2017). According to current case law, however, free services are not considered a market, and thus cannot be pursued by antitrust law. Consequently, this raises the question whether free services required a price tag? The initial suspicion was that the terms and conditions for the use of respective platform services would violate valid data protection regulations. As user profiles for targeted advertising are created, those require the prior informed consent of the user. However, those terms are often lengthy, difficult to understand and it is hard to assess the scope of the agreement accepted by the users.[6] There is considerable doubt as to the admissibility of this procedure, in particular under applicable national data protection law. Thus, platforms may be accused of utilising their dominant market position to impose certain contractual provisions upon users, concerning the further use of their data, provisions that are unfair and disadvantageous for those users and violate or undermine data protection standards. When assessing the relevance of data for competition law enforcement, the joint paper of the authorities identified two aspects of particular relevance: (i) whether the data under consideration can easily be obtained by rivals and (ii) whether the scale and scope of data matter. As a result, the necessity of a differentiated approach and a case-by-case analysis is highlighted (Bundeskartellamt 2016b). In terms of practical action, the French *Autorité de la concurrence* announced the launch of a full-blown sector inquiry into data-related markets and strategies. The German *Bundeskartellamt* has already launched a proceeding against Facebook and will investigate whether Facebook has abused its possibly dominant position in the market for social networks with its specific terms of service on the use of user data. The infringement claims that Facebook does not properly inform its users about the type and extent of the collection and use of their personal data, and according to the accusation, thus undermines data protection law. The *Bundeskartellamt* will examine to what extent a connection exists between the possibly dominant position of the company and the use of such unlawful terms and conditions clauses. If there is a connection between such an infringement of data protection law and market dominance, this could also constitute an abusive practice under competition law (Bundeskartellamt 2016a).

Evaluation: the interface between data protection and competition law as a new regulatory path

The possibility of convergence between data protection, competition, and consumer policies provides interesting elements to reflect upon, while leaving open a number of theoretical challenges. Assessing mergers by using the metric of turnover fails to capture the potential of a tech start-up that has zero revenues, yet has high numbers of users and big market potential. Therefore, the number of consumers affected by a merger should be assessed in evaluating whether it would create a monopoly. However, it is very tricky to find a persuasive alternative metric to turnover for assets such as knowledge, patents, or data. 'We try to prepare ourselves to make sure we have the right set of glasses to make sure we can see what is going on when it comes to data,' EU commissioner Vestager promised. 'Data is a currency, it is a resource, it is an asset, and it will play an enormous role in the entire economy which is why with other colleagues here we are playing close attention to it' (Rankin 2017).

This approach constitutes a new regulatory perspective, as the interface between data protection and competition law is targeted, and hence competition law is extended. Competition regulation would not be based solely on the question of whether monopolistic structures are detrimental to consumers with regard to price and quality of products and services, but would also encompass the handling of their personal data (Pozzato 2014: 469). In addition, competition authorities may become active if competition between companies is jeopardised, in case some companies are complying with data protection rules and others are not. US Economist Eric Clemons, for example, has pointed to the fact that Google Search's dominant position in Europe is only partly based on technological superiority, and much more on the systematic breach of European data protection laws (Clemons 2015). If Google and other monopolists were required to adhere to the rules, other companies, such as those that pay particular attention to data protection and data security, would also have a chance to increase their market shares. Therefore, in 2014, the European Data Protection Supervisor (EDPS) issued a report in which he called for joined forces between antitrust, consumer welfare and data protection authorities, 'to facilitate a "race to the top" on privacy standards' (EDPS 2014: 33). More specifically, the EDPS focuses on abuse of dominance and merger control-related aspects, but also acknowledges the difficulties of identifying parameters on which to calculate market shares in free online services. What is also recognised is that the value of large data sets is not in the collection of data as such, but rather in the combination of aggregated data and Big Data tools to organise and exploit these data (Pozzato 2014: 469).

To this purpose, the German *Bundeskartellamt* in 2015 set up a think tank of lawyers and economists in order to establish criteria for assessing the market power of data-based platforms and networks. In their first report, they analysed problems and proposed possible conceptualisations to catch up with the peculiarities and challenges posed by the Big Data-based economy.

First, they call for including the non-monetary user side for the economic calculation of market power. Second, while some innovative start-ups that offer their products free of charge or have low sales are taken over by large, established companies, this has happened without the control of the antitrust authorities. The reason for this is that merger control so far has only included mergers of companies whose sales exceed a certain threshold. This is often not the case for start-ups. Nevertheless, due to their high market potential, their business ideas can have a great economic significance for the purchaser. Such acquisitions may also lead to an undesirable obstacle to effective competition. At present, it is uncertain whether non-monetary exchanges can also legally be regarded as markets. In order to overcome these uncertainties, the Federal Cartel Office sees the need for a legal clarification that takes transaction costs into account. Another proposal targets the thresholds in the merger control, which need to be complemented, according to the report. To allow adequate control by cartel authorities, they propose extending merger control to cases where the transaction value of a takeover is particularly high. Thus, it would be possible to record cases where a participating company generates no or only low turnover, but at the same time the competitive potential and market significance of the merger are particularly large. A third recommendation considers the clarification of market power criteria. Thus, according to the report, it should be clarified by law that the factors (a) direct and indirect network effects, (b) economies of scale, (c) the prevailing form of data usage and the degree of differentiation, (d) access to data, and (e) the potential for innovation in digital markets are particularly important when assessing the market position of a company that operates a platform or a network (Bundeskartellamt 2016c).

First legislative adaptations have followed. In Germany, on 9 March 2017, a novel act extended the criteria for merger control to cases in which the price for purchase is over US$400 million, despite small turnovers. In addition, non-remunerated services are taken into account, as well as cooperation in advertising, marketing and distribution (BmWi 2017).

It remains to be discussed whether these new conceptualisations will be adequate not only to assess but also to effectively tackle the new power asymmetries in the Big Data-based digital economy. While some scholars welcome the interplay between competition law, data protection, and consumer welfare, others warn that this would overstretch distinct legal categories and confuse their boundaries, with the effect of legal fuzziness (Kuner *et al.* 2014; Graef and Alsenoy 2016; Pozzato 2014; Ulbricht 2017). At the very least, these reports provide food for thought in the context of the ongoing policy debate on Big Data and digital platforms' economic role in contemporary capitalism.

Having contemplated data protection and competition law, I turn to another area of regulatory control that tackles high profit margins.

Another regulatory approach: combatting tax avoidance

Internet giants are well known for sophisticated tax avoidance strategies. Apple pays only 1%, Google 3%, and Amazon 5% on taxes abroad. Apple also keeps its cash reserve of US$150 billion abroad to avoid taxation in the US (Wever 2014: 222). Tax avoidance schemes by large platform corporations is another issue on which EU authorities have started to act. Companies like Google, Amazon, PayPal, eBay, Microsoft, Twitter and Facebook have been found to be using the so-called 'Double Irish With a Dutch Sandwich' scheme, which reduces taxes by routing profits through Irish subsidiaries and the Netherlands and then to the Caribbean. These and similar tax avoidance schemes have enabled the US-companies to pay little to no corporate tax across Europe (Bowers 2016).

Apple may serve as an example that will illustrate the concerns: Apple sells an iPhone for about US$650, while the costs for the physical parts amount to only US$200. The question is, how much of the difference of US$450 is due to knowledge, Big Data analytics, software or marketing and how much just due to profit and rent-seeking (Bernau 2017). Digital technology giants have taken advantage of the fact that some or even most of their profits derive not from physical goods but from software and royalties on intellectual property, like the patents on design or technical details or on software that makes devices work. Often, the products themselves are digital, like apps, search results, videos, or downloaded songs. It is relatively easy for businesses with royalties and digital products to move profits to low-tax countries like Ireland, the Netherlands, or to tax-free states like the Bahamas. Such arrangements also allow them to send patent royalties from one part of the company, for example, in California, to another overseas, in particular in Ireland (The 'First Irish'). As a result, some profits are taxed at the Irish rate of approximately 12.5%, rather than at the US statutory rate of 35%. Thus, in 2004 for instance, Ireland, a nation of less than five million inhabitants, was home to more than one-third of Apple's worldwide revenues. Moreover, another Irish subsidiary – the 'Double' – allows other profits to flow to tax-free companies in the Caribbean. Finally, because of Ireland's treaties with other EU members states, some of the companies' profits could travel virtually tax-free through the Netherlands – the 'Dutch Sandwich' – making them essentially invisible to outside observers and tax authorities (Kocieniewski and Duhigg 2012; *New York Times* 2012). Ireland thus, for many years, has worked both as a tax oasis and a data protection desert, due to its very low privacy standards.

Google is another prominent case. As a response and countermeasure to such tax avoidance schemes, in 2016, French tax authorities had been seeking €1.6 billion (US$1.76 billion) in back taxes from Google, which was criticised for its use of 'aggressive tax optimisation techniques'. However, in July 2017, Google won its fight against the French tax bill with the decision that Google Ireland Ltd. wasn't taxable in France over the period 2005–2010. The Paris administrative court rejected claims that the search engine giant abused loopholes to avoid paying its fair share. The judges ruled that Google's European headquarters in Ireland couldn't be taxed as if it also had a permanent base in France, as requested by the nation's administration (Sebag 2017). In the UK, on similar issues, Google reached a £130 million (US$181 million) settlement with British tax authorities for the period since 2005, which was criticised by British politicians as 'disproportionately small' (Agence France-Presse 2016).

But let us return to Apple. Measured in market capitalisation, Apple is the world's most valuable company. In August 2016, the European Commission ordered Apple to pay a record-breaking €13 billion in back taxes to Ireland, arguing that a tax deal between Apple and the Irish tax authorities amounted to illegal state aid. The Commission said the deal allowed Apple to pay a maximum tax rate of just 1%. In 2014, the tech firm paid tax at just 0.005%. As already mentioned, the usual rate of corporation tax in Ireland is 12.5%. The Commission said Ireland's tax arrangements with Apple between 1991 and 2015 had allowed the US company to attribute sales to a 'head office' that existed only on paper and could not have generated such profits. According to the Commission, the result was that Apple avoided tax on almost all profits generated from its multi-billion euro sales of iPhones and other products across the EU's single market. It booked the profits in Ireland rather than the country where the product was sold. Apple, which changed its tax arrangements with Ireland in 2015, should easily be able to pay the huge tax bill because in 2016, it owned a mountain of more than US$230 billion in cash and securities, mostly held outside the US. The tech group keeps the money outside the US because it incurred US tax charges if it repatriated the money. The €13 billion figure covers only the ten years before the Commission first requested information in 2013. The Commission, which does not have the authority to go back any further, said it was up to Ireland to collect the tax from Apple. The Irish government, however, wants the ruling reversed because it wants to preserve its status as a low-tax base for overseas companies. Apple and Ireland appealed against the ruling. EU commissioner Margrethe Vestager suggested other countries, including the US, might examine how Apple did business within their borders. These other jurisdictions might then claim a share of the unpaid tax from Apple for the same period. This would reduce the bill owed to Ireland (Farrell and McDonald 2017). However, the European Commission in October 2017 also filed the case at the CJEU, because Ireland resisted collecting the €13 million back taxes from Apple.

In 2016 alone, Apple made a profit of US$62 billion. Worldwide, Apple paid US$16 billion as company taxes, of which only US$2 billion were paid outside the US. In Germany, however, only €25 million were paid to the tax offices, which amounts to only 0.2% of Apple's tax burden. The US federal government levies high taxes on the domestic profit of Apple; the international profits, however, are only taxed when the company brings them home, which companies seek to avoid at any price. In 2016 alone, Apple saved US$5 billion in taxes by not bringing 'parked money' to the US (Bernau 2017).

In October 2017, the European Commission also ordered that Amazon must pay €250 million in back taxes to Luxembourg because of an illegal deal struck in 2003 (Smith 2017).

The EU Commission's rulings on Apple and Amazon send a warning to countries that facilitate hard-edged corporate tax minimisation strategies and are a serious attempt at curtailing the power that large digital platforms have in avoiding their tax liabilities. Whether such attempts will succeed will depend on the further willingness of the countries to engage in 'race to the bottom games' to attract foreign companies. As yet, the EU member states have not achieved a common strategy to shut down their tax havens. Brexit, however, might incite the UK to enter a new round of such tax undercutting. These national strategies undermine trust in fair taxation and just distribution of wealth. Tax evasion undermines social welfare and democracy. It demoralises citizens and erodes trust in the public good.

A new initiative on fair taxation was spearheaded by France and backed by Germany, Italy, Spain, Romania, Bulgaria, Slovenia, Greece, Portugal, and Austria at a gathering of EU finance ministers in Tallinn, Estonia in September 2017. The ten countries urged the European Commission to explore EU law compatible options for establishing an 'equalisation tax' based on turnover generated in Europe by the digital companies. Other EU countries like Luxembourg, however, expressed scepticism over the overhauling of a tax system that targets profits rather than revenue to make tech companies pay their fair share of taxes in Europe (Smith-Meyer *et al.* 2017).

Judicial regulation: the jurisdiction of the Court of Justice of the European Union

Another vital actor that may become more important in taming the powers and asymmetries of Big Data-based digital capitalism is the Court of Justice of the

European Union (CJEU). In past decades, the Court has often been criticised for fostering neoliberal policies. However, in several judgments in the area of digital rights and freedoms, the CJEU has gained a prominent profile as a fundamental rights court (Schneider and Rehder 2016). Due to restrictions in scope, this chapter cannot dig deeply into the judgements. But it will name at least some important decisions.

In April 2014, the CJEU (2014b) struck down the EU's Data Retention Directive (Digital Rights Ireland, Cases C-293/12 und C-594/12). Another ruling concerning Data retention and national law in December 2016, again reiterated the Court's strong reliance on the EU Charter of Fundamental Rights and further clarified what safeguards are required for data retention to be lawful (Joined Cases C-203/15 and C-698/15 Tele2 and Watson) (CJEU 2017c).

Google Spain v. *Gonzalez* was another landmark decision in 2014 (C-131/12). It held that an Internet search engine operator is responsible for the processing that it carries out, of personal information that appears on web pages published by third parties. The decision inferred from Article 7 (respect for private and family life) and Article 8 (protection of personal data) of the Charter of Fundamental Rights of the European Union that the data subject has a 'right to be forgotten'. Therefore, an Internet search engine must consider requests from individuals to remove links to freely accessible web pages resulting from a search on their name. Grounds for removal include cases where the search result(s) 'appear to be inadequate, irrelevant or no longer relevant or excessive in relation to those purposes and in the light of the time that has elapsed' (CJEU 2014c: 93). If the search engine rejects the request, the individual may ask relevant data protection authorities to consider the case. Under certain conditions, the search engine may be ordered to remove the links from search results (European Commission 2015a).

To allow individuals to exercise their right to be forgotten, Google has set up a removal request process available online. However, the review process is opaque to the general public. It is therefore unknown how Google weighs the damage to the person making the request against any public interest in the information being available. Some scholars have criticised that Google is performing sovereign tasks that should rather be performed by a state or a state-mandated agency. Another concern is the territorial scope of the delinkings. The European Commission has been pushing for the delinkings requested by EU citizens to be implemented by Google not just in European versions of Google (as in google.co.uk, google.fr, etc.), but on google.com and other international subdomains. Regulators want delinkings to be implemented globally, so that the law cannot be circumvented in any way. However, to date, Google has refused the French Data Protection Agency's demand to apply the right internationally.

The *Google Spain* v. *Gonzalez* case also codified the market location principle instead of the seat country principle. Operators of search engines thus must act according to the respective national data protection laws when they are processing data in Europe. As already mentioned, this principle was further codified in the General Data Protection Regulation.

A further important ruling of the CJEU (2014a) was *Max Schrems* v. *Data Protection Commissioner* (C-362/14). The final judgement in 2014 settled a complaint filed against Facebook Ireland by Austrian law student Max Schrems. The complaint aimed at prohibiting Facebook from further transferring data from Ireland to the United States, given the alleged involvement of Facebook USA in the PRISM mass surveillance programme. Schrems based his complaint on EU data protection law, which does not allow data transfers to non-EU countries, unless the data handler can guarantee 'adequate protection'. In October 2015, the CJEU decided the Safe Harbour framework to be invalid. It was later replaced by the EU–US Privacy Shield as a new framework for exchanges of personal data for commercial purposes between the EU and the US. The new Privacy Shield agreement, however, has been criticised by members of the European Parliament and by Max Schrems, who find citizens' data inadequately protected. Privacy Shield may also eventually be challenged before the CJEU.

One last case worth noting: in July 2017, the CJEU declared that the agreement envisaged between the EU and Canada on the systematic transfer, retention and use of all Passenger Name Record data of airlines may not be concluded in its current form, because several provisions of the draft agreement do not meet requirements stemming from the fundamental rights of the EU (CJEU 2017a and 2017b).

We can expect further litigation and judgments of the CJEU. The future will show whether the CJEU holds firm to European fundamental rights and freedoms and defends citizens from privacy intrusion.

Conclusion

We have seen that Big Data practices – whatever benefits they might confer in terms of convenience, medical discoveries, efficiency, etc. – also represent a number of threats to liberal democracy, civil society and to individuals' privacy, security, and social integration. In terms of political economy, digital platforms tend towards oligopolisation. Media pluralism and a deliberative public sphere is endangered. Big Data-related algorithmic ratings, rankings, and scorings expand competition, commodify social realities, produce new forms of subjectivation and moral ordering, and are prone to exacerbate power inequalities, thus possibly leading to further fragmentation and polarisation of society.

However, we have also seen that society and the state are not helpless or passive in the face of these threats. Nor are we relegated to dealing with them individually. Big Data has become a salient policy issue. Politicians, data protection agencies, cartel offices, and courts have started to engage with the challenges of Big Data-based digital capitalism.

Given strict enforcement, the General Data Protection Regulation may, if not eliminate, then at least mitigate, the most egregious practices of third-party tracking and open up ways to make corporate platforms' data practices more transparent and accountable. Furthermore, its impact may reach beyond the European Union. Antitrust measures from applying competition law and emerging interpretations of this law to include data protection and consumer rights are also innovative and promising steps forward. Authorities are also seeking ways to counteract tax avoidance – a category of ploys particularly available to companies dealing in 'virtual', abstract goods and services. Restricting tax avoidance is also important to hold companies accountable to contribute their fair share to infrastructure, welfare, and the common good. The jurisdiction of the CJEU is proving important to framing and executing Big Data politics in the framework of fundamental rights and freedoms, and not only in frameworks of innovation and economic growth.

So, even though ultimate answers to the political and social challenges of Big Data have not (yet) been found, step by step, incrementally, old regulations are being adapted and novel regulations are being developed to tame the disruptive and socially undesirable aspects of Big Data-based digital capitalism. Scholarly phantasy, political creativity, and civil society's inventiveness will further be necessary to provide compelling analyses and novel regulatory approaches.

Notes

1 Social scientists at Facebook had deliberately manipulated some people's news feeds to see what effect, if any, it had on their emotions. The resulting paper was a study of 'social contagion' of positive and negative posts (Kramer *et al.* 2014). It may be important to note that in another study that received much less public attention, researchers found that 1% increase in 'likes', clicks, and status updates was correlated with a 5 to 8% decrease in self-reported mental health. The study found that the positive effect of real-world interactions, which enhance well-being, was accurately paralleled by the 'negative associations of Facebook use' (Shakya and Christakis 2017).
2 It is worthwhile mentioning that Kolinski's data and analytics have also been used by Cambridge Analytica and are said to have contributed to the election victory of US president Donald Trump (Grasegger and Krogerius 2016).
3 The Matthew effect takes its name from the parable of the talents in the biblical Gospel of Matthew. It is named from the biblical sentence 'For he that hath, to him shall be given' (Matthew 25:29). Robert Merton credited his collaborator and second wife, sociologist Harriet Zuckerman, as co-author of the concept of the Matthew effect.
4 In EU law, a Recital sets out reasons and arguments formally given for the new legal act; conventionally, Recitals start with the word 'whereas'. In contrast to the Articles of a legal act, the Recitals in themselves are not binding EU law but should be taken into account by courts, lawyers, and the European Data Protection Board (EDPB), when interpreting the meaning of the General Data Protection Regulation.
5 Namely in Recitals 24, 60, 63, 70, 71, 72, 73, 91 as well as in Articles 13 (f) and in 14 (g), 15 (h) and 21 (1) and (2).
6 A study by McDonald and Cranor (2008: 18) has calculated that it would take on average each Internet user 244 hours per year, or 40 minutes a day, to read the privacy policy belonging to each website they view, which is more than 50% of the time (72 minutes a day) that the average user spends on the Internet. 'These policies typically contain statements about the future use of data which are concealed in legal small print or which require decoding due to vague, elastic terms like "improving customer experience"' (EDPS 2014: 34).

References

AEPD (Agencia Española de Protección de Datos) (2017). The Spanish DPA fines Facebook for violating data protection regulations. 11 September. Available at: www.agpd.es/portalwebAGPD/revista_prensa/revista_prensa/2017/notas_prensa/news/2017_09_11-iden-idphp.php. [Accessed 4 October 2017].

Agence France-Presse (2016). France to seek €1.6bn in back taxes from Google, says official. *Guardian*, 24 February. Available at: www.theguardian.com/technology/2016/feb/24/france-google-tax-avoidance-back-taxes. [Accessed 24 August 2017].

Albrecht, J.P. (2015). *The EU's Data Protection Reform*. Brussels: European Parliament.

Amoore, L. (2013). *The Politics of Possibility: Risk and Security Beyond Probability*. Durham, NC: Duke University Press.

Anon, V. (2015). Google has over a billion users of Android, Chrome, YouTube, and search. 28 May. Available at: www.theverge.com/2015/5/28/8676599/google-io-2015-vital-statistics. [Accessed 15 September 2017].

Baker, D. (2014). Don't buy the 'sharing economy' hype: Airbnb and Uber are facilitating rip-offs, *Guardian*, 27 May, www.theguardian.com/commentisfree/2014/may/27/airbnb-uber-taxes-regulation.

Barocas, S. and Selbst, A.D. (2016). Big Data's Disparate Impact. *California Law Review*, 104(3), 671–732.

Bauman, Z., Bigo, D., Esteves, P., Guild, E., Jabri, V., Lyon, D. and Walker, R.B.J. (2014). After Snowden: Rethinking the Impact of Surveillance. *International Political Sociology*, 8(2), 121–144.

Becker, A. (2017). Everything we know about US investigations into Russian election hacking. *The Independent*, 18 May. Available at: www.independent.co.uk/news/world/americas/russia-election-hacking-us-investigations-everything-we-know-interference-donald-trump-hillary-a7742426.html. [Accessed 10 October 2017].

Bernau, P. (2017). Warum zahlt Apple so wenig Steuern? *Frankfurter Allgemeine Sonntagszeitung*, 25 June, p. 29.

BmWi (2017). 9. GWB-Novelle – ein modernes Wettbewerbsrecht im Zeitalter der Digitalisierung. Available at: www.bmwi.de/Redaktion/DE/Artikel/Wirtschaft/gwb-novelle.html. [Accessed 15 September 2017].

Boffey, D. (2017). Google appeals against EU's €2.4bn fine over search engine results. *Guardian*, 11 September 2017. Available at: www.theguardian.com/technology/2017/sep/11/google-appeals-eu-fine-search-engine-results-shopping-service. [Accessed 15 September 2017].

Bolukbasi, T., Chang, K.W, Zou, J., Saligrama, V. and Kalai, A. (2016). Man is to computer programmer as woman is to homemaker? Debiasing word embeddings. *Advances in Neural Information Processing Systems 29 (NIPS 2016)*, https://papers.nips.cc/paper/6228-man-is-to-computer-programmer-as-woman-is-to-homemaker-debiasing-word-embeddings.pdf.

Bowers S. (2016). Google pays €47m in tax in Ireland on €22bn sales revenue, *Guardian*, November 4. Available at: www.theguardian.com/business/2016/nov/04/google-pays-47m-euros-tax-ireland-22bn-euros-revenue. [Accessed 2 January 2018].

boyd, d. and Crawford, K. (2012). Critical Questions for Big Data. Provocations for a Cultural, Technological, and Scholarly Phenomenon. *Information, Communication, & Society*, 15(5), 662–679.

Bundeskartellamt (2016a). Bundeskartellamt initiates proceeding against Facebook on suspicion of having abused its market power by infringing data protection rules. Available at: www.bundeskartellamt.de/SharedDocs/Meldung/EN/Pressemitteilungen/2016/02_03_2016_Facebook.html?nn=3591568. [Accessed 24 August 2017].

Bundeskartellamt. (2016b). The French Autorité de la concurrence and the German Bundeskartellamt publish joint paper on data and its implications for Competition Law. Available at: www.bundeskartellamt.de/SharedDocs/Meldung/DE/Pressemitteilungen/2016/10_05_2016_Big%20Data.html. [Accessed 24 August 2017].

Bundeskartellamt.de. (2016c). Market power of platforms and networks. Working Paper, June. Available at: www.bundeskartellamt.de/SharedDocs/Publikation/EN/Berichte/Think-Tank-Bericht-Langfassung.pdf?__blob=publicationFile&v=2. [Accessed 28 August 2017].

Business Insider (2017). Amazon accounts for 43% of US online retail sales. *Business Insider*, 3 February. Available at: www.businessinsider.de/amazon-accounts-for-43-of-us-online-retail-sales-2017-2?r=US&IR=T. [Accessed 30 August 2017].

Caliskan, A., Bryson, J. and Narayanan, A. (2017). Semantics Derived Automatically from Language Corpora Contain Human-like Biases. *Science*, 356(6334), 183–186.

Christl, W. (2017). Corporate surveillance in everyday life. Available at: http://cracked labs.org/en/corporate-surveillance. [Accessed 24 August 2017].

Christl, W. and Spiekermann, S. (2016). Networks of control. A report on corporate surveillance, digital tracking, Big Data & privacy. Available at: http://crackedlabs.org/en/networksofcontrol. [Accessed 24 August 2017].

CJEU (2014a). Max Schrems v Data Protection Commissioner (C-362/14).

CJEU (2014b). Digital Rights Ireland (Cases C-293/12 und C-594/12).

CJEU (2014c). Google Spain SL, Google Inc. v Agencia Española de Protección de Datos (AEPD), Mario Costeja González, 13 May 2014. (C-131/12).

CJEU (2017a). Passenger name record data. Court of Justice of the European Union Press. Release No 84/17. Available at: https://curia.europa.eu/jcms/upload/docs/application/pdf/2017-07/cp170084en.pdf. [Accessed 15 September 2017].

CJEU (2017b). The Member States may not impose a general obligation to retain data on providers of electronic communications services. Court of Justice of the European Union. Press Release No 145/16, Luxembourg, 21 December 2016. Available at: https://curia.europa.eu/jcms/upload/docs/application/pdf/2016-12/cp160145en.pdf. [Accessed 29 August 2017].

CJEU (2017c). Tele2 and Watson (Joined Cases C-203/15 and C-698/15).

Clemons, E.K. (2015). The EU files complaints against Google, and it's about time! *Huffington Post*. Available at: www.huffingtonpost.com/eric-k-clemons/the-eu-files-complaints-against-google_b_7069780.html. [Accessed 24 August 2017].

CNIL (2017b). Facebook sanctioned for several breaches of the French Data Protection Act, 16 May 2017. Available at: www.cnil.fr/en/facebook-sanctioned-several-breaches-french-data-protection-act. [Accessed 24 August 2017].

CNIL (Commission Nationale de l'Informatique et des Libertés) (2017a). Common Statement by the Contact Group of the Data Protection Authorities of The Netherlands, France, Spain, Hamburg and Belgium, 16 May 2017. Available at: www.cnil.fr/fr/node/23602. [Accessed 24 August 2017].

Constine, J. (2017). Facebook now has 2 billion monthly users ... and responsibility. *TechCrunch*. Available at: https://techcrunch.com/2017/06/27/facebook-2-billion-users/. [Accessed 15 September 2017].

Council of the EU (2016). The general data protection regulation. Available at: www.
consilium.europa.eu/de/policies/data-protection-reform/data-protection-regulation/.
[Accessed 21 August 2017].

Datta, A., Tschantz, M.C. and Datta, A. (2015). Automated Experiments on Ad Privacy
Settings. *Proceedings on Privacy Enhancing Technologies*, 2015(1). doi:10.1515/popets-
2015-0007.

David (2015). Apple Music – Locking customers in through network effects, 4 October.
Available at: https://digit.hbs.org/submission/apple-music-locking-customers-in-through-
network-effects/. [Accessed 15 October 2017].

Dolata, U. (2017). Internetkonzerne: Konzentration, Konkurrenz und Macht, in: Dolata,
U. and Schrape, J.V. (eds) *Kollektivität und Macht im Internet*. Wiesbaden: Springer
VS, pp. 101–130.

Döpfner, M. (2014). An open letter to Eric Schmidt: Why we fear Google. *Frankfurter
Allgemeine*, 17 April. Available at: www.faz.net/aktuell/feuilleton/debatten/mathias-
doepfner-s-open-letter-to-eric-schmidt-12900860.html. [Accessed 15 September 2017].

Dueck, G. (2013). *Wild Duck: Empirische Philosophie der Mensch-Computer-Vernetzung*
(4. Aufl.). Berlin: Springer.

Ecommerce News. (2017). Ecommerce in Europe. Available at: https://ecommercenews.
eu/ecommerce-per-country/ecommerce-in-europe/. [Accessed 15 September 2017].

EDPS (2014). Preliminary Opinion of the European Data Protection Supervisor. Privacy
and competitiveness in the age of big data: The interplay between data protection, competition law and consumer protection in the Digital Economy. March.

EDPS (European Data Protection Supervisor) (2015). Meeting the challenges of big data: A
call for transparency, user control, data protection by design and accountability. Available at: https://secure.edps.europa.eu/EDPSWEB/webdav/site/mySite/shared/Documents/
Consultation/Opinions/2015/15-11-19_Big_Data_EN.pdf. [Accessed 24 August 2017].

Elgin, M. and Silver, M. (2017). Facebook and Google helped anti-refugee campaign in
swing states. Available at: www.bloomberg.com/news/articles/2017-10-18/facebook-
and-google-helped-anti-refugee-campaign-in-swing-states. [Accessed 31 October 2017].

EU (2016). Regulation on the protection of natural persons with regard to the processing
of personal data and on the free movement of such data, (Regulation (EU) 2016/679 of
27 April 2016). Available at: http://eur-lex.europa.eu/legal-content/EN/TXT/PDF/?uri=
CELEX:32016R0679&from=EN. [Accessed 31 October 2017].

Eurobarometer (2015). Data protection. *PublicOpinion – European Commission*. 431.
Available at: http://ec.europa.eu/commfrontoffice/publicopinion/index.cfm/Survey/get
SurveyDetail/yearFrom/1974/yearTo/2015/surveyKy/2075. [Accessed 12 September
2017].

Eurobarometer (2016). Online platforms. *PublicOpinion – European Commission*. 447.
Available at: http://ec.europa.eu/COMMFrontOffice/publicopinion/index.cfm/Survey/
getSurveyDetail/instruments/SPECIAL/surveyKy/2126. [Accessed 12 September 2017].

European Commission (2015a). Factsheet on the 'Right to be Forgotten' ruling
(C-131/12). Available at: http://ec.europa.eu/justice/data-protection/files/factsheets/
factsheet_data_protection_en.pdf. [Accessed 29 August 2017].

European Commission (2015b). Antitrust: Commission opens formal investigation against
Google in relation to Android mobile operating system. Press Release, 15 April 2015.

European Commission (2016). Antitrust: Commission sends Statement of Objections to
Google on Android operating system and applications. Press Release, 20 April 2016.

European Commission (2017a). Reform of EU data protection rules. Available at: http://
ec.europa.eu/justice/data-protection/reform/index_en.htm. [Accessed 21 August 2017].

European Commission (2017b). Antitrust: Commission fines Google €2.42 billion for abusing dominance as search engine by giving illegal advantage to own comparison shopping service – Factsheet. Available at: http://europa.eu/rapid/press-release_MEMO-17-1785_en.htm. [Accessed 24 August 2017].

European Parliament (2017). Resolution of 14 March 2017. Fundamental rights implications of Big Data: privacy, data protection, non-discrimination, security and law-enforcement. Available at: www.europarl.europa.eu/oeil/popups/ficheprocedure.do?reference=2016/2225(INI)&l=en#documentGateway. [Accessed 21 August 2017].

Farrell, S. and McDonald, H. (2017). Apple ordered to pay up to €13bn after EU rules Ireland broke state aid laws. *Guardian*. Available at: www.theguardian.com/business/2016/aug/30/apple-pay-back-taxes-eu-ruling-ireland-state-aid. [Accessed 28 August 2017].

Federal Trade Commission (2016). Big Data. A Tool for Inclusion or Exclusion? Understanding the Issues – FTC Report. Available at: www.ftc.gov/system/files/documents/reports/big-data-tool-inclusion-or-exclusion-understanding-issues/160106big-data-rpt.pdf. [Accessed 4 October 2017].

Felschen, Ch. (2017). Lobbyismus: Der Google-Staat. Available at: www.zeit.de/digital/internet/2017-09/lobbyismus-google-usa-einfluss-politik/komplettansicht. [Accessed 15 September 2017].

Fourcade, M. and Healy, K. (2017). Seeing Like a Market. *Socio-Economic Review*, 15, 9–29.

Gao, G. and Madden, M. (2017). Privacy and cybersecurity: Key findings from Pew Research. Pew Research Center. 16 January 2015. Available at: www.pewresearch.org/fact-tank/2015/01/16/privacy/. [Accessed 15 September 2017].

García Martínez, A. (2016). *Chaos Monkeys: Obscene Fortune and Random Failure in Silicon Valley*. New York: Harper.

Gibbs, S. (2017). Germany orders Facebook to stop collecting WhatsApp user data. *Guardian*. Available at: www.theguardian.com/technology/2016/sep/27/germany-orders-facebook-stop-collecting-whatsapp-phone-numbers-user-data. [Accessed 15 September 2017].

GitHub (2017). Snowden Archive. Available at: https://github.com/iamcryptoki/snowden-archive. [Accessed 10 October 2017].

Goodwin, T. (2015). The battle is for the customer interface. *TechCrunch*. Available at: https://techcrunch.com/2015/03/03/in-the-age-of-disintermediation-the-battle-is-all-for-the-customer-interface/. [Accessed 4 October 2017].

Graef, I. and van Alsenoy, B. (2016). Data protection through the lens of competition law. Available at: http://blogs.lse.ac.uk/mediapolicyproject/2016/03/23/data-protection-through-the-lens-of-competition-law-will-germany-lead-the-way. [Accessed 24 August 2017].

Grasegger, H. and Krogerius, M. (2017). The data that turned the world upside down. Available at: https://motherboard.vice.com/en_us/article/mg9vvn/how-our-likes-helped-trump-win. [Accessed 21 August 2017].

Greenwald, G. (2014). *No Place to Hide: Edward Snowden, the NSA, and the U.S. Surveillance State*. New York: Metropolitan.

Gumbus, A. and Grodzinsky, F. (2015). Era of Big Data: Danger of Discrimination. *SIGCAS Computers & Society*, September, 45(3), 118–125.

Habermas, J. (1991). *The Structural Transformation of the Public Sphere: An Inquiry into a Category of Bourgeois Society*. Burger, T. (Trans.). Cambridge, MA: MIT Press.

Heath, R. (2017). Tech's European judge, jury and executioner. *Politico*, 27 June. Available at: www.politico.eu/pro/techs-european-judge-jury-and-executioner/. [Accessed 11 October 2017].

Hofmann, J. and Bergemann, B. (2016). Die informierte Einwilligung. Ein Datenschutzphantom. *Spektrum der Wissenschaft Kompakt*, October 4, pp. 50–59.

Hofstetter, Y. (2016). *Das Ende der Demokratie. Wie künstliche Intelligenz die Politik übernimmt und uns entmündigt.* Gütersloh: C. Bertelsmann.

Jasanoff, S. (2006). *States of Knowledge: The Co-Production of Science and the Social Order.* London: Routledge.

Kergueno, R. (2017). The Über-lobbyists: How Silicon Valley is changing Brussels lobbying. *Transparency International EU*, 4 May. Available at: http://transparency.eu/uber-lobbyists/Article. [Accessed 21 August 2017].

Khan, L. (2017). Amazon bites off even more monopoly power. *New York Times* 21 June. Available at: www.nytimes.com/2017/06/21/opinion/amazon-whole-foods-jeff-bezos.html. [Accessed 15 September 2017].

Kiely, E. (2017). Timeline of Russia investigation Available at: www.factcheck.org/2017/06/timeline-russia-investigation/. [Accessed 10 October 2017].

Kitchin, R. (2014). *The Data Revolution.* London: Sage.

Knüwer T. (2013). Springer, Funke und das Schlimmste, das noch kommt, 25 July. Available at: www.indiskretionehrensache.de/2013/07/springer-funke-zeitungskrise/. [Accessed 15 September 2017].

Kocieniewski, C. and Duhigg, C. (2012). Apple's tax strategy aims at low-tax states and nations. *New York Times*, 28 April. Available at: www.nytimes.com/2012/04/29/business/apples-tax-strategy-aims-at-low-tax-states-and-nations.html. [Accessed 29 August 2017].

Kosinski, M., Stillwell, D. and Græpel, T. (2013). Private Traits and Attributes Are Predictable from Digital Records of Human Behavior. *Proceedings of the National Academy of Sciences of the United States of America*, 110(15), 5802–5805.

Kramer, A., Guillory, J. and Hancock, J. (2014). Experimental Evidence of Massive-Scale Emotional Contagion Through Social Networks. *PNAS*, 24(111), 8788–8790, doi: 10.1073/pnas.1320040111.

Kuner, C., Cate, F.H., Millard, C., Svantesson, D.J.B. & Lynskey, O. (2014). When Two Worlds Collide: The Interface Between Competition Law and Data Protection. *International Data Privacy Law*, 4(4), 247–248.

Lanchester, John (2017). You Are The Product. *London Review of Books*, 39(17), 7 September, 3–11. Available at: www.lrb.co.uk/v39/n16/john-lanchester/you-are-the-product. [Accessed 29 September 2017].

Lane, J., Stodden, V., Bender, S. and Nissenbaum, H. (2014). *Privacy, Big Data, and the Public Good: Frameworks for Engagement.* New York: Cambridge University Press.

Leggewie, C. and Maar, C. (1998). Internet und Politik. Von der Zuschauer- zur Beteiligungsdemokratie? Braunschweig: Bollmann.

Lobigs, F. (2017). Paradigmenwechsel in der Ökonomie gesellschaftlich relevanter digitaler Medieninhalte. Expertise im Auftrag der Schweizer Eidgenössischen Medienkommission EMEK. Available at: www.emek.admin.ch/fileadmin/dateien/pdf/Expertise_EMEK_Frank_Lobigs.pdf.

Lyon, D. (2003). *Surveillance as Social Sorting: Privacy, Risk and Digital Discrimination.* London and New York: Routledge.

Lyon, D. (2014). Surveillance, Snowden, and Big Data: Capacities, Consequences, Critique. *Big Data & Society*, 1(2), 1–13.

Mau, S. (2017). *Das metrische Wir. Über die Quantifizierung des Sozialen*. Berlin: Suhrkamp.

McDonald, A.M. and Cranor, L.F. (2008). The Cost of Reading Privacy Policies, *A Journal of Law and Policy for the Information Society*. Available at: http://lorrie. cranor.org/pubs/readingPolicyCost-authorDraft.pdf. [Accessed 31 December 2017].

McRae, H. (2015). Facebook, Airbnb, Uber, and the unstoppable rise of the content non-generators, *The Independent*, 5 May. Available at: www.independent.co.uk/news/business/ comment/hamish-mcrae/facebook-airbnb-uber-and-the-unstoppable-rise-of-the-content-non-generators-10227207.html. [Accessed 15 September 2017].

Merton, R.K. (1968). The Matthew Effect in Science. *Science*, 159(3810), 56–63.

Mohsin, M. (2017). The Next White House Could Be Staffed With Silicon Valley Veterans. *Bloomberg*. Available at: www.bloomberg.com/news/articles/2016-10-18/ outspending-wall-street-2-to-1-silicon-valley-takes-washington. [Accessed 15 September 2017].

Morozov, E. (2017). To tackle Google's power, regulators have to go after its ownership of data. *Guardian*, 1 July. Available at: www.theguardian.com/technology/2017/jul/01/ google-european-commission-fine-search-engines. [Accessed 4 October 2017].

New York Times (2012). 'Double Irish with a Dutch sandwich'. *New York Times*, 28 April. Available at: www.nytimes.com/interactive/2012/04/28/business/Double-Irish-With-A-Dutch-Sandwich.html?_r=0. [Accessed 29 August 2017].

O'Neil, C. (2016). *Weapons of Math Destruction: How Big Data Increases Inequality and Threatens Democracy*. New York: Crown.

OECD (2013). The digital economy. February 2013. Available at: www.oecd.org/daf/ competition/The-Digital-Economy-2012.pdf. [Accessed 30 August 2017].

Pariser, E. (2012). *The Filter Bubble: What the Internet is Hiding From You*. London: Penguin Books.

Pasquale, F. (2015). *The Black Box Society: The Secret Algorithms that Control Money and Information*. Cambridge, MA: Harvard University Press.

Patterson, M.R. (2017). *Antitrust Law in the New Economy: Google, Yelp, LIBOR, and the Control of Information*. Cambridge, MA: Harvard University Press.

Perry, D. (2014). Sex and Uber's 'Rides of Glory': The company tracks your one-night stands – and much more. *The Oregonian*, 20 November. Available at: www. oregonlive.com/today/index.ssf/2014/11/sex_the_single_girl_and_ubers.html. [Accessed 11 October 2017].

Porter, T.M. (1996). *Trust in Numbers: The Pursuit of Objectivity in Science and Public Life*. Princeton, NJ: Princeton University Press.

Power, M. (2010). *The Audit Society: Rituals of Verification*. Oxford: Oxford University Press.

Pozzato, V. (2014). Opinion of the European Data Protection Supervisor: Interplay Between Data Protection and Competition Law. *Journal of European Competition Law & Practice*, 5(7), 468–470.

Rankin, J. (2017). Facebook fined £94m for 'misleading' EU over WhatsApp takeover. *Guardian*, 18 May. Available at: www.theguardian.com/business/2017/may/18/ facebook-fined-eu-whatsapp-european-commission. [Accessed 24 August 2017].

Reuters (2017). EU to conclude Google antitrust cases in next few months. Available at: www.reuters.com/article/us-eu-google-antitrust-idUSKBN18I1EV. [Accessed 24 August 2017].

Richter, Ph. (ed.). (2015). *Privatheit, Öffentlichkeit und demokratische Willensbildung in Zeiten von Big Data*. Baden-Baden: Nomos.

Rifkin, Jeremy (2014). *The Zero Marginal Cost Society: The Internet of Things, the Collaborative Commons, and the Eclipse of Capitalism.* 1st edn. New York: Palgrave Macmillan.

Rosenbach, M. and Stark, H. (2014). *Der NSA-Komplex – Edward Snowden und der Weg in die totale Überwachung.* Hamburg: Spiegel.

Rouvroy, A. (2016). 'Of Data and Men'. Fundamental rights and freedoms in a world of Big Data. Council of Europe, Directorate General of Human Rights and Rule of Law. Available at: https://works.bepress.com/antoinette_rouvroy/64/. [Accessed 4 October 2017].

Schneider, I. and Rehder, B. (2016). *Gerichtsverbünde, Grundrechte und Politikfelder in Europa.* Baden-Baden: Nomos.

Schneider, I. and Ulbricht, L. (2017). Ist Big Data fair? Normativ hergestellte Erwartungen an Big Data, in: Heil, R., Kolany-Raiser, B. and Orwat, C. (eds) *Big Data und Gesellschaft. Eine multidisziplinäre Annäherung.* Wiesbaden: Springer (forthcoming).

Scott, M. (2017). E.U. fines Facebook $122 million over disclosures in WhatsApp deal. Available at: www.nytimes.com/2017/05/18/technology/facebook-european-union-fine-whatsapp.html. [Accessed 24 August 2017].

Sebag, M. (2017). Google spared $1.3 billion tax bill with victory in French court. Available at: www.bloomberg.com/news/articles/2017-07-12/google-wins-french-court-fight-over-1-3-billion-tax-bill. [Accessed 28 August 2017].

Shakya, H.B. and Christakis, N.A. (2017). Association of Facebook Use With Compromised Well-Being: A Longitudinal Study, *American Journal of Epidemiology*, 1 February, 185(3), 203–211. doi: 10.1093/aje/kww189.

Smith, M. (2017). EU orders Amazon to repay $295 million in Luxembourg back taxes. Available at: www.reuters.com/article/us-eu-amazon-taxavoidance/eu-orders-amazon-to-repay-295-million-in-luxembourg-back-taxes-idUSKCN1C913S. [Accessed 11 October 2017].

Smith-Meyer, B., Vinocur, N. and Scott, M. (2017). 10 EU nations back new plan to tax digital giants. *Politico*, 16 September. Available at: www.politico.eu/article/ten-eu-nations-back-new-plan-to-tax-digital-giants-google-amazon-facebook/amp/. [Accessed 11 October 2017].

Srnicek, N. (2017). *Platform Capitalism.* Malden, MA: Polity.

Stone, M. and Silver, M. (2017). Google's $6 billion miscalculation on the EU. 6 August 2015. *Bloomberg Business.* Available at: www.bloomberg.com/news/features/2015-08-06/google-s-6-billion-miscalculation-on-the-eu. [Accessed 15 September 2017].

Swan, M. (2013). The Quantified Self: Fundamental Disruption in Big Data Science and Biological Discovery. *Big Data*, 1(2), 85–89.

Taplin, J. (2017a). Why is Google spending record sums on lobbying Washington? *Guardian*, 30 July. Available at: www.theguardian.com/technology/2017/jul/30/google-silicon-valley-corporate-lobbying-washington-dc-politics. [Accessed 15 September 2017].

Taplin, J. (2017b). *Move Fast and Break Things: How Facebook, Google and Amazon have Cornered Culture and What It Means for All of Us.* New York: Hachette.

The Verge (2017). Google's next EU fine could be even bigger for Android violations. Available at: www.theverge.com/2017/7/6/15927400/eu-google-android-antitrust-fine-rumors. [Accessed 24 August 2017].

U.S. Bureau of Labor Statistics (2017). Newspaper publishers lose over half their employment from January 2001 to September 2016. Available at: www.bls.gov/opub/ted/2017/newspaper-publishers-lose-over-half-their-employment-from-january-2001-to-september-2016.htm. [Accessed 15 September 2017].

Ulbricht, L. (2017). Regulativ hergestellte Erwartungen an Big Data: Regulierung von Big Data als Deutungskonflikt, in: Heil, R., Kolany-Raiser, B. and Orwat, C. (eds) *Big Data und Gesellschaft. Eine multidisziplinäre Annäherung*. Wiesbaden: Springer (forthcoming).

Van de Rijt, A., Kang, S.M., Restivo, M. and Patil, A. (2014). Field Experiments of Success-Breeds-Success Dynamics. *Proceedings of the National Academy of Sciences*, 111(19), 6934–6939.

Weiser, Marc (1991). The Computer for the 21st Century. *Scientific American*, September, 94–104.

Wever, G. (2014). *Open Government, Staat und Demokratie*. Baden-Baden: Nomos.

White House (2014). Big Data: Seizing Opportunities, Preserving Values. Available at: http://purl.fdlp.gov/GPO/gpo64868. [Accessed 4 October 2017].

White House (2016). Big Data: A Report on Algorithmic Systems, Opportunity, and Civil Rights. Available at: www.whitehouse.gov/sites/default/files/microsites/ostp/2016_0504_data_discrimination.pdf. [Accessed 4 October 2017].

World Bank (2016). Digital Dividends. World Development Report 2016. Washington, DC.

Wu, T. (2008). The International Privacy Regime, in: Chander, A., Gelman, L., Radin, M.J. (eds) *Securing Privacy in the Internet Age*. Stanford, CA: Stanford University Press, pp. 91–107.

Wu, T. (2017). *The Attention Merchants: From the Daily Newspaper to Social Media, How Our Time and Attention Is Harvested and Sold*. London: Atlantic.

Yeung, K. (2016). 'Hypernudge': Big Data as a Mode of Regulation by Design. *Information, Communication & Society*, 1–19.

Zuboff, S. (2015). Big Other. Surveillance Capitalism and the Prospects of an Information Civilization. *Journal of Information Technology*, 30(1), 75–89.

Zuiderveen Borgesius, F., Trilling, D., Möller, J., Bodó, B., de Vreese, C. and Helberger, N. (2016). Should We Worry About Filter Bubbles? *Internet Policy Review*, 5(1). DOI: 10.14763/2016.1.401.

9 Rear window – transparent citizens versus political participation

Maria João Simões and Nuno Amaral Jerónimo

Introduction

In this chapter,[1] more focused on the constraints on citizens' political participation, we intend to address the challenges – some of them already enunciated by Simões (2011) – that political participation is facing. We will consider the increasing spread and depth of ICTs and other technologies as surveillance devices – spreading extensively through all spheres of social activity, as well as intensively penetrating the routines of our daily lives – and provide a comprehensive analysis of the ways that surveillance can constrain political participation, or even make it impracticable, at least as we recognise it in contemporary democratic societies.

Concerning the threats to democracy caused by surveillance, most current studies mainly emphasise democracy/privacy interdependency, as is largely the case of Lyon (1988, 2001), Raab (1997) and Rouvroy and Poullet (2009). Our approach relies on a different assumption: that surveillance challenges our *autonomy* as social and political actors, and that loss of or decrease in autonomy poses major threats to political participation. Most certainly, such a decrease is largely due to the growing loss of privacy, as we do not deny the importance of privacy as a condition for autonomy.

When most people face privacy–security trade-offs, they rapidly choose security over privacy. Are they aware of the consequences that loss of privacy has on their autonomy, like losing their faculty and power to make political choices and to participate in decision-making within the public domain? Autonomy is a central issue regarding threats to political participation. Transparent citizens may hardly be politically autonomous, and consequently free. This chapter intends to explain how and why this is the case.

Surprisingly, albeit being a crucial condition in the performance of free political action, most authors in political sociology have underestimated the concept of autonomy. In actual fact, this concept provides a better understanding of how social structural constraints work in order to restrain or prevent political participation.

Accordingly, to engage in the discussion about political participation we will take into account a more transversal and all-encompassing idea: political participation in all spheres of public everyday life. Facing the challenges to participation presented by surveillance, it is important to be aware of major types of politics, which entail several kinds of participation.[2] The concept of politics that has arisen from Athenian democracy and from the Renaissance republican tradition – which involves every public matter in which every citizen should participate and through which their abilities and skills are developed and expressed – has a wider conception than the current liberal ones. In a similar way, in contemporary societies, Beck (1999) and Giddens (1992) share a concept of wideranging politics, respectively sub-politics and life politics. Politics is

> about power; that is, it is about the *capacity* of social agents, agencies and institutions to maintain or transform their environment, social or physical. (…) It is expressed in all activities of cooperation, negotiation and struggle over the use and distribution of resources. It is involved in all relations, institutions and structures which are implicated in activities of production and reproduction in the life of societies. Politics creates and conditions all aspects of our lives and it is at the core of the development of problems in society and the collective modes of their resolution.
>
> (Held 1996: 309–310)

Politics is, above all, a domain of human action.[3] It is action and it is about action, something done by citizens and not for citizens; but, as Barber (1984) argues, not every action is politics – politics only concerns areas that require appropriate public action and choices in the presence of conflict, and from which public consequences are expected.

Citizens with higher levels of participation, or who are interested in a wider vision of politics, may be under more systematic, more permanent and broader forms of surveillance than those who rely on more liberal views on politics.

To these liberal points of view, politics is a hampered sphere restricted to the world of government; politics is seen as a thing, a place, an aggregate of institutions, or, if action is considered, actions of politicians, specialists, bureaucrats and political parties. Politics is established, thus, out of the cultural, economic or family realms, matters that are understood as non-political (Barber 1984; Held 1996).[4]

By way of contrast to mainstream studies on e-participation and e-democracy, we do not underestimate acquired knowledge in the field of political sociology prior to the emergence of ICTs (cf. Bourdieu 1979; Memmi 1985; Mayer and Perrineau 1992). We also take into consideration that strengths and weaknesses of online public participation are not disconnected from other social issues, as they accrue from offline political contexts. Democratic history and culture have not disappeared due to the simple emergence of a new technology, and even though they may be changeable, change is always operated within the framework of the existing democratic culture.

Given our own initial framework, the chapter will proceed as follows: a first section examines the required conditions for citizens to participate and engage in politics, taking mainly into consideration the discussion around the issue of autonomy; a second section will present the main concerns on the essential subject of surveillance; the third, an incisive examination of the increasing transparency of our daily lives and the ensuing decrease of autonomy. Finally, the chapter presents some summary considerations on these critical debates regarding the challenges superimposed by surveillance and sousveillance with respect to political participation.

Political participation requirements and the autonomy issue

People need resources to engage in politics. From the point of view of liberal individualism, individuals need civil, political and legal rights. Other approaches, that adopt the republican tradition and are more active regarding the citizenship issues, emphasise social and economic resources. In this latter tradition, without reasonable income, education, health, cultural capital, political skills and others alike, it is difficult to become a political actor (Oldfield 1998).

We can link the necessity of social and economic resources with Marshall's perspective. In his evolutionist argument back in 1964, Marshall (1998) identified three kinds of citizenship – civil, political and social – that have emerged in a sequential way in the eighteenth, nineteenth and twentieth centuries. Civil citizenship established the necessary rights for exercising individual freedom, namely personal freedom, freedom of thought, speech and religion, the right to justice, to private property and to establish contracts. Individual liberty is only possible when there is no interference from the state or other organisations in individual private life, or when, in public contexts, individuals are not systematically watched. It is only when individual private life is far from the gaze of those organisations, and subsequently away from unequal power relations, that individuals can become more autonomous, make their choices and acquire opinions about their lives and the world – the right to privacy and the right to be unbothered are therefore fundamental issues of civil rights.

Political citizenship, following Marshall (1998), embraces the right to vote, the right of association and the right to participate in politics, whether as a voter or as an elected member (thus with political authority). Political citizenship – one dimension of democratic societies – also implies that neither the state nor any other organisations interfere with or watch over citizens' political activities.

This gradual evolution of citizenship should have been concluded with the development of the welfare state in the twentieth century, through the attribution of social rights, for example, health, education, employment and social security rights.

Beyond the guarantee of civil, political and social rights, however, other conditions are also crucial for political participation in democratic societies, being all of which necessary, but none sufficient by itself. Participation opportunities have to be assured, which implies the creation and widening of appropriate institutional settings at several levels (local, national, global and also horizontal and specialised levels). The aim of these institutional settings is to stimulate civic participation in general and, in a more particular way, to promote a rational understanding of, and better information about, public issues and participation in decision-making – thus encouraging participation in decision-making choices to become more widespread within the frame of a more participative democracy (Barber 1984; Held 1996; Oldfield 1998).

The predominant institutional frame in contemporary democratic societies envisaged so far provides the guarantee that citizens could participate in politics without being harassed, interfered with or even watched by their own or others' governments, or by any other organisation – a guarantee secured by civil and political rights. Voting by secret ballot is the best example of such an institutional frame. The intensive and extensive upgrade of surveillance, however, questions the ground rules of such institutional frames in the realm of conventional political participation, and also challenges alternative modes of participation, thus creating constraints to citizen's political action through invested political and economic groups and organisations.

On the other hand, individuals also have to be encouraged to participate, to execute their political rights and duties, that is, to be citizens. In contemporary societies, where we are simultaneously facing a crisis in political participation, as well as an increasing distancing between rulers and ruled, is it possible to mobilise citizens to politically participate in contexts where they are simultaneously aware that they are also being watched?

The autonomy issue

In pre-capitalist societies, personal autonomy was not an available possibility, as political rights and duties were connected to property rights and religious tradition. The bourgeois order in fact created the conditions for an increased participation amongst an up-and-coming class – the bourgeoisie – but not for the majority of the population, who instead found themselves submerged in new kinds of social relationships, with new challenges and constraints, which are not simply overcome just by stating that everyone is equal before the law (Held 1996).

Within that new order, liberals proposed a challenging perspective, according to which every individual was born equal and free, and able to choose, determine and justify one's own actions. For liberal thought, individuals, regarded as citizens, are considered from the start as responsible and autonomous moral agents. It is taken for granted that they possess control over their lives, and that they also possess the resources and opportunities to politically participate, therefore not requiring any kind of support. This theoretical assumption has led to a systematic undervaluing of the issue of individual autonomy. Liberal theorists assume from the start that a defensible political order is one in which individuals might develop their abilities, desires and interests free from the arbitrary usage of political authority and coercive power. But, within this perspective, they neglected to address the fact that modern societies were not civil societies of totally autonomous people (van Gunsteren 1994). They have never taken into consideration the effective circumstances of how individuals live – how fully connected people are within complex networks of relationships and institutions where relations of domination and subordination are established[5] (Held 1996).

Besides the dominance of the liberal conception of democracy in contemporary societies, the Internet's libertarian ideology also leads to a devaluation of the autonomy issue. This libertarian ideology has contributed, until the turn of the millennium and in large extent, nowadays, to a gap between the supposed potentialities of ICTs and the practices that have developed in all domains of life, including political participation (see Pasquale, Chapter 7 in this volume). Several authors, such as Breindl (2010), Simões, Barriga and Jerónimo (2011), Han (2014) and Harcourt (2015), state that libertarian theories regarding the Internet have a rhetorical and speculative nature. It is enough to refer to, for example, the great optimism of Rheingold (1996) and Barlow (1996), for whom cyberspace empowers – and where individuals are assumed to become more equal and free of State and corporate interference.

Rousseau (1981), writing in 1726 and following the republican tradition, had already established a connection between liberty and participation, as well as developing a concern regarding autonomy and participation – thereafter revived by Marshall (1998). Although Marshall may have been criticised for his evolutionist conception of citizenship, he had already made a clear distinction between formal rights and their effective application, arguing that the effective exercise of citizenship would only be possible whenever social rights were also assured. Without social rights, that is, a certain level of well-being (income, health, education, and others), people would not have material grounds to participate as equals in political and social life, because they would live economically and politically subordinated to others. In this sense, when dispossessed of social rights, the impact of the formal equality of civil and political rights will always be undermined. The author was therefore one of the first sociologists to pay attention to the issue of autonomy, even if only implicitly.

Surprisingly, even after Marshall's contributions, political sociologists still have not paid sufficient attention to the issue of autonomy from a theoretical and conceptual point of view. Thus, sociological theory has not deepened or specified all conditions under which participation could be assured when individuals face the concentration of State power, or power relations in the economic and/or religious realms, against the weakness of political institutions and their citizens. These issues were later readdressed and increasingly developed by Barber (1984), Held (1996), Roche (1998) and Oldfield (1998), according to whom the effective achievement of autonomy is a necessary condition for engaging in political participation.

These authors, by contrast with voluntarist action theorists, start with a crucial assumption: an unequal distribution of economic, social and political resources limits the possibility for autonomous choices, judgement and political actions – as Bourdieu (1979, 1994) had also understood. Such resources aim to enable individuals to become effective agents in the world, that is, to make decisions autonomously, unconditioned by relations of domination. Also, the political

common good could only be understood through political interaction and deliberation, which supposes, according to Held (1996), that autonomy should be
understood as a social acquisition and not as a given feature.

To Simões (2005, 2011), the major discussion is *how* citizens act politically,
not if they do it or not. Here is where it turns crucial to reiterate the efficiency of
civil, political and social rights, but also to pronounce the concept of autonomy
and under which conditions it becomes effective. Barber (1984: 134) states that
'consent without autonomy is not consent. (…) While clients or voters or con-
stituents or masses may be characterised in ways that omit their free agency,
participants cannot'. This statement leads to the idea of autonomy and the necessity of assuring its existence to citizens. But what does autonomy actually
consist of?

As Roche (1998) argued, citizens are autonomous when they are rational
agents and free moral individuals, which not only requires a theoretical conception of autonomy but also the enumeration of necessities and preconditions to its
effectiveness. Autonomy 'connotes the capacity of human beings to reason self-
consciously, to be self-reflective and to be self-determining. It involves the
ability to deliberate, judge, choose and act upon different possible courses of
action in private as well as public life' (Held 1996: 300). Its effectiveness,
according to this author, is closely dependent on the material and cognitive
resources, amongst others, that people are able to achieve, and on facilities that
allow (or prevent) access to these resources. It also depends on liberating individuals from the potential constraints on action arising from relationships of economic, political and social domination.

To Oldfield (1998), the concept of action is the starting point – actions are
autonomous when they show characteristics such as self-determination and
authenticity. Action, distinguishable from behaviour, identifies the importance of
motives, purposes and will. An action is self-determined when it is a product of
a person's will. This requires the skills of being unconstrained by others, or by
the demands of the institutions one belongs to. It is authentic when it is built and
chosen by each person, not by others, and rationally presented. Autonomy also
requires some kind of moral dimension, which hints at the proficiency of individuals to make and proclaim political judgements.[6]

Surveillance is becoming a major threat to autonomy in newer and more
diverse forms, undermining the possibilities for freer political actions within
contemporary societies. The concept of autonomy, regarding the debate around
these threats, appears as more heuristic than the concept of privacy. For now,
within this reflexive approach, we take as our starting point the definition of
privacy proposed by Westin (1967: 7): 'privacy is the claim of individuals,
groups or institutions determining themselves, when, how, and to what extent of
information about them is communicated to others', plus a proposed short addition, 'or can be extracted by others'.[7]

When discussing privacy–security trade-offs, most people would choose
security over privacy, asserting that they have nothing to hide. As Simões (2011:
95) has already questioned, 'Are they aware of the consequences brought to their

autonomy by losing privacy? Are they aware of the loss on their faculty and power to make political choices and participate in decision-making within the public domain?' As we can see comprehensively in the following sections, the central issue around this debate is the concept of autonomy.

Certainly, autonomy is nowadays largely threatened by the invasion of privacy enabled by ICTs and other technologies used as surveillance devices. In this sense, it is crucial to analyse how autonomy and privacy interweave, but also to look more closely to privacy issues in contemporary societies. We are therefore facing a double challenge in the domain of political participation: the reconfiguration of political participation caused by surveillance, and the threats posed to privacy. Indeed, the characteristics of privacy are changing, and its theorisation is currently very open-ended. In this domain, there is an enriching and widespread debate, where theories on privacy and current common-sense conceptions of privacy are reshaped, akin to the continuing changes in contemporary societies, namely with respect to the intensive and extensive increase of surveillance.

Surveillance: crucial issues and threats

In contemporary societies, we are facing two kinds of surveillance: top-down and bottom-up surveillance, both of which have implications with respect to autonomy and political participation, although in different ways and with different consequences. To distinguish top-down from bottom-up observing technologies, as Timan and Oudshoorn (2012) note, Surveillance Studies has formulated new terminology. The term 'surveillance' 'is restricted to refer to observing activities executed from above, e.g. organisations observing people. (...) In contrast, the terms "sousveillance" or "inverse surveillance" refer to observing practices in which the watching is performed by ordinary people' (Timan and Oudshoorn 2012: 169). The former is also designated by other authors such as Mann *et al.* (2003) and Ganascia (2010), as organisational surveillance. The term enunciated in the latter form also allows us to understand that surveillance is not only in the hands of formal surveillance organisations.

In a surveillance environment, information is gathered with precise goals and by agents that can impose their power and/or domination, for example, the State, while in a sousveillance context, as Timan and Oudshoorn (2012) have pointed out, people's recording practices do not necessarily have any explicit objective. In the first, individual citizens are configured as passive and subordinate subjects, whereas in the second, they are configured as active subjects.

Let us analyse first the top-down or organisational surveillance. In contemporary societies, this kind of surveillance has expanded both intensively (it enters deeply in the routines of our private lives) and extensively (it embraces almost every sphere of social activity). Organisational surveillance has two faces; it is both an enabler and a constrainer to our action (Giddens 1992; Lyon 1994, 2001). A good example of this ambivalent process is how surveillance has spread alongside the development of democracy and the emergence of social rights. To establish liberal democratic regimes, States had to collect population data to categorise and classify their citizens. Another example is the case of the mandatory electronic Citizen Card in Portugal, which was presented as an instrument to ease access to public services, such as its national health service or public education, while enabling State bureaucracy to observe citizens at will. Private and public powers can use surveillance devices with positive or negative impacts, depending on the interests and purposes they were designed and created for.

We should also examine the historical context in which such devices can be found, because technological systems do not produce the same effects in all their contexts of usage. Knowing about each person's and organisations' ideologies throughout time and space helps us to understand the goals towards which surveillance devices are aimed, how they are used and to identify specific forms of resistance that allow for change (Lyon 1994, 2001). Some technologies may even overhaul their initial purposes. Besides, even when someone creates these technologies and uses them with no harm intended, they may bring undesirable and unintended consequences, namely the unpredicted use of several technologies in newer and more profound or more extensive forms of surveillance, for example, the use of smartphones to control children's online and offline actions and interactions.

Opposite to what Marxist approaches have stated, reinforcing and spreading of surveillance practices cannot be understood as a product of a capitalist conspiracy. They are a result of the complex way our society is organised. Our societies explicitly value consumption freedom, productivity, efficacy, speed, mobility, efficiency and security. In this sense, in contemporary societies, most organisations employ devices used as surveillance technologies (STs) in a systematic way, in order to control production outcome, to reduce uncertainties, and specially to prevent threatening behaviours and risks on security grounds (Lyon 2001).

STs were intensified after September 11, 2001, a landmark for an assumed increase in terrorist threats. The belief that technology may contribute to reducing potential risks and controlling outcomes increases the pressure to progressively create more sophisticated means of surveillance. The twofold state of affairs we currently live in involves, on the one hand, a stimulation of technology development carried out by powerful economic interest groups, and intensified by alarming news, systematically presented by the media. On the other hand, governments and increasingly specialised agencies are gradually using more and more sophisticated means in order to collect people's data regularly, turning everyone into targets of monitoring and suspicion. Such technologies ostensibly strengthen the extensive and intensive advances of organisational surveillance and permit their spread into previously unforeseen areas beyond the aims they were allegedly created and designed for.

Surveillance is therefore the contemporary outcome of a process that has been disseminated, scattered and refined throughout history. The 1800s turned out to be fundamentally groundbreaking, as state bureaucracies used the development of statistics to count, categorise, classify and administer citizens. Its emergence already set, to a large extent, the framework and models of how surveillance should develop in the next centuries, which was largely facilitated in the late twentieth century by the development of computer science and ICTs. With the introduction of statistics, Castel (1991) emphasises a change from the 'observable' to the 'deduced' in the construction of individual selves. Thus, administrative practices increasingly focused on risks rather than on danger. Data gathering, initially used to watch over specific suspects and thwart danger, widened to monitor everyone in order to prevent risk. Risk management is associated to statistics. Castel (1991) reminds us that statistical techniques were used to produce personal profiles that were not under the immediate glance of those who watch.

Preventive policies of surveillance, along with statistical techniques, base their profiling methods on the deconstruction of the subject and its reconstruction as a matrix cell using a combination of statistical correlations of different kinds of elements and facts, which allows checking each person's proneness for producing risk.

When paper surveillance was replaced by electronic surveillance, it gained 'the potential to erode liberties and freedoms, because those technologies changed the balance of power in our society' (Davies 1992: iv). In the late 1980s, before the increasing sophistication of ICTs and the emergence of other STs, Gary Marx (1988) highlighted that computers were not only spreading the scope of surveillance, but were also allowing more regular and deepened forms of surveillance – also emphasising that the way STs are to be used in contemporary societies reaffirms an increasing totalitarian potential, regardless of who controls these surveillance means.

Marx (2008) asserts that control practice and culture are changing, because 'hard' forms of control are not reducing as 'soft' forms are simultaneously expanding in different ways. As Marx (2008) points out, we deal with data collection processes that encompass the use of misleading information, with benefits offered in exchange for information, the gathering of 'false' volunteers with the stratagem of appealing to good citizenship, and even the use of hidden or disguised collection techniques.

Citizens are interested in avoiding discrimination, manipulation and an inappropriate classification of themselves that could be the result of an inadequate combination of our personal data (Marx 2008). As Solove affirms (2004: 49), 'the information in databases often fails to capture the texture of our lives'. The problematic issue, as we see above, is that citizen profiling is constructed by connecting decontextualised data – as discussed also by Matzner, Chapter 5 in this volume. This does not translate to a variety of personal and social contexts, as well as the reasons for action, because these are reduced to a limited number of variables. This limitation is rather based on the need for predictive and scientific generalisation capacities. Given that any data can be classified by a statistical model as comprising higher or lower risk, it is assumed that risk is understood and consequently controllable on probabilistic grounds. Identities constructed with decontextualised data are not equal to our own identities (Solove 2004; Marx 2008).

As Simões says (2011), we can be considered political activists or opposition-ists when actually we are not, or activists with characteristics we do not possess. The worst is that these identities can never be questioned and, despite this fact, they can therefore be deployed to prescribe and proscribe our political behaviour. This inappropriate classification can even be deliberately obtained for political ends – for example, inducing certain political behaviour.

So, we are currently facing a paradoxical situation – the use of STs for pre-venting risk has itself increasingly become a risk; a risk to be taken into account in the exercise of citizenship. The question, as Lyon (2001) poses it, is whether we are witnessing either an increase in their negative dimensions or a growing imbalance of power between 'vigilant' and 'monitored' citizens, thus subse-quently thickening increasing risks of a totalitarian and/or unequal society, com-posed of what we label as 'transparent' citizens.

But, as stated above, not only organisational surveillance has implications in the political sphere. Due to a number of reasons, people take part in surveillance and sousveillance and involuntarily contribute through this process to the sys-tematic recollection of information by organisations with political aims. On the one hand, large sections of the population are more willing to give away their personal data, believing more in the benefits of surveillance than in its potential risks, claiming that they have nothing to hide or fear (Lyon 2001). Governments, companies and/or the media contribute to this situation because news highlights and exaggerates stories of crime, war and terrorism. This contributes to increas-ing feelings of insecurity, encouraging people to accept surveillance devices.

On the other hand, we can look at cultural changes characterised by the fasci-nation entailed in exposing aspects of private and public lives (Marx 2008; Ganascia 2010; Morozov 2013; Han 2014; Harcourt 2015). This has been the case in television, for example reality shows and, in an alarmingly increasing way, in online social networks, with Facebook a significant example. Everybody can communicate with everybody, everybody can express their opinions, feel-ings, meetings, pictures, trips on social networks, and everybody is able to take pictures in everyone's public and private spaces, copy sayings from known and unknown friends, record sounds and share and disseminate all these on the Inter-net. And as Ganascia (2010) stresses, these processes are facilitated by the massive ongoing development of ICTs, and the widespread dissemination of information through radio and TV, books, newspapers, photos or movies is therefore no longer a privilege of powerful organisations such as states or corpo-rations. As Han (2014: 95) puts it, 'Each one willingly offers himself to the pan-optic gaze. We contribute to the digital panoptic, given that we disclose and expose ourselves.' Such assumptions allow a rejection of the simplistic view that available data only serve the interest groups that have technological devices to collect it, although we need to take into account that the agents of these two kinds of surveillance are very different according to their power, intentionality and consequences of their actions.

Furthermore, the Internet of Things, 'the network of physical objects that contain embedded technology to communicate and sense or interact with their internal states or the external environment' (Gartner 2013b), has been received with both cheering acclaims and careful criticism. The Internet of Things, that a Gartner, Inc. report from 2013 predicts to grow into 26 billion units by 2020 (Gartner 2013b), is seen by some authors as enabling more efficient machine-to-machine cooperation (daCosta 2013; Gaglio and Lo Re 2014) or as performing a radical transformation of capitalism (Rifkin 2014), whereas others point to the risks thereby posed to privacy, social control and political manipulation (Sterling 2014; Howard 2015).

STs' design and programming are never neutral when regarding the intended data outcome. As Lyon (2001) highlights, the intended effects of STs aim to reinforce the regimes they were designed and programmed for. Organisational surveillance has always been a source of power and is even more so today. But it would be simplistic to think that STs endlessly reinforce the position of the most powerful social actors, as according to the structural perspective of Foucault, expressed in the panopticon metaphor, where individuals passively act in accordance to the established rules, being their behaviours forever determined by settled surveillance systems. Human beings, despite the rigidity of social structures and power inequalities, are cognitive beings and endowed with some opportunities to resist, reduce, change and reshape the constraints imposed by dominant groups (Burns and Flam 2000). As Giddens (1987) states, in the field of dialectic control, power is not always absolute. However, it would also be simplistic to think, according to the voluntarist theories of action, that surveillance implies no constraints to individual and collective political action, as if people were able to choose their actions freely.

Increasingly 'transparent' citizens in everyday life

Until the turn of the nineteenth century, most of people's everyday life and privacy was not the target of watching, collecting data, categorisation and classification by the state or other organisations. Due to the aforementioned social changes, the situation shifted: individuals' everyday lives and privacy have rather become increasingly monitored via various means. This section has both descriptive and analytical dimensions, aiming to highlight how devices are becoming growingly diversified and sophisticated, with wider range and depth, further rendering the individuals more and more transparent.

Commercial surveillance is one of the major contributors to the erosion of boundaries between private and public spaces and to the intensification of surveillance that begins to embrace the routines of our everyday life and our privacy (Lyon 1994). Let us just consider credit and debit cards, data from insurance companies, or frequent customer cards provided by all kinds of shops, including bookshops and cinemas. Certainly, commercial surveillance devices are aimed at persuading people, as consumers, to voluntarily provide information about themselves in exchange for discounts and other benefits. Notwithstanding, these cards can hold other purposes, for example, political ones. These cards 'allow knowing where, when and what we consume, thus revealing our political and ideological preferences: precious information to detect political activists in some democratic countries and even more in (potential) authoritarian and totalitarian regimes' (Simões 2011: 96). As has happened with others, these technological devices may be used to ends not initially intended for.

Biosurveillance is another growing field of surveillance through the collection of DNA, eyes, face, hands, fingers, voice and body data, thus allowing, with tiny margins for error, to associate a singular being to a set of characteristics (Nelkin and Andrews 1993; van der Ploeg 2003; Ceyhan 2008). The capability of linking bodies to names and numbers enables individual distinctions and the enrichment of categorisation, classification and profiling of citizens. This possibility may be used to strengthen social and political control. As Simões states (2011: 97),

> Such processes cause not only inequalities accessing social and other rights, thus reducing necessary resources to political participation, but such data can also be used more directly to achieve political goals, namely to identify people who were in specific places involved in political activities.'

Since September 11, States have increased the implementation of ID cards that, particularly the most recent ones, became the most important and most sophisticated devices in performing social classification and control from a technological point of view (Lyon 2009). These devices, as Lyon argues, combine, on the one hand, more innovative characteristics of identification (e.g. biometric data) with traditional characteristics (e.g. social security databases). On the other hand, we can find programmable chips on ID cards that collect more data and that can easily be linked to remote authentication mechanisms (Stalder and Lyon 2003). The same is happening with electronic passports. As aforementioned, electronic IDs enable citizens to vote, travel or access health services, as well as, depending on the political context, allowing the State to mount surveillance systems.

The emergence and increasing number of CCTV devices over city centre streets is the most visible sign of surveillance being disseminated from prisons to factories, schools and other public, semi-public, or private places, and is embracing all urban landscapes (Coleman and Sim 2000; Norris 2003; Sætnan *et al.* 2004; Germain *et al.* 2013). Thus, thousands of CCTV systems collect data about millions of citizens on a daily basis, alongside advances in the technological precision and sophistication of those devices. Regarding the already discussed liberty–security trade-offs, citizens can feel safer with CCTV after some criminal and terrorist attacks that have occurred in several countries. Nevertheless, as argued before (Simões 2011), despite the safety reasons these devices were created for in this ambivalent social world, they can extend their action into the political sphere, recording encounters and gatherings where the people involved would not be aware of it and would possibly not be interested.

Surveillance in urban and other public spaces is no longer restricted to CCTV cameras installed by governments and other organisations. People in those public spaces may be watched not only by anonymous CCTV cameras, but also by the cameras carried by other people. With the introduction and proliferation of personal recording and storing devices (including mobile phones with photographing and filming cameras) public spaces are now invaded by more devices that can end up as surveillance technologies. These devices allow for an increase in 'sousveillant' recordings of public spaces that can be 'publicly shared on local computers, between phones, or on the internet, thus becoming a form of Open Circuit TV (OCTV)' (Timan and Oudshoorn 2012: 167). Following these reflections, our assessment is that these data can also be captured and recompiled for political purposes, an idea reinforced by some documented practices by governmental agencies, for instance, the American secret information agency NSA.

If surveillance has spread in fixed places, the same has happened in offline and online mobility areas (Bennett *et al.* 2003). This kind of surveillance is made possible with technologies that allow the tracking of people. In the domain of offline mobility, embedded chips in vehicles, automatic systems of highway tolls, GISs (Geographic Information Systems), RFID (Radio Frequency Identification) chips and GPSs (Global Positioning Systems) allow for the detection of people's locations or destinations. Using triangulation through a set of satellites, GPSs allow us to know what our geographical positions are. As Lahlou (2008: 303) argues,

> There are now many other techniques which enable position location in space: triangulation can be done with ground antennas, e.g. mobile phone antennas or Wi-Fi base stations; by beaconing (identifying a close element of the environment whose position is already known); dead reckoning (calculating the trajectory from a known position based on inertia and measurement of displacement); scene analysis (recognition of a previously known setting that had already been geolocated); etc.

As the author adds, these mature techniques are growing in precision in all countries where mobile phone providers or other entities can instantly geolocate mobile phone users. As Lahlou (2008: 303) says, a number of current surveillance possibilities are relatively benign when 'compared to the possibility afforded by continuous geolocation to provide individual *trajectories*'.[8] As the author says, a route provides much more data than a mere set of positions. A route provides a direction and can lead to intentionality. Locating someone chronologically as well as spatially might facilitate access to indications of causality. Sequential positioning can reveal a pattern, or a route, much easier to identify and recognise. A series of routes harvested from the same individual is 'even more revealing, because it yields access to habits. Intersections or convergences in trajectories can reveal a lot about social networks and communities of interest' (Lahlou 2008: 303).

In the virtual domain, online mobility 'also allows for the recording of not only what we search, but also what we read, with whom we speak and what is said, which is invasive concerning civil and political rights' (Simões 2011: 96).

Notwithstanding all the surveillance devices referred to here, the discussion around ICTs remains fundamental as they aggregate data from all forms of surveillance, including their own. ICTs have made it possible to collect personal data and to build large and widely interconnected databases, allowing the categorisation and the predictive classification of individuals aimed at social control. Without ICTs, there would be no Big Data.

Surveillance currently takes place mostly within digital realms, thus making it more imperceptible and unaccountable. Often, most people are unaware of the trails of data 'crumbs' they leave behind them in their daily lives. Excessive information on citizens progressively flows without their knowledge and permission. On the other hand, digital surveillance does not always work in a concealed way, but within the common moments and places of our everyday life. Digital surveillance is at once both open and invisible. Moreover, ICTs also enabled the deletion of data, carried out either without trace, or traceable only by experts, which raises critical and ethical issues concerning data reliability (Lyon 1994). Furthermore, regarding political participation, be it within totalitarian regimes, or wherever the Rule of Law principles are not present, data can also be manipulated, even as criminal 'evidence', for purposes of political persecution, as several secret police forces have done within authoritarian regimes (Simões 2011).

However, in several different ways, large sectors of the population do not resist this access to their everyday life and privacy. When requested by organisations, they convey their personal data, believing more in the paybacks of the supposed benefits they get from surveillance, disregarding its potential risks (Lyon 1994, 2001; Marx 2008; Harcourt 2015).

Additionally, due to cultural and social changes mentioned in the previous section, some population groups tend to exhibit their personal life, and are also fascinated with knowing the private lives of famous people, friends and even strangers. 'We want to be loved, we want to be popular, we want to be desired' (Harcourt 2015: 41), People, in an illusory autonomy position, voluntarily take part in sousveillance and both project and contribute to the strength of Big Data.

The current development of social networks, especially Facebook, provides the 'ideal' means to these fascination forms. The architecture of Facebook is based on the disclosure that gives answer to Zuckerberg's transparency ideology.

> Through likes, status update, photos and other applications, users are crafting a pastiche of their daily life by *disclosing* elements of themselves. The emphasis on the site is on providing the *individuals* with a venue to explore and present themselves to others.
>
> (Marichal 2012: 28)

Some sections of the population, such as children and teenagers, are more concerned about authenticity and less about privacy. More than anything,

> they fear anonymity and want to be distinguished from others. Attracting attention is in itself considered important and is worth sacrificing privacy for. (…) A continuous record of all individual data, e.g., constitution of

personal digital archives, and their free public dissemination through the Web, can also be seen as an example of such tremendous exhibitionism, since every gesture and instant of life is available to everybody.

(Ganascia 2010: 492)

Ganascia's and Marichal's assumptions may be considered excessive, as people also use Facebook for other purposes, such as political ones.

This cultural tendency is contradictory to another emphasised by Ganascia (2010) and other authors: most citizens fear the risk of surveillance, which leads them to worry about ethical issues related to the restriction of liberty and privacy. This fluidness is also part of this contemporary globalised societal form which Bauman (2000) has designated 'liquid modernity'.

All surveillance processes and devices lead us to the Big Data phenomenon, upon which a detailed reflection can be found previously in this volume. Does Big Data imply new senses or modalities of surveillance? Big Data is not a new phenomenon, nor is it related to some specific surveillance device or dimension. It looks like a reassessment of a well-known trend. As Klauser and Albrechts-lund (2014: 273) state, 'discourses surrounding Big Data usually refer to the ever increasing possibilities of gathering, interconnecting and analysing huge amounts of data relating to a wide range of fields and domains of everyday life.' A Gartner, Inc. (2013a) report underlines three main attributes of Big Data: high-velocity, high-volume and high variety of data assets for decision-making. Lipovetsky (2016: 140–141) also reminds us that 'the Internet's new macro-actors are built from this enormous amount of tiny scattered information, after-wards guided to data centres'. In the Big Data universe of personal data, the Internet giants feed themselves from lightness and smallness.

The Big Data concept has been well exemplified by the Snowden affair when, on 10 June 2013, Snowden

exposed NSA practices of routine surveillance to the news media, [and] he described in detail the 'architecture of oppression' that enabled him and many other NSA contractors to intercept the metadata of three billion phone calls and interactions recorded by Facebook, Google, Apple, and other tech companies.

(van Dijck 2014: 197)

The information revealed by Snowden brought to our understanding the gigantic size of data collected by information agencies and corporations. 'Big Brother and Big Deal become allies. The vigilant State and the market merge with one another' (Han 2015: 74).

Nowadays, more than ever, it might be accurate to consider a 'progressive "disappearance of disappearance" – a process whereby it is increasingly difficult for individuals to maintain their anonymity, or to escape the monitoring of social institutions' (Haggerty and Ericson 2000: 619). The possibilities for anyone to get out of sight are becoming increasingly narrow.

The devices explored above allow tracking, enabling to know where we are, where we were, where we are going or where we went, what we are reading, and clearly whom we talk to or meet up with, permitting the disclosure of our everyday political activity. As citizens become aware that their political activity can be more and more watched, political activity may come to be self-constrained or, fearing the consequences, citizens may even choose to demobilise from political activity altogether. A transparent citizen in such circumstances is therefore not a free moral agent. As Harcourt (2015: 187) states, 'The digital economy has torn down the conventional boundaries between governing, commerce, and private life. (...) The collapse of these different spheres is disempowering to us as individuals.'

In an unequal world, there are inequalities in political participation with respect to ethnicity, social class, gender, place, and political resources. Maybe surveillance levels can differ, to some extent, regarding these social variables; however, surveillance constraints to political activity are more transversal and identical across the social span, regardless of social and economic conditions, cultural capital, and so on. When facing the risk of a totalitarian society, or even the one of a muscled democracy, almost every one of us may be affected.

Final considerations

As Lyon (1994) first questioned and others (Han 2014; Harcourt 2015) restated, can we be facing the emergence of a more totalitarian society, a prison society? We tend to think we are. But, it is also crucial to assert that even in a less dystopian scenario, surveillance can threaten the functioning of democracy, as we know it in contemporary societies, whether in a democratic system based on a more liberal political participation model or on a more active one, or by questioning the core principles of political participation that potentially turn democracy into a redundancy.

The future of democratic political participation is an open-ended path. In a realistic way, it is more appropriate to speak about social and political tendencies than about scenarios. A more comprehensive analysis of these tendencies has to focus research more on the way surveillance challenges autonomy than on privacy. It is the reduction of autonomy that can not only increasingly condition political actions and citizens' choice (certainly in politics, but in the education, work or health realms too), but can also lead to a totalitarian society.

Thus, it is also important to set out the following question: do 'transparent' citizens have the autonomy to participate in the political life of their cities, regions, countries or even globally? Most certainly not. A 'transparent' citizen is not a free moral agent; one is not an agent who could actually make a political difference in our world.

The never-ending expansion of surveillance forms and range, particularly due to its increasing sophistication, and the people's compliance with their transformation into more 'transparent' citizens, gives surveillance technologies the capacity to undergird and shape a social world characterised by permanent and conscious visibility, at least for many. This state of affairs is an uttermost guarantee for established powers, providing the latter with the capacity to constrain undesired (if any) political activity, to determine a mandatory status quo, by which political participation must abide, and to threaten citizens' autonomy.

In the panopticon metaphor, the subjects of surveillance know who and where the watcher is; in contemporary societies, we are facing a worse situation. As Lyon (1994) states, watched citizens are dominated by uncertainty, since they do not know where, when, about what and whom is watching over and collecting information about them, so they simply have to comply. What Solove wrote about Orwell's Big Brother can be said about total surveillance in the contemporary context of Big Data. Total surveillance 'constructs the language, rewrites the history, purges its critics, indoctrinates the population, burns books, and obliterates all disagreeable relics from the past. (...) Any trace of individualism is quickly suffocated' (Solove 2004: 29). As Han wrote, 'total control annihilates the freedom of action and leads, definitely, to uniformity' (Han 2014: 91).

Certainly, invasion of privacy is nowadays the main way of threatening autonomy, merging itself with other forms such as economic domination. Political participation depends primarily on autonomy. Another crucial issue for further research is therefore how privacy intertwines with autonomy. The concept of autonomy also has more heuristic potential for research on the perceptions of people about the threats of surveillance to political participation. This can be a first step to public debate. Focusing the debate on autonomy makes it easier to mobilise citizens to participate in public debate concerning expanding surveillance and threats to autonomy, and therefore to political participation. As we saw throughout the discussion, when citizens are faced with security–privacy trade-offs, they choose security, saying that they have nothing to hide. But are they really aware of the consequences that loss of privacy has on autonomy (and thus on their political participation)? For this reason as well, research and public debate should be refocused on the issue of autonomy.

As stated early in this chapter, through civil and political rights, institutionally and lawfully guaranteed, democratic societies have so far assured that citizens are able to participate in political affairs without being harassed, interfered with, or even watched by their government or any other organisation. This assurance is currently at its lowest point in contemporary democratic societies. Harcourt (2015), also considering Tocqueville's cautions about 'democratic despotism', warns that living in liberal democracies might be precisely what leads to little resistance. 'It may be that democratic practices themselves facilitate our complacency' (Harcourt 2015: 254).

When security and military concerns are at the top of the political agenda, democracy and freedom are underestimated. However, these two sets of priorities should not even be considered at the same level. From an ethical point of view, democracy should prevail over security (Lyon 2003). Placing democracy at the top of the agenda might thwart the devices created to provide safety and security, becoming a threat to democratic principles. As Winner reminds us, different ideas of social and political life entail different technologies for their realization. One can create systems of production, energy, transportation, information handling, and so forth that are compatible with the growth of autonomous, self-determining individuals in a democratic polity. Or one can build, perhaps unwittingly, technical forms that are incompatible with this end and then wonder how things went strangely wrong.

(Winner (1979) in Eubanks 2006, 105–106)

The increasing breadth and depth of modes of surveillance occur most of the time with absent or insufficient public debate about established policies, but also with such haste that legal and political efforts that could safeguard certain social and political implications are limited.

The public debate and the participation in decision-making processes will be necessary to think alternative designs and programming of STs, in order to challenge the unevenness of power between the 'vigilant' and the 'monitored'. Citizens may mobilise others unaware of surveillance threats, and even engage in forms of resistance and refusal of some surveillance modes. This involvement is mandatory for an authentic autonomous participation that assures our democracy and our freedom.

Notes

1 This chapter is a much-extended work that further explores the arguments made in an earlier article: Simões, M. J. (2011). Surveillance: A (Potential) Threat to Political Participation? In: *ICDS 2011: The Fifth International Conference on Digital Society*, pp. 94–99.
2 Taking into account the Weberian methodology of the ideal type, two opposite types of politics are considered, constructed for clarification purposes, knowing that there are other models between the two ideal types, where different combinations of both can be found.
3 Action implies building (or not), doing (or not) something in the world in which one lives. Action implies energy, activity, work and organisation (Barber 1984: 122).
4 This perspective on politics, which lies in the clear distinction amongst civil servants and citizens, between the State and society, did not exist in the Athenian tradition. It has only arisen in the fifteenth and sixteenth centuries, respectively with Machiavelli and Hobbes, and has been deepened, from both theoretical and practical points of view, as the liberal model of citizenship became dominant, and in which an active involvement from citizens is not required (Held 1996).
5 These relations of domination both pre-exist and are continuously reconstructed.
6 Judgements may have, according to Oldfield (1998: 25), two directions: on one side, they are posterior to the object of judgement, on the other, judgements precede the course of action.
7 To a deeper approach on this discussion, Nissenbaum (1998, 2004) and Solove (2004, 2009) are must-read authors.
8 The trajectory concept referred to comprises the sense given by Lahlou (2008) and not the sense of social trajectory used in sociology. Although respecting the author's terminology, we would prefer phrasing it as 'routes'.

Bibliography

Barber, B. (1984). *Strong Democracy: Participatory Politics for a New Age*. Berkeley, CA: University of California Press.

Barlow, J. P. (1996). *A Cyberspace Independence Declaration*. Electronic Frontier Foundation. Available at: www.eff.org/cyberspace-independence. [Accessed 28 July 2002].

Bauman, Z. (2000). *Liquid Modernity*. Cambridge: Polity Press.

Beck, U. (1999). *The Reinvention of Politics – Rethinking Modernity in the Global Social Order*. Cambridge: Polity Press.

Bennett, C., Raab, C. and Regan, P. (2003). People and Place: Patterns of Individual Identification within Intelligent Transportation Systems. In: D. Lyon, ed., *Surveillance as Social Sorting – Privacy, Risk and Digital Discrimination*. London: Routledge, pp. 153–175.

Bourdieu, P. (1979). *La Distinction. Critique sociale du jugement*. Paris: Ed. Minuit.

Bourdieu, P. (1994). *O Poder Simbólico*. Lisbon: Difel.

Breindl, Y. (2010). Critique of the Democratic Potentialities of the Internet: A Review of Current Theory and Practice. *tripleC*, 8(1), pp. 43–59.

Burns, T. and Flam, H. (2000). *Sistemas de Regras Sociais – Teorias e Aplicações*. Oeiras: Celta.

Castel, R. (1991). From Dangerousness to Risk. In: G. Bruchell, C. Gordon and P. Miller, eds., *The Foucault Effect: Studies in Governamentality with Two Lectures by and Interview with Michel Foucault*. Chicago, IL: University of Chicago Press, pp. 281–298.

Ceyhan, A. (2008). Technologization of Security: Management of Uncertainty and Risk in the Age of Biometrics. *Surveillance & Society*, 5(2), pp. 102–123.

Coleman, R. and Sim, J. (2000). 'You'll never talk alone': CCTV Surveillance, Order and Neo-liberal Rule in Liverpool City Centre. *British Journal Sociology*, 51(4), pp. 621–639.

daCosta, F. (2013). *Rethinking the Internet of Things: A Scalable Approach to Connecting Everything*. New York: Apress Books.

Davies, S. (1992). *Big Brother: Australia's Growing Web of Surveillance*. Sydney: Simon and Schuster.

Eubanks, V. (2006). Technologies of Citizenship: Surveillance and Political Learning in the Welfare System. In: T. Monahan, ed., *Surveillance and Security – Technological Politics and Power in Everyday Life*. New York: Routledge, pp. 89–107.

Gaglio, S. and Lo Re, G. (2014). *Advances onto the Internet of Things: How Ontologies Make the Internet of Things Meaningful*. Basel: Springer International.

Ganascia, J.-G. (2010). The Generalized Sousveillance Society. *Social Science Information*, 49, pp. 489–507.

Gartner, Inc. (2013a). *IT Glossary*. Available at: www.gartner.com/it-glossary/big-data/. [Accessed 5 May 2016].

Gartner, Inc. (2013b). *Gartner Says the Internet of Things Installed Base Will Grow to 26 Billion Units By 2020*. Available at: www.gartner.com/newsroom/id/2636073. [Accessed 5 May 2016].

Germain, S., Dumoulin, L. and Douillet, A.-C. (2013). A Prosperous 'Business': The Success of CCTV Through the Eyes of International Literature. *Surveillance & Society*, 11(1/2), pp. 134–147.

Giddens, A. (1987). *The Nation-State and Violence*. Cambridge: Polity Press.

Giddens, A. (1992). *As Consequências da Modernidade*. Oeiras: Celta.

Haggerty, K. and Ericson, R. (2000). The Surveillant Assemblage. *British Journal Sociology*, 51(4), pp. 605–622.

Han, B.-C. (2014). *A Sociedade da Transparência*. Lisbon: Relógio D'Água.

Han, B.-C. (2015). *Psicopolítica*. Lisbon: Relógio D'Água.

Harcourt, B. E. (2015). *Exposed – Desire and Disobedience in the Digital Age*. Cambridge, MA: Harvard University Press.

Held, D. (1996). *Models of Democracy*. 2nd edn. Cambridge: Polity Press.

Howard, P. N. (2015). *Pax Technica: How the Internet of Things May Set Us Free, Or Lock Us Up*. New Haven, CT: Yale University Press.

Klauser, F. and Albrechtslund, A. (2014). From Self-tracking to Smart Urban Infrastructures: Towards an Interdisciplinary Research Agenda on Big Data. *Surveillance & Society*, 12(2), pp. 273–286.

Lahlou, S. (2008). Identity, Social Status, Privacy and Face-keeping in Digital Society. *Social Science Information*, 47, pp. 299–330.

Lipovetsky, G. (2016). *Da Leveza – Para uma civilização do ligeiro*. Lisbon: Edições 70.

Lyon, D. (1988). *The Information Society*. Cambridge, MA: Blackwell.

Lyon, D. (1994). *The Electronic Eye – The Rise of Surveillance Society*. Cambridge: Polity Press.

Lyon, D. (2001). *Surveillance Society – Monitoring Everyday Life*. Buckingham: Open University Press.

Lyon, D. (2003). *Resisting Surveillance, Surveillance after September, 11*. Cambridge: Polity Press.

Lyon, D. (2009). *Identifying Citizens – ID Cards as Surveillance*. Cambridge: Polity Press.

Mann, S., Nolan, J. and Wellman, B. (2003). Sousveillance: Inventing and Using Wearable Computing Devices for Data Collection in Surveillance Environments. *Surveillance & Society*, 1(3), pp. 331–355.

Marichal, J. (2012). *Facebook Democracy – The Architecture of Disclosure and the Threat to Public Life*. Farnham: Ashgate.

Marshall, T. (1998). Citizenship and Social Class. In: G. Shafir, ed., *The Citizenship Debates*. Minneapolis, MN: University of Minnesota Press, pp. 93–111. (Paper originally published in 1964).

Marx, G. (1988). *Undercover: Police Surveillance in America*. Berkeley, CA: University of California Press.

Marx, G. (2008). Vigilância Soft. In: C. Frois, ed., *A Sociedade Vigilante – Ensaios sobre identificação, vigilância e privacidade*. Lisbon: ICS, pp. 87–109.

Mayer, N. and Perrineau, P. (1992). *Les comportments politiques*. Paris: Armand Colin.

Memmi, D. (1985). L'engagement politique. In: M. Grawitz and J. Leca, *Traité de science politique* (V. 3: *Action Politique*). Paris: PUF, pp. 310–366.

Morozov, E. (2013). *To Save Everything Click Here*. London: Allan Lane.

Nelkin, D. and Andrews, L. (1993). Surveillance Creep in the Genetic Age. In: D. Lyon, ed., *Surveillance as Social Sorting – Privacy, Risk and Digital Discrimination*. London: Routledge, pp. 94–110.

Nissenbaum, H. (1998). Protecting Privacy in an Information Age: The Problem of Privacy in Public. *Law and Philosophy*, 17, pp. 559–596.

Nissenbaum, H. (2004). Privacy as Contextual Integrity. *Washington Law Review*, 79, pp. 101–139.

Norris, C. (2003). From Personal to Digital: CCTV, the Panopticon, and the Technological Mediation of Suspicion and Social Control. In: D. Lyon, ed., *Surveillance as Social Sorting – Privacy, Risk and Digital Discrimination.* London: Routledge, pp. 249–281.

Oldfield, A. (1998). *Citizenship and Community: Civil Republicanism and the Modern World.* 2nd edn. London: Routledge.

Raab, C. (1997). Privacy, Democracy, Information. In: B. D. Loader, ed., *The Governance of Cyberspace – Politics, Technology and Global Restructuring.* London: Routledge, pp. 153–172.

Rheingold, H. (1996). *Electronic Democracy Toolkit.* The Well. Available at: www.well.com/user/hlr/electrondemoc.html. [Accessed 6 June 2000].

Rifkin, J. (2014). *The Zero Marginal Cost Society: The Internet of Things, the Collaborative Commons, and the Eclipse of Capitalism.* London: Palgrave Macmillan.

Roche, M. (1998). Citizenship, Social Theory and Social Change. In: B. Turner and P. Hamilton, ed., *Citizenship: Critical Concepts.* 2nd edn. London: Routledge, pp. 80–110.

Rousseau, J.-J. (1981). *O Contrato Social.* Lisbon: Publicações Europa-América. (Book originally published in 1726).

Rouvroy, A. and Poullet, Y. (2009). The Right to Informational Self-Determination and the Value of Self-Development: Reassessing the Importance of Privacy for Democracy. In: Reinventing Data Protection: Proceedings of the International Conference (Brussels, 12–13 October 2007). Dordrecht: Springer, pp. 45–76.

Sætnan, A. R., Lomell, H. M. and Wiecek, C. (2004). Controlling CCTV in Public Spaces: Is Privacy the (Only) Issue? Reflections on Norwegian and Danish Observations. *Surveillance & Society*, 2(2/3), pp. 396–414.

Simões, M. J. (2005). *Política e Tecnologia – Tecnologias da Informação e da Comunicação e Participação Política em Portugal.* Oeiras: Celta.

Simões, M. J. (2011). Surveillance: A (Potential) Threat to Political Participation? In: *ICDS 2011: The Fifth International Conference on Digital Society*, pp. 94–99.

Simões, M. J., Barriga, A. and Jerónimo, N. A. (2011). Brave New World? Political Participation and New Media. *SOTICS 2011: The First International Conference on Social Eco-Informatics*, pp. 55–60.

Solove, D. (2004). *The Digital Person – Technology and Privacy in the Information Age.* New York: New York University Press.

Solove, D. (2009). *Understanding Privacy.* Cambridge, MA: Harvard University Press.

Stalder, F. and Lyon, D. (2003). Electronic Identity Cards and Social Classification. In: D. Lyon, ed., *Surveillance as Social Sorting – Privacy, Risk and Digital Discrimination.* London: Routledge, pp. 77–93.

Sterling, B. (2014). *The Epic Struggle of the Internet of Things.* Moscow: Strelka Press.

Timan, T. and Oudshoorn, N. (2012). Mobile Cameras as New Technologies of Surveillance? How Citizens Experience the Use of Mobile Cameras in Public Nightscape. *Surveillance & Society*, 10(2), pp. 167–181.

van der Ploeg, I. (2003). Biometrics and the Body as Information: Normative Issues of the Socio-technical Coding of the Body. In: D. Lyon, ed., *Surveillance as Social Sorting – Privacy, Risk and Digital Discrimination.* London: Routledge, pp. 57–73.

van Dijck, J. (2014). Datafication, Dataism and Dataveillance: Big Data Between Scientific Paradigm and Ideology. *Surveillance & Society*, 12 (2), pp. 197–208.

van Gunsteren, H. (1994). Four Conceptions of Citizenship. In: B. van Steenbergen, ed., *The Condition of Citizenship.* London: Sage, pp. 36–48.

Westin, A. (1967). *Privacy and Liberty.* New York: Atheneum.

10 Fading dots, disappearing lines – surveillance and Big Data in news media after the Snowden revelations

Gunhild Tøndel and Ann Rudinow Sætnan

Introducing the story

Any event, person, place, stack of papers, object, any data set worth a story at all can be the basis for thousands of stories. Nothing has only one story to tell. Which stories we get to hear depends on the telling, which in turn depends on the tellers, the listeners and the re-tellers. This chapter presents an analysis of the changing shape of Norwegian surveillance and Big Data discourse, with a story told by Edward Snowden as our device and empirical departure. The story has since been retold innumerable times – first by Glenn Greenwald and Laura Poitras, then by other journalists who picked up the story and retold it to their audiences, then by those audiences … and now again by us.

Stories exist within a socio-historical matrix. As representations, they structure incidents, events and meanings – for instance through the presentation of a beginning, while even a beginning has antecedents. A story could always be told otherwise – resembling Everett Hughes' (1984) familiar old mantra. A story could be told with flashbacks, flash-forwards, or chronologically. It could also be told as if no alternative story were possible, as if there existed a path-dependent pattern (Bennett and Elman 2006) in the discourse that connected the dots in the first place – but of course, without executing full control over the readers' or listeners' convictions. Although our story will glance backwards to antecedents, to explore the surveillance/Big Data discourse, we choose to begin with Edward Snowden's decision to blow the whistle on US domestic surveillance.

Edward Snowden, in the course of his work as a cybersecurity analyst for various US surveillance agencies and contractors, became disenchanted with the workings of US surveillance, especially surveillance of US citizens' communications with one another. He chose not to tell his own narrative based in the documents he downloaded. He chose to leave that to carefully chosen storytellers – journalists. To leave the telling to others is a strategy that has had success in many different storytelling traditions – from fairy tales to criminal investigations. He was also strategic in choosing which documents to reveal or not, carefully evaluating every document he disclosed to ensure that each was legitimately in the public interest – as harming people was not his goal, but transparency (Greenwald, MacAskill and Poitras 2013).

Over the course of retellings, any story is constantly changing. Stories change their shapes, their messages, their morals. They can also have many layers – stories in the stories in the stories. Our story is not like the original; for instance, it is not about US surveillance in itself, but about the *retelling* of that story in Norwegian newspapers in the months following the initial telling. That retelling consists of thousands of individual stories. Taken together, they make up a meta-story, which evolves as constituent elements, themselves stories in their own right, are added to and abandoned from the whole. We have followed the evolution of this story in Norwegian national and regional print newspapers.

Print newspapers are at once both lasting and ephemeral. Their stories are lastingly archived on paper and electronically. Yet most of those stories fade from public discourse in a matter of weeks, days, or even hours. This means that abandoned stories can always be revived by further retellings, but also that they *must* be retold and revived if they are not to fade into oblivion. Thus, over time the size and shape of the larger meta-story changes. Unless retold, it becomes smaller, thinner, somewhat ghostlike and frail. It may end up as a bunch of anecdotes without any obvious connections, or tamed from 'lion' to 'kitten', or even totally silenced. In this chapter, we explore both the duration of this meta-story in Norwegian print newspapers and the changes in how the story frames surveillance and Big Data over time. We will be focusing on two aspects of the evolving Snowden meta-story in the chosen newspapers, starting with the *Guardian*'s intended storyline – as (re-)told by editor Alan Rusbridger when receiving an honorary doctorate in Oslo. We ask: which issues raised by Rusbridger were included in Norwegian journalists' initial retellings of the story, which issues have since faded from later retellings – and especially, how has the retold story in the Norwegian press dealt with the original story's Big Data issues?

Rusbridger's reasons

Again, many stories could be told about why Snowden took and leaked secret documents. Many stories could be told about why those he leaked them to released (some of) them to the public. The journalists chose to let documents 'speak for themselves', although some storyline is implied by the choices they made as to which documents to reveal and in what order. Both Greenwald and Poitras deferred, not only by choice but also of necessity, to further journalists who would take on their stories to be reframed and republished. Thus responsibility for the narrative was handed over from whistle-blower to journalists to further journalists to readers and (it was hoped) onto kitchen-table discourses (Gullestad 1984) and from there (it was further hoped) to activism.

For our story, we chose the *Guardian* as our focal point, not least because the *Guardian* was the source for so many of the further retellings in Norwegian newspapers. We chose the *Guardian*'s editor, Alan Rusbridger, as spokesperson for the staff's journalistic reasoning as they chose which of Snowden's materials to publish. From various occasions and formats where he has discussed those choices (e.g. Rusbridger 2013), we then chose to cite the acceptance lecture for his honorary doctorate from the University of Oslo (*ABC News* 2014). In this lecture, he conveniently listed the following 12 reasons (Table 10.1) as criteria for selection of documents being worthwhile to use in news stories, in accordance with Snowden's instructions.

Rusbridger ends his list here, indicating that these 12 points are probably the most important, though perhaps not the only points he wished to open up for public discourse by publishing material from the documents Snowden provided. In a UK context, Dencik *et al.* (2016) found that the post-Snowden debate predominantly centred on techno-legal responses relating to the development and use of encryption, and policy advocacy around privacy and data protection. Regarding the impact of that cumulative story in a Norwegian context, we will now explore two questions: (i) which issues were repeated in the ongoing

Table 10.1 Rusbridger's 12 reasons

Reason	Argument
The nature of consent	'What role do we citizens have in consenting to what's going to be done? Are we allowed a knowledge of what's going to happen to our emails, our text messages, our photographs ... the intrusive capacities of this technology? ... [I]t may be that we're prepared to give away that privacy in return for security, but is there a meaningful nature of consent?'
The role of parliaments	The British Parliament does not have sufficient understanding of the technology, of their having rejected this type of data collection the one time it was actually offered for them to vote on, and their not being told that it was already being used and continued to be used since. Is there a meaningful form of Parliamentary control over governments' digital intelligence practices?
Legality across technologies	If the police were 'suddenly [given] powers to come into our houses and seize our papers, we would be horrified ... [W]here is it written that the digital world is to be treated separately from the physical world?' Which assumptions about the physical world are taken to apply to the digital? Is an email to be seen and treated the same as a letter in a sealed envelope, requiring a warrant issued by a judge on the basis of probable cause before police can open it? Or is it equivalent to a postcard left lying in the open, or a loud conversation in a public space?
The role of the private sector	Governmental digital surveillance 'piggybacks' on private sector telecom and internet service providers. How many went beyond what they were legally required to do, and do the customers and shareholders of these companies have the right to know how their information is being used and whether that's on a legal or a voluntary basis?

continued

Table 10.1 Continued

Reason	Argument
Encryption and the integrity of the Web	This aspect concerns 'all our bank statements, all our medical records, all our emails ... [I]f what has happened is that the NSA has gone around creating trapdoors and weaknesses in the encryption of the Web itself, then the system that we all use has been compromised, because you can't produce trapdoors that are used by the good guys but not by the bad guys.'
Risks to the digital economy	Potential impacts on Western technology companies of the rest of the world thinking that these technologies are being used as spyware. Other economic dangers may be added, such as the potential harms for businesses of industrial spies using the same 'trapdoors and weaknesses' that government intel agencies such as the NSA have created.
International relations	Is it OK to be bugging the president's phone of a country that is supposedly a friend?
Truthfulness	Have those in positions of authority 'told the truth in public about what they've been doing?' As we now know, they haven't, which can render consent and/or parliamentary control meaningless.
Privacy	According to Rusbridger, 'The collection of billions of events per day is the most staggering potential invasion of privacy in history'. This concerns not only communications content, but also 'metadata' – the content-accompanying technical information that shows who has been in contact with whom, where, and for how long. Because '[c]ontent is often confusing and troublesome, "metadata" is the stuff you want. But they treat metadata as something you don't need a warrant to get a look at.'
Confidentiality	Similar but not identical to privacy, confidentiality refers to certain privileged forms of communication, such as between doctor and patient, lawyer and client, priest and parishioner, or journalist and source. 'Anybody who has a confidential relationship, or thinks [Rusbridger's emphasis] they have a confidential relationship, is going to have to change the way they communicate and learn about encryption.'
Proportionality	This hinges on *effectiveness*. The costs, including social costs, of this massive endeavor, can only be defended if results are reasonable in proportion to those costs. And yet, the effectiveness of the NSA mass surveillance programs and of similar programs elsewhere has been an 'evidence-free zone' [Rusbridger's term]. As with truthfulness, this impinges critically on consent and the role of parliaments.
Information security	The accumulation of whistleblowers from the NSA data collection programs and related programs shows that 'even the most secure databases in the world are evidently not secure.' Can we trust these agencies with all our most personal and sensitive data? What further risks to our data integrity and security do these massive databases represent, even beyond the invasion of our privacy that the databases in themselves may constitute?

retellings of and about the Snowden leaks, and (ii) where did the media discourse on Snowden and NSA hit or miss its relevance to Big Data issues? But first, we describe how we accessed, read, interpreted and related the stories.

Tracing issues, reading stories as data material

Mapping the formation, stretching, clustering and twisting of issues both in traditional and social-digital media is a well-known methodological and analytical task in social science. Recently, a social media research approach to controversy analysis has been developed within Science and Technology Studies (STS) and related fields (Marres and Moats 2015). This approach offers a growing repertoire of promising sophisticated quali-quantitative techniques for studying controversies within social media (Moats 2015). Inspired by this approach, we have done an analysis of the Snowden revelations in Norwegian news media stories, which clearly qualifies as a controversial matter. We have approached the collected articles related to the controversy as 'containers of content' (Prior 2004). When making this clear, it is with reference to the dichotomy of content and materiality being a recurring problem for STS and media studies (Gillespie *et al.* 2014). For instance, one topic of discussion has been whether the recent move towards materiality has been at the expense of content (Moats 2015). Yet, as Suchman (2014) argues (and as we sympathise as well), in any given empirical case study, the content-material distinction is moot, at least for Actor Network Theory-inspired approaches.

As for the core work of data collection and sorting concerns, we have done this manually through searchable electronic archives and readily available figure and table calculations. The Norwegian and Swedish telegram bureaus, NTB and TT, operate a daily updated, searchable electronic archive of all Scandinavian print news media stories, Atekst–Retriever. Using the search terms 'Snowden OR NSA', we searched all Norwegian media in this archive for the years 2013–2015. This gave us the basic month-by-month numbers of article hits where either of these two words appeared. Then, for national and regional print news media, we downloaded the articles themselves from June of each of those years for closer reading. Reading through the articles, we systematically recorded reference details (newspaper, date, article title, page number) and a brief description of the central topic of each article. Simultaneously, we did analytical interpretations of: (i) the article's thematic relationship to the NSA, to surveillance and/or to the Snowden leaks and Big Data issues; (ii) the article's modality (positive, neutral, negative) towards Snowden and towards any surveillance practices referred to; and (iii) which (if any) of Rusbridger's 12 points of public interest were mentioned in the text. We also recorded excerpts from the article illustrating the analytical points.

Of course, the analytical data result from our own readings and judgement calls. We will enable readers to assess our judgements and form their own by illustrating two points about our judgement calls as regards which of Rusbridger's issues any given article addressed and our assignment of modalities to the articles. First, when deciding which (if any) of Rusbridger's issues to code as addressed, we did not consider it sufficient that we, as presumably more-than-averagely interested readers, recognised a statement in an article as relevant to one of those issues. We only coded an issue as addressed if the journalist/author of an article or some person quoted within the article specifically mentioned that issue. For instance, an article mentioning the size of the NSA budget was not necessarily addressing the issues of proportionality and effectiveness, not unless they also mentioned the effectiveness side of that equation. However, we did code articles mentioning the presence or lack of effects of NSA surveillance as addressing this issue even if it did not mention costs, since claims of the presence or absence of effects – even independent of costs – are claims about effectiveness. We did not expect all contributions to a discourse on a given issue to fully represent Rusbridger's presentation of those issues in the Oslo lecture – or, for that matter, even to agree with Rusbridger. We coded for contributions to debate on a theme, not for the specifics of those contributions.

Then, we coded each article for the overall modality of its references to Snowden and to the surveillance measures discussed in the article. We coded modalities as *positive* towards Snowden when texts referred to him – either exclusively, predominantly, or in conclusion – with positive-laden characterisations. *Negative* modalities towards Snowden referred to him – either exclusively, predominantly, or in conclusion – with negative-laden characterisations. Modalities were coded as *neutral* when Snowden was not mentioned at all; when he was mentioned in terms of simple facts such as his age, or where he was seeking asylum; or when he was mentioned in the form of quotes from various sources with both positive and negative sources cited and the journalist/newspaper not weighing in on the assessment through explicit conclusions, choice of article title, or selective use of sarcasm. Similarly, modalities on surveillance were coded as neutral, with the addition that claims of fact, based on surveillance as a source of those facts, would be coded as positive. Care had to be taken to recognise any reversals of apparent modality made through the use of irony, which several news reports played upon.

In the text that follows, excerpts may contain our re-translations from Norwegian translations of statements or texts originally in English. Obviously, as in the children's game called 'Chinese Whispers' in the UK, or 'Telegraph' in the US, our translations may not revert to precisely the same words originally used. All such translations are therefore marked as our re-translations.

Now, we proceed to how the meta-story about surveillance after Snowden in Norwegian news media unfolds from 2013–2015, starting with surveillance in the media before Snowden, and then after Snowden year for year and issue for issue.

The story unfolds

The prequels

Snowden was not the first NSA whistle-blower. Critical stories about US domestic and foreign surveillance had been launched in Norwegian news media prior to Snowden's document leaks, but retellings of these were few and far between – at least in Norway by 2013 when we started our archive search (see Figure 10.1 below). Using our search terms (Snowden OR NSA) we found four stories from January through May 2013, prior to the first story about Snowden's leaked documents. Each of these mentioned one or more of the earlier whistle-blowers.

During the five months before Snowden entered the public scene, the phenomenon of whistle-blowing appeared mostly in small fonts in the shadows of the daily news reports. On 25 January 2013, the newspaper *Dag og Tid* wrote about controversy in the wake of the film *Zero Dark Thirty*. Pentagon officials suspected one of the film-makers' sources of being overly generous with details. But, as the film was flattering towards the CIA and the military, it was seen as unlikely that this source would be prosecuted and punished as other leakers/whistle-blowers had been.

Two weeks later, the left-wing daily *Klassekampen* ran a full-page story about the US hunting down whistle-blowers. They list six whistle-blower cases in the preceding five years, all convicted or still under prosecution. One of these, former NSA executive Thomas Drake, had been sentenced to one year in prison for revealing information about domestic surveillance. All but one of the charges against him had been dropped, so the one-year sentence seemed quite stiff.

On 27 March 2013, the business newspaper *Dagens Næringsliv* published a multi-page feature article about William Binney under the title 'The man who

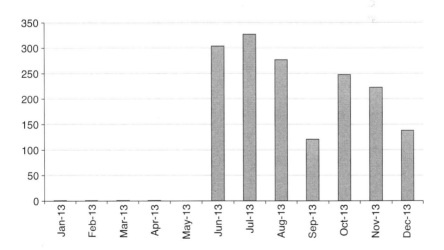

Figure 10.1 Numbers of articles in Norwegian print news, 2013, found in A-Tekst/ Retriever using search terms 'NSA OR Snowden'.

knew too much'. Like Drake, Binney had revealed information quite similar to some of what Snowden was soon about to reveal, but the newspaper didn't know that at the time.

On 3 April 2013, Norway's largest newspaper, the conservative broadsheet *Aftenposten*, published a full-page commentary by their political editor, Harald Stanghelle, about Norwegian domestic surveillance. The Norwegian Parliamentary Control Committee on Investigative, Surveillance and Security Services was to deliver their annual report to the Parliament. Stanghelle predicted that the meeting would be 'interesting' (Stanghelle's term and quote marks), as the report included incidents the committee had uncovered where surveillance organisations had targeted domestic journalists critical of their operations. Stanghelle highlighted parallels to William Binney's revelations about the NSA.

May was a quiet month as far as NSA-related surveillance stories were concerned. Then, in June, the Snowden revelations began to draw Norwegian newspaper attention.

One leak at a time

As Snowden's revelations begin to appear, with Norwegian journalists picking up the story from the *Guardian* and (over time) also from other sources, references to the NSA and (once he reveals himself as the whistle-blower) to Snowden leap from one to hundreds per month. Already in June that year, starting a day after the *Guardian*, on 7 June, Norwegian print media are registered in Atekst/Retriever with over 300 hits for our search terms. Of these, discounting front-page teasers with only title and page reference, we downloaded and studied more closely the 275 that were in national and regional newspapers.

As one would expect in news media, article production is noticeably event-driven. At this time, the chronology of the leaks followed first from the documentation that NSA had data on millions of telephone calls via Verizon. Then came the leaks that NSA's so-called 'PRISM' programme had accessed tele- and Internet-traffic data from all the major service providers, that US agencies were hacking Chinese tele- and Internet services, and that the British agency GCHQ had hacked tele- and email-communications of delegates to the G20 summit meeting. Besides the leaks themselves, there were also spin-off events from these and tangent events that related to these. Spin-off events that generated hits were Snowden revealing his identity, Snowden's flight from Hong Kong to Moscow and search for asylum, Senate and Congressional hearings, a Norwegian defence lawyer being denied a visa to the US after communications with one of his clients were intercepted, and Norway and the EU demanding and receiving information and assurances from the US regarding how their citizens were being affected. In addition, President Obama's visit to Berlin was coloured by the Snowden leaks that preceded it.

All but one of the 275 articles refers to one or more of these events, either explicitly or in recognisable hints. The one exception mentions the NSA in relation to a murder case from several decades earlier. While the initial leakages already struck Norwegian journalists as significant, resulting in dozens of articles, the discourse really picked up momentum when the Norwegian lawyer's communications were intercepted and his visa application denied. This obviously made the closeness to and relevance for Norway more visible. From then on, the matter remained a hot news item throughout the month, with the exception of Sundays, since Norway had few and thin Sunday newspapers at the time.

One would also expect that journalists, at least initially, might hesitate to jump to conclusions. This, too, appears to be born out in the data, as shown in Table 10.2 where, in keeping with that expectation, we see predominantly neutral modalities regarding the surveillance measures discussed and (once his identity is known), Snowden as whistle-blower or leaker. However, it is worth noting that even though neutral modalities dominate overall, negative modalities regarding the surveillance practices in question far exceed positive ones. This is at first glance strikingly different from what we, together with colleagues from Sweden and Denmark, found to be the case for Scandinavian media discourse on surveillance in general (Backman, Johnson, Sætnan *et al.* 2015). Using various terms for surveillance as search terms, we found predominantly positive modalities in Scandinavian media discourse. However, a close examination of those data showed that modalities differentiated between various goals and scopes of surveillance: Targeted surveillance based on reasonable suspicion was discussed in positive or neutral terms; mass surveillance of whole swaths of the population was discussed more often in negative terms. Thus, the findings in our Snowden-related data are not so surprising after all.

We must also caution that our findings may, to some extent, have been coloured by those earlier findings, which may have enabled (or prejudiced?) us to recognise certain subtle expressions of modalities. For instance, we saw the recurring use of 'massive' and 'millions of citizens' in descriptions of the Verizon and PRISM data sweeps as expressions of shock and dismay and as references to privacy issues. For example, some might read the following statement from the first article produced by our search as a bland, neutral statement of fact, revealing neither value judgements nor issues affecting those judgements: 'It makes no difference whether they are suspected of anything illegal or not. The many millions of cell phone customers of Verizon … are all under surveillance' (*Dagsavisen* 2013a). Thus, when we coded the above-excerpted article as engaging with the issues of privacy, legality and the role of the private sector, and as carrying a negative modality towards the surveillance in question, our coding choices may reflect our earlier research experience. But then again, even an

Table 10.2 Norwegian print news article modalities re: surveillance and Snowden, June 2013

Referring to	Positive	Neutral	Negative
Surveillance	11	180	78
Snowden	31	230	8

ordinary fluent-foreigner knowledge of Norwegian language[1] points in the same direction. Norwegians tend to avoid superlatives, so the frequent occurrence of a word such as 'massive' is, by Norwegian standards, exceptional. Our modality reading becomes an even more obvious choice as the terms 'massive' and 'millions' are repeated in story after story, such as in the following excerpt from *Klassekampen* (2013a), with the title 'This is how the USA surveilles the world':

> In the book *1984* where Big Brother sees everything, the Party says that 'war is peace, freedom is slavery and ignorance is strength'. In today's USA Obama's positive-laden term 'openness' masks the development of a top secret and massive surveillance machinery with the capacity to surveille millions, perhaps billions, of people over the entire planet.

On the whole, we would characterise Norwegian newspapers' initial coverage of the Snowden leaks as shocked, cautious but trending negative towards the practices unveiled, and taking a broad view of the implications of those practices. Given Rusbridger's self-proclaimed goals for publishing from Snowden's materials, and assuming that those goals are similar to Snowden's own goals in obtaining and releasing them, Rusbridger and Snowden would have reason to be pleased with the initial coverage of the leaks in Norway – not only by its quantity and modalities, but also by the breadth of issues discussed in relation to the revealed surveillance practices. Of the 275 articles we read from June 2013, 66 touch on three or more of the issues Rusbridger wished to raise, often showing how the various issues intertwined with one another, as in the code-annotated excerpt below:

> President Barack Obama used the press conference and his speech in Berlin to attempt to calm criticisms of the USA's surveillance of telephone and internet traffic. But so far, he has not succeeded [*foreign relations*]. According to the recent Congress hearings [*role of Congress*] with the leadership of the National Security Agency (NSA), it has been stated that a number of terrorist actions have been averted as a result of this surveillance [*effectiveness*]. In that connection it was supposedly the internet traffic, rather than surveillance of telephone traffic, that was helpful. But not so much help that it averted the Boston terrorism, The Economist notes [*effectiveness*]. The NSA leadership demands to be believed when they say that terrorist actions have been averted, but they couldn't say anything about specifics [*truth*]. It's a matter of confidential documents. Congress is more concerned with surveillance of American citizens than of what the USA does to the rest of us in the world [*foreign relations*] who use Twitter or Google [*role of private sector*]. Merkel and other European leaders see that their citizens are free prey for American surveillance since they are customers of American multinational companies [*foreign relations, role of private sector*]. This is obviously a matter for concern. What long-term effects this may have on trust in American companies, everything from Apple to Facebook, is

unknown [*risks to digital economy*]. So far, their stock values don't seem to have been impacted by the furore. But European competitors may start using as a sales argument that they are outside the reach of American intelligence [*risks to digital economy*].

(*Aftenposten* 2013a)

Table 10.3 shows that almost all of the 12 issues raised by Rusbridger in his Oslo lecture were already included in Norwegian media discourse on the Snowden leaks in the week of the first two leaks – the one exception being the 'nerdy' issue of the integrity of the web and the need for encryption. That issue may well have been discussed in other media, such as technology journals or the tech web pages of online newspapers. It was also discussed in the mainstream media later, when brought up by Snowden in his televised lecture for the South by Southwest conference (Backman, Sætnan, Svenonius *et al.* 2015).

However, the figure also shows that not all issues received equal attention. Table 10.4 shows that the articles displayed a degree of complexity, with about two-fifths of them mentioning and linking multiple aspects of the overall story. However, attention to even the most prominent issues was soon deflected by discussions of Snowden's character and his asylum situation once his identity was revealed. This is also bemoaned in several editorials and op-ed pieces towards the end of that month. New leaks did, however, revive attention to the issues. Thus the distribution of leaks over time appears to have been a successful strategy.

Table 10.3 'Rusbridger reasons' mentioned in Norwegian national and regional print news coverage of NSA and Snowden leaks, June 2013

Rusbridger reason	Number of mentions
1 Consent	37
2 Role of Parliament	20
3 Legality	49
4 Role of private sector	61
5 Encryption	–
6 Risks to digital economy	12
7 International relations	64
8 Truthfulness	22
9 Privacy	78
10 Confidentiality	7
11 Proportionality	32
12 Information security	18

Table 10.4 Number of 'Rusbridger reasons' mentioned per article of NSA OR Snowden coverage in Norwegian national and regional print news, June 2013

Number of 'Rusbridger reasons' mentioned	0 (of these, number focused on Snowden as person)	1	2	3	4	5	6	7 or more
Number of articles	120 (88)	45	43	26	19	14	5	3

Connecting the dots – a closer look at how the issues were discussed

Most of the 275 articles we included in our data material for 2013 were short and simple, neither elaborating on the issues nor linking them. Looking through the material issue by issue, we found that the journalists and other writers largely expressed agreement on most of the issues raised, but that there was debate on some, and that they occasionally raised further aspects of these issues than those pointed out by Rusbridger in his Oslo lecture. We also see that some issues received far more attention than others.

To simplify our presentation here, we have grouped Rusbridger's themes into several clusters (Table 10.5) according to how they relate to Big Data practices. This depends, of course, on our own framings of those issues. The clusters are thus groupings of convenience for the analysis at hand; for another analysis, they could have been clustered otherwise. To prioritise our presentation, we have further grouped the clusters according to how pertinent they are to current Big Data debates. The five issues in what we have called the framing cluster are core issues in Big Data critiques, for instance, the question of informed consent for personal data (re-)use in a Big Data context, or the question of how Big Data practices affect privacy. The four themes in the regulation and measurement clusters are overarching issues across many technologies. The remaining themes, while not irrelevant, are more peripheral to core Big Data concerns. Of course, this peripheral status may be temporary. For instance, encryption as a defensive strategy against Big Data inclusion may become more common, or customers (even whole countries) may begin to boycott companies engaged in Big Data practices, making Big Data a real and immediate threat to the digital economy. For now, however, that threat is more latent or theoretical, with even surveillance usage of Big Data seen as a commercial opportunity. In other words,

Table 10.5 Issue clusters

Relationship to Big Data debates	Cluster name	'Rusbridger reasons' within cluster
Core issues in current Big Data debates	Framing	The nature of consent Privacy Confidentiality Legality across technologies The role of the private sector
Overarching issues of technology regulation	Regulation	The role of Parliaments International relations
Overarching issues of technology regulation	Measurement	Truthfulness Proportionality
Peripheral issues	Management	Encryption and the integrity of the Web Risks to digital economy Information security

each of the issues Rusbridger points out as being of public interest when it comes to NSA surveillance is also of public interest when it comes to Big Data more generally, but some are currently discussed more than others in Big Data debates.

All these issues are mutually entangled one way and another. Thus, media discourses on them may cut across themes and clusters. In what follows, we describe how Rusbridger's issues combined (or not) in Norwegian news media in the first weeks after the Snowden revelations. We begin with the framing cluster, as the issues there are at the core of Big Data debates.

Framing issues

It is not surprising that issues such as consent, privacy, confidentiality, legality across technologies and the role of the private sector came up with primary relevance in our analysis – with privacy looming largest. With the revelations of Snowden internationally, privacy has risen in the general public discourse (Epstein, Roth and Baumer 2014) – while also being a traditionally debated political concern. Looking at those articles in our material that elaborated on the issues and even on mechanisms that linked them, we found that privacy was linked to just about all the other issues mentioned by Rusbridger – with the exception of the encryption issue, which was not mentioned at all. But not all links received equal attention. Surprisingly, the connection to confidentiality, for instance, was rarely raised. Less surprisingly, when it did come up, it was most often mentioned regarding protection of journalistic sources.[2] When stating that most attention was devoted to privacy in our data material, however, we must caution that we included references to freedom of expression as conflations with the issue of privacy rather than separating them out as a thirteenth issue. Only a few articles made this link to freedom of expression explicit, but enough did so that we took the link as given for others. As one excerpt, primarily concerned with political communications, states: 'When legal communications are surveilled, this threatens freedom of information and expression' (*Adresseavisen* 2013). Other articles were more concerned with the everyday communications of ordinary citizens:

> You thought perhaps that the picture of your baby that you posted on Facebook was only of interest to the nearest family? That your chat with your girlfriend on Skype was a matter between the two of you? ... Indications are that you were wrong. While Uncle Sam's watchers may not necessarily be interested in the miniscule details of your personal tracks online, evidence is that they do have access to whatever of it they may wish to see.
>
> (*Klassekampen* 2013b)

In the same vein, at least three writers (a Norwegian left-wing politician, a refugee from South Africa and a China correspondent) reflected from personal experience as to how surveillance had impacted their lives and sense of independence. Note the links the China correspondent, excerpted below, makes to both freedom of expression and to foreign affairs (the latter an issue we will get back to later):

> Once I was sitting in my kitchen in Beijing, talking about 'girl stuff' with my young daughter, when all of a sudden she put her finger to her lips and pointed up at the ceiling with her other hand, up to an imagined, hidden microphone: – Hush, mamma! They can hear us. That's how ingrained the awareness of 'Big Brother' is in China, that even children behave in accordance with his presence. If you want to exchange sensitive information with anyone, you make plans to meet in a park. My e-mails were of course hacked and all my electronic communications forwarded to some, for me unknown, address. That was simply how it was. But the USA? As bad as China? … It seems ironic that news of this surveillance scandal should break just as China's Xi Jinping and USA's Barack Obama are to meet in California and argue over internet espionage. The watchers in Beijing must have been rubbing their hands with glee.
>
> (*Dagbladet* 2013)

While the connection to confidentiality was nearly invisible, far more frequently, the privacy issue was linked with the question of whether our voluntary use of digital services implied our consent to surveillance. The nature of consent was not discussed in great depth or breadth, focusing primarily on user naiveté, as in the examples below:

> They didn't have cell phones back when Stasi was surveilling German citizens. It's easier for the American NSA, now that we make our lives transparent. [NSA] gathers information from the servers for Facebook, Google, Yahoo, Microsoft, Skype, Apple and YouTube. That means that our e-mails, Facebook updates, documents stored in the cloud and chats with friends are surveilled and picked through with an eye for suspicious content. … So where are the protests? Why is there so little anger to be found over the USA invading our privacy in a manner that means they could just as well have had cameras and microphones in our apartments? Could it be because, deep down, we already knew? … Perhaps we've thought it's a good thing it's the USA that's first out with the technology … they defend many of the values we hold dear. Aside from privacy.… I would bet that for every person who's paranoid in this area, there are ten thousand who are naïve.
>
> (*Vårt Land* 2013)

Most people perceive their own internet activities as something deeply personal. And yet, we sign digital contracts with Facebook, Twitter, Instagram, Google and Apple without a peep of protest. Just to tell God and everyman what we ate for dinner, how it feels to lose a lover and what we did on the weekend, we readily hand over broad powers to commercial actors, so they can use our metadata to earn even more money. When security forces do the same, it's a big scandal. What should they have done? Asked first? 'Are you a terrorist?' We are comfortable with Mark Zuckerberg capitalising our lives voraciously, while our reflex is to damn to Hell those supposed to protect our security. It's a paradox. When it comes down to it, it's our own stupidity, and not spies, that constitutes the greatest threat to our privacy.

(*Nordlys* 2013)

The other context that came up with some frequency and that we coded as addressing the issue of consent was when opinion polls were cited regarding whether people were inclined to accept or reject the surveillance practices revealed. For instance, according to *VG* (2013), an opinion poll recently published showed that Obama's government had support for their surveillance policies, where '56 percent find that the authorities having access to their telephone data is "acceptable" ... and 62 percent respond that it is more important to investigate terrorist threats, even at the cost of privacy'. Of course, opinion polls are very sensitive to context (which one of the articles did mention) and to question phrasing and sampling techniques (which none mentioned). As one article wrote:

I think it's fairly certain that if an opinion poll had been conducted without the Boston terror fresh in mind, the numbers would have been different.... It is possible that the surveillance cases ... may lead to a change ... and that we will see the usual scepticism towards authorities turning up again.

(*Aftenposten* 2013b)

Overarching and peripheral attention

Many different themes brought the issue of *international relations* into Norwegian Snowden/NSA-related media coverage that month: one was whenever one country or another lodged a formal query or complaint. At the opposite end of the scale was the news of which countries were collaborating with NSA data collection. Related to that was the question of which countries' data were being collected. And finally, other collaborative events were noticeably uncomfortable with espionage being so firmly and clearly in view. This was particularly ironic if the negotiations in question were about *data security*, or if cosy (even espionage-collaborative) relationships were being disrupted, such as the relationships described here: 'NSA works closely with Australia, Canada, New Zealand and Great Britain' (*Klassekampen* 2013c). Our data material contained quite an extensive list of such cosinesses, or at least, the importance of a frontstage appearance of cosiness:

Iran, Pakistan and Jordan top the list over countries USA's military intelligence service NSA gathers information from, according to the *Guardian*

(…). The overview shows that Norway is among the countries American intelligence is least interested in.

(*Aftenposten* 2013c)

News articles about American surveillance of telephone conversations and data traffic are highly inconvenient for European and American bureaucrats. In July they should, according to plans, be embarking on difficult tug-of-wars over a free trade agreement. Privacy and information exchange are among the most difficult points on that agenda.

(*Nationen* 2013)

Of course, our data material also contained a list of obvious *un*cosiness:

A spokesperson for the Turkish foreign minister writes in a comment that 'the accusations in the *Guardian* are very worrisome, and we want an official and adequate explanation'. He states that it is alarming if the British have been spying on a NATO member nation.

(*Dagens Næringsliv* 2013)

It was the head of USA's national security agency NSA, General Keith Alexander, who last year described the theft of American economic secrets – by among others China – as 'history's greatest transfer of wealth'. But it doesn't exactly make things easier for Obama to confront the Chinese now that the unveiling of NSA's widespread internet surveillance world-wide came on the same day that they began their summit meeting.

(*Aftenposten* 2013d)

The role of the Parliament in all this was a topic at least one journalist thought Norwegians might need some help understanding. Here, that role is coupled intimately with the role of the private sector – which, otherwise, was often related to our main cluster, concerning the question of leakage of information over borders and industry boundaries related to consent and security:

There is one growth industry in the USA … large portions of that industry are growing with no others than a trusted few knowing what it's doing. Not even US senators with marginal insight into its activities can tell anything about it in public without risking criminal proceedings against them. The security industry has achieved optimum status: A state-financed secret operation that is protected against any debate whatsoever as to the industry's scale or methods.

(*Dagsavisen* 2013b)

Finally, the issue of *truth* came up in two forms. One was about accusations of lying, tied to issues of parliamentary oversight, legality and the nature of consent: how can oversight and consent be practised if the truth of what we are regulating and consenting to is deliberately concealed? The other form concerned whether the data themselves revealed truths about the world under surveillance – a question almost identical to the issue of effectiveness and proportionality. Not infrequently, the two aspects were linked, for instance because the statements being questioned as possible lies concerned the effectiveness of the surveillance efforts. As one article concluded:

> As long as the debate about privacy and security is based on documents stamped 'confidential', lies, and secrecy – then it's not worth much. In addition, there is much to indicate that the controversial data surveillance by all evidence is very ineffective.
>
> (Dagsavisen 2013c)

Full circle

Within three weeks of media analysis, we seemed to have come full circle. Norwegian press coverage of the Snowden leaks and of linked events rippling out from those leaks, began by touching on almost all of the themes the *Guardian* editor Rusbridger later cited as grounds to publish from the leaked documents in the first place. Then, the coverage drifted for a time away from those topics and onto the subject of Snowden as a person. At the end of June, a new leak from the Snowden documents brought the Norwegian press back on topic. Again, the themes were linked together – not in detail, as journalistic texts are brief and simple after all, but with a concise clarity. The themes were being brought 'home', shown as relevant for Norwegian daily lives. This quote from June 29 is a fitting example:

> The Norwegian state's surveillance of its own citizens is strictly regulated by Norwegian law. The police, for instance, are not allowed to listen in on citizens' conversations however they might please, but must get a warrant based on actual grounds for suspicion. Lately, however, intelligence services have found a way around this: through collaboration with other countries' security services they can whitewash information they themselves are not allowed to collect ... the USA's explanations to Cabinet Secretary Pål Lønseth that their surveillance has been conducted legally is one we have growing reasons not to put faith in. Yesterday the news broke that the PRISM program, outside of all legal controls, has surveilled American citizens. By using information that has 'been out for a walk', PST [Norway's security police] accepts the USA's surveillance.
>
> (*Klassekampen* 2013d)

Coverage that first month was dense and comprehensive. What happened as time and the news moved on?

Retellings taper off

Looking back at Figure 10.1, we can see that retellings of stories generated by the Snowden revelations had already tapered off after a few months. First, there is a marked dip in September. Norway held municipal and county elections early in October that year, so September's newspapers were filled with election news, and surveillance had not become a Norwegian election issue, at least not at the municipal and county levels. Reporting on Snowden's leaks and NSA surveillance surged back onto the news scene after the election – but not quite to the level of intensity from the summer – and again thereafter continued to taper off in terms of numbers of stories.

One particular leakage may have signalled the end of the first, and most intense, half-year of Snowden/NSA coverage. On 29 November 2013, a story appeared in Norwegian news that NSA may have been spying specifically on Norwegian citizens. One of Snowden's leaked documents contained a table of numbers of conversations recorded and a figure of several tens of thousands appeared in the column marked 'against Norway'. The public was aghast, but only briefly. The next day an officer in Norwegian military intelligence claimed to recognise the number as corresponding to the number of conversations intercepted by Norwegian forces in Afghanistan and reported by them to the NSA. Could it be that 'against' in this instance was merely an accountancy term, as in 'credited against the account of…'? Whether that episode somehow deflated a balloon of indignation, or caused journalists to be suddenly more cautious, or was simply a coincidence to other factors that pushed the Snowden/NSA story to the margins of the news, is hard to say. Whether a cause or a coincidence, the number of stories fell steeply at around that time. And yet, the theme has still not entirely disappeared from view.

One year later

Figure 10.2 shows that 'hit' numbers continued to fall off in 2014, but remained in double digits per month throughout the year with an apparent surge to 92 articles per month in June and again in July. We have chosen to take a closer look at the articles from June 2014, one year after the initial document releases.

That month our archive search produced 92 hits for the search terms 'Snowden OR NSA' in Norwegian print newspapers overall, 74 of these in national and regional print newspapers. Though markedly fewer than the 300+ hits per month the summer before, it is still obviously far more than the single-if-any hits regarding earlier NSA whistle-blowers in the first months of 2013.

Reading through the 74 articles in national and regional newspapers, we see some of the impact of Snowden's leaks and also some of their limitations as instigators of an ongoing public discourse. On the one hand, they show Snowden and the NSA to have become standard references, metaphors if you wish, invoking certain storyline positions. For the most part, references to Snowden invoke a David-fighting-the-giant-Goliath-on-behalf-of-us-all image, whereas NSA and

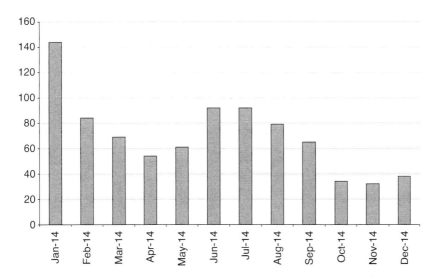

Figure 10.2 Numbers of articles in Norwegian print news, 2014, found in A-Tekst/ Retriever using search terms 'Snowden OR NSA'.

the US are cast as the giant, the oppressor, or a once-benevolent-leader-unfortunately-run-amok. We see this, for instance, when Snowden's name comes up as a comparison in the context of a computer game review (3 June). Similarly, in *Dagsavisen*'s regular listings of Oslo cinema schedules – 15 of the month's 74 hits – the blurb for the film *Captain America: The Winter Soldier* reads: 'Sci-fi-drama that goes further in its criticism of Obama's drones and the NSA than most Hollywood productions have dared, and gets away with it since the message is wrapped up in a superhero film' (*Dagsavisen* 2014 and 14 other hits starting 2 June 2014). To have become a pop culture icon, one's name serving as metaphor for a more ideal hero (or, in the story of the abandoned cat given the name 'Snowden' by its rescuers (*Aftenposten* 25 June 2014b, p. 22), serving as metaphor for a persecuted individual worth saving), and to see the agency one set out to rein in stamped as a pop culture 'bad guy', is certainly some indication of success in establishing a popular discourse.

Another indication of discourse success is that only two of the 74 hits lean towards a negative modality when referring to Snowden. For one of these, negativity is only a matter of the article's title (*Adresseavisen* 2014): 'Snowden er en forræder' [Snowden is a traitor]. The body of the article is neutral in that it states a number of opinions on Snowden's historical, political and judicial status and uses named sources to voice each of these. Multiple nearly identical articles in other newspapers have neutral or positive-leaning headlines – for example, 'Professors wish to give Snowden the peace prize' (*Aftenposten* 2014a) or 'Snowden must receive the peace prize' (*Dagsavisen* 2014). The other negative article is a letter to the editor arguing against awarding the Nobel Peace Prize to Snowden

(Matlary 2014). Aside from these two, all remaining articles lean either positive or maintain a neutral stance regarding Snowden and lean either negative or neutral regarding mass surveillance. Given the generally positive modalities used in Norwegian newspaper articles regarding surveillance more generally (Backman, Sætnan *et al.* 2015), this negative take on surveillance when coupled with Snowden's leaks and the NSA is remarkable.

And yet, these same 74 hits also reveal some of the limitations of the post-Snowden discourse one year on. One is that it takes various sorts of events to keep reviving the story. June 2014 saw several such events. One was the publication of nominations for that year's Nobel Peace Prize, with Snowden amongst the 278 nominated individuals and organisations. Another was that some of those who nominated him released to the press a detailed letter arguing for his candidacy. Others came out in support, thus generating a story within the larger story. This story accounts for 17 of the 74 hits. An interview with Snowden where he mentions having sought asylum in various countries, including Brazil, generated seven of the hits. Announcement of plans for a film about Snowden to be directed by Oliver Stone accounts for five hits. Publication and reviews of Greenwald's book about Snowden generated three more. A German decision to investigate the purported US hacking of Angela Merkel's cell phone generated four hits, one of them a more general analysis of what we should now know about our susceptibility to surveillance online and on phone. The Merkel cell phone investigation can be seen as a downstream event or 'ripple effect' from earlier Snowden leakages. A more direct new leakage event generated two hits about Denmark's collection and transmission of tele- and Internet-traffic data for the US.

In sum, through this month of articles, the Snowden/NSA story has been simplified. Almost all the 'dots' and lines drawn between them have disappeared. Only seven of Rusbridger's 12 points of public interest are discussed at all (Table 10.6). Only one article links three of them, eight articles pair two themes each, the rest mention a single theme or none at all (Table 10.7). The theme

Table 10.6 'Rusbridger reasons' mentioned in Norwegian national and regional print news coverage of NSA and Snowden leaks, June 2014

Rusbridger reason	Number of mentions
1 Consent	1
2 Role of Parliament	–
3 Legality	3
4 Role of private sector	2
5 Encryption	1
6 Risks to digital economy	–
7 Internat'l relations	9
8 Truthfulness	2
9 Privacy	6
10 Confidentiality	–
11 Proportionality	–
12 Information security	1

Table 10.7 Number of 'Rusbridger reasons' mentioned per article of NSA or Snowden leak coverage in Norwegian national and regional print news, June 2014

Number of 'Rusbridger reasons' mentioned	0 (of these, number focused on Snowden as person)	1	2	3	4	5	6	7 or more
Number of articles	58 (48)	9	8	–	–	–	–	–

garnering the most attention is that of international relations, which is touched on ten times, mostly in connection with the issue of Angela Merkel's telephone. The issue of privacy is raised in six articles, legality and the role of the private sector in three each, consent and truthfulness in two each, and encryption once. The remainder of the stories concern Snowden as a person or secondary media events such as a book release or film plans. In other words, the issues Snowden and Rusbridger were hoping we would discuss are either fading from view, or those discussions have come to be so taken for granted that they are hardly any longer mentioned.

Two years later

The following year saw a further decline in the numbers of stories about 'Snowden OR NSA', with another surge at the two-year mark in June (see Figure 10.3). From hit numbers in the low double digits, suddenly June 2015 produced 126 hits in our search of all Norwegian print sources indexed by Atekst/Retriever, 115 of these in national and regional newspapers.

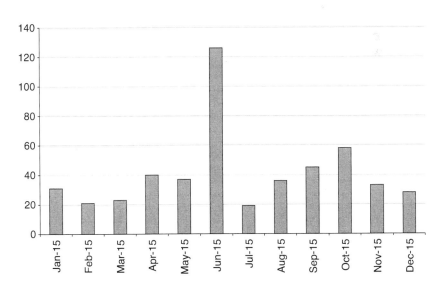

Figure 10.3 Numbers of articles in Norwegian print news, 2015, found in A-Tekst/Retriever using search terms 'Snowden OR NSA'.

Reading through those 115 June stories in national and regional newspapers, we find that some of what we saw the year before still holds true. First, the resurge remains event-driven. On 2 June we see nine stories about US Senator Rand Paul's filibuster which delayed voting on the so-called FREEDOM Act and prevented unamended renewal of the similarly euphemised and acronymed PATRIOT Act which it was to replace. Two further stories on the same event followed on 3 June, another two followed several days later when the FREEDOM Act was passed, after which that event faded to an occasional indirect mention as an aside in other stories.

In response to the next event, 45 stories focus on the conservative Norwegian cabinet not being willing to guarantee safe passage for Snowden to receive the Bjørnstjerne Bjørnson Prize (a Norwegian prize honouring efforts for freedom of speech) at the annual awards ceremony. This story hit the news on 3 June, triggered by the Bjørnson committee's letter to the cabinet requesting such a guarantee and initial responses from the Minister of Justice declining to offer one. After a flurry of articles for a couple of days, the story continued to generate a trickle of mentions in various forms (letters to the editor, questions in weekly news quizzes), then surged to a new two-day flurry two weeks later when a written reply from the cabinet reiterated that no such guarantee would be offered.

Other events triggered smaller numbers of articles. Four were in response to Norwegian security police ransacking the home of film journalist Ulrik Imtiaz Rolfsen in search of tapes from his interview with a Norwegian Islamist activist. Two reported on a purportedly Chinese hacker attack on US federal websites containing data about millions of employees. Six mentioned or commented on a proposal by Norway's Socialist Party to establish safe web zones for whistle-blowers on the Norwegian-owned domains .bv (Bouvet Island) and .sj (Svalbard). Another six were about new Wikileaks revelations concerning US espionage against allied countries' leaders. In all, these five events accounted for two-thirds of that month's search hits.

The stories are also, for the most part, kept short and simple and raise few, if any, of Rusbridger's points of public interest regarding surveillance (see Tables 10.8 and 10.9). For instance, two of the articles on Senator Rand Paul's filibuster against the FREEDOM and PATRIOT Acts do not mention any of Rusbridger's points. For example, *Aftenposten*'s article of 2 June 2015 on page 16, in which the reference to the NSA simply states that 'Central portions of the anti-terror law Patriot Act, which amongst other things authorises the National Security Agency (NSA) to collect telephone data on a grand scale, expired at midnight.' However, where the Rusbridger issues had all but disappeared as of June 2014, the June 2015 articles show that, given new events and stories, they could still be revived, at least to some extent.

Most of the articles about that event mention only one of Rusbridger's points, namely the issue of privacy. Even then, the mention is fleeting. For instance, *Klassekampen* on 2 June 2015, page 16, writes:

Critics are calling it a 'zombie version of the Patriot-Act', a law that will live on even if the current version dies. Many, including Paul, hold that the reform does little to limit the NSA's ability to invade privacy or conduct espionage.

However, the article in *Dagbladet* (2 June 2015: 12) manages to squeeze in references to (or at least hints at) the nature of consent, the role of Congress, the role of the private sector, legality across technologies, and privacy by tucking some key words and quotes into a few short sentences:

> Congress has passed a solution [*role of Congress*] where collection of cell phone data is done by the service providers themselves [*role of private sector*], and not by central authorities, says Melby. The Act will, if it in fact passes, imply that investigators will have to get a warrant to access specific information [*legality across technologies*] … The judgment emphasised that surveillance before the leak was illegal because it wasn't authorised by Congress [*role of Congress*]. The judge, Gerard Lynch, wrote at the time, according to Reuters, that an authorisation would have represented an 'unprecedented contraction of the privacy [*privacy*] expectations [*nature of consent*] of all Americans'.

The paucity and brevity of references touching on the points Rusbridger aimed to raise was typical throughout the material. All of Rusbridger's points were

Table 10.8 'Rusbridger reasons' mentioned in Norwegian national and regional print news coverage of NSA and Snowden leaks, June 2015

Rusbridger reason	Number of mentions
1 Consent	7
2 Role of Parliament	7
3 Legality	24
4 Role of private sector	6
5 Encryption	3
6 Risks to digital economy	1
7 Internat'l relations	16
8 Truthfulness	6
9 Privacy	40
10 Confidentiality	5
11 Proportionality	6
12 Information security	10

Table 10.9 Number of 'Rusbridger reasons' mentioned per article of NSA or Snowden leak coverage in Norwegian national and regional print news, June 2015

Number of 'Rusbridger reasons' mentioned	0 (of these, number focused on Snowden as person)	1	2	3	4	5	6	7 or more
Number of articles	43 (37)	45	10	8	3	6	–	–

mentioned at least once during that month, but almost only in fleeting terms – a single sentence, a phrase, or even just a single word. In contrast to the first month of coverage of the Snowden leaks, the importance of these issues for democracy or for people's daily lives was hardly discussed at all in the newspaper material two years after the initial leaks.

Conclusions

Stories matter. Snowden and the journalists he channelled his leaks through had goals in telling those stories. They intended to engender public discourse, not only for the sake of discourse itself, but also with the idea that the discourse might lead to activism and thus to self-protective online behaviours (such as those discussed by Fleischhack, Chapter 12 in this volume) and legal reforms (as discussed by Schneider, Chapter 8 in this volume). Given Rusbridger's specific theme goals for publishing from Snowden's materials, and assuming that those goals are similar to Snowden's own goals in obtaining and releasing them, Rusbridger and Snowden would have reason to be pleased with the initial news media coverage of the leaks in Norway – not only by its quantity and modalities, but also by the breadth of issues discussed in relation to the revealed surveillance practices. First, measured in presence, the story of surveillance after Snowden has had much greater and more lasting success than earlier NSA whistle-blowers had in the Norwegian news media. Snowden's whistle-blowing has also had more political effectiveness internationally than earlier whistle-blowers have managed to create. Clearly, Snowden strategised well with his choice of documentary method, together with the other actors enrolled into the network of leakage activity that Snowden set up. Thick documentation with solid provenance, followed up by journalistic craftsmanship worthy of a chess grand master did pay off, to some extent. As Bauman *et al.* (2014) state, to keep the issues raised by Snowden in the public eye over a longer term than the usual brief media interest normally permits is an achievement of some very canny whistle-blowing. Even though the story later became event-driven in the Norwegian news, new leaks did revive attention to the issues. Thus, the distribution of leaks over time appears to have been a successful strategy, as described in several books, amongst others by Greenwald (2015) himself and in Laura Poitras' (2014) documentary *Citizenfour*. Our analysis clearly illustrates the complexity and emergent character of the subject matter from when the leaks were launched in June and the immediately following months in 2013, to how it was further retold in the following years, in a Norwegian context.

Nevertheless, in the Norwegian context, the story shrank and withered under the pressures of time, counter-stories, and just plain reduction down to a news article format. The political and judicial reforms are also limited in scope. The story became event-driven and, in the end, also mainly a story of Snowden, the person. When Snowden flew from Hong Kong seeking asylum and wound up stuck in Moscow, the consequences of exposing the whistle-blower became bodily and geographically very visible, containing both human sweat, nervousness *and* high-stake international politics. This is a much easier story to manage than the spiderweb of high stakes politics, institutions, concerns and values first sketched by the revelations. The transition in frame and message – typically a result of practical media logic in action (and perhaps especially so in the post-fact society) – seems in our data to be an especial drawback in terms of the opportunity for the consideration of Big Data to more thoroughly enter the general public debate. The relevance of the revelations to Big Data crumbled early in the coverage. However, it may also express how we – of necessity – deal with the world. Both the sociotechnical network of Big Data and the data itself are messy (Cukier and Mayer-Schoenberger 2013). Even descriptions of individual cases and controversies within the larger picture are likely to share that characteristic. In compressing such messy, complex issues down to media size, simplification seems inevitable – even for issues with serious and immediate consequences (Bauman *et al.* 2014). In this instance, Snowden contributed to the simplification himself when presenting the case as about Big Data in the hands of the State rather than Big Data writ large. But, perhaps simplification is also how larger, messier messages get out, bit by bit.

What then of distractions and simplifications that also entail a change of theme? While the turn from issues of surveillance, state power and Big Data to Snowden the person may be a sign of messaging failure, it is also to some extent a sign of success. Looking at the overall trajectory of the story, journalists began by using vague and dramatic terms such as 'massive' and 'millions' to describe the horizon of data collection or people concerned. While such terms more than hint that processes referred to as Big Data are actually in play (Lyon 2014), they can make it difficult for newsreaders to identify how surveillance relates to individuals. After the initial weeks of broad framing of the leaks, the journalistic coverage of the case derails, so to speak, into concentration on Snowden as a person. However, simultaneously, we find that Snowden and the NSA have become standard references or metaphors in the public discourse, invoking certain storyline positions, with Snowden as David and the NSA and the US as the giant oppressor or Goliath. With only a handful of articles leaning towards a negative modality when referring to Snowden, readers are invited to identify with Snowden as a folk hero. Given the generally positive modalities used in Norwegian and other Scandinavian newspaper articles regarding surveillance more generally (Backman, Johnson *et al.* 2015), the negative take on broad, warrantless surveillance, as when coupled with Snowden's leaks and the NSA, is worth noting.

The term 'story' gives familiar associations to narrative accounts of events or, for instance, a work of history, a real or fictional incident or an anecdote. Our analysis shows that this term is representative for the fate of the Snowden revelations in Norwegian surveillance discourse, and also for the framing of the NSA and other secret services' mass surveillance practices and of the miserable situation of Edward Snowden. As we sketched in the introduction, stories are phenomena that must be retold and revived if they are to remain prominent in public discourse. Unless retold, they become smaller, thinner, somewhat ghostlike and frail – perhaps even devolving into a frazzle of anecdotes without any obvious connections. However, silences produced through such fading away processes are not necessarily synonymous with the story becoming powerless on behalf of those it concerns. Silence can have several important functions in discourses, such as representing the invisible that ties the visible together. Silence may even represent the opposite of the lack of sound, turning from absence of voices into screams for attention.

Notes

1 Tøndel is a native speaker of Norwegian with acquired fluency in English. Sætnan is a native speaker of American English with acquired fluency in Norwegian. The contrast between American usage and Norwegian non-usage of superlatives is especially striking when seen from these complementary fluent but non-native perspectives.
2 As in the article excerpted here:

> The so-called PRISM-program enables the NSA to gather all types of information, such as search histories, the contents of e-mails, file transfers and live chats. The matter has enormous principled importance, and represents an overwhelming threat against privacy, protection of sources, national security and the right to independent political activity the world over. Its impact increases apace with the companies in question taking control over more and more public and private communications in an increasing proportion of the world.
>
> (Klassekampen 2013b)

References

ABC News (2014). Se hele Snowden-foredraget i Oslo [See the entire Snowden lecture in Oslo]. *ABC Nyheter* [*ABC News*], September 2. Available at: www.abcnyheter.no/video/2014/09/02/207155/se-hele-snowden-foredraget-i-oslo. [Accessed 12 October 2017].

Adresseavisen (2013). Global heksejakt på media [Global witchhunt on the media], June 29, p. 23.

Adresseavisen (2014). Snowden er en forræder [Snowden is a traitor], June 7, p. 18.

Aftenposten (2013a). Kommer storebror til å lære? [Will Big Brother ever learn?], June 21, p. 3.

Aftenposten (2013b). Kan bety et skille i synet på overvåking [May cause a shift in views on surveillance], June 12, p. 19.

Aftenposten (2013c). Mest interessert i Irans hemmeligheter [Most interested in Iran's secrets], June 10, p. 17.

Aftenposten (2013d). *Hvis det hadde vært så enkelt* [If it had been so simple] June 11, p. 20.

Aftenposten (2014a). Professorer vil gi Snowden fredsprisen [Professors wish to give Snowden the peace prize], June 22, p. 11.

Aftenposten (2014b). 'Snowden' ble dumpet av eierne – men reddet av Dyrebeskyttelsen. ['Snowden' was dumped by the owners – but saved by Animal Rescue], June 25, p. 22.

Backman, C., Johnson, E., Sætnan, A.R., Tøndel, G., Svenonius, O. and Yngvesson, S.W. (2015). Post-Snowden Surveillance Journalism in Scandinavia, Paper presented at conference: Surveillance and Citizenship: State-Media-Citizen Relations after the Snowden Leaks, Cardiff: Cardiff University, June 18–19.

Backman, C., Sætnan, A.R., Svenonius, O., Tøndel, G., Yngvesson, S.W., Johnson, E.M. and Jerak-Zuiderent, S. (2015). A Blue-Eyed Look at Surveillance? Paper presented at workshop: Trust, distrust and surveillance: The Scandinavian network on surveillance and society, Göteborg, October 5–6.

Bauman, Z., Bigo, D., Esteves, P., Guild, E., Jabri, V., Lyon, D. and Walker, R.B.J. (2014). After Snowden: Rethinking the Impact of Surveillance, *International Political Sociology*, 8, pp. 121–144.

Bennett, A. and Elman, C. (2006). Complex Causal Relations and Case Study Methods: The Example of Path Dependence, *Political Analysis*, 14(3), pp. 250–267.

Cukier, K. and Mayer-Schoenberger, V. (2013). The Rise of Big Data: How It's Changing the Way We Think About the World, *Foreign Affairs*, 92(3), pp. 28–40.

Dagbladet (2013). Joss! USA like ille som Kina? [OMG! USA as bad as China?], June 13, p. 2.

Dagbladet (2015). En varslet krise [A warned crisis], June 2, p. 12.

Dagens Næringsliv (2013). Refser britisk 'spionjobb' [Scolds British 'spy job'], June 18, p. 29.

Dagsavisen (2013a). Overvåker millioner [Surveillance of millions], June 7, p. 18.

Dagsavisen (2013b). USAs hemmelige verden [USA's secret world], June 20, p. 20.

Dagsavisen (2013c). En hverdagslig sak [An everyday affair] June 28, p. 2.

Dagsavisen (2014). Snowden må få fredsprisen [Snowden must receive the peace prize]), June 23, p. 7.

Dencik, L., Hintz, A. and Cable, J. (2016). Towards Data Justice? The Ambivalence of Anti-surveillance Resistance in Political Activism, *Big Data & Society*, pp. 1–12.

Epstein, D., Roth, M.C. and Baumer, E.P.S. (2014). It's the Definition, Stupid! Framing of Online Privacy in the Internet Governance Forum Debates, *Journal of Information Policy*, 4, pp. 144–172.

Gillespie, T., Boczowski, P.J. and Foot, K.A. (2014). *Media Technologies: Essays on Communication, Materiality, and Society*. Cambridge, MA: MIT Press.

Greenwald, G. (2015). *No Place to Hide: Edward Snowden, the NSA, and the U.S. Surveillance State*. New York: Metropolitan Books.

Greenwald, G., MacAskill, E. and Poitras, L. (2013). Edward Snowden: The Whistleblower Behind the NSA Surveillance Revelations, *Guardian*, June 11. Available at: www.theguardian.com/world/2013/jun/09/edward-snowden-nsa-whistleblower-surveillance. [Accessed 12 October 2017].

Gullestad, M. (1984). *Kitchen-Table Society*. Oslo: Scandinavian University Press.

Hughes, E. (1984). *The Sociological Eye: Selected Papers*. New Brunswick, NJ: Transaction Books.

Klassekampen (2013a). Slik overvåker USA verden [This is how the USA surveilles the world], 12 June, p. 16.

Klassekampen (2013b). Lisens til å snoke [Licence to spy], June 8, p. 21.

Klassekampen (2013c). Overvåking [Surveillance], June 14, p. 2.

Klassekampen (2013d). NSA: Stort og skjult [NSA: Big and hidden] June 8, p. 21.

Klassekampen (2015). NSA sikrer seg zombie-lov [NSA gets zombie-law], June 2, p. 16.

Lyon, D. (2014). Surveillance, Snowden, and Big Data: Capacities, Consequences, Critique, *Big Data & Society*, pp. 1–13.

Marres, N. and Moats, D. (2015). Mapping Controversies with Social Media: The Case for Symmetry, *Social Media + Society*, pp. 1–17.

Matlary, J.H. (2014). Fortjener ikke fredspris [Doesn't deserve peace prize]. *VG*, 26 June, pp. 36–37.

Moats, D. (2015). *Decentring Devices: Developing Quali-Quantitative Techniques for Studying Controversies with Online Platforms*. PhD-thesis in sociology. Goldsmiths, University of London.

Nationen (2013). Nettovervåking bekymrer EU [Internet surveillance worries the EU], June 12, p. 16.

Nordlys (2013). Spion-paradokset [The spy paradox], June 10, pp. 2–3.

Poitras, L. (2014). *Citizenfour*. Documentary film.

Prior, L. (2004). Doing Things with Documents, in Silverman, D. (ed.) *Qualitative Research: Theory, Method and Practice*. London: Sage Publications, pp. 76–94.

Rusbridger, A. (2013). The Snowden Leaks and the Public, *New York Review of Books*, November 21. Available at: www.nybooks.com/articles/2013/11/21/snowden-leaks-and-public/. [Accessed October 12, 2017].

Suchman, L. (2014). Mediations and Their Others, in Gillespie, T., Boczowski, P.J. and Foot, K.A. (eds.) *Media Technologies: Essays on Communication, Materiality, and Society*. Cambridge, MA: MIT Press, pp. 129–139.

Vårt Land (2013). Med Stasi i lomma [With Stasi in your pocket], June 21, p. 2.

VG (2013). Varsleren blir trolig sendt rett hjem [The whistleblower will likely be sent straight home], June 11, p. 30.

Part III

Performance is political

Big Data practices, performance, and resistance

11 No (Big) Data, no fiction?

Thinking surveillance with/against Netflix

Rocco Bellanova and Gloria González Fuster[1]

> The *trouble de l'archive* stems from a *mal d'archive*. We are *en mal d'archive*: in need of archives. Listening to the French idiom, and in it the attribute *en mal-de*, to be *en mal d'archive* can mean something else than to suffer from a sickness, from a trouble or from what the noun *mal* might name. It is to burn with a passion. It is never to rest, interminably, from searching for the archive right where it slips away. [...] No desire, no passion, no drive, no compulsion, indeed no repetition compulsion, no '*mal-de*' can arise for a person who is not already, in one way or another, *en mal d'archive*.
>
> (Derrida 1996: 91)

Introduction

It all starts with binge-watching TV series on Netflix. In particular, it all began watching the fourth season of *House of Cards* in March 2016, and thinking something like, 'Wow! I can learn so much about surveillance and politics just by watching this series'. And then, it is about immediately reckoning that, 'Well, actually, perhaps we can learn even more about politics and surveillance by watching me here, under Netflix's constant monitoring, watching *House of Cards* and trying to think about surveillance.' This critical, reflective movement is the trigger of this chapter, and thus also of our efforts to better understand surveillance between what is brought and performed on stage and what is performed and done to create the stage itself.

House of Cards is a series produced by the United States (US) company Netflix, which released at once all the episodes of the first season on its online platform in February 2013 (Klarer 2014; Nussbaum 2013). The series is a 'political drama' in the sense that it follows the ambitions of a couple of politicians portraying multiple strategies of influence and manipulation to secure their political ambitions (Crouch 2016). To make a long story short, in the fourth season of the series, released in March 2016, the TV show brings to the forefront of its narrative several techniques concerning the massive gathering and processing of data about individuals. By focusing on mass surveillance, *House of Cards* became a sort of 'Big Data drama' too.

Netflix is an 'international Internet video streaming subscription service' (Amatriain and Basilico 2015: 390). Increasingly, it also produces its own original content, that is, series, movies and documentaries that are directly funded by the company, or whose rights have been acquired to allow for new creations (Napoli 2014). Its interest in marketing surveillance-related content was also confirmed in 2015 with the commissioning of a number of episodes of the British dystopian series *Black Mirror* (Plunkett 2015).

Netflix has not only a vast archive of films and metadata about them (Madrigal 2014), but also a continuously growing database of information about users, especially when it comes to their interaction with the platform's interface (Amatriain 2013; Amatriain and Basilico 2015). Hence, Netflix has over time acquired the means and the tools to infer its users' preferences, and to design cultural products tailored to an identified market. As such, Netflix explicitly shows that online platforms are far from mere intermediaries (on the growing role of online platforms in shaping our contemporary political economy, see Schneider, Chapter 8 in this volume). As Gillespie puts it,

> their choices about what can appear, how it is organised, how it is monetised, what can be removed and why, and what the technical architecture allows and prohibits, are all real and substantive interventions into the contours of public discourse.
>
> (2010: 359)

If we are to understand digital surveillance, our attention should focus both on the organisation of the stage (i.e. how the company organises the capture of users' behavioural data) and on the content of what is staged (i.e. the kinds of narratives that are promoted through the platform).

Netflix's investment in *House of Cards* was as a matter of fact portrayed as a prime example of the way in which its programme commissioning is directly based on personal data mining (Baldwin 2012; Carr 2013; Leonard 2013; Sweney 2014). It marked indeed a decisive and clear shift from the mere streaming of content to its active production, and a production which is directly grounded on the statistical analysis of massive amounts of data (Lycett 2013: 384). Netflix, in this sense, announced that it had decided to buy the rights of this TV series, and then to produce this specific kind of political drama with a particular lead actor and a particular director because its own data showed there was a public for such a concrete combination (Carr 2013; Leonard 2013; Hallinan and Striphas 2016: 128).

While media scholars have already highlighted the role of 'data generated as a by-product of new forms of popular cultural engagement' (Beer and Burrows 2013: 49), surveillance studies have only marginally engaged with the epistemic and political implications of the affinities between the surveillance at work for cultural production, on the one hand, and the surveillance depicted in cultural products, on the other. This is certainly not a completely new theme in surveillance studies and, even more explicitly, in popular culture itself. As Kammerer notes:

It is easy to see how surveillance and cinema relate to each other. Techno-
logically, both rely on apparatuses of (acoustic and visual) recording. Struc-
turally, both create situations where one side is watching and the other is
being watched. It is no wonder that surveillance also plays an important
thematic role in many films.

(Kammerer 2012: 101)

However, in surveillance studies and social discussions, popular culture mainly
operates, and it is used, as an heuristic and pedagogical device, exposing surveillance practices and rationalities by staging them through the means of fiction (cf.
inter alia: Lyon 2007: 139ff.). From this perspective, dystopic and utopic works
acquire quite an immediate conceptual relevance for surveillance studies (Marks
2005, 2015). Some iconic images have moved from popular culture to social analysis. Probably the most evident example is the figure of the Big Brother, introduced by Orwell in his novel *1984*, which is often mobilised by social actors and
commentators to discuss governmental and corporate surveillance. The focus on
the plot and its speculation upon the emergence of 'surveillance societies' may
facilitate the bringing together of a public around given issues, such as the spread
of wiretapping and the outreach of governmental powers into the private lives of
individuals, or the ubiquity of CCTV surveillance in public spaces.

What is generally left out of sight, is the fact that surveillance techniques,
besides the very use of video and audio recording technologies, may be mobilised
to create and produce cultural products. For instance, pop culture products are
generally designed so as to capture a vast audience, especially in the case of blockbuster movies (Odello 2013: 7–8), and the collection of information about their
possible reception may influence their very production. However, film-makers or
producers rarely push the surveillance aspects of the 'making of' to the forefront of
the public presentation. And, when the surveillance aspects of their 'making of' is
brought to the stage, as is the case with reality shows where footage is explicitly
based on a seemingly continuous CCTV surveillance, the main theme is rarely surveillance as such. Now, as the case of Netflix illustrates, the surveillance-like
rationale of data mining is openly embraced by the producer and distributor
(Amatriain and Basilico 2015). The company processes the data collected (about
the movies and about the users) so as to produce and suggest cultural artefacts that
may please manifold diverse users' profiles rather than address a one-size-fits-all
audience. These practices are presented in terms of 'personalisation' of a service
and a product rather than in terms of users' surveillance (Amatriain 2013: 1).

In the Netflix-watching setting described above, we find ourselves in front of,
and embedded in, several forms of surveillance: those at play in the plot of
House of Cards, and those at play in the making of *House of Cards*. When we
watch the surveillance practices depicted by the storyline, we may understand
better how we are tracked by, and trapped in, multiple public and private high-
tech surveillance systems. But when we realise how Netflix actually works, we
may come to finally visualise algorithmic surveillance as an 'embodied' practice,
a perception overall too rare in many other social settings. Every move our

fingers make on the platform is a trace for an archive about users' behaviours, and these data, once properly mined, will 'feed back' into what we (and others) will be suggested to watch.

On the one hand we are thus facing a narrative that points to the crucial role of databases and algorithms in the fabric of politics. On the other, we realise we are feeding the databases (and thus the algorithms) that ultimately contribute to the making of a narrative that, in the case of *House of Cards*, speaks to us about the role of databases and algorithms in the fabric of politics. In both cases, what is at play is the ambition to collect and process Big Data. This chapter is a tentative exploration of Big Data surveillance as a '*mal d'archive*' (Derrida 1996: 91). We aim to pinpoint this drive to translate the world into a seemingly consistent, yet never complete, archive where data will be ultimately able to shape the coming into being of events (Rouvroy 2013). Our journey attempts to chart the main practices at work on and beyond the stage, so as to understand whether we can 'rescue' a narrative or an image that may help us to think about surveillance without dragging ourselves into a *mal d'archive*, where the database drive erodes and erases any possible imaging of surveillance.

The chapter is divided into three main parts. In the first we identify and discuss key conceptual resources for thinking (Big) Data, surveillance and the database-narrative tensions at work in digital media. Next we delve deeper into the plot of season four of *House of Cards*, offering an analytical description of the main Big Data techniques presented there and their political rationales. Finally, we move our analysis to the functioning of Netflix as a platform, discussing its Big Data features and its own staging of the same. In the concluding section, we summarise the main insights of our exploration.

Conceptual resources for thinking Big Data surveillance and the database-narrative tension

By focusing on algorithmic surveillance in a Netflix series and through the online entertainment platform itself, this work finds itself at the crossroads of critical media studies and surveillance studies. Both fields are so conceptually rich that it might be useful to clarify some of the basic notions used in this chapter. Hence, this section has a twofold aspiration: first, to walk through the conceptual thicket surrounding Big Data surveillance; second, to propose a conceptual approach to think surveillance through and against Netflix, in order to go beyond more traditional surveillance studies' readings of pop culture and fiction.

A key term requiring definition and clarification is 'data'. Kitchin states that:

> Data are commonly understood to be the raw material produced by abstracting the world into categories, measures and other representational forms – numbers, characters, symbols, images, sounds, electromagnetic waves, bits – that constitute the building blocks from which information and knowledge are created.
>
> (Kitchin 2014: 1)

Data are thus, despite the term's Latin etymological roots, not a given. They are something that must be produced, out of a gesture of 'capture'. Kitchin notes that we should rather speak of 'capta' (Kitchin 2014: 2). For this very reason, they are not as 'raw' as one might think (Gitelman and Jackson 2013: 2), or as Kitchin's above definition paradoxically hints at, when he refers to a 'raw material' that is 'produced' (2014: 1). Data are generated and manufactured in pre-determined formats ('by abstracting the world into ... forms', ibid.), and thus may become recalcitrant to other forms and formats, or modes of processing initially not foreseen. They might even become silent, or simply decay and disappear if their material support is no more readable or computable for technical or physical reasons (Borgman 2015). In sum, data can only be assembled as a set by pre-existing representations, and might require an often invisible labour of maintenance, adjustment and elaboration informed by such representations if they are to contribute to any form of knowledge generation and action.

Data are not merely extracted from passive individuals. In many instances, data are produced in settings that facilitate their generation through transactions that are seldom based on the full understanding of what is happening. Interactive media services, for example online platforms such as Netflix, can thus collect data generated with the help of individuals who are to be *datafied*, that is, transformed into 'a quantified format [that] can be tabulated and analysed' (Mayer-Schönberger and Cukier 2013: 78). Participation to datafication practices is not without echoes of the conception of online users as *prosumers*, that is, the consumers that contribute to the production of a product that they are supposed to consume (Ritzer and Jurgenson 2010). When it comes to online or digital interactions, media scholars note that '[t]he information produced by these acts of participatory consumption clearly generate a form of transactional data that is available for companies to harvest and data mine' (Beer and Burrows 2010: 9). Users are not inactive, even if most of their actions ultimately feed the *datafication* actively pursued by the online services, and do so in the terms of these services.

In order to account for the 'fragility' and 'power' of data (Borgman 2015: 4), as well as their relational nature, we propose to think of digital data as '*translations* of people, things, behaviours and relations, into information that can be stored, computed and visualised by computers' (Bellanova 2017: 331, emphasis added). Translation is a process that 'gives new life' (Barry 2013: 415), but also one that requires extensive work to be carried out. While '[t]ranslation is a significant medium of subject re-formation and political change' (Apter 2006: 6), not everybody has the same means to perform and impact these transformations.

Data, and especially 'personal data' understood as data referring to identifiable persons, lie at the very core of modern practices of surveillance. In this context, Lyon proposed the following working definition of surveillance:

> [Surveillance is] the focused, systematic and routine attention to personal details for purposes of influence, management, protection or direction. Surveillance directs its attention in the end to individuals (even though

aggregate data, such as those available in the public domain, may be used to build up a background picture). [...] Beyond this, surveillance is routine; it occurs as a 'normal' part of everyday life in all societies that depend on bureaucratic administration and some kinds of information technology.

(Lyon 2007: 14)

As Lyon (2007: 14) notes, 'personal details', 'aggregated data' or, more in general, what is produced by nearly ubiquitous 'information technolog[ies]' facilitate the governing of people (and things). From the translation perspective sketched earlier, we can say that data sit between the 'real' and its possible quantification and calculability, as well as between the production of diverse forms of knowledge and the governing and shaping of the 'real' at stake (cf. Desrosières 2011; Rouvroy 2013).

In the last few years, the term 'Big Data' has become part of (almost) everyday parlance, dubbed in the title of a popular book as the 'revolution that will transform how we live, work, and think' (Mayer-Schönberger and Cukier 2013). It has also given rise to a growing number of academic debates, diffused well beyond the realm of computer sciences. As a matter of fact, probably all fields of social sciences and humanities have by now engaged in at least some discussion about the role and possible effects of Big Data in their discipline, be it (critical) security studies (Amoore and Piotukh 2015; Aradau and Blanke 2015), criminology (Chan and Bennett Moses 2016), information studies (Borgman 2015), media studies (boyd and Crawford 2012) or geography (Kitchin 2013). An academic, reflexive debate is particularly important in the areas for which Big Data is potentially both a research object and a research method, such as 'digital sociology' (Lupton 2015; Orton-Johnson and Prior 2013).

The field of surveillance studies is not an exception. So far, it seems to be mostly leaning towards an engagement with Big Data in terms of the research object, and only to a limited extent as a potential conceptual or methodological revolution (Andrejevic and Gates 2014; Degli Esposti 2014; Lyon 2014). In the introduction to a dedicated special issue of *Surveillance & Society*, Andrejevic and Gates note that 'the notion of "big data" refers to both the unprecedented size of contemporary databases and the emerging techniques for making sense of them' (2014: 186). They also point to another feature of Big Data: it tends in fact to push data out of the original linear translation process where they were generated, facilitating their processing in response to a given query (in view of enacting a purpose defined (and limited) in advance). In their words, '[t]o refer to big data is [...] also to consider the new uses to which that data is put – the novel forms of "actionable intelligence" that emerge from the analysis of ever-expanding data sets' (Andrejevic and Gates 2014: 186).

Albeit only implicit in their reflection, this way of thinking about Big Data connects this specific form of data-led governance with the recent history of the statistical techniques and algorithms whose ambition is to crunch whatever digits are available (Desrosières 2011; Rouvroy and Berns 2013). It also highlights the frictions between the unbounded computational ambition of 'machine learning' and the premise about the *material* limitations of data described above. Despite the eagerness of Big Data machines and those devising and operating them, data are generally generated in pre-determined forms, and thus they often remain in need of re-engineering before further processing. Hence, Big Data sounds rather as a kind of magic wand through which data shall be liberated from the constraints that made them what they were, and confined them to pre-established purposes. Big Data is, from this perspective, the force of data without its inhibitions.

But, how can Big Data be defined more precisely? Drawing from several works, Kitchin has offered one of the most exhaustive definitions (Kitchin 2013). It would be, inter alia, 'huge in volume, consisting of terabytes or petabytes of data' and 'exhaustive in scope, striving to capture entire populations or systems', as well as 'relational in nature, containing common fields that enable the conjoining of different data sets' (Kitchin 2013: 262). Yet, and this is particularly relevant for the purposes of this chapter, boyd and Crawford emphasise that Big Data is not only characterised by its technical features, but also represents 'a cultural, technological, and scholarly phenomenon' (boyd and Crawford 2012: 663). Indeed, Big Data relies on its own 'mythology', described as 'the widespread belief that large data sets offer a higher form of intelligence and knowledge that can generate insights that were previously impossible, with the aura of truth, objectivity, and accuracy' (boyd and Crawford 2012: 663). In our view, this mythology is further reinforced by the difficulty to fully grasp and visualise Big Data beyond the tropes of a supernatural and ineffable power.

However, this mythical image of Big Data can be conceptually approached in light of what used to be the traditional container (and multiplier) of data, that is, the database. While social sciences seem increasingly fascinated with the role of algorithms (Amoore and Raley 2017; Cardon 2015; Pasquale 2015; Ziewitz 2016), these cannot operate without appropriate data structures and databases (Gillespie 2014). As Manovich notes, 'In computer programming, data structures and algorithms need each other; they are equally important for a program to work' (2002: 226). However – still following the reasoning proposed by Manovich (2002) – once databases are brought to the fore, we should also consider whether databases and narratives are compatible. In fact, Manovich argues that there is a crucial tension between the database and the notion of narrative:

> As a cultural form, the database represents the world as a list of items, and it refuses to order this list. In contrast, a narrative creates a cause-and-effect trajectory of seemingly unordered items (events). Therefore, database and narrative are natural enemies. Competing for the same territory of human culture, each claims an exclusive right to make meaning out of the world.
> (Manovich 2002: 225)

In other terms, the rationale of the database leans towards the widening of its collection outreach and the continuous effort to make the world indexical, akin to the mechanisms set in motion by the older technology of knowing and governing that is the list (Eco 2009; de Goede *et al.* 2016). It is the algorithm that is supposed to counter-balance and steer this *mal d'archive*. It offers the means to exploit the possibility of translation provided by the data in the database, and it keeps alive the feasibility of prospective readings. As such, algorithms become similar to narratives, that are supposed to bring forward, and thus sometimes expose to critique, a given order (Hayles 2012). Yet, according to Manovich, the problem triggered by the diffusion of digital devices and digitalisation in general, is that everything becomes a database, at least 'on the level of material organization' (2002: 228), and thus narratives function only insofar as they can operate as algorithms.

Understanding the interactions between narratives and the digital requires taking seriously how technologies of media production and consumption have always affected the design and dissemination of consumed content. Before algorithms, there already existed other technologies of digital/material organisation. One can think, for instance, of the physical limitations inscribed into DVDs, artificially limiting in which devices they can be used, and enabling what Guins described as morality management by DVD players (2009: 19), or of the implications of the MP3's format for music (Sterne 2012). Whole cultural practices and genres, in fact, must be contextualised in the technologies that helped them co-create them. Popular music, in this sense, can be seen as a product of the radio and the parallel emergence of audience surveys, which, by the development of refined demographics, impacted the way in which radio content was imagined and produced (see notably Volcler 2017).

These considerations remind us that cultural products, including fictions, never 'purely' emanate from an unconnected, romantically inspired author, or even a series of interconnected inspired creators. Cultural products are co-determined, to some extent, by inferences and presumptions about the publics' preferences, increasingly on the basis of their monitoring, study and surveillance. Modern data-driven cultural productions might thus be seen not as a disruption, but as a continuation of previous practices. What remains to be done, in any case, is to inquire into how nowadays (the mythical powers of) Big Data might impact the construction of narratives that animate our societies, and thus indirectly delineate any critical thinking of society through such narratives. Navigating through all these insights, we aim to connect them to the exploration of Big Data through the lens of the constitution of data, taking seriously that data is not a given, but rather a site of translation, and thus possibly also of contestation.

Thinking surveillance through *House of Cards*

The fourth season of the Netflix series *House of Cards* was released worldwide on 4 March 2016. This season of the show can help us better understand the rise of a new mode of governing, where vast amounts of personal and behavioural data are becoming as important as more traditional 'cards' for playing politics. At the end of the third season, viewers already knew what was going to be on the menu in the fourth season. Claire Underwood – the first lady – had left both the White House and her husband, thus altering old power relations. Frank Underwood – then acting president of the US – was fighting to win the primaries for the Democratic Party presidential nomination, while his grasp on present and future events weakened. In sum, we already expected *House of Cards* to bring us into a fictional world that largely resembles and echoes the one we see on the evening news (i.e. when we are not watching Netflix).

The explicit connection between the fictional world of *House of Cards* and the 'real' world of politics as we knew it is secured by reference to quite traditional themes and practices: primary elections, decisions over the appointment of new justices or charges, diplomacy, a never-ending Middle East crisis, or the deliberation over new legislation. More particularly, in this fourth season our attention is brought to topics such as the relations between the US and Russia, federal efforts to increase gun control, the beginning of the presidential primary elections, the struggle to secure campaign funding, etc. Actually, the series shows us a very familiar setting, and then provides us with a privileged access to what happens behind the façade, so that the fiction seems to cast a light on what happens in the shadows of (world) politics. Sometimes the narrative brings us literally behind the screen, as when Frank – the main character – looks directly into our eyes and speaks to us – the viewers – explaining what is really going on, how the machinery of power works and how it has to be worked by those interested in power (Klarer 2014). And he shows his mastery of the game by mustering allies and playing his cards well, time and time again, against all odds and antagonists.

Much has been said in the press about the vision of politics that *House of Cards* brings forward and contributes to popularising (e.g. Crouch 2016). And, given the increasing attention towards popular culture in social sciences (amongst others: Kiersey and Neumann 2013; Potter and Marshall 2008; Marks 2015; Regazzoni 2014), we can expect to read more about the politics represented in *House of Cards* and other Netflix-produced TV shows in the near future. In this chapter, we mostly focus on a specific (dis-)continuity brought about by the fourth season: the staging of Big Data surveillance techniques next to more traditional political practices. This is probably only a slight modification of the usual underlying rationale in *House of Cards*. In fact, the choice of introducing domestic mass surveillance of telecommunications amongst the key themes of *House of Cards* is far from surprising, especially since the use of this and other forms of data-driven surveillance have become public issues following the Snowden revelations. More important, these novelties in the series' plot coincide with the progressive realisation by the media and society in general of the significance of data-driven analytics for the allocation of political power worldwide. These practices have been notably embodied by the widely mediatised data-mining firm Cambridge Analytica. This US company specialises in both 'audience behaviour' and influencing electoral processes, and its slogan is 'Data drives all that we do' (Cambridge Analytica 2017). The use of the company's services has notably been connected to the election of US President Donald

Trump and the United Kingdom's vote to leave the European Union (Doward and Gibbs 2017).

Apparently, *House of Cards* is once again echoing and leveraging on themes that are widely discussed in real-world debates. From this perspective, giving prominence to these issues highlights how high-tech surveillance and security practices have become the 'new normal' of world and domestic politics (Čas *et al.* 2017: 1). Nonetheless, we believe that the staging of Big Data surveillance in a popular series like *House of Cards* deserves to be framed as showing the potential of this kind of popular culture products to make researchers and social critics think more thoroughly about worldviews on politics and power, as well as about the relationship between politics and power and data-driven fiction.

What matters most to the scope of this chapter is that the show gives a subtle but important twist to the topic of data surveillance. On the one side, we see the US Acting President extending further domestic surveillance and, on the other, we find his main political opponent deliberately using data generated by people's online searches. In pure *House of Cards*' style, the President's team tries to win the data race against the other candidate by further processing citizens' data syphoned by counter-terrorist agencies. From this (somewhat tortuous) perspective, the question of domestic mass surveillance is introduced in a slightly different way than to what we are now accustomed. Boosting counter-terrorism surveillance is not only presented as a perverse solution to hijack the attention of the electorate in crucial moments. Nor is it merely portrayed as a problem of civil liberties and of ambiguous public/private partnerships. It is (re)presented, first and foremost, in relation to the emergence of a new mode of knowledge generation, and thus in relation to the need to 'sense' and better affect the electorate.

The discovery of dirty secrets, of political plots or of the whereabouts of a potentially dangerous witness are no longer the central focus of the plot, contrary to the previous seasons of the series. What is now at stake is the capacity to detect and register how the mass of potential voters reacts 'spontaneously'. Said otherwise, the ambition of both rival candidates is to know which keywords US citizens type into the search bar of an online search engine and what political discourse or action may thus resonate with their everyday digital life and thus influence their electoral behaviour. This kind of mass surveillance is presented as definitely important for politics, be it in the struggles amongst different actors, their everyday political actions, or the attempts to govern people. This new form of knowledge generation is different from the more classical forms of acquiring information about competing actors. It works less through the surveillance of each individual than through the analysis of aggregated data and the identification of profiles. It relies on, and promises, a double adjustment: that of politicians in response to emerging trends of the electorate, and that of voting behaviour in response to stimuli coming from political speeches and actions.

This seems to be a brave new world even for Frank Underwood, and it may require a major readjustment of his 'arts' of governing. The show suggests to us that polls, focus groups, scheming and blackmail are no longer enough to guarantee the success of a speech act, at least when performed in public. The analysis of vast amounts of (meta-)data seems now to provide a much more solid ground to perform politics. Hence, Underwood's speeches now have to include specific words if the goal is to appeal to and mobilise previously unknown audiences. His own performance is tailored on and for '[t]he production of calculated publics', where 'the algorithmic presentation of publics back to themselves shape a public's sense of itself' (Gillespie 2014: 168, emphasis in original). Still, the need for the Underwood couple to adjust speeches and actions also shows how this 'production of calculated publics' influences the behaviour of 'who is best positioned to benefit from that knowledge' (Gillespie 2014: 168). In the show, this is presented as a subtle alteration of the routine practice of politics. It is actually the Republican Party candidate that has first secured his own data sources and learned to work this machinery with the support of a major corporation whose core business is an online search engine. And it is Claire Underwood, now back into the White House and seemingly supporting her husband, who chiefly integrates data analytics in support of her political speeches, thus both adopting and adapting to this new art of governing by literally rewording her communication strategy.

Several researchers have already pointed to the crucial political role played by data collection and data analytics, as well as their somewhat mythical functioning (Ziewitz 2016). Bennett (2015) has notably worked on the use of data-driven technologies in electoral campaigns. Some scholars invite us to better understand the rationales underlying Big Data – and the 'dreams' of algorithms, as Cardon (2015) has suggested in a beautiful book – if we are to understand the rationales at play in 'algorithmic governmentality' (Rouvroy 2013; Rouvroy and Berns 2013). But the importance of a show such as *House of Cards* is that it attempts to visualise both the shift towards a new form of knowledge generation and to question its limits and its everyday integration into current political practices. And it does so while being, itself, a data-driven product supported and distributed by a company grounded on pervasive data collection. Albeit powerful, databases and algorithms are here nested in fiction, which remains a largely 'traditional' narrative that brings them to the stage in a more mundane, and less mythical, fashion.

So far, the key to the success of the main characters (and, by extension, of all those that seem able to play politics) is, indeed, *performance*. This is a term that can be used in many ways. Here it should be understood in its most theatrical sense. In many episodes, *House of Cards* shows us how the Underwood couple overcome an obstacle or 'turn the tables'. It often does so by juxtaposing in the same sequence both the rehearsal and the enactment of speeches and political interactions. The Underwood couple continuously ponder how to play their cards. However, faced with the challenge of governing the mass of potential voters, and not only governing the 'House', in the fourth season they discover that they need to learn how to play data (analytics) too. As such, this challenge should be no surprise to *House of Cards* fans. Unforeseen consequences or obstacles are introduced via the overall narrative of the show as tests to be passed. They may cause trouble or open new opportunities – but, ultimately, power is represented as the ability to succeed at these tests and of capitalising upon this success. When it comes to data analytics, one solution to pass the test is to adapt the text of public speeches so as to include terms that correlate with desired voting postures. While initially successful, this solution quickly shows its limits: 'producing' a public through numbers alone is not enough. This is where *House of Cards* offers a counterpoint to a mythical rendering of Big Data. As another character, a data scientist, recognises: 'People didn't know they wanted jazz until they heard it for the first time. I can get them to like the music – I can't compose it. Give me something I can work with' (cited also in: Brems 2017). In other words, one needs more than numbers: one needs to 'spell' new fictions not only to make sense of the data already collected and organised in the database, but also to provoke a reaction amongst people so that they can co-produce more data to be collected. The question that *House of Cards* invites us to posit is thus how Big Data practices, with all their potential and their limits too, are included in a wider palette of arts of governing. In particular, the series brings to the stage the tension between the database and the narrative, and it does so in a narrative fashion. It pinpoints the need to supplement algorithms with fictions if the purpose is to steer people's behaviour.

Thinking surveillance 'against' Netflix

To watch Netflix in search of new insights about surveillance requires not only watching what Netflix wants us to see, but also how that is determined, and organised. It demands that we understand how (Big) Data dictates its content, and thus the fictional spaces where its publics might – potentially – think about surveillance.

Originally, Netflix was a mail order-based disc rental service, specialising in the renting of DVDs and Blu-rays through a dedicated website. Its operating model was based on requiring subscribers to create and maintain a queue of media content they wished to rent. They rented a disc with a movie, and after they had mailed it back to Netflix, the company sent the next available disc as listed in their subscribers' 'wish list' queue (Lycett 2013: 383). The management of such subscribers' queues quickly became a crucial business goal, leading to a strong interest in all the metadata around them, and, eventually, the introduction of movie recommendations to users (Lycett 2013: 383).

In 2006, Netflix announced a US$1 million prize for improving its movie recommendation service (Hallinan and Striphas 2016; Amatriain 2013; Amatriain and Basilico 2015). In the context of the competition, Netflix publicly released a dataset containing 100,480,507 movie ratings, created by 480,189 Netflix subscribers between December 1999 and December 2005, while declaring that all customer-identifying information had been removed from the dataset. The prize publicly embodied Netflix's commitment to an unabashed data-driven business model, in which the core of its service and the users' experience would be determined by innovative algorithms on the basis of the screening and interpretation of users' preferences and behaviour (Amatriain 2013; Amatriain and Basilico 2015). The prize, however, was also a failure in terms of reassuring about the privacy compliance of such a data-driven business model. Indeed, and despite Netflix's assurances regarding the inexistence of any customer-identifying information in the publicly shared dataset, experiments showed that in cross-correlating that data with non-anonymous records from the Internet Movie Database it was possible to learn sensitive non-public information about a person's political preferences, and even their sexual orientation (Narayanan and Shmatikov 2008).

The Netflix algorithm contest was actually only a first sign of possible privacy problems triggered by the massive amount of data processed by the company, some of which can be highly sensitive. It was also only one of the many occasions in which it has publicly boasted about its pervasive data-mining practices. 'Data is invaluable in making Netflix such an exceptional service for our customers', states the Netflix Open Source Software Centre website, before adding that '[b]ehind the scenes, we have a rich ecosystem of (big) data technologies facilitating our algorithms and analytics' (Netflix 2017a).

Nowadays, viewers' wishes and ratings are only a (relatively small) piece of the mass of data collected and processed by Netflix (Amatriain 2013; Amatriain and Basilico 2015). As detailed by its Privacy Statement (Netflix 2017b), the company collects three types of data: some are actively and consciously provided by users (named '[i]nformation you provide to us'), some are taken from them as they use the service (defined as '[i]nformation we collect automatically'), and some are taken from other, third-party sources (referred to as '[i]nformation from other sources'). Information actively provided by users includes data such as name, email and postal addresses, payment method or telephone number, as well as data actively provided by them on their self-declared preferences and tastes, for instance by rating films. This fundamentally corresponds to the information that users are aware of sharing (what they know they have accepted to share), because they enter it themselves into the system – although they might not be completely aware of with whom they are actually sharing it.

Information collected from users without their 'active' involvement relates to data about their activities on the Netflix service, 'such as title selections, watch history and search queries', and their interactions with ads, as well as different types of data related to their devices and their connection, including IP addresses (Netflix 2017b). This refers to all the data that is collected while they watch content, and about how they watch it: at what time, until which second, when again (if twice or more), from which devices, and where they could be located. Amatriain and Basilico label these data 'play data', stating that 'as of 2013 we [i.e. Netflix] had around 50 million play events coming into the service every day' (Amatriain and Basilico 2015: 398). Many users might not be fully aware of the total extent of such continuous data collection, unless, of course, they happened to read and fully understand the Netflix Privacy Statement, and could also interpret what is said between its lines (cf. also: Hallinan and Striphas 2016).

In addition to all this information, Netflix also collects data from other sources, including from both online and offline data providers. This is 'supplemental information' that 'could include demographic data, interest based data, and Internet browsing behaviour' (Netflix 2017b), as well as, possibly, any other data deemed relevant (Amatriain 2013; Amatriain and Basilico 2015). A majority of users will never know exactly how this is happening: which data were sought for complementing the already massive and fine-grained information obtained about them concretely, and about users' reactions in general, by the monitoring of all of their interactions with the service. The Netflix Privacy Statement notes that the data collected is used inter alia to offer 'personalized viewing recommendations for movies and TV shows we think will be enjoyable', but also for, generally, 'analyzing and understanding our audience; improving our service (including our user interface experiences), delivery optimization, content selection, and recommendation algorithms' (Netflix 2017b). In short, Netflix seems to operate in a growing condition of *mal d'archive*, where the drive to expand the database and introduce indexes never rests.

All these data collection practices, as well as the multiplicity of purposes they serve, are not as such a phenomenon specific to Netflix. Napoli notes that '[t]wo of the primary functions that algorithms are performing in the media production realm at this point are: (a) serving as a demand predictor and (b) serving as a content creator' (2014: 348). While Netflix is probably one of the clearest examples of a company already engaged in both practices, other online providers of popular culture follow similar paths. The digital music service Spotify, for instance, also relies on a combination of data provided by users, data obtained through the monitoring of their behaviour, and data gathered through other sources – most notably Facebook (Spotify 2017). Spotify, as a matter of fact, claims for instance that, for the sake of providing the best possible music recommendations to its users, it is also necessary to systematically monitor whether they are running, as running listeners would have different musical expectations than listeners who are walking, or just sitting (Spotify 2017).

As Beer and Burrows (2013: 67) note, this data pressure on users is different from traditional use of market research to design cultural products. They argue that while '[w]e might say that there has always been a performativity of circulation of data in popular culture[,] this circulation has accelerated, the data has hyper-multiplied and the connections and linkages forged have been beyond any previous comprehension' (Beer and Burrows 2013: 67). In our view, the 'circulation of data' (Beer and Burrows 2013: 67) has not only exploded in quantitative terms, but has also reached a qualitative shift, precisely in asserting and strengthening its circularity. Such circularity affects content design – users are surveilled to know what they might want, so it can be produced – and the purposes of such tailoring: users are to be given what they want, so they might continue to be under surveillance, to make sure what they want can be produced. As documented by *House of Cards*, the purpose of all the data collection practices in place is not limited to suggesting to users certain choices, but to enabling and modulating the possible choices. As noted by Hallinan and Striphas, the company ran its algorithms to decompose the property to determine whether an audience might exist for some combination of 'David Fincher,' his 'style,' the collection of genres across which he has worked, 'Kevin Spacey,' the specific genre of political thriller, and so forth.

(Hallinan and Striphas 2016: 128)

Thus, these permissible choices might include the very definition of future available content, determining casting decisions, or the evolution of plots.

Moreover, such an algorithmic mobilisation of diverse datasets (movies, users' behaviour informations, etc.) shows that 'Netflix [is] moving away from an undifferentiated mass toward an aggregation for highly differentiated micro-audiences' (Hallinan and Striphas 2016: 128). The audiences that Netflix cherishes and monitors might be micro or macro; that is not the decisive factor. What is key is that they are audiences, fully disciplined into a constant (conscious and unconscious) participation, to the production of data about them, thereby silently acquiescing to the mythical image of (Big) Data as a magic enabler of better fictions – about the world and about themselves. Their cooperation for translating their behaviour into what they want (and thus must see) is part of the very plot which is attracting them.

Concluding remarks

House of Cards is more than an artefact of popular culture in which data surveillance is represented. It is also an exemplary instance of how the large-scale collection and processing of data about users' behaviour can be determinant in producing contemporary popular culture. This chapter has attempted to show how, by watching *House of Cards* while at the same time looking into how Netflix watches us watching it, it is possible to discover even more tropes of contemporary surveillance. The fourth season of *House of Cards* stages digital surveillance beyond the visual clichés of graphs showing the relations between datapoints (Cardon 2012; Galloway 2011) or those resonating with an 'algorithmic drama' (Ziewitz 2016). It offers a way of imaging Big Data surveillance that somewhat bypasses the 'mythology' of Big Data (boyd and Crawford 2012). Its images and its storyline make visible something more relatable and diverse than pseudoscientific maps of digital connections and relations.

A key notion that emerges in this co-constitutive and bidirectional watching is the notion of created and creating publics (Gillespie 2014). Streaming services pursue and create publics, and publics facilitate the creation of the fiction that shall be streamed, for a better understanding of its publics. And all this streaming and being *streamed-to-public* ultimately come into being through something called data, which is what holds everything together – or separate, as necessary. They are data-driven, data-drawn publics that are mobilised for, and disciplined into, sustained personal data production, that is, as data-breeding publics. In this sense, the drama of current business strategies would not be that there is not enough data to generate fiction, but rather that there is not enough fiction to generate data, and thus to partially satisfy this *mal d'archive*.

In this spiral of public(s)-data creation, some might want to attribute to the new publics a promise of self-consciousness, if not agency. As exemplified by Gillespie (2014: 168), algorithms could be portrayed as contributing to 'produce' new kinds of 'calculated publics' that are somehow specular to networks of users, even if very different in their sociotechnical and political engineering. The question remains, however, to what extent the algorithmic (re-)presentation of publics echoes something more, or something different from (and potentially in contestation of) the data-generating publics. Thinking surveillance with and against Netflix, through and besides its fiction, obliges us to interrogate the role allocated to individuals in the shared production of data. Publics can be viewed as consumers of content, but mainly as co-producers of data, which, in the end, is what shall be produced, unless what is ultimately to be produced is a public that is perhaps not able to see itself as such. We might think of Netflix as surveillance, to the extent that surveillance is a process of data generation, but on the condition that we understand it as a complex process occurring with and via its users/viewers/watchers.

Watchers are, indeed, a classical conceptual category of surveillance studies, generally understood as those who perform surveillance, those who surveil (as in watch over) the others who are being surveilled (the watched). This dyad of watcher/watched has been put into question by the analysis of other practices of surveillance, where the somewhat vertical visual diagrams of watcher/watched is put into discussion by 'lateral' surveillance (as the watched are also watching others being watched, thus becoming co-watchers) or by the uptake of the surveillance performance (e.g. cases of self-exposure) (cf. González Fuster *et al.* 2015). In the present case, the picture is complicated by the fact that individuals wishing to look into a depiction of surveillance are taken over as members of a public that might be unable to perceive itself as such.

In this blurring of watching vectors, data play a critical role as mediators: they are what is extracted from individuals before these are transformed into new, invisible, data-built entities. Data thus here translate people into publics, and publics potentially into fictions – or, in the case of real-life data-driven electoral processes, political realities. Individuals might be pictured as trapped inside data bubbles (on this metaphor, see Schneider, Chapter 8 in this volume), but also as being dissolved into the very soap that makes up the bubbles built around them and others.

These reflections are crucial to engage in a discussion about the possible role of data-driven and data-breeding publics as potentially 'emancipated spectators' (Rancière 2009) – that is, their political relation to the databases and the narratives with which they are confronted and thrown into. If we are to accept the link between political emancipation and fiction (and thus, by extension, the narrative), or, in Rancière's words, the idea that '[the political] begins with fiction' (2014: 50), then we definitely need new forms of collective and creative imaging to reappropriate the contemporary database drive for emancipatory purposes. We need to keep thinking while (or in spite of, or instead of) watching fiction on the fictional nature of our translations into data, and our possible emancipation through it.

Note

1 Authors' note: Authors are listed in alphabetical order. They sincerely thank the editors of this volume for encouraging and constructively accompanying the preparation of this contribution. The first reflections about this work were presented at the session 'Data as Things: Dis/assembling the Stuff of Data and Data's Coming to Matter' of the *London Conference on Critical Thought* in June 2016. An earlier version of the section 'Thinking surveillance through *House of Cards*' was released as a blog post with the title 'From House of Cards to House of Data?' (available at: https://blogs.prio. org/2016/03/from-the-house-of-cards-to-house-of-data/). Rocco Bellanova's research has been carried out in the framework of the research project DIGICOM: Communicating Risk in the Digital Age (funded by the Norwegian Research Council, grant number: 233867) and of the research project *FOLLOW: Following the Money from Transaction to Trial* (funded by the European Research Council, grant number: ERC-2015-CoG 682317). Gloria González Fuster is not subscribed to Netflix.

References

Amatriain, X. (2013). *Big & Personal: Data and Models Behind Netflix Recommendations. BigMine '13*. New York: ACM.

Amatriain, X. and Basilico, J. (2015). Recommender Systems in Industry: A Netflix Case Study. *In:* Ricci, F., Rokach, L. and Shapira, B. (eds.) *Recommender Systems Handbook*. 2nd edition. New York: Springer.

Amoore, L. and Piotukh, V. (2015). Life beyond big data: Governing with little analytics. *Economy and Society*, 44, 3, 341–366.

Amoore, L. and Raley, R. (2017). Securing with algorithms: Knowledge, decision, sovereignty. *Security Dialogue*, 48, 1, 3–10.

Andrejevic, M. and Gates, K. (2014). Big Data surveillance: Introduction. *Surveillance & Society*, 12, 2, 185–196.

Apter, E. (2006). *The Translation Zone*. Princeton, NJ: Princeton University Press.

Aradau, C. and Blanke, T. (2015). The (Big) Data-security assemblage: Knowledge and critique. *Big Data & Society*, 2, 2, 1–12.

Baldwin, R. (2012). Netflix gambles on Big Data to become the HBO of streaming. *Wired*, 29 November.

Barry, A. (2013). The Translation Zone: Between actor-network theory and international relations. *Millennium – Journal of International Studies*, 41, 3, 413–429.

Beer, D. and Burrows, R. (2010). Consumption, prosumption and participatory web cultures. An introduction. *Journal of Consumer Culture*, 10, 1, 3–12.

Beer, D. and Burrows, R. (2013). Popular culture, digital archives and the new social life of data. *Theory, Culture & Society*, 30, 4, 47–71.

Bellanova, R. (2017). Digital, politics, and algorithms: Governing digital data through the lens of data protection. *European Journal of Social Theory*, 20, 3, 329–347.

Bennett, C.J. (2015). Trends in voter surveillance in Western societies: Privacy intrusions and democratic implications. *Surveillance & Society*, 13, 3/4, 370–384.

Borgman, C.L. (2015). *Big Data, Little Data, No Data. Scholarship in the Networked World*. Cambridge, MA: MIT Press.

boyd, d. and Crawford, K. (2012). Critical questions for Big Data. Provocations for a cultural, technological, and scholarly phenomenon. *Information, Communication & Society*, 15, 5, 662–679.

Brems, M. (2017). *What House of Cards Got Right (and Wrong) About Data Science.* Available at: https://medium.com/towards-data-science/what-house-of-cards-got-right-and-wrong-about-data-science-41218f69c7f5. [Accessed 6 October 2017].

Cambridge Analytica. (2017). *Data Drives All We Do*. New York: Cambridge Analytica. Available at: https://cambridgeanalytica.org/. [Accessed 6 October 2017].

Cardon, D. (2012). Regarder les données. *Multitudes*, 2, 49, 138–142.

Cardon, D. (2015). *À quoi rêvent les algorithmes*. Paris: Seuil.

Carr, D. (2013). *Giving Viewers What They Want*. New York: *New York Times*. Available at: www.nytimes.com/2013/02/25/business/media/for-house-of-cards-using-big-data-to-guarantee-its-popularity.html. [Accessed 5 October 2017].

Čas, J., Bellanova, R., Burgess, J.P., Friedewald, M. and Peissl, W. (2017). Introduction. Surveillance, Privacy and Security. *In:* Friedewald, M., Burgess, J.P., Čas, J., Bellanova, R. and Peissl, W. (eds.) *Surveillance, Privacy and Security. Citizens' Perspectives.* London: Routledge.

Chan, J. and Bennett Moses, L. (2016). Is Big Data challenging criminology? *Theoretical Criminology*, 20, 1, 21–39.

Crouch, I. (2016). *'House of Cards' Season 4 Is Less Vulgar Than Real Politics*. New York: New Yorker. Available at: www.newyorker.com/culture/culture-desk/house-of-cards-season-4-is-less-vulgar-than-real-politics. [Accessed 5 October 2017].

De Goede, M., Leander, A. and Sullivan, G. (2016). Introduction: The politics of the list. *Environment and Planning D: Society and Space*, 34, 1, 3–13.

Degli Esposti, S. (2014). When big data meets dataveillance: The hidden side of analytics. *Surveillance & Society*, 12, 2, 209–225.

Derrida, J. (1996). *Archive Fever. A Freudian Impression*. Chicago, IL: The University of Chicago Press.

Desrosières, A. (2011). Words and Numbers: For a Sociology of the Statistical Argument. *In:* Sætnan, A.R., Lomell, H.M. and Hammer, S. (eds.) *The Mutual Construction of Statistics and Society*. New York: Routledge.

Doward, J. and Gibbs, A. (2017). *Did Cambridge Analytica influence the Brexit vote and the US election?* London: *Guardian*. Available at: www.theguardian.com/politics/2017/mar/04/nigel-oakes-cambridge-analytica-what-role-brexit-trump. [Accessed 6 October 2017].

Eco, U. (2009). *The Infinity of Lists*. New York: Rizzoli.

Galloway, A. (2011). Are some things unrepresentable? *Theory, Culture & Society*, 28, 7–8, 85–102.

Gillespie, T. (2010). The politics of 'platforms'. *New Media & Society*, 12, 3, 347–364.

Gillespie, T. (2014). The Relevance of Algorithms. *In:* Gillespie, T., Boczkowski, P.J. and Foot, K.A. (eds.) *Media Technologies. Essays on Communication, Materiality, and Society.* Cambridge, MA: MIT Press.

Gitelman, L. and Jackson, V. (2013). Introduction. *In:* Gitelman, L. (ed.) *'Raw Data' is an Oxymoron.* Cambridge, MA: MIT Press.

González Fuster, G., Bellanova, R. and Gellert, R. (2015). Nurturing ob-scene politics: Surveillance practices between in/visibilities and disappearances. *Surveillance & Society*, 13, 3/4, 512–527.

Guins, R. (2009). *Edited Clean Version: Technology and the Culture of Control*. Minneapolis, MN: University of Minnesota Press.

Hallinan, B. and Striphas, T. (2016). Recommended for you: The Netflix Prize and the production of algorithmic culture. *New Media & Society*, 18, 1, 117–137.

Hayles, K.N. (2012). *How We Think. Digital Media and Contemporary Technogenesis*. Chicago, IL: University of Chicago Press.

Kammerer, D. (2012). Surveillance in Literature, Film and Television. *In:* Ball, K., Haggerty, K. and Lyon, D. (eds.) *Routledge Handbook of Surveillance Studies*. Abingdon, Oxon: Routledge.

Kiersey, N.J. and Neumann, I.B. (eds.) (2013). *Battlestar Galactica and International Relations*. London/New York: Routledge.

Kitchin, R. (2013). Big data and human geography. *Dialogues in Human Geography*, 3, 3, 262–267.

Kitchin, R. (2014). *The Data Revolution. Big Data, Open Data, Data Infrastructures & Their Consequences*. London: Sage.

Klarer, M. (2014). Putting television 'aside': Novel narration in House of Cards. *New Review of Film and Television Studies*, 12, 2, 203–220.

Leonard, A. (2013). *How Netflix is Turning Viewers Into Puppets*. Salon. Available at: www.salon.com/2013/02/01/how_netflix_is_turning_viewers_into_puppets/. [Accessed 1 January 2018].

Lupton, D. (2015). *Digital Sociology*. London/New York: Routledge.

Lycett, M. (2013). Datafication: Making sense of (Big) Data in a complex world. *European Journal of Information Systems*, 22, 4, 381–386.

Lyon, D. (2007). *Surveillance Studies. An Overview*. Cambridge: Polity.

Lyon, D. (2014). Surveillance, Snowden, and big data: Capacities, consequences, critique. *Big Data & Society*, 1, 2, 1–13.

Madrigal, A.C. (2014). How Netflix Reverse Engineered Hollywood. *The Atlantic*, 02.01.2014.

Manovich, L. (2002). *The Language of New Media*. Cambridge, MA: MIT Press.

Marks, P. (2005). Imagining surveillance: Utopian visions and surveillance studies. *Surveillance & Society*, 3, 2/3, 222–239.

Marks, P. (2015). *Imagining Surveillance. Utopian and Dystopian Literature and Film*. Edinburgh: Edinburgh University Press.

Mayer-Schönberger, V. and Cukier, K. (2013). *Big Data: A Revolution That Will Transform How We Live, Work, and Think*. Boston: Eamon Dolan.

Napoli, P.M. (2014). Automated media: An institutional theory perspective on algorithmic media production and consumption. *Communication Theory*, 24, 3, 340–360.

Narayanan, A. and Shmatikov, V. (2008). Robust De-anonymization of Large Datasets (How to Break Anonymity of the Netflix Prize Dataset). *arXiv*.

Netflix. (2017a). *Netflix OSS*. Netflix. Available at: http://netflix.github.io/. [Accessed 6 October 2017].

Netflix. (2017b). *Privacy Statement*. Amsterdam: Netflix International B.V. Available at: https://help.netflix.com/legal/privacy?locale=en&docType=privacy. [Accessed 6 October 2017].

Nussbaum, E. (2013). *Shark Week. 'House of Cards', 'Scandal', and the Political Game*. New York: New Yorker. Available at: www.newyorker.com/magazine/2013/02/25/shark-week. [Accessed 5 October 2017].

Odello, L. (2013). Exploser les images, saboter l'écran. *In:* Odello, L. (ed.) *Blockbuster. Philosophie & cinéma*. Paris: Les Prairies ordinaires.

Orton-Johnson, K. and Prior, N. (eds.) (2013). *Digital Sociology. Critical Perspectives*. Basingstoke: Palgrave.

Pasquale, F. (2015). *The Black Box Society. The Secret Algorithms That Control Money and Information*. Cambridge, MA: Harvard University Press.

Plunkett, J. (2015). *Netflix Set to Make New Series of Charlie Brooker's Dystopian Drama Black Mirror*. London: *Guardian*. Available at: www.theguardian.com/media/2015/sep/08/netflix-new-series-charlie-brooker-dystopian-drama-black-mirror. [Accessed 5 October 2017].

Potter, T. and Marshall, C.W. (eds.) (2008). *Cylons in America. Critical Studies In Battlestar Galactica*. New York/London: Continuum.

Rancière, J. (2009). *The Emancipated Spectator*. London/New York: Verso.

Rancière, J. (2014). *Moments Politiques. Interventions 1977–2009*. New York: Seven Stories Press.

Regazzoni, S. (2014). La déconstruction à l'époque de la pop culture. *Rue Descartes*, 3, 82, 121–124.

Ritzer, G. and Jurgenson, N. (2010). Production, consumption, prosumption: The nature of capitalism in the age of the digital 'prosumer'. *Journal of Consumer Culture*, 10, 1, 13–36.

Rouvroy, A. (2013). The End(s) of Critique. *In:* Hildebrandt, M. and De Vries, K. (eds.) *Privacy, Due Process and the Computational Turn*. Oxon: Routledge.

Rouvroy, A. and Berns, T. (2013). 'Gouvernementalité algorithmique et perspectives d'émancipation' Le disparate comme condition d'individuation par la relation? *Réseaux*, 1, 177, 163–196.

Spotify. (2017). *Politique de confidentialité de Spotify*. Stockholm: Spotify AB. Available at: www.spotify.com/be-fr/legal/privacy-policy/. [Accessed 6 October 2017].

Sterne, J. (2012). *MP3: The Meaning of a Format*. Durham, NC: Duke University Press.

Sweney, M. (2014). Netflix Gathers Detailed Viewer Data to guide its Search for the Next Hit. *Guardian*, 23 February.

Volcler, J. (2017). *Contrôle: Comment s'inventa l'art de la manipulation sonore*. Paris: La Découverte.

Ziewitz, M. (2016). Governing algorithms. Myth, mess, and methods. *Science, Technology, & Human Values*, 41, 1, 3–16.

12 'Data trainings' in German schools – learning empowerment from hackers

Julia Fleischhack

Introduction

'Fight for your digital rights' was one of the slogans on stickers and handouts from civil society organisations, such as 'Netzpolitik' or the 'Digital Rights Foundation', lying around at a workshop on mobile phone security that I attended in the summer of 2017, together with a group of eight teenage girls and boys in Berlin. The workshop was led by two young women in their mid-twenties, both members and co-founders of a Berlin female-only hackerspace. Their aim was to present the participants with ways of how to protect their individual privacy and personal data on mobile phones. One of them also worked as an IT security consultant.

We were all sitting around a long table. On one of the shorter ends of the table, behind the two women, was a big screen, displaying the topics of the workshop. Focusing on the security of the phone in their workshops, as they explained to the group, is important for them, because of its widespread use in everyday life and its popularity amongst young people. Carrying it around every day makes it one of the best 'tracking devices', as one of the women argued, employing a term coined by the German 'Chaos Computer Club e.V.' (CCC).[1] In addition, they named further 'problematic' issues concerning the mobile phone: according to them, there are fewer options to update and tinker with the operating systems of mobile phones than with computers, thereby making the device more vulnerable technically. The two educators involved the students in the analysis of the 'vulnerabilities' of the phone. When asked by the two women what they know about the modes of tracking through the mobile device, the students presented a range of responses. Amongst the terms the students named and explained in their functions are 'WLAN', 'SIM-based', 'web tracking' and communication with the 'GPS', while the women offered helpful comments. During the two-hour workshop, we discussed ways of creating safe passwords, of how particular communication apps are affecting the personal data on our mobile phones and what kind of browsers are considered 'independent' in their workings.

The workshop described here exemplifies the forms of empowerments these two women provided for the students in the form of technical knowledge, support and discussion on issues such as data security, personal privacy settings and data-tracking mechanisms in the online world. However, it also displays the rising civil society engagement of hacker groups or 'maker spaces' in – what the groups themselves often define as – 'digital literacy' (in contrast to 'media literacy') in Germany, in addition to schools and state-run media centres.

In this chapter, I analyse how these digital literacy initiatives by hacker and digital rights groups in Germany promote and appropriate a sovereign and safe Internet use in the era of Big Data and increased data surveillance. A great deal of literature in anthropology, sociology and media studies addresses the societal and cultural challenges of Big Data, and highlights how

> the tools of big data research are increasingly woven into our daily lives, including mining digital medical records for scientific and economic insights, mapping relationships via social media, capturing individuals' speech and action via sensors, tracking movement across space, shaping police and security policy via 'predictive policing', and much more.
>
> (Zook *et al.* 2017)

These works often 'interrogate the ethics of big data use and critically consider who gets access to big data and how access (or lack of it) matters to the issues of class, race, gender, sexuality, and geography' (Crawford *et al.* 2014). Studies point to problems of 'data discrimination', to cultural bias in the work of data scientists or to the imbalance of control and power over data (boyd 2011, 2012, 2016; boyd and Crawford 2011; boyd *et al.* 2014). A substantial body of scholarship on Big Data makes these ethical challenges and the imbalance of control and power over personal data visible. My contribution brings into focus the forms of empowerment digital rights activists and educators discuss and promote in their digital literacy initiatives. I am interested in how they interpret and translate the current challenges and risks of Big Data, as described in scholarship above, in media, and in their work and advocacy. By drawing on my ethnographic research in digital literacy initiatives and workshops in Germany, I will analyse how their members discuss ideas of online vulnerability and safety in relation to Big Data in their daily work, and how they understand, teach and encourage control over personal data.[2] How do they envision forms and practices of safe data use for young people in digital media and the Internet? What are the goals, motivations and resources in their work? What are their strategies of empowerment for the era of Big Data?

The work and engagement of these civil society organisations and hacker groups in digital literacy initiatives are the main focus, as they allow for a perspective on how their members, offering long-standing expertise in 'human rights technology activism' (Coleman 2012, 2015) and advocacy for 'digital justice' (Gray and Couldry 2012), do not 'translate'[3] merely the current challenges and risks of Big Data in their engagement in digital literacy, but what is central to their understanding of contemporary digital literacy programmes for young people in schools. I focus especially on the digital literacy initiative

'Chaos macht Schule' of Germany's largest hacker club, the CCC, and their concepts and ideas for a reform of digital literacy education in German schools.[4] The initiative has a strong focus on issues of data safety and privacy in their advocacy work and digital literacy campaigns (Landeszentrale für Medien und Kommunikation Rheinland-Pfalz 2016). I show how its members define current approaches and goals in digital literacy by exploring their work and expert perspectives. What kind of cultural ideas, practices and norms are incorporated in their teaching? What does it mean for them to have digital skills and knowledge? How are these skills achieved across different groups, especially amongst kids with varied skills and knowledge?

I argue that examining current approaches and concepts of digital literacy from the perspective of educators, digital literacy and rights experts opens up new avenues for thinking about the relationship of Big Data and everyday forms of empowerment in digital and media settings, and about the ways literacy and skills can be promoted in school curricula and other educational spaces, such as maker spaces.[5]

I have conducted ethnographic research in different digital literacy initiatives programmes and digital rights organisations in Germany since 2016. I attended several digital literacy workshops and youth conferences on such topics as online hate, mobile phone security, Nazism in Rap music, and safe YouTube tutorials that were directed at either students or parents and teachers. In addition, I attended meetings of pedagogical expert and literacy campaigns, where the experts presented and discussed their work. I have conducted several semi-structured interviews and informal conversations with educators, digital literacy and rights experts, teachers and policymakers over the past years, and learned about their visions and goals in promoting digital literacy, their own work, engagement and experiences in this field. I also incorporate written material from handbooks and brochures from digital literacy initiatives and media reports on these issues.

This chapter starts with a review of recent anthropological studies of digital literacy that give insight into the ways in which media literacy is conceptualised, defined, discussed and promoted. Next, I present examples from my fieldwork in digital literacy initiatives and show how these discuss the challenges of Big Data issues (for the individual) in their work, pointing out how they present new ideas and approaches. I will then move on to discuss current calls for media literacy reforms, their goals and new approaches, to the current scene of digital literacy. Finally, I will turn to the forms of empowerment in the digital world that the media literacy initiatives display and discuss in their work.

On media and digital literacies

The fundamental importance of digital literacy in a highly mediated world is repeatedly highlighted in media pedagogy and amongst policymakers. An expert report from a special committee of the German ministry of education on digital literacy in 2009 defines, for example, digital literacy as an integral part of a general education and educational training (e.g. Schelhowe *et al.* 2009: 2). These accounts of digital literacy often note how meaningful digital literacy is for personality development and identity-building (Esken 2015, 2016a, 2016b; Körber-Stiftung 2017; Kultusministerkonferenz 2012; Zorn 2011).

Pointing to the new challenges in education and learning caused by digital media, these works often use the term 'digital literacy' instead of the older and more commonly known term 'media literacy', often used to describe the 'ability to "access, analyse, and evaluate media" in multiple forms and "communicate competently" within these' (Bulger 2012: 84). While there is a lot of attention paid to the promotion of digital literacy on the national and European level, Bulger shows that there are ongoing debates 'as to what constitutes "literacy" generally, and digital literacy in particular' (Bulger 2014). Looking back to the early stages of her dissertation research in 2006 when ' "digital literacy" as a term had not been formalized', she notes that researchers 'were still determining the basic components of this emerging practice' (Bulger 2012: 84). Zorn argues similarly in her analysis of existing 'media literacy models' in German media pedagogy. Zorn, highlighting that many of them have emerged in pre-digital times, calls for new approaches in media pedagogy that address the challenges caused by digital media (Zorn 2011: 176).[6] Following Zorn or Bulger, we can see that the elements of what constitutes digital literacy today are still a matter for ongoing debates. I will take up these issues in a more ethnographic register, drawing on my fieldwork conducted amongst digital literacy initiatives and by contributing to anthropological scholarship on 'digital literacies'.

There has been a range of anthropological studies in the last two decades that have explored how 'young people acquire various forms of technical and media literacy by exploring new interest, tinkering, and "messing around" with new forms of media' (Ito *et al.* 2008: 1, 2). The 'Digital Youth Project' carried out a large, multi-site ethnographic study to try to understand the mechanisms of informal learning in digital environments. The research focused especially on the youths' 'engagement with social network sites, media fandom, and gaming', asking what kinds of literacy and social competence they are defining with their media engagements (Ito *et al.* 2008: 7). Using the term 'new media', they want to highlight a 'media ecology where more traditional media such as books, television, and radio, are "converging" with digital media, specifically interactive media and media for social communication' (Ito *et al.* 2008: 8).

By following an ethnographic approach, the studies consider the social and cultural ideas, meanings and experiences that young people themselves articulate about their kinds of literacy and social competence 'with this set of new media technologies' (Ito *et al.* 2008: 11). Patricia G. Lange, one member of the Digital Youth team, places, for instance, a strong emphasis on video-making as a space of learning, particularly regarding the ways how and where youths are learning (Lange 2007, 2014). Lange, in her book 'Kids on YouTube: Technical Identities and Digital Literacies', which draws on a two-year, deeply engaged ethnographic project on YouTube and video bloggers, for instance, pushes back on conceptions of 'digital natives': 'The term would imply that all kids are equally well versed in all technologies', however, such was not the case in her study. On the contrary, she points to the youths' diverse digital skills and interests, and the 'vastly different media dispositions they exhibit with regard to how comfortable they feel sharing videos of themselves' (Jenkins 2014a). Lange's study examines the ways in which these skills are achieved across different groups, amongst youths with varied skills and knowledge, and of different gender, highlighting, for instance how boys and girls 'share certain ideas about what it means to be technical' (Jenkins 2014b).[7] Her account also draws crucial attention to the role of peer-to-peer learning and its limits in her own research. Relating to her own observations from her field, she argues that 'peer-to-peer mentorships may or may not always provide the kind of encouragement they need' (Jenkins 2014b). For her, adults, schools and other mentors can provide the perspective and experience to develop these skills (Jenkins 2014b).

While these studies focus more on informal learning spaces, peer-to-peer learning, and 'what kind of literacies and social competencies they are defining with this set of new media technologies' – on 'what they see themselves as important' (Ito *et al.* 2008: 11) – they provide fewer clues for understanding the interplay within a 'context of explicit instruction' (Ito *et al.* 2008: 8) and how the literacy and engagement with new media amongst young people can be shaped, for instance, in particular school curricula or digital literacy initiatives, and on which my research focuses.

This context of explicit instruction came into focus in a essay entitled 'Did Media Literacy Backfire?' by media scholar danah boyd (2017). Analysing how media literacy has been understood and taught within the last 30 years in the US, boyd shows the long-standing and powerful effects of media literacy approaches – taught, for instance, in schools or higher education programmes – can have on information consumption and information behaviour in society (boyd 2017). She argues that the problems of fake news and conspiracy news 'have in parts their origin in efforts to educate people against misinformation' (boyd 2017). She wrote in response to recent calls for a political regulation of fake news and calls for an increased commitment to media literacy programmes. There, she warns about quick solutions for the problems. According to her, these approaches would not be successful, 'because they fail to take into consideration the cultural context of information consumption that we've created over the last thirty years' (boyd 2017). Boyd points to the changing values and norms in education and literacy: what is seen as important literacy at a certain time in society, can be considered a decade later as wrong or ineffective. Similarly, the authors of the 'Digital Youth Project' argue in their report: 'Not only are literacy standards diverse and culturally specific, but they are constantly changing in tandem with technical changes and a rising bar of cultural sophistication' (Ito *et al.* 2008: 38). Monica E. Bulger argues in her practice-oriented approach that 'understanding the cultural, regulatory, economic, and educational context in which media literacy is developed and enacted is essential to further developments in policy and training' (Bulger 2012: 98).

What is worth noting is that the studies point to the importance of considering the different cultural and societal contexts, and to new challenges in literacy and education 'by a shifting landscape of media and communications in which youth are central actors' (Ito *et al.* 2008: 4). I will expand these studies by analysing the civil society engagement in digital literacy education and programmes in Germany, analysing their concepts, ideas, and practices and how they relate these to the contemporary challenges of the online world and media devices. Throughout my analysis, I will mainly use the terms 'digital literacy' and 'new media literacy' instead of media literacy, because it captures the usage of many experts in my ethnographic field and research literature (Bulger 2012, 2014; Bulger *et al.* 2014; Lange 2014; Ito *et al.* 2008). This distinction is not just as a matter of new technologies, but also reflects new claims and approaches. Consequently, the terminological distinction between media and digital literacy is ethnographically productive.

Promoting 'digital maturity' – hackers as teachers

A range of government and educational institutions, schools and civil society organisations are currently engaged in digital literacy education in Germany. The *Landesmedienanstalten*, the media agencies of the federal states that supervise German-speaking media content on television, radio and Internet programmes, offer a cluster of digital literacy programmes and campaigns. The federal state of North Rhine-Westphalia, for instance, launched the project *Medienscouts* in 2012, where students are taught in workshops on media issues aimed to support other peers through their knowledge.[8] It is one of the largest peer-to-peer programmes in Germany (Landesanstalt für Medien Nordrhein-Westfalen 2017). In addition, there is the European initiative and 'Awareness Centre' called *klicksafe* (a mutual project run by the Central Authority for Media and Communication Rhineland Palatinate, the coordinator, and the Media Authority for North Rhine-Westphalia) to promote a 'safe use of modern communication media and to protect consumers from undesirable content'.[9] Many of the organisations and institutions above offer workshops in schools. Media literacy has been a component of school curricula, often in the form of computing or programming classes, since the 1990s (Kultusministerkonferenz 2012).

Moreover, a broad range of civil society groups and organisations also engage in media literacy programmes and campaigns. In the following, I will present the CCC, a civil society actor with a ten-year-long experience in digital literacy programmes in schools. When the CCC members started their volunteer engagement in schools in 2007, there were, as one of their members states in a presentation, not many similar digital literacy initiatives by civil society actors. Today there is a significant range of initiatives, often – as in my example from the introduction – based on volunteer engagement and rather locally active (CCC Video 2016). However, some of them have grown into supraregional projects such as 'Jugend hackt', 'CoderDojo', 'Hacker School' or 'Datarun', many of them focusing on promoting coding skills.[10] How did it come about that a hacker community with several thousand members, standing for technical research, policy advice, whistle-blower support – they also operate anonymisation services

(*Anonymisierungsdienste*) and communication platforms – became engaged in the field of digital literacy? How do they situate their activism and work in this field?

Members and regional groups of the CCC began with singular sessions and engagements in schools in 2007. At that time, teachers had approached the 'hacker community' and asked them for help and expertise because they felt overstrained by the task (CCC Video 2016). Since then, their activities in schools, youth centres and public libraries have turned into a continuous and regular engagement in the field of digital literacy. And it gained a name: 'Chaos macht Schule [Chaos makes school]'.

'Chaos macht Schule' currently offers a workshop, lecture and literacy programme for schools, directed at the younger generation, mainly students, though they also train teachers. Their topics are safe Internet usage, social media risks and raising awareness concerning issues of data protection, data security or Internet policy (CCC Video 2016; Landeszentrale für Medien und Kommunikation, Rheinland-Pfalz 2016). In the following, I will analyse the specific features and qualities they address in their media literacy programmes and presentations. What are their goals and visions in their work? How do they define them?

The literacy initiative does not have a fixed programme or agenda set; many of the regional communities of 'Chaos macht Schule' work independently at the request of schools or youth organisations (CCC München n.d. a, b, c; Chaos macht Schule Hamburg n.d. a, b). However, their members have a shared aim and vision in their work that is summarised in the mission statement for their initiative and has been repeatedly expressed by members of the initiative (CCC Video 2016; CCC, Chaos macht Schule: Forderungen 2017).[11]

They want to promote a critical, curious and confident usage of the Internet in their workshops. That includes the fact that young people 'can move competently through the Internet, can form their own opinion about technical devices and developments, and most importantly can take independent and autonomous decisions in the digital world' (CCC, Chaos macht Schule, Forderungen 2017). Parents, as one member of the initiative states, often want to have suggestions from them on specific protective software, so that their kids can only access special websites and other sites are blocked (CCC Video 2016). However, they are voicing reservations regarding that task, and they would prefer to promote what they call 'digital maturity' (CCC, Chaos macht Schule, Forderungen 2017).

A female member of 'Chaos macht Schule' outlines what the notion 'digital maturity' means in their work context and how they understand and discuss it in their community by referring to a joint project with the German civil society organisation Körber-Stiftung, that works with the same concept in their digital literacy campaigns (Körber-Stiftung n.d. a, n.d. b). What is important to them is that young people develop, in addition to an 'openness for technology', a 'basic understanding' of the digital world and the skill to question it critically. They argue for a better knowledge of how these device platforms work on not only the technical, but also the social and ethical level. Moreover, they should know about digital policies and developments, what to make of them and can ask questions about these. In their ideal version it means that young people can then shape these worlds technically, ethically and creatively (CCC, Chaos macht Schule, Forderungen 2017; CCC Video 2016).

However, their idea of 'digital maturity' is strongly related to the idea that young people can control the digital devices they use. For them, it is important that youths not only learn to use digital devices, but they should also be taught how to 'control' them (CCC, Chaos macht Schule, Forderungen 2017). The following fieldnote excerpt, documenting a two-hour workshop they gave at the Berlin youth conference 'Tincon' in June 2017, offers insights into how this form of 'control' is discussed and envisioned in their work, and how they translate the complex phenomena and dangers of Big Data in their workshops.[12]

(Personal) data training: 'let's have a look at the data we leave behind'

'Let's have a look at the data we leave behind on different online applications, mobile phones, computers and other digital devices', announced one of the two workshop organisers. It was the third morning of the youth Internet conference 'Tincon' in Berlin. The workshop took place in a small corner of the conference hall and was led by two male members from 'Chaos macht Schule'. Eight youths, aged 13 to 15 years, sat on small benches around them. The net activist Daniel Domscheid-Berg, who also engages in the programme, was also present. The workshop was entitled 'Digital traces' and exemplified – through presenting case studies, research and joint discussion – ways of data tracking on social media sites, such as Facebook, Instagram and Twitter (Chaos macht Schule Hamburg n.d. a).

We started with a short video sequence. Using the video, the two men leading the workshop on data security wanted to demonstrate to us the importance of privacy settings of social media services. It shows how Instagram users having open, non-private Instagram accounts can be easily tracked and located by the geodata of their accounts. The tracking of Instagram users took place in Berlin. Prior to the tracking, the film-makers had selected a random site in Berlin and searched for posts from there within the last 45 minutes. Most of the people who had posted something during that time were still in the area. When confronted by the film team, nearly all the tracked users shown in the video were surprised or even shocked that they were so easily identified by their last post, which gave the location and the time. In the video, one guy, clearly caught by surprise and shocked, stated that his Instagram photos were only meant for his friends.

Subsequently, we discussed the film example. The two members from 'Chaos macht Schule' wanted to know what we made of the example and whether we understood the problem shown. Two of the students – one girl, one boy – gave a detailed account of the key issues seen in the film. Instagram is apparently also popular and common amongst the young workshop participants. When asked by the two workshop leaders what kind of apps and social media they use, three of them also used Instagram. After the film, we switched to the next topic, which was encryption or what we understand of encryption. Again, we were asked what modes of encryption we knew and how these worked. One student named 'end-to-end encryption' and described its basic workings and the apps that offer it. The two workshop leaders seemed satisfied with his explanation, however, they asked the students to review the product's instructions on encryption critically. Both argued that some manufacturers and companies have quite different understandings of what encryption, especially end-to-end encryption, means. We also discussed our options for safe and encrypted communication and messenger services. Both gave advice for alternatives.

There is a range of further data issues that we addressed during the 90-minute workshop: we discussed the technical and organisational possibilities of securing our mobile phones, devices and data. We reviewed different privacy and security settings, what they stand for and what they offer. The two members explained the current business model for many websites that offer free content in exchange for personal data and the user's compliance with this business model. They presented a research study on WhatsApp that demonstrates what can be found out about users who have not turned off their online status, of how their online behaviour can be tracked throughout the day and night, giving a lot of information about sleep behaviour. We considered the pervasiveness of the GPS in digital devices that track our location all the time and case examples of apps that demand access to personal contact lists without any obvious reasons. Another important topic was whom do we accept as a friend on social media and who from the private sector could be interested in our online behaviour.

The workshop consisted of a mixture of demonstration, advising, discussing and sharing data privacy practices and experiences. The team illuminated the ways of data tracking by using all kinds of examples from our digital everyday life, discussed developments in the field of Big Data and data surveillance and their significance for privacy, clarified complicated technical settings, gave feedback and advice to students' questions, tested the knowledge of the students and discussed solutions with the youths. Additionally, their members showed the youths technical and organisational possibilities of protecting their personal data and how to make use of them.

My ethnographic account of the workshop by 'Chaos macht Schule' shows that the 'networked' character of Big Data (boyd and Crawford 2011: 2) and its potential harms for the individual, particularly young people, are presented, taught, discussed and exemplified through the media devices, applications and services the young people use on a daily basis. By relating and translating the workings of Big Data tools and methods to the young people's own social online practices in digital contexts and by focusing explicitly on their social online worlds, they make the quite abstract workings of Big Data palpable. In the work of 'Chaos macht Schule', the notion of data is not abstract artefacts such as Big Data, but rather data which are situated as something personal and deeply social: data are private messages, post, contact info or photos of friends. Data privacy and security are here not abstract legal or technical terms, but these terms are related to personal decisions and everyday practices in social media or other web services.[13]

By looking at their work, it becomes apparent that this kind of data training forms an essential component of their work and of their conceptual under-standing of what digital literacy should constitute today. Patricia G. Lange sees 'knowing what to post' as crucial digital literacy 'in today's self-image-laden media environment' in her study on young YouTube bloggers (Jenkins 2014b). In the work of 'Chaos macht Schule', knowing how to protect personal privacy and personal data is articulated as an important skill and literacy in the digital world. This is also highlighted in conversations and presentations of their work (CCC Video 2016; Landeszentrale für Medien und Kommunikation, Rheinland-Pfalz 2016). The titles of their workshops for students and youths are 'Digital Traces' or 'Why data protection is not a question of good manners/behaviour' (Landeszentrale für Medien und Kommunikation, Rheinland-Pfalz 2016).[14]

'Digital empowerment' in the era of 'Big Data': learning to control personal devices and data

The analysis of what 'digital literacy' means in the work of 'Chaos Macht Schule' gives an insight into not only the challenges of the current online world, but also the forms of empowerments their members – and other like-minded initiatives – promote. It becomes apparent by looking at their concepts and ideas that learning how to control one's own digital devices might be seen as an essen-tial feature of their educational and advocacy work to promote 'digital maturity'. However, that degree of control they are promoting in their workshops espe-cially concerns the data we leave behind by using online devices, services and applications. Their aim is for young people to have control over their data life. They give suggestions and solutions so that the youths can assess and review their own personal data management and make their own personal decisions about it. They offer young people a means of taking 'control' over their data by calling attention to data-tracking mechanisms by websites or in pointing out the limits of encryption modes. Dawn Nafus and Jamie Sherman have argued this of the 'Quantified Self Movement', explaining that 'self-trackers assert greater control over what their data ultimately means' by often resisting 'the categories that are built into devices and into the market for data' (Nafus and Sherman 2014: 1791).

In that way, the initiative's 'data training' also consists of modes of resisting data-tracking mechanisms that are built into devices and web services.

However, I argue that their way of promoting digital literacy is more than a kind of basic online safety education. Their workshops demonstrate methods of encouragement and empowerment to deal with the challenges of Big Data in young people's own personal way. The authors of the 'Digital Youth Project' argue much the same about what new media literacy programmes should look like in the future according to their research findings:

> It is important to understand the diverse genre conventions of youth new media literacy before developing educational programs in this space.

Particularly when addressing learning and literacy that grows out of informal, peer-driven practices, we must realize that norms and standards are deeply situated in investments and identities of kids' own cultural worlds.

(Ito *et al.* 2008: 38)

It is important for the members of 'Chaos macht Schule' that the students find their own way of dealing with the ambiguities of, for instance, 'free' online services that will make use of their data. Their message to the students is without any restrictive or moral undertones. It is more an encouragement to get to know the devices they want to use, and to take well-thought-out decisions about to whom they want to disclose their personal data or to which online service they want to give their data in exchange for a free service. They encourage the students to decide what is important to them in their usage.

Their approach is not about risk-framing, rather it displays a form of encouragement to explore the online world, of experimenting and tinkering with the devices which young people use. I will illustrate it once more with an example from the workshop I attended in June 2017. The older of the two workshop leaders handed out some advice to the students at the end of the workshop:

Use the technology wisely. Spread your data through the usage of different browsers, email services. Be careful whom you give access to your private accounts. Just use the different services, but protect yourselves as best as you can! We do not want to prevent you from using these services, rather create an awareness for these issues.[15]

Redefining digital literacy – a digital literacy manifesto

There has been an increased political interest in the status and promotion of digital literacy education in Germany and Europe in the last decade, along with calls for broader reforms of 'media' literacy programmes in schools and the educational sector (Esken 2015, 2016a, 2016b; Körber-Stiftung n.d., b; Kultusministerkonferenz 2012). The most obvious place to start understanding the broader social context in which these calls for reform for digital literacy in Germany took hold is probably the widespread concern about the state of information consumption and the social climate online. Alarming stories about 'fake news' and 'digital propaganda' have become a regular feature of media stories. Many media and political reports, not only from Germany but also the US, linked this development to failed approaches in media literacy programmes (boyd 2017; CCC, Chaos macht Schule Forderungen 2017; Esken 2015, 2016a).

In Germany, the widespread rise of online hate in German-speaking social media platforms added concern (Fleischhack 2017). However, there are further long-term concerns about the 'digital gap' – or 'digital divide' – in society that have added to that increased political attention to digital literacy (Esken 2016b).

The politician Saskia Esken, for example, in a report from 2016, names data misuse and disinformation which result in threats for people who lack digital skills (Esken 2016a, 2016b). Many of these accounts called for an increased commitment to media literacy programmes (Esken 2016b; Körber-Stiftung n.d. a, b; Kultusministerkonferenz 2012).

It is this specific context that also prompted the German CCC to outline their vision for digital literacy in a manifesto in 2016.[16] The statement calls for a radical change of its format and contents, expressing its discontent with the ways 'media literacy' is understood and taught in most schools (CCC, Chaos macht Schule Forderungen 2017). Its authors see it as an urgent and necessary step to start an – in their words – overdue reform process. Pointing to the recent debates on fake news, they argue that these stand for the consequences of failed media literacy initiatives and neglected policy measures in that domain. Media literacy for the CCC starts in, and with, schools. The text presents their ideas and claims for new media literacy programmes in German schools, based on their long-term engagement in schools and observations of computing classes and the media literacy approaches.

Among the improvements the CCC points out in its reform agenda, are that students should be introduced to open source tools and open extendable platforms, to prevent them from becoming advertising targets of commercialised platforms that track and assess their behaviour (CCC, Chaos macht Schule Forderungen 2017). Additionally, topics and issues from the digital world, such as 'net neutrality', should not be taught in specific isolated classes, but become part of different school subjects or class schedules. Regarding the challenges of the digital era and the technical infrastructure in schools, they argue not only for a better education of teachers, but also for more technical and personal resources in schools to create an ideal environment for digital learning.[17] The agenda particularly stresses the role of teachers (CCC, Chaos macht Schule Forderungen 2017). Lange also highlights in her study, the additional role that schools can play in promoting these skills. For Lange, 'School can supplement informal learning by teaching kids how to provide meaningful commentary in online sites. Classroom exercises could include ways to learn how to comment and present oneself online' (Jenkins 2014b). Yet, the manifesto sees teachers even as role models for the students by promoting digital security practices and a responsible handling of data. According to 'Chaos macht Schule', teachers would not often pay sufficient attention to these issues (CCC Video 2016). They suggest that schools should cooperate with external experts from 'maker spaces' or civil society organisations that have a long-standing expertise and experience in promoting digital literacy to implement the reforms quickly (CCC, Chaos macht Schule Forderungen 2017).

Their manifesto for reform emerged in a special context: as mentioned before, their statement came at a time when digital literacy had received massive political attention because of the dramatic increase in fake news and social bots in social media. However, the field of media literacy is changing rapidly at this stage: an increasing number of media literacy initiatives from the private sector, mainly giant Internet companies, are entering the field. Industry giants such Apple, Microsoft and Google have created their own initiatives: Apple announced so-called 'Free Hour of Code' workshops for youths and adults in many Apple shops across the world in December 2016, while Google opened its first training centre in Munich, calling it euphemistically a *'Zukunftswerkstatt'*, a 'future workshop' (Deyerler and Rausch 2017; Schwan 2016). Further hubs will follow in Berlin and Hamburg. Their goal is to reach about two million people by 2020 with their media literacy initiative.[18] Consequently, the CCC's claim is not without a political message directed at the government to take action and a warning that the field will soon be taken over by powerful private actors, whose engagement is not altruistic, but based on economic interest. It is, as the CCC puts it, learning with the company's products (CCC Video 2016). The field of digital literacy has become highly diverse, and so are the political agendas and interests of the different actors involved – whether they are from civil society, the private or public sector. Promoting digital literacy has become a highly contested normative and political site, and so are the understandings of what 'digital literacy' means.

I wanted to highlight here the work of 'Chaos macht Schule' in digital literacy because of its long-standing experience and engagement in this domain. Their members bring their technical knowledge and long-standing expertise about the online world to society, especially to the younger generation. Through their advocacy work on issues of data protection, privacy and data surveillance, they monitor present developments in the industry and field of Big Data and how the latter might affect individual online behaviour: this can include phenomena of how our newsfeed on Facebook can be manipulated or how Google tracks and works with our search results to improve their services or to sell them to interested companies (e.g. Kurz and Rieger 2009). I argue that these initiatives act as 'translators' of complex and often abstract sets of Big Data phenomena and tools that can influence and shape our online behaviour by highlighting how they play out in the application and services we use on a daily basis. With their volunteer engagement in schools or in hacker spaces, the local teams from the CCC or the female hacker group from Berlin provide a kind of 'community service 3.0' to promote online safety for, and – to draw on their own concept – 'digital maturity' amongst, the next generation.

Conclusion

My analysis gives insights into how members of 'Chaos macht Schule' are translating the workings and meanings of Big Data here into the contexts of the children's own social and cultural online worlds, and how they are mapping out the opportunities for empowerment and the chances of harm – related to personal data – in their workshops. However, as Bulger notes, 'neither of those are happening in a vacuum'. She argues that 'digital literacy alone is not the sole tool for empowering and it is also not the sole tool for protecting' (Dumancela 2015). Bulger, in her practice-oriented research on digital literacy and children's rights online, looks 'at what aspects of child protection can be enhanced by digital literacy and then, what is left' (Dumancela 2015).

The limits of individual empowerment (for more on these, see Ochs, Chapter 13 in this volume) were always present and made transparent by the initiatives in my own ethnographic research into digital literacy initiatives. It is worth noting here that the 'Chaos macht Schule' approach in its message to students is without myths and empty promises about the online safety that is possible for them. They claim that 'data safety' is a process and is not something fixed.[19] 'Data safety' is a relatively relational category in their work, one that has to be continuously adapted to different contexts and developments in the online world.

I have demonstrated, with my example of 'Chaos macht Schule', that their engagement in the promotion of digital literacy in schools has become a means of sharing their knowledge and expertise of the online world with the broader society, in particular the younger generation, and with parents and teachers. Their concept of 'digital maturity' and the ideas and skills related to it are reflections of their advocacy for digital rights and for transparent communication infrastructures (CCC n.d., *Self-description*). All of them present a quest for more online autonomy and more sovereignty for young people. However, their ultimate goal is to convey the instrumental values of knowing how to control the devices and their personal data, without undermining the freedom of using different services and limiting online practices. They are well aware that this goal is often a transient and difficult one in the reality of the online world.

In my ethnographic research, digital literacy is seen not only as an instrument that gives, at least to a certain degree, protection from several 'online vulnerabilities' (Lange 2007), from harassment or false information to data tracking, but also as a form of empowerment for the younger generation. The young people in the workshops I attended for my research learned how to deal with potential online harm or risks in technical, social or even legal and emotional terms: knowing how to protect oneself through the choice of a safe password and privacy settings, knowing ways in which to react to mean comments or finding social support or help for particular problems online form all-important digital literacies in today's online and media use. The current online and media world – I do not want to exclude here more traditional media such as newspapers, radio or television – demands 'this diversity in forms of literacy' (Ito *et al.* 2008: 2) and in forms of empowerments – may it be through formal contexts, such as the literacy initiatives I discussed in this chapter, or through peers and parents.

Notes

1 Most of the empirical material I use in this chapter is originally in German. I translated all of my interview material, field notes and sources.
2 Many of their members have long-standing expertise and background in the field of IT security, programming, hacking, media literacy and digital rights advocacy.
3 See here for anthropological and ethnographic accounts of 'translation processes' in the human rights sector: Sally Engle Merry (2006): Human Rights & Gender Violence. Translating International Law into Local Justice. Chicago.

4 See a self-representation here: www.ccc.de/de/club. The CCC is the biggest European Hacker community with several thousand members and was founded in 1981. The CCC, as it is called, has regional offices/communities in various cities across Germany, Switzerland and Austria. Yet, regional groups and initiatives of the CCC plan their activities and outreach independently, following their own interests and key activities. Their areas of activism address – to name just a few – privacy, surveillance, censoring, discrimination, consumer rights, open source software and includes technology development. In their work, they monitor, for instance, potential privacy threats, they review and analyse current developments in the Internet, they create information campaigns for raising awareness on issues of digital rights and do lobbying work for (inter)national legalisation, or create technological tools to make the online space safer for its users. Sharing their know-how with young people and children has become a further site of activity.

5 Nearly every bigger city in Germany has 'Maker spaces' or 'Fablab'. See an overview here: www.medienpaedagogik-praxis.de/2014/05/27/fablabs-makerspace-und-co-was-ist-das-eigentlich-maker-movement-teil-12/.

6 Zorn presents different models of what media literacy means from different expert perspectives in media pedagogy in her essay. Amongst the most popular and well-known theoretical approaches is the model by the media educator Baacke from the early 1990s. He lists four criteria of 'media literacy', namely media critique, knowledge about media and media systems, the use of media, and the ability to develop and shape media (see Fischnaller 2013: 21). He was the first to highlight the 'critical awareness of the individual' as an important skill in his model, providing the individual with the skill to select media services autonomously and critically. He is said to be the first to coin the term *Medienkompetenz* in German scholarship on media literacy.

7 Consequently, Lange argues that, 'More attention should be paid to how girls attain and achieve a sense of pride in mastering technical ideas, devices, and systems rather than only analysing what participation online means for the construction of their "femininity"' (Jenkins 2014b).

8 See the project here: www.medienscouts-nrw.de/.

9 See the project here: www.klicksafe.de/ueber-klicksafe/die-initiative/project-information-en/what-is-klicksafe/.

10 See the initiatives here: www.ccc.de/de/schule; https://jugendhackt.org/; http://data-run.de/.

11 A recent video presentation of their work can be found here: https://news.rpi-virtuell.de/2016/12/29/chaos-macht-schule-schulbesuche-vom-ccc/. Further, http://schule.muc.ccc.de/.

12 The following is based on my field notes from the youth Internet conference 'Tincon' in Berlin, where I conducted participant observation in June 2017. The conference is for young people between 13 and 21 years of age and created by Tanja and Johnny Haeusler, the co-founders of re:publica.

13 See Carsten Ochs, Chapter 13 in this volume.

14 The original titles in German are: '*Spuren im Netz*' and '*Warum Datenschutz keine Frage des guten Tons ist*'. www.klicksafe.de/service/aktuelles/news/detail/experten interview-zum-ccc-projekt-chaos-macht-schule/.

15 See note 12.

16 The full statement by the CCC can be found here: www.ccc.de/de/cms-forderungen-lang.

17 So far, the Ministry of Education supports schools only technically, such as with WLAN and other devices.

18 Microsoft also offers a broad programme of online courses in 'digital literacy' See here: www.microsoft.com/en-us/digitalliteracy/overview.aspx.

19 See note 12.

References

boyd, d. (2011). *Privacy and Publicity in the Context of Big Data.* Available at: www.danah.org/papers/talks/2010/WWW2010.html. [Accessed 12 October 2017].

boyd, d. (2012). Networked Privacy. *Surveillance & Society*, 103(4), pp. 348–350.

boyd, d. (2016). Undoing the Neutrality of Big Data. *Florida Law Review*, 67, pp. 226–232.

boyd, d. (2017). *Did Media Literacy Backfire?* Available at: https://points.datasociety.net/did-media-literacy-backfire-7418c084d88d. [Accessed 30 September 2017].

boyd, d. and Crawford, K. (2011). *Six Provocations for Big Data.* Available at: https://papers.ssrn.com/sol3/papers.cfm?abstract_id=1926431. [Accessed 12 October 2017].

boyd, d., Levy, K. and Marwick, A. (2014). The Networked Nature of Algorithmic Discrimination. In: S. Peña Gangadharan, V. Eubanks and S. Barocas, eds. *Data & Discrimination: Collected Essays*. Washington, DC: Open Technology Institute, pp. 43–57.

Bulger, M. E. (2012). Measuring Media Literacy in a National Context: Challenges of Definition, Method, and Implementation. *Media Studies*, 3(6), pp. 83–104.

Bulger, M. E. (2014). *Knowledge and processes that predict proficiency in digital literacy article published today.* Available at: http://monicabulger.com/2014/08/knowledge-and-processes-that-predict-proficiency-in-digital-literacy-article-published-today/. [Accessed 30 September 2017].

Bulger, M. E., Mayer, R. E. and Metzger, M. J. (2014). Knowledge and Processes that Predict Proficiency in Digital Literacy. *Reading and Writing*, 27(9), pp. 1567–1583.

CCC: Chaos Computer Club e.V., ed. (2016). *Zwischen Technikbegeisterung und kritischer Reflexion: Chaos macht Schule.* [video]. Available at: https://media.ccc.de/v/33c3-8262-zwischen_technikbegeisterung_und_kritischer_reflexion_chaos_macht_schule. [Accessed 30 September 2017].

CCC: Chaos Computer Club e.V., ed. (2017). *Chaos macht Schule: Forderungen für eine zeitgemäße digitale Bildung an unseren Schulen.* Available at: www.ccc.de/de/cms-forderungen-lang. [Accessed 30 September 2017].

CCC: Chaos Computer Club e.V., ed. (n.d.). *Chaos Computer Club: Chaos Computer Club's Official Website: Self-Description.* Available at: http://ccc.de/de/club. [Accessed 12 October 2017].

CCC München: Chaos Computer Club München, ed. (n.d. a). *Chaos macht Schule.* Available at: http://schule.muc.ccc.de/. [Accessed 11 October 2017].

CCC München: Chaos Computer Club München, ed. (n.d. b). *Chaos macht Schule.* Available at: https://cdn.rawgit.com/muccc/cms/5a9dca95/20170515_cms_eltern_planegg.html. [Accessed 11 October 2017].

CCC München: Chaos Computer Club München, ed. (n.d. c). *CmS auf dem Regionaljugendkonvent München Nord.* Available at: http://schule.muc.ccc.de/chaosmachtschule:ejm. [Accessed 11 October 2017].

Chaos macht Schule Hamburg (n.d. a). *Was ist 'Chaos macht Schule'?* Available at: https://cms.hamburg.ccc.de/. [Accessed 30 September 2017].

Chaos macht Schule Hamburg (n.d. b). *Auf den Spuren unserer Daten mit Chaos macht Schule.* Available at: http://tincon.org/session_ber/spurensuche-im-netz-mit-chaos-macht-schule/. [Accessed 30 September 2017].

Coleman, E. G. (2012). *Am I Anonymous?* Available at: https://limn.it/am-i-anonymous/. [Accessed 30 September 2017].

Coleman, E. G. (2015). *Hacker, hoaxer, whistleblower, spy: The many faces of Anonymous.* London, Brooklyn, NJ: Verso.

Crawford, K., Gray, M. and Miltner, K. (2014). Critiquing Big Data: Politics, Ethics, Epistemology. Special Section Introduction. *International Journal of Communication*, 8, pp. 1663–1672.

Deyerler, F. and Rausch, L. (2017). *Digitale Bildung.* [video]. Available at: www.faz. net/aktuell/wirtschaft/digitale-bildung-google-eroeffnet-zukunftswerkstatt-in-muenchen-15110213.html. [Accessed 30 September 2017].

Dumancela, G. (2015). Monica Bulger: Questions About Digital Literacy. [pdf] Available at: https://cyber.harvard.edu/sites/cyber.harvard.edu/files/bulger_research_overview_0. pdf. [Accessed 11 October 2017].

Esken, S., ed. (2015). *Digitale Bildung und Medienkompetenz muss gestärkt werden.* Available at: www.saskiaesken.de/aktuelle-artikel/digitale-bildung-und-medienkompetenz-muss-gestaerkt-werden. [Accessed 30 September 2017].

Esken, S., ed. (2016a). *Digitale Souveränität statt Angst vor der Digitalisierung! SPD-Abgeordnete Saskia Esken macht Vorschläge zur digitalen Wende im Bildungssystem.* Available at: www.saskiaesken.de/aktuelle-artikel/digitale-souveraenitaet-statt-angst-vor-der-digitalisierung. [Accessed 30 September 2017].

Esken, S. (2016b). Konzeptpapier, 16.11.2016: Offensive Digitale Souveränität für alle. [pdf] Available at: www.saskiaesken.de/aktuelle-artikel/digitale-souveraenitaet-statt-angst-vor-der-digitalisierung?file=files/aktuelles/16_November/161116%20Offensive %20Digitale%20Souver%C3%A4nit%C3%A4t.pdf. [Accessed 30 September 2017].

Fischschnaller, L. (2013). *Mediennutzungsverhalten und Medienkompetenz der Digital Natives.* Magisterarbeit. Universität Wien. Fakultät für Sozialwissenschaften. Available at: http://othes.univie.ac.at/28001/1/2013-03-17_0609600.pdf. [Accessed 29 September 2017].

Fleischhack, J. (2017). *Seeing evil differently.* Available at: https://culanth.org/ fieldsights/1113-seeing-evil-differently. [Accessed 30 September 2017].

Gray, M. and Couldry, N. (2012). Digital In/Justice. [blog] Available at: http://culture digitally.org/2012/09/digital-injustice/. [Accessed 29 September 2017].

Ito, M. and Baumer, S. (2008). *Living and learning with new media: Summary of findings from the digital youth project.* Available at: http://digitalyouth.ischool.berkeley.edu/ files/report/digitalyouth-WhitePaper.pdf. [Accessed 30 September 2017].

Ito, M., Horst, H., Bittanti, M., boyd, d., Herr-Stephenson, B., Lange, P.G., Pascoe, C.J. and Robinson, L. (with Baumer, S., Cody, R., Mahendran, D., Martínez, K., Perkel, D., Sims, C. and Tripp, L. (2008). Living and Learning with New Media: Summary of Findings from the Digital Youth Project. Available at: http://digitalyouth.ischool. berkeley.edu/files/report/digitalyouth-WhitePaper.pdf. [Accessed 30 September 2017].

Jenkins, H. (2014a). Kids on YouTube: An Interview with Patricia Lange (Part One). [blog] Available at: http://henryjenkins.org/blog/2014/03/kids-on-youtube-an-interview-with-patricia-lange-part-one.html. [Accessed 30 September 2017].

Jenkins, H. (2014b). Kids on YouTube: An Interview with Patricia Lange (Part Two). [blog] Available at: http://henryjenkins.org/blog/2014/03/kids-on-youtube-an-interview-with-patricia-lange-part-two.html. [Accessed 30 September 2017].

Körber-Stiftung, ed. (2017). *Digitale Bildung in Deutschland braucht ein Update.* Available at: www.koerber-stiftung.de/themen/digitale-muendigkeit/news-detailseite/ digitale-bildung-in-deutschland-braucht-ein-update-1082.html. [Accessed 30 September 2017].

Körber-Stiftung, ed. (n.d. a). *Im Fokus Digitale Mündigkeit.* Available at: www.koerber-stiftung.de/themen/digitale-muendigkeit.html. [Accessed 30 September 2017].

Körber-Stiftung, ed. (n.d. b). *Thesenpapier.* www.koerber-stiftung.de/fileadmin/user_ upload/koerber-stiftung/redaktion/fokusthema_digitale-muendigkeit/pdf/2017/

Hintergrund-Fokusthema-digitale-Muendigkeit_Thesenpapier.pdf. [Accessed 30 September 2017].

Kultusministerkonferenz (2012). Medienbildung in der Schule: Beschluss der Kultusministerkonferenz vom 8. März 2012. [pdf] Available at: www.kmk.org/fileadmin/Dateien/ veroeffentlichungen_beschluesse/2012/2012_03_08_Medienbildung.pdf. [Accessed 30 September 2017].

Kurz, C. and Rieger, F. (2009). Stellungnahme des Chaos Computer Clubs zur Vorratsdatenspeicherung. [pdf] Available at: https://www.ccc.de/de/vds/VDSfinal18.pdf. [Accessed 30 September 2017].

Landesanstalt für Medien Nordrhein-Westfalen (LfM), ed. (2017). *Auszeichnung für gelungene Medienkompetenzvermittlung: 105 Schulen aus dem ganzen Land erhalten Abzeichen des Projekts Medienscouts NRW.* Available at: www.lfm-nrw.de/service/ pressemitteilungen/pressemitteilungen-2017/2017/september/auszeichnung-fuer-gelungene-medienkompetenzvermittlung-105-schulen-aus-dem-ganzen-land-erhalten-abzeichen-des-projekts-medienscouts-nrw.html. [Accessed 30 September 2017].

Landeszentrale für Medien und Kommunikation (LMK) Rheinland-Pfalz, ed. (2016). *Experteninterview zum CCC – Projekt 'Chaos macht Schule'.* Available at: www. klicksafe.de/service/aktuelles/news/detail/experteninterview-zum-ccc-projekt-chaos-macht-schule/. [Accessed 30 September 2017].

Lange, P. G. (2007). The Vulnerable Video Blogger: Promoting Social Change through Intimacy: Promoting Social Change through Intimacy, 5(2). Available at: http:// sfonline.barnard.edu/blogs/lange_01.htm. [Accessed 29 September 2017].

Lange, P. G. (2014). *Kids on YouTube: Technical identities and digital literacies.* Walnut Creek, CA: Left Coast Press.

Merry, S. E. (2006). *Human rights and gender violence: Translating international law into local justice.* Chicago, IL: University of Chicago Press.

Nafus, D. and Sherman, J. (2014). This One Does Not Go Up To 11: The Quantified Self Movement as an Alternative Big Data Practice. *International Journal of Communication,* 8, pp. 1784–1794.

Schelhowe, H., Grafe, S., Herzig, B., Koubeck, J., Niesyto, H., Vom Berg, A., Coy, W., Hagel, H., Hasebrook, J., Kiesel, K., Reinmann, G. and Schäfer, M. (2009). Kompetenzen in einer digital geprägten Kultur: Medienbildung für die Persönlichkeitsentwicklung, für die gesellschaftliche Teilhabe und für die Entwicklung von Ausbildungs- und Erwerbsfähigkeit. [pdf] Available at: www.dlr.de/pt/Portaldata/45/Resources/a_ dokumente/bildungsforschung/Expertenkommission_Maerz_2009.pdf. [Accessed 11 October 2017].

Schwan, B. (2016). *Kostenloser Programmierunterricht in allen Apple-Läden.* Available at: www.heise.de/mac-and-i/meldung/Kostenloser-Programmierunterricht-in-allen-Apple-Laeden-3491213.html. [Accessed 30 September 2017].

Zook, M., Barocas, S., boyd, d., Crawford, K., Keller, E., Peña Gangadharan, S., Goldman, A., Hollander, R., Koenig, B. A., Metcalf, J., Narayanan, A., Nelson, A. and Pasquale, F. (2017). *Ten simple rules for responsible big data research.* Available at: https://datasociety.net/output/ten-simple-rules-for-responsible-big-data-research/. [Accessed 30 September 2017].

Zorn, I. (2011). Medienkompetenz und Medienbildung mit Fokus auf Digitale Medien, In: H. Moser, P. Grell and H. Niesyto, eds. *Medienbildung und Medienkompetenz: Beiträge zu Schlüsselbegriffen der Medienpädagogik.* München, Kopaed Verlag, pp. 175–209. Available at: www.socialnet.de/rezensionen/isbn.php?isbn=978-3-86736-205-4. [Accessed 30 September 2017].

13 Self-protection beyond the self

Collective privacy practices in (Big) datascapes

Carsten Ochs

Introduction[1]

In a 2014 interview, MIT's computational social science expert Alexander Pentland was quite positive about Big Data techniques' potential to improve society by providing 'a complete picture of social interactions' (Der Spiegel 2014). He thus echoed a hope attached to the analysis of huge data sets, a hope which had already been expressed more than 120 years before by Durkheim's now famous opponent Gabriel Tarde. For, in 1890, when writing *The Laws of Imitation*, Tarde profoundly grappled with the phenomenon of statistics. It is quite remarkable that he stated at the time:

> If statistics continues to progress as it has done for several years, if the information which it gives us continues to gain in accuracy, in dispatch, in bulk, and in regularity, a time may come when upon the accomplishment of every social event a figure will at once issue forth automatically, so to speak, to take its place on the statistical registers that will be continuously communicated to the public and spread abroad pictorially by the daily press. Then, at every step, at every glance cast upon poster or newspaper, we shall be assailed, as it were, with statistical facts, with precise and condensed knowledge of all the peculiarities of actual social conditions (...) Let us hope that the day will come when the representative or legislator who is called upon to reform the justiciary or the penal code and yet who is, hypothetically, ignorant of juridical statistics, will be as rare and inconceivable a being as a blind omnibus driver or a deaf orchestral leader would be to-day.
>
> (Tarde 1903: 133, 134)

Not only in Tarde, but in general there is a widespread belief that *more* data allows us to generate *more* information, *more* knowledge – thereby allowing us to have a *more* functional society. So it seems that bigger is better, after all, when it comes to data: Big Data sets are better than little ones. And as this is apparently the received opinion it is not surprising, then, that plenty of 'folks are buzzing around wondering what they can do with all of the data they've got their hands on' – that there is even an actual 'obsession with Big Data' (boyd 2010[2]).

However, what is Big Data in the first place? There is, of course, the well-known computer science listing of the aspects characterising Big Data, a listing that amounts to the description of Wittgensteinian 'family resemblances' (Wittgenstein 1958: §66–67) in absence of a commonly agreed-upon definition:[3] the infamous '4 Vs' – that is, volume, velocity, variety of data, and perhaps also their veracity (Simo 2015: 14; Grimm 2015: 127, 128; see also Chapter 1 of this volume). With the help of 'low-cost infrastructures and powerful data-mining techniques and statistical correlation algorithms' (Simo 2015: 15) such data may be recombined, related to each other, and thoroughly analysed. All of this is the well-known computer science view, and STS scholars are, of course, well advised to become acquainted with this view. Still, besides the character of the data sets ('the 4 Vs') and techniques ('storage, data-mining, algorithms') there is a third aspect to Big Data worth mentioning, and one that is at times accounted for by computer science scholars, too: the multiplicity of sociotechnical contexts from where the desirable data stem (ibid.: 15). For some researchers, it is in fact this very correlation of data stemming from so many diverse contexts that defines the real difference that Big Data makes:

> There is little doubt that the quantities of data now available are indeed large, but that's not the most relevant characteristic of this new data eco-system. Big Data is notable not because of its size, but because of its relationality to other data. Due to efforts to mine and aggregate data, Big Data is fundamentally networked. Its value comes from the patterns that can be derived by making connections between pieces of data, about an individual, about individuals in relation to others, about groups of people, or simply about the structure of information itself.
>
> (boyd and Crawford 2011: 1, 2)

Hence, what quite obviously provides the basis for the occurrence of Big Data techniques in the first place is the emergence of sociotechnical environments that are packed with digital networked technologies: datascapes constituted by human (massively data emitting subjects) and non-human (massively data recording sensor technologies) agents producing the data which then might be correlated.

In this contribution, I proceed from the well-established premise that, at least in the wealthy and extensively digitised regions of the world, most people now almost ubiquitously live a life within such Big Data-based digital datascapes, a tendency that is likely to gain momentum as a manifold of more or less novel sociotechnical systems are introduced – such as the Internet of Things, Cyber-physical Systems, Wearable Technologies, Smart Cars, Smart Homes, or Smart Factories. Focusing on datascapes, the utopian promises of Big Data lead quickly into dystopian visions of total surveillance, as from the latter perspective, Big Datascapes present a whole range of potential problems – from privacy issues via social sorting, to questions of algorithmic accountability (Simo 2015: 24–37). As far as these problems are concerned, it is a commonly held assumption that informational self-protection (*Selbstdatenschutz* in German), especially through encryption, is an appropriate antidote to at least mitigate some of the issues that go along with life in (Big) datascapes, especially privacy-related issues (Grimm 2015: 129). In this sense, informational self-protection (from now on ISP) is considered a means to prevent the emergence of a Big Data-driven Big Brother; distinguished advocates of this approach, such as PGP[4] developer Phil Zimmermann, therefore even regard the usage of encryption tools as a 'civic duty' (Gruber 2013).

Having said this, ISP discourses are contested. On the one hand there is a discourse on ISP that makes certain claims as to how the latter helps to protect privacy, what privacy is, and what functions privacy is supposed to fulfil. On the other hand, ISP discourses also refer to a set of specific sociotechnical practices that are to be realised in order to practically achieve a certain form of privacy in a specific way. The question to be addressed here therefore concerns: *how does ISP discourse relate to ISP practices?* The posing of this question is motivated by the fact that although there have been great emancipatory hopes attached to ISP in discourse over at least the past 20 years, the relevant techniques quite obviously do not spread as advocates wish them to.

To illustrate this, we may turn to some of the reactions that occurred in response to Edward Snowden's revelations concerning the data-gathering activities of a range of Western intelligence services, such as the NSA. Snowden himself stated that '[Operational Security Practices] is important even if you're not worried about the NSA. (…) It's to reclaim a level of privacy' (quoted in Lee 2015). In line with this view, at the time Snowden's leaks were published, so-called 'crypto parties' were staged in diverse countries and places. Amsterdam based crypto party organiser, Jurre van Berg, expressed his hopes as follows: 'At first, some people visit crypto parties, then they will be helping other newcomers, to the point where eventually the relevant know-how spreads all by itself' (quoted in Reißmann 2012[5]). Irrespective of whether or not one may embrace wholeheartedly the realisation of the development presaged in the quote, there is little evidence that 'the massive spread of know-how' is somehow inevitable. Focusing on the US, Snowden's country of origin, evidence suggests that: 'Despite continuing media coverage, the public's privacy behaviors have hardly changed' (Preibusch 2015). While a representative survey in 2014 found that 'most adults express a desire to take additional steps to protect their data online' (Pew Research Center 2014: 5), the follow-up study of 2015 headlines 'Americans' Privacy Strategies Post-Snowden: Some are changing their behaviors with technology, but few are making big changes using sophisticated tools' (Shelton *et al.* 2015).

Similar studies in other countries (see below) tend to confirm that the number of people who turned to ISP techniques when learning about the global surveillance disclosures is remarkably low, especially given that ISP raises such high hopes. The thesis that I attempt to establish in this chapter is that the non-appearance of an increase as regards the adoption of ISP techniques is due at least in part to a fundamental divergence between the in-built *individualism of*

ISP discourses compared to the constitutional *collectivism of ISP practices*. As a result, responsibility for the emergence of ISP practices is depoliticised and shifted to the individual – who is, in turn, necessarily overburdened with the task of developing appropriate practices. I will argue that this has everything to do with the essentially individualistic notion of privacy that is so widespread in contemporary discourses on digitisation and surveillance (Bennett 2011). What follows, then, from the argument in terms of conceptualising privacy is the necessity to develop notions that, instead of being based on the individual, set out from collectivity.[6]

To make my case I will therefore proceed as follows: In the first section I will provide a cursory analysis of the German discourse on *ISP* (*Selbstdatenschutz*), followed in the second section by a discussion of a practice theory-based analysis of the components constituting ISP. In performing such analysis, the divergences between individualistic discourses and collective practices of privacies and protections become visible. I will argue that the problematic is inherited from the exaggerated individualism built into the discourse on ISP in particular and on privacy in general. Finally, I will sum up, draw political conclusions and plead for a re-politicisation of privacies as practices.

The individualised (German) discourse on informational self-protection

The global surveillance disclosures unleashed by Snowden invoked a global public (Privacy International/Amnesty International 2015: 3). Since an analysis of such a wide-ranging discourse exceeds my research capacities I will focus largely on the German fraction. The latter lends itself well to investigation since, due to Germany's Nazi past and Eastern Germany's subsequent totalitarian history, privacy and surveillance sensitivities are distinctive:

> The experience of these oppressive states and the societal decomposition caused by intensive spying activities of the Nazi secret police and the GDR 'Staatssicherheitsdienst' (…) has left a deep mistrust in German citizens towards governmental surveillance for security purposes. This mistrust has diminished after the 9/11 terrorist attack and follow-up events. But it noticeably returned to the attention of the public and seeped into controversial media discourse after the revelations of whistle-blower Edward Snowden about the spying activities of the U.S. National Security Agency (NSA).
>
> (SurPRISE 2014: ii)

However, given these sensitivities, still the few available studies on ISP suggest that, in spite of German secret services' involvement in the global surveillance disclosures, widespread adoption of actual ISP techniques did not occur. For example, a representative survey ordered by Germany's digital industry association BITKOM e.V. in 2011 revealed that only 14% of the respondents made use of encryption tools, while 10% indicated they relied on anonymisation techniques (BITKOM 2011: 36). After the Snowden revelations in 2013, another survey was conducted, saying that only 9% made use of mail encryption, and only 13% of anonymisation techniques (BITKOM 2013a). In 2014, German market research institute *Gesellschaft für Konsumforschung* drew a representative sample by posing the following 'query of the month': 'Have you changed your ways of handling personal data since the NSA affair's disclosure?'[7] 76.9% of the respondents answered 'no', and only 12.2% 'yes'. What is even more revealing is that it was only 3.8% of respondents who chose the response option 'yes, I now make use of other programs and devices' (Heuzeroth 2014). Of course, surveys such as these should be taken with a pinch of salt; still, they suggest that even when a rather surveillance-sensitive social formation learns about massive privacy intrusions, ISP techniques do not start to flourish. Thus we may find out about the drivers preventing users from widespread ISP adoption by focusing in our analysis on this very environment. I will restrict the analysis, therefore, in large part to discourses occurring in Germany.

In the German context, ISP (*Selbstdatenschutz*) is usually conceived as the entirety of all the technical, organisational, and legal measures taken by individuals in order to protect and realise their basic data protection rights (Sächsischer Datenschutzbeauftragter 2014). Such measures can be further distinguished into *passive* and *active* ones: while the former refer to the avoidance of emitting personal data (data minimisation, pseudonymisation), the latter concern usage of privacy-friendly applications or *Privacy Enhancing Technologies* (PETs, used for encryption, anonymisation etc.) as well as organisational (e.g. running particular applications offline) and legal measures (a posteriori, in the event of damage occurring to the data subject). Active ISP was particularly hailed in answer to the global surveillance disclosures (Bernold 2012; Reißmann 2012; Beuth 2013; Peikert 2013) as a bundle of techniques and practices allowing the safeguarding of informational privacy (Rössler 2001: 25).

I will now provide a cursory analysis of the German discourse on these techniques, that is, on active ISP. I focus on the latter because passive ISP implies a tendency to *refrain* from digital networking, whereas I am mainly interested in digital, networked privacy practices. The corpus being analysed here consists of empirical data that were collected between 1 January and 15 April 2014. The material was gained from public sources (websites, booklets, official documents etc.), systematically assembled, coded and analysed according to Grounded Theory procedures (Strauss and Corbin 1996). I do not claim to provide a global or exhaustive analysis of the discourse that interests me here; research and analysis were only pushed up to a point where it became possible to clarify whether or not there was a certain congruity between the discourse and the practice of ISP. Divergences between discourses and practices are so prevalent in the field of privacy studies that they have even acquired a label: the 'privacy paradox'. The latter designates the frequent empirical finding that research subjects might rhetorically praise privacy, say, in interviews, while acting in a way that seems to disregard privacy considerations (see, for example, Dienlin and Trepte 2015). Giddens (1984: 4) refers to such discrepancies as the divergence of discursive and practical consciousness: 'the commonplace observation that the reasons actors offer discursively for what they do may diverge from the rationalisation of action as actually involved in the stream of conduct of those actors.' In sum, then, my practice theory-informed analysis focuses on the discourse–practice relationship, and when I call the analysis 'cursory' I mean that it is restricted to providing evidence as regards a discourse–practice relationship with a view to possible 'differences between what can be said and what is characteristically simply done' (ibid.: 7).

When scanning the Internet for discursive statements on ISP it became obvious quickly that there are four main groups actively participating in the public discourse:

- self-organised initiatives and activists (e.g. Chaos Computer Club, Digital Courage e.V., Jacob Applebaum etc.);
- institutional data protection authorities of the federal and state governments;
- political parties constituting the parliament;[8]
- industrial associations.

Obviously all these groups differ significantly in terms of worldviews, interests and normative frames. Very roughly we may delineate these differences as shown in Table 13.1.

In spite of these differences, what is striking is that the great majority of discursive statements – regardless of the group from which a given statement emanates – in fact tend to address the individual as the relevant entity for developing ISP practices. In what follows I will compare the respective groups' discourses in terms of their various characterisations of individualisms.

Table 13.1 A very rough characterisation of the main groups participating in the discourse on ISP

Group	Worldview	Interest	Normative framework	Users' portrayal
Self-Organised Activists & Initiatives	Techy leftist background	Fostering civil society	Hacker ethics and civic rights	Users as actors within civil society
Institutional Data Protection Authorities	Ambivalent role: state-run, protecting from the state	Rule of law	Constitutional law (right to informational self-determination)	Users as citizens
Political Parties	... diverse ...	Winning the election	The state	Users as voters
Industrial Associations	Market economy	Realising profit	The market	Users as consumers

Self-organised activists and initiatives

As far as self-organised activists and initiatives[9] are concerned, their central point of reference is oftentimes the debate about and struggle around the German census conducted in the early 1980s (the so-called '*Volkszählung*') to which large parts of the population offered resistance (see Berlinghoff 2013; Frohman 2013), leading to a complaint of unconstitutionality that resulted in the Federal Constitutional Court's issuing of *the right to informational self-determination* (BVerfG 1983). Many activists and initiatives have a left-wing oppositional background, and they explicitly refer to ISP as part of democratic practices (ccc. de/de/club n.d.), thereby somewhat harnessing the Court's legislation as a kind of legalistic resource providing legitimation (Digital Courage n.d.). At the same time, activists tend to submit to the 'rules' of *hacker ethics*, and there is an explicit imperative in this normative framework to '[d]istrust authorities – foster decentralisation' (ccc.de/de/hackerethik n.d.).[10] The political drive of activists and initiatives to that effect is based on the idea of technical elucidation (*Aufklärung*), and part of this is to unveil the actual interests and practices of governmental and economic surveillance agencies. The frequent reference to civil rights (Aktion-Freiheit-statt-Angst n.d.) indicates the ambivalent and reserved stance this group takes vis-à-vis the state, but also illustrates this group's idea of users as social actors with a political role: users are 'configured' (Woolgar 1991) as civil society's citizens who are, or shall be, elucidated – with the process of elucidation requiring actors' own initiative (Deutsche Vereinigung für Datenschutz n.d.). Privacy is consequently conceptualised as having control over devices to be exercised by active citizens (Lechtenbörger 2017). Whereas such control is considered a basic right, backed-up by legal guarantees, some doubt is expressed as to whether legislation still plays the role of a robust resource one may rely on (selbstdatenschutz.info n.d.):

> Those who want to or must play safe shouldn't rely on governments ignoring basic rights, on authorities, secret services, on companies ignoring data protection law, but instead take care for themselves of their digital self-defence and technical data protection respectively.
>
> (Ibid.[11])

Self-organised activists' and initiatives' discourses thus contain a *civic individualism*, that is, one that is born out of a scepticism towards societal institutions and the power asymmetries they create in relation to users/citizens. Against this background, activists and initiatives advocate the individual use of diverse techniques and technologies supporting the emergence of ISP practices. Informational privacy here counts as an intrinsic value, and activists and initiatives have the skills required to safeguard such privacy with the help of technical means. However, as these organisations do not have at their disposal the institutional (power) and financial resources (money) to establish the conditions that are required for the flourishing and widespread diffusion of ISP practices, the only option left is to address the individual.

Institutional data protection authorities

Institutional data protection authorities (of federal or state governments, and also foundations funded by government) draw on the right to informational self-determination in the sense of a fixed, legalistic, normative framework.[12] Legislation is considered the decisive element in creating a situation in which individuals may determine for themselves the knowledge a given entity has about them at any given time, and at any given occasion (BVerfG 1983: 43[13]). Yet, due to *structural* contradictions, institutionalised data protection, at least potentially, plays a contradictory role, especially vis-à-vis the state. On the one hand, public agencies (e.g. Federal Office for Information Security), data protection authorities (e.g. Federal Commissioner for Data Protection and Freedom of Information), and foundations (e.g. Federal Foundation for Data Protection) act *as* governmental bodies. On the other hand, however, it is these organisations' task to protect citizens *from* governmental surveillance. Thus, the task of state-aided protection of citizens against 'external threats' goes hand in hand with the task of protecting citizens against the government itself – a double requirement that may play out in a paradoxical fashion.[14] Insofar as institutionalised data protection is bound to legal-normative specifications provided by the state, it has to submit to existing law; and, as regards the latter, there are two things to be noticed. First, the reference to law is usually accompanied by calling upon the individual to 'self-activate' (Berliner Beauftragte für den Datenschutz).[15] Second, numerous statements in these authorities' discourses, in fact, account for the considerable limits of juridical means for the practice of data protection (Voßhof 2014). Consequently, data protectionists' ISP discourse frequently includes the explicit suggestion to also apply technical means (Scholz 2014), as well as the requirement to strengthen awareness and new media literacy.

As both federal and governmental data protection authorities have a close structural relationship to Ministries of the Interior, we may assume that it is rather problematic for them to put forward radical claims for the widespread development of ISP practices. As, for example, techniques of encryption for privacy/protection purposes might also be harnessed for criminal or seditious activities, this obviously conflicts with governmental authority.[16] What is more, data protection authorities are not in charge of providing citizens with the skills required to build ISP practices. As their influence in this regard is pretty limited, they explicitly call upon government to provide for the structural conditions that are required (Konferenz der Datenschutzbeauftragten des Bundes und der Länder 2010, 2013; Hamburgischer Datenschutzbeauftragter 2011). In this sense, institutional data protectionists, while acting as spokespersons for data protection and to some extent considering the collective effort that must be made to achieve effective data protection, may propagate the development of ISP practices only to a certain degree, and they definitely lack the structural resources to foster the development of such practices. As a result, the individualism of the legalistic reasoning[17] may at times lead data protectionists to determine *collective* data protection responsibilities being based on *individual* rights.[18] Still, the legalistic base of the data protectionists' reasoning results in addressing the individual in the first place, as is exemplified in the following quote from the Berlin Data Protection Authority: 'Data protection realises your basic right to informational self-determination. However, you may only benefit from the manifold of laws that were issued for the sake of data protection if you (...) exercise your rights yourself' (Berliner Beauftragte für den Datenschutz). Quite in this spirit we may call the data protectionists' approach a *legalistic individualism*.

Political parties and government

Parties of the parliament[19] obviously have at their disposal the structural resources and institutional power that is needed to foster the development of ISP practices; however, at the same time they also face, again, *structural contradictions*, which is likely to contravene their support for such practices. We may distinguish two such contradictions: first, there is the task of politics to reconcile the diverging interests of so many different social groups and actors. Informational privacy is traded against other relevant goods, especially against economic ones. Thus, political parties – while broadly recognising a 'right to privacy', propagating measures to maintain such a right, and rhetorically calling for a strengthening of media literacy – differ from each other in terms of the normative weight they give to informational privacy in relation to (primarily) economic interests. The conservative party CDU, for instance, implies a tension between those two goods in their manifesto for the 2013 parliamentary elections (CDU/CSU 2013a: 35); stress is laid explicitly on self-regulation of the economy, on individual responsibility, and also on ISP (*Selbstdatenschutz*; see CDU/CSU 2013b: 5–6). When following the political spectrum towards the left-wing, from SPD (similar to Britain's Labour Party), Bündnis 90/Die Grünen (The Green Party) to Die Linke (The Leftists), there is a steady decrease in the emphasis of individual responsibility. For all of that however, political parties – once they are elected and in government – may be expected to rank economic goals higher in relation to privacy protection (I will return to this issue below).

The second structural contradiction arises from tensions between the state and society. As far as government is concerned, this tension especially arises as conflicts between ministries representing different interests. For example, while the Ministry of the Interior is responsible for ensuring security, the Ministry of Justice and Consumer Protection is the central entity to protect Internet users' informational privacy (see Maas 2014). These contradictions between the respective Ministries' responsibilities notwithstanding, it is clear that modern states are now, to a certain extent, dependent on sophisticated surveillance techniques so as to be able to administer and manage large populations (Giddens 1984). States' security interests are aligned with this task, and political discourses would have it that widespread ISP practices would largely contravene such security interests.

So, insofar as ISP, if applied widely, tends to be in stark contrast to surveillance purposes of economies and governments, there is a tendency for political parties, once they are in power, not to foster the development of such practices to the same extent as they support them rhetorically when they form part of the parliamentary opposition. Conducting a discourse analysis of parliamentary documents (speech protocols, proposals, draft laws, reports of committees, and commissions), Baumann (2013: 47) comes to the conclusion that, 'The more power an actor [here: a parliamentary member of a political party; CO] possesses, i.e. the more he is involved in administering the state, the less he might be inclined to indulge in data protection' (my translation[20]). However, if, empirically speaking, even those parties and politicians, once they are in government, do not or even cannot support data protection to the same extent as they actually wish, then there must be a structural explanation for this discrepancy. And, in fact, it is the trade-off amongst diverse interests and goals as well as governments' interest in surveillance that provides such an explanation.

Where political parties and their members nevertheless cling to data protection, they highlight the strengthening of media literacy so as to enable informational self-determination – this goes for all parliamentary parties (Baumann 2015: 86). Thus, whether intentionally or not, they tend to practically delegate responsibility for protecting privacy to the individual (ibid.: 86–87). This clears the way for some parties to even energetically propagate this approach. Accordingly, a CDU/CSU response to a query which was posed by the German Federation of the Digital Economy (*Bundesverband Digitale Wirtschaft* e.V.) in the run-up to the 2014 parliamentary elections went:

> The state cannot take responsibility off the citizens when they are busy with surfing, emailing, chatting or posting. (…) Basic pillars of [the conservative party's] data protection policy therefore are: 1. Individual responsibility and informational self-protection (*Selbstdatenschutz*) of the citizens. 2. Self-regulation and proactive measures of the economy.[21]
>
> (CDU/CSU 2013b: 5, 6–7)

As the stance taken here results in the deliberate shifting of responsibilities to the individual in the image of Foucauldian governmentality, we may speak in this case of a *governmental individualism* (I will return to this later).

Industrial associations

Industrial associations representing the digital economy, such as BITKOM e.V. or the aforementioned Federation of the Digital Economy, tend to consider social actors as consumers and clients within data-driven markets (BVDW 2013). The discourse of these associations centres on self-determination, the latter designating in this context most notably consumption decisions as regards the purchasing of goods and services. As far as market economy practices are concerned, associations have a rather strong interest in creating an atmosphere of trust, since the latter is considered a precondition for the functioning of market mechanisms. The absence of trust, representatives hold, has deleterious effects on the utilisation of digital technologies, and therefore on economy and society (BITKOM

2013b: 1). Associations consequently regard data protection as an appropriate instrument to (re-)create confidence in data-driven markets. Yet data protection also seems to play a double-edged role for the representatives of business, as a great many business models of the digital economy are based on the reception, processing, and exploitation of personal data. Considering themselves to be involved in global competition, companies have a strong incentive to exploit such data.

Thus, here again we encounter a structural contradiction, insofar as data protection seems to be a precondition for establishing trust, but at the same time is a potential threat to business models. Consequently, businesses call for a 'balanced relationship between security on the one hand, and freedom of individuals and involved businesses on the other hand'.[22] Furthermore, industrial associations call for an extension of their right to process personal data, and for the restriction of the concept of personal, or 'person-related' data.[23] In this sense, these associations sometimes demand the weakening of one of the central pillars of informational self-determination. Against this background, and given that industry is mainly responsible for the design and shaping of sociotechnical infrastructures – including the 'privacy friendliness' of those infrastructures – the call for 'capabilities for self-protection' of the users (BITKOM 2013b: 6) seems somewhat paradoxical. Due to the business models in place, for structural reasons industry can have only limited interest in the widespread diffusion and application of ISP practices. However, as such practices are currently not established to a significant degree and as their diffusion under current sociotechnical conditions seems rather unlikely, it seems to be a matter of rhetoric in the first place to call upon individual users to develop such practices. Having said this, BITKOM states:

> Consumers could improve individual data protection too. BITKOM explicitly welcomes awareness-raising, the improvement of media literacy, and public and private initiatives to increase security (...) for this reason, we support training activities and the like, so as to enable business staff as well as citizens to correctly handle sensitive data.[24]
>
> (Ibid.: 6)

All in all, then, we may call the industrial associations' take on ISP *consumer individualism*.

The analysis thus reveals four types of individualism: a civic, legalistic, governmental, and consumer type. The way the sequence of individualisms was arranged, moreover, illustrates the ease of shifting the discourse from the idea of individual empowerment to governmentality-like requests directed at the individual (Foucault 2000: 66), threatening to result in a factual coercion to individually act and make decisions (Lemke *et al.* 2000: 30). Yet, regardless of whether or not the whole of the discourse of informational self-protection is to be considered as articulating the techniques of governmentality (*quod esset demonstrandum*), all the individualisms identified above end up in a request that the individual 'self-activate', so to speak. As all the discourses, one way or another, tend to address the individual, this facilitates governmentality-type ideas to prevail.

In the next section I will attempt to explain why it is so easy to address the individual when it comes to ISP – and why delegating the task to the individual seems mistaken.

Informational self-protection as collective practice

The discourse on ISP, as carried by the mass media and social movements – such as the 'crypto party movement' – frequently refers back to the so-called 'Cypherpunks' of the 1990s, who are oftentimes deemed to be the 'inventors' of ISP (e.g. see Bernold 2012; Beuth 2013; Peikert 2013; Reißmann 2012). Regardless of whether or not it is at all possible to determine in such a way a definite point of origin of ISP,[25] the Cypherpunks may legitimately be considered rather early and prominent proponents of ISP. As a start, we may take a closer look at the Cypherpunks so as to learn about the 'historic ancestry' of contemporary ISP discourses and practices.

Generally speaking, the Cypherpunk movement features strong leanings towards libertarian ideas,[26] and insofar as the libertarian worldview basically rests on the concept of 'self-ownership', Cypherpunks demonstrate a significant appreciation of individualism and proprietorship. The Cypherpunks' high profile is not least due to the well-known *A Cypherpunk's Manifesto*,[27] authored and published by American mathematician Eric Hughes (1993) at the time when Internet usage was in its early, but dynamic, stages.[28] It seems worthwhile to set out with an analysis of the *Manifesto* since some of the Cypherpunks' basic premises are articulated there. Doing so, we may realise that the *Manifesto* contains a three-step argument, holding that:

- open society presupposes privacy;
- privacy presupposes anonymous transaction systems;
- anonymous transaction systems presuppose the application of cryptographic techniques.

Privacy in this context is defined as 'to selectively reveal oneself to the world' (ibid.). This is precisely what anonymous transactions allow for, according to Hughes, thus they are best suited to safeguarding the 'essence' of privacy. While the individual is celebrated in the *Manifesto*, there also is a certain scepticism towards large governmental and economic organisations; in fact, people must shield themselves from their influence:

> We cannot expect governments, corporations, or other large, faceless organizations to grant us privacy out of their beneficence. It is to their advantage to speak of us, and we should expect that they will speak. To try to prevent their speech is to fight against the realities of information. (...) We must

defend our own privacy if we expect to have any. We must come together and create systems which allow anonymous transactions to take place. People have been defending their own privacy for centuries with whispers, darkness, envelopes, closed doors, secret handshakes, and couriers. The technologies of the past did not allow for strong privacy, but electronic technologies do.

(Ibid.)

So as becomes clear, while there is distrust of 'large, faceless organisations', there is trust in digital technologies. The Cypherpunks believe technical procedures to be the appropriate measures in order to render ISP possible, and thus, in turn, to support a libertarian social order: 'We the Cypherpunks', the *Manifesto* reads, 'We are defending our privacy with cryptography, with anonymous mail forwarding systems, with digital signatures, and with electronic money' (ibid.). We can find here the same type of optimism concerning the spread of cryptographic knowledge that we encountered already above in the 'crypto party' activists' reasoning:[29] 'Cryptography will ineluctably spread over the whole globe, and with it the anonymous transaction systems that it makes possible' (ibid.). To paraphrase, the quote articulates Cypherpunks' strong belief in the idea that social actors *ineluctably* adopt cryptographic tools and knowledge individually, so as to globally perform ISP practices.

In sum, the Cypherpunks' worldview tends to feature libertarian leanings, including an extreme individualism and general distrust in large organisations; we may furthermore presume that Cypherpunks dispose of considerable techno-mathematical skills. The normative and semiotic framework of this group conceives privacy as an 'intrinsic value' that pertains to the individual and is aligned with the idea of private property. Individual adoption of particular techniques and procedures are considered key to safeguarding this type of privacy.

In the Cypherpunks' discourse we come across a range of characteristics that we also find again in contemporary debates on ISP. In particular, the stubborn individualism seems discursively 'hard-wired', and thus is also preserved in current debates: it is this individualism that was built into the ISP discourse right from the outset, and that subsequently allows us to address the individual as the very entity who is responsible for the development of ISP practices. Whatever the Cypherpunks' motivation has been, one only has to omit a fraction of their reasoning so as to arrive at some unrealistic, governmental individualism that delegates all responsibility to isolated humans. For of course, while the Cypherpunks imply some collective dimension ('we must come together to create systems...'), a position that believes in the 'ineluctable' spread (i.e. 'automatic' distribution) of anything obviously falls short of some of the most convincing lessons of STS: namely the empirically grounded acknowledgement that in fact nothing at all spreads all by itself, that nothing is ineluctable, and that there is never automatic distribution of anything (Latour 1986). In other words, sociotechnical practices in general, and thus also ISP, must be understood as a collective achievement, which is why the idea of individual activation is fairly misguided.

To get things analytically straight, we may continue by conceptualising the world of the Cypherpunks as a *social world*. According to Strauss (1978), social worlds are scalable social formations with rather fluid boundaries. In this sense, they are

> groups with shared commitments to certain activities, sharing resources of many kinds to achieve their goals, and building shared ideologies about how to go about their business. Social worlds form fundamental building blocks of collective action and are the units of analysis in many interactionist studies of collective action. (…) Society as a whole, then, can be conceptualised as consisting of a mosaic of social worlds.
>
> (Clarke 1991: 131)

Social worlds are built and maintained through collective action: they rest on so-called core practices. The social world of alpine winter sport, for instance, is built via alpine winter sport practices; obviously, however, this social world is sub-divided into sub-worlds constituted by differentiated alpine sports practices, such as snowboarding, downhill skiing, cross-country skiing etc. Consequently, the actors participating in the practices of a social world usually belong to a manifold of such worlds at once. Moreover, it is not only humans who contribute to some practice but also non-human elements (Clarke 2012: 101–105), such as technologies, techniques, procedures, codes, virtual or physical places, and specific modes of organising a given social world. The social world of the Cypherpunks is most obviously made up of human actors with considerable cryptographic skills, but also of the techniques themselves, of cryptographic tools and so on; Cypherpunks' place of gathering, as well as the place where their practices are performed, is the Internet, where their core practice is constituted by encrypted communication. Non-human encryption tools, anonymisation services, digital signatures, and electronic currencies participate in constituting these practices. Insofar as privacy in this world is strongly tied to libertarian ideas of the 'self-owning' individual, the hope that, say, cryptographic techniques may spread from one individual self-owner to the next, are at least consistent.

Yet, what is discursively consistent, is not necessarily so in terms of the 'practical logic' (Bourdieu 1979: 228). In fact, the Cypherpunks' behaviour can be considered a blueprint for the Giddensian divergence of discursive and practical consciousness. As far as the Cypherpunks are concerned, their discursively established individualistic self-image clashes with the collective nature of their practices. Empirically, this clash materialises as the non-occurrence of the once expected spread of ISP practices. Hughes, for example, stated in a 2012 interview, that is, about 20 years after having authored *A Cypherpunk's Manifesto*, that, 'People do not encrypt their Emails as a matter of course. (…) Nobody is going to eventually start encrypting because it's so cool'[30] (quoted in Reißmann 2012). The reasons behind this non-diffusion become visible when we scrutinise the matter with the help of practice theory: stating that people do not encrypt emails 'as a matter of course' indicates that encryption in most social worlds does not play the role of a quasi-automatically performed routine – in other words, a practice – embedded into practical consciousness (Giddens 1984: 5–7). Not counting as 'cool' meanwhile concerns the semiotic dimension: outside the social world of the Cypherpunks, performing encryption is not attached with a similar meaning, neither is it embedded into a similar normative framework.[31] Whereas Cypherpunks are equipped with robust techno-mathematical skills, average users more often than not find encryption compli-cated and cumbersome.[32]

And it *is* complicated. The latter term stems from the same root, the Latin 'complicare', as the word 'complice'. 'Complicare' refers (amongst other things) to the activity of interweaving. Hence, saying that encryption is complicated equates to stating that it is a convoluted affair, as well as to suggest that to be performed it requires a range of other (human and non-human) fellows that are, as it were, complicit in this affair. To illustrate this, I would like to turn to some basics of encryption. For instance, end-to-end encryption, that is, the encryption of the semantic content of, say, an email being exchanged between two users, first of all requires a key. For the sake of convenience we may think of a very simple symmetrical key, the so-called Caesar Key that the Roman military made use of. The Caesar Key encrypts messages via the very simple algorithm 'shift any letter that is used three positions to the right'. Thus, the letter 'A' is to be represented as letter 'D', the letter 'B' as 'E' and so on; in order to decrypt a message encrypted with the aid of the Caesar Key one only needs the symmetri-cal key specifying the backwards operation: 'shift any letter that is used three positions to the left' (Grimm 2015: 131). We can present this in Table 13.2 as a simple scheme.

Thus, if one of the correspondents wants to let the other know secretly about the name of a person she will vote for in an election, and the name of the person is Abe, she will send a message saying DEH. The receiver, knowing the key, will shift the letters back to the original position and thus obtain the original ABE.

Obviously, the Caesar Key is so simple that it can be broken very easily, and, of course, current encryption makes use of much more complicated procedures, including asymmetrical procedures consisting of a pair of keys: the public one, that is, one that is publicly available and can be used to encrypt a message, and

Table 13.2 The encryption scheme of the Caesar key

1	2	3	4	5
A	B	C	D	E
Shift any letter three positions to the right				
4	5	6	7	8
D	E	F	G	H
Shift any letter three positions to the left				
1	2	3	4	5
A	B	C	D	E

the private one that only the receiver holds and that can be used to decrypt the message (Grimm 2015: 132–133). As the pair of keys is not symmetrical, it is not possible to deduce the private decryption key from the public encryption key. However, as Grimm explains (ibid.: 139–140), to implement the whole procedure, a range of provisions has to be made:

- *algorithms* that are mathematically sound must be developed;
- *hardware* must be functioning and able to process the algorithms;
- *software applications* must be compatible with encryption and up to date as regards IT security; this includes frequent firewall updates, software patches etc.;
- *remote maintenance staff* taking care of updates, patches etc. must be trustworthy;
- the same goes for *software engineers* who do the coding of operating systems, the software applications and so on;
- when it comes to key management, an independent entity, a so-called *Trusted Third Party* must certify the authenticity of the public key;
- and, last but not least, *users* must also be capable of handling the software, a task that is not necessarily easy, as even cryptography experts readily admit.[33]

While I do not claim this list to be exhaustive, we can already see at this point that indulging in ISP, the core practice of the Cypherpunks, requires the coordinated pre-installation of numerous human and non-human entities: actors, things, programmes, codes, norms, meanings, skills, institutions etc. It is the collectivity of all these entities that allows for the establishment of the actual practice – in this sense, the core practice constituting the social world of the Cypherpunks features a pattern that is constituted by the whole collective involved in the establishment of the practice in question. Hence, insofar as encrypting emails counts as ISP practice, the former must be considered a form of collective action: those who want to communicate with their peers in an encrypted fashion are not only required to interact, but what's more, their interaction also relies on a huge network of the most diverse elements. The same goes for similar ISP practices. Anonymous surfing of the web using *Tor*, for example, requires further elements that are part of a collectively generated, sociotechnical infrastructure (Leigh Star 1999), and that must be in place in order to perform the practice in question. We may call this in a Latourian style 'A Collective of Humans and Nonhumans' (Latour 1999: 174), a sociotechnical constellation, the stable performance of which presupposes the coordinated distribution of a whole range of agencies. The irony we encounter here, is that, while Actor Network Theory scholars introduced the notion of collectivity so as to include non-human agency in the analysis, we may refer to this notion precisely to get rid of the one-sided (non-human) technical solutionism so often found in ISP discourse in particular, and in privacy discourse more generally: the belief that the provision of individuals with *Privacy Enhancing Technologies* will readily transform contemporary sociotechnical constellations into more privacy-friendly ones is hardly sustainable.

To sum up, it is not only collective norms, sanctioning apparatuses, competencies, meaning structures, and political worldviews, but also algorithms, protocols, programmes, software applications, hardware devices, institutional orderings (and so on and so forth) that carry a given practice. In the case of the Cypherpunks – and, in fact, in case of large parts of the informational privacy discourse – these elements are simply discursively suppressed. While the discourse preaches radical individualism, at the same time it calls for collective practices that are required to achieve the propagated individualism in the first place (see also Fleischhack, Chapter 12 in this volume). An STS analysis in this sense renders visible the fact that even for those actors for whom individualism and privacy plays the role of an intrinsic value, to realise these values they must collectively generate ISP practices, thereby relying on a vast sociotechnical infrastructure – they act under sociotechnical circumstances encountered, given and transmitted from the past. Thus, if it is true that '[r]esponsibility for action must be shared among the various actants' (Latour 1999: 180), we must detach the issue of privacy from civic, legalistic, governmental, or consumer individualism and re-politicise it: What responsibilities? Whose rights and obligations? Which entities? The collective seems to be in need of reinvention – a process that includes, but still goes way beyond equipping individuals with a range of tools.

Conclusion: de-individualise/re-politicise privacies!

When former Minister of the Interior, Hans-Peter Friedrich, was interrogated in 2013 by the German Parliamentary Investigation Committee that was dealing with the so-called 'NSA scandal', he appeared before the public after having given his testimony. Facing the media, he addressed German citizens:

> Encryption techniques, antivirus software – all these issues must be brought much more into focus. People must become aware of the fact that internet communications also need to be protected. And it is the debate on these issues that we will push forward.[34]

While the Minister was interrogated so as to shed some light on, allegedly, one of the most sophisticated IT security attacks in history – an attack on Internet-based communication in general, that is, the collectively orchestrated Advanced Persistent Threat of an intelligence service equipped with, practically speaking, unlimited resources – in the face of this global 'surveillant assemblage' (Haggerty and Ericson 2000) he still referred the public to the responsibility of the individual to perform informational self-protection.[35]

The analysis provided above allows us to answer the question as to why it was so remarkably easy – why it was at all possible – for the Minister to shift the spotlight to the individual, although what was at stake was a massive attack on the part of intelligence services. It is the divergence of the discourse–practice link that enables actors to shift the burden of developing ISP practices onto the individual, despite the fact that the efforts to be made towards 'self' protection are very much collective in nature.[36] The problem identified not only characterises the phenomenon of informational self-protection, but also large parts of the privacy discourse: exaggerated individualism is the spectre that haunts this discourse.[37]

The phenomenon of ISP makes the discrepancy between traditionally modern privacy notions and actual practices perfectly visible as it indicates that whereas individualistic notions of privacy may be considered a relic of bourgeois cultural modes of subject formation (Bennett 2011; Ochs 2015), contemporary practices of digital networking require novel, post-individualistic conceptions of privacy setting out from collectivity (Dourish and Anderson 2006; boyd 2012; Rössler and Mokrosinska 2015; Ochs 2018). In this sense, the analysis outlined above is not at all a plea against encryption, but rather an attempt to highlight the technopolitical dimension of ISP: as we see above, terms such as '*Selbstdatenschutz*' allow for the discursive de-politicisation of practically political issues (Baumann 2015: 87). Technical democracy presupposes re-politicising the issue; re-politicising the issue in turn requires us to set out from a notion of privacy as collective practice rather than individual responsibility.

In this sense, then, we may conclude by pointing out somewhat polemically: *there is no such thing as informational self-protection*, just as *there is no such thing as individual privacy*; what there may be, however, is collective privacy practices in (Big) Datascapes.

Notes

1 This contribution was enabled by a grant of the German Federal Ministry of Education and Research awarded to the interdisciplinary research project Privacy Forum (see www.forum-privatheit.de/forum-privatheit-de/index.php), support code 16KIS0103. Sincere thanks are given to the editors for their very useful comments and valuable suggestions. The conclusions benefit strongly from discussing privacy issues for years with Jörn Lamla.

2 This contribution will refer to, and quote from, a great variety of sources and page numbers will be given where available.

3 In §66 of *Philosophical Investigations*, Wittgenstein considers a range of games and wonders whether it is possible, not to conceive, but to determine what they have in common by *looking at* how they work in practice:

> And the result of this examination is: we see a complicated network of similarities overlapping and criss-crossing: sometimes overall similarities, sometimes similarities of detail. (…) I can think of no better expression to characterize these similarities than 'family resemblances'.
>
> (Wittgenstein 1958, §66, §67)

4 'PGP' (stands for 'Pretty Good Privacy') is a well-known software for encrypting emails etc.

5 In this article when quoting from German sources I will provide translations in the main text, and indicate the original version in a footnote. The quotation just presented originally reads: 'Erst besuchen die Leute Cryptoparties, dann helfen sie anderen

Anfängern, bis wir an einen Punkt kommen, an dem sich das Wissen von selbst verbreitet' (quoted in Reißmann 2012).

6 In a way, my contribution thus simply demonstrates the pitfalls of what boyd (2012: 350) has called 'our cultural fetishisation with the individual as the unit of analysis'. What is more, boyd claims that basing privacy notions on individual control only 'reinforces the power of those who already have enough status and privilege to meaningfully assert control over their own networks' (ibid.). We will see in the course of the article how such power asymmetries may play out in the case of ISP, thus supporting her demand to develop privacy conceptions that are based on collective aggregates (social formations, such as groups).

7 The original German question was: 'Haben Sie Ihren Umgang mit persönlichen Daten seit dem NSA-Skandal geändert?'

8 Of course, there are also parties that are not represented in the German Parliament but still participate in the ISP discourse. For *Die Piraten*, for instance, the topic is of utmost importance; however, as my selection criteria for taking or not taking into account a given party's contribution was whether the party is represented in the Parliament, I will omit their positioning here.

9 Included in this category are also websites, such as www.informationelle-selbstbestimmung-im-internet.de; www.selbstdatenschutz.info; www.netzausglas.de; www.daten-speicherung.de and so on.

10 In German: 'Mißtraue Autoritäten – fördere Dezentralisierung'.

11 In German: 'Wer wirklich sicher gehen möchte oder muss, sollte sich nicht auf Grundrechte ignorierende Regierungen, Behörden, Geheimdienste und Datenschutzgesetze ignorierende Wirtschaft verlassen, sondern sich selbst um digitale Selbstverteidigung bzw. technischen Datenschutz kümmern.' (selbstdatenschutz.info).

12 We include diverse groups with differing legal status into this category. The main criteria for inclusion is the strong attachment of the actors to legal norms as prescribed by public authorities. In this sense, all the organisations falling into this category feature a certain closeness to the state.

13 I do refer here to the 'Volkszählungsurteil'. Translating legal text is difficult at best, thus I will also provide the German version: 'Mit dem Recht auf informationelle Selbstbestimmung wären eine Gesellschaftsordnung und eine diese ermöglichende Rechtsordnung nicht vereinbar, in der Bürger nicht mehr wissen können, wer was wann und bei welcher Gelegenheit über sie weiß' (BVerfG 1983: 43).

14 See, for instance, the statement of the Federal Chief Commissioner for Data Protection and Informational Freedom (Voßhoff 2014).

15 Similar statements can be found in a booklet of the governmental foundation *Stiftung Datenschutz:* 'Data Protection – It's Your Turn' ('Datenschutz – es liegt an Ihnen').

16 This tension is made explicit by the Commissioner for Data Protection of Thuringia (Thüringer Datenschutzbeauftragter n.d.).

17 The individualistic core of the verdict is expressed in the following quote: 'Individual self-determination, however, presupposes (…) everybody's opportunity to free decision-making regarding things to be done or left undone respectively, including the opportunity to act indeed according to the decision being made' ('Individuelle Selbstbestimmung setzt aber (…) voraus, dass dem Einzelnen Entscheidungsfreiheit über vorzunehmende oder zu unterlassende Handlungen einschließlich der Möglichkeit gegeben ist, sich auch entsprechend dieser Entscheidungen tatsächlich zu verhalten') (BVerfG 1983: 45).

18 Of course, the practices of the German data protection authorities – supervising organisations, reviewing information systems, fining violators – may be understood as the collective shaping of privacy practices. Still, early data protection discourses in Germany seem to have featured a much higher degree of awareness of the collective and societal dimension of data protection, compared to the current rather individualistic framing. For example, Steinmüller, one of the pioneers, wrote already in 1986:

It is an absurd situation: From the first wave of industrialisation, targeted on manual labour, there emerged modern capitalism and the labour movement – in the end (…) contemporary labour unions arose. Currently, the second phase of industrialisation is underway by means of information and communication technologies, targeted at mental work and communication. However, who is going to stand up for the newly deprived?

(Steinmüller 1988: 12; my translation)

19 The following specifications are based on an analysis of the relevant parties' manifestos prepared for the parliamentary elections 2013 (CDU/CSU 2013a; SPD 2013; Die Linke 2013; Bündnis 90/Die Grünen 2013). In addition the coalition agreement was analysed (CDU/CSU/SPD 2013). At the time research was conducted and the manuscript for this contribution was prepared, similar documents allowing for comparison were not available. Generally speaking, the 2017 elections occur against a somewhat shifted background, shaped by the passing of the EU Data Protection Directive, the emergence of an influential discourse concerning Industry 4.0, and strong emphasis on public safety issues. However, the structural contradictions identified in this section are still operative.

20 In German: 'Je mehr politische Macht ein Akteur besitzt, d.h. je mehr er den Staat verwaltet, desto geringer dürfte seine Bereitschaft zum Datenschutz sein' (Baumann 2013: 47). In general Baumann's analysis is congruent with the one presented here, although the former is focused on a slightly different subject and time-span: political parties' discourse on privacy in Online Social Networks (OSNs) 2009–2012.

21 In German:

Der Staat kann dem Bürger beim Surfen, Mailen, Chatten oder Posten seine Eigenverantwortung nicht abnehmen. (…) Die Grundpfeiler für die Datenschutzpolitik von CDU und CSU sind daher: 1. Eigenverantwortung und Selbstdatenschutz der Bürgerinnen und Bürger. 2. Selbstverpflichtung und Eigeninitiative der Wirtschaft.

(CDU/CSU 2013b: 5)

22 In German: 'Balance zwischen der Sicherheit auf der einen und Freiheit des Einzelnen sowie der Berufsausübungsfreiheit der betroffenen Unternehmen auf der anderen Seite' (BITKOM 2013b: 5).

23 See the definition of person-related data of the Federal Chief Commissioner for Data Protection and Informational Freedom (BfDI n.d.). Only data that are related to *individual persons* count as 'personal data' in German law. Data that are not, but in principle could be related to some individual person, are called 'person-relatable' (*personenbeziehbare*) data. In any case, personal or person-relatable data *per definitionem* do not concern legal persons.

24 In German:

Auch Verbraucher können ihre Daten besser schützen. Eine weitere Sensibilisierung, Medienkompetenz, öffentliche und private Initiativen zur Erhöhung der Sicherheit begrüßt BITKOM ausdrücklich (…) aus diesem Grund werden auch Schulungen oder ähnliche Weiterbildungsmaßnahmen unterstützt, die Unternehmensmitarbeiter und Bürger in die Lage versetzen, mit sensiblen Daten richtig umzugehen

(BITKOM 2013b: 6)

25 For example, as regards Germany already in the 1980s there were IT security experts dealing with ISP issues (see Pfitzmann and Waidner 1986; Pfitzmann, Pfitzmann and Waidner 1988).

26 For instance, the author of 'CYPHERNOMICON: Cypherpunk FAQ and More' states: 'My libertarian, even anarchist, views surely come through' (unknown author n.d.).

27 Note that the manifesto is entitled '*A* Cypherpunk's Manifesto', and not '*The* Cypher-
    punks' Manifesto' – another indication of the deep-rooted individualism of the
    movement.
28 I would like to mention in passing that the *Cypherpunks* were also active participants
    in the international controversy on cryptography of the 1990s, an international dispute
    concerning the establishment of global norms specifying the (il)legal use of cryptog-
    raphy (see Winkel 2000).
29 See the quoting of van Berg in Reißmann (2012) as it was presented in the introduc-
    tion to this chapter.
30 My translation; the original reads: 'Die Leute verschlüsseln ihre Emails nicht selb-
    stverständlich. (…) Niemand wird plötzlich mit Verschlüsselung anfangen, weil es
    cool ist' (quoted in Reißmann 2012).
31 Garfinkel has repeatedly pointed out the normative quality of routinised practices,
    perceived by social actors as 'the world of daily life':

> They refer to this world as "natural facts of life" which, for members, are through
> and through moral facts of life. For members not only are matters so about famil-
> iar scenes, but they are so because it is morally right or wrong that they are so.
>
> (Garfinkel 1984: 35)

    Thus, violations of 'normal courses of action' (ibid.) are tantamount to the violation
    of norms.
32 Computer science scholars still aim to identify the reasons for the non-occurrence of
    widespread active, technical ISP practices, with usability difficulties belonging to the
    chief explanations; a classic study is Whitten/Tygar (1999).
33 It is consequently not too surprising that aforementioned PGP developer Phil Zim-
    mermann states: 'Even I have to admit: as a Macintosh user encrypting via PGP, the
    software that I have invented myself, is *complicated*' (Gruber 2013, my emphasis). In
    German: 'Sogar ich muss gestehen: Als Nutzer mit einem MacIntosh ist Verschlüsse-
    lung über das Programm PGP, das ich selbst erfunden habe, kompliziert.'
34 In German: 'Verschlüsselungstechniken, Virenabwehrprogramme – all diese Fragen
    müssen noch mehr in den Fokus gerückt werden. Die Menschen müssen sich bewusst
    werden, dass auch Kommunikation im Netz eines Schutzes bedarf. Und auch das ist
    eine Diskussion, die wir vorantreiben werden' (Rabhansl 2013).
35 The final report of the Parliamentary Investigation Committee by now has been com-
    pleted, a preliminary version has been published (Deutscher Bundestag 2017). The
    controversy about encryption goes on, as Islamist groups increasingly make use of
    encryption techniques, while German authorities attempt to legalise the use of an
    Online Trojan called 'Staatstrojaner' (Flade 2016). The way the Minister of the Inte-
    rior tried to achieve this by passing somewhat sneakily a correspondent law without
    public debate raised a lot of criticism (e.g. see Prantl 2017). The whole issue confirms
    once more that what is lacking is a political debate about the reinvention of the (now
    digitised) society.
36 As far as encryption is concerned, the example of WhatsApp shows how easy and
    widespread the use of end-to-end encryption becomes if the technical mechanism is
    directly inscribed into the technical infrastructure instead of overcharging users in a
    governmentality fashion. Still, the WhatsApp case cannot serve as an example for re-
    politicising the shaping of sociotechnical infrastructures: as there is no public access
    to the WhatsApp source code, users are still bound to simply trust Facebook as the
    provider (Scherschel 2016). Moreover, WhatsApp's end-to-end encryption is not the
    result of a public negotiation but the consequence of the strategic decision of a
    monopoly-like multi-billion dollar company that is able to afford to focus on the
    exploitation in this case only of metadata instead of analysing semantic content. In
    this sense, then, the WhatsApp case may be understood as the very reverse of ISP:
    instead of overburdening the individuals they have no voice at all.

37 This statement should not be misunderstood as a plea to shift all responsibility to national or international authorities. While regulation is certainly in need of modification – with efforts to adjust regulatory frameworks already being underway (see Schneider, Chapter 8 in this volume) – exaggerated *governmental paternalism* may be understood as the flipside of *governmentality*. The public negotiation of privacy issues therefore at best succeeds in reinventing appropriate institutional *ecologies* that allow for the *redistribution of responsibilities* (see Ochs and Lamla 2017). However, as privacy discourse for the most part propagates excessive individualism rather than collectivism it seems essential to highlight the collective character of the issue.

Bibliography

Aktion-Freiheit-statt-Angst (n.d.). *Aktion Freiheit statt Angst*. Available at: http://aktion-freiheitstattangst.org/. [Accessed 15 August 2017].

Baumann, M.-O. (2013). Datenschutz im Web 2.0: Der politische Diskurs über Privatsphäre in sozialen Netzwerken. In: U. Ackermann, ed., *Im Sog des Internets. Öffentlichkeit und Privatheit im digitalen Zeitalter*. Frankfurt/M.: Humanities Online, pp. 15–52.

Baumann, M.-O. (2015). Datenschutzversagen. *Merkur. Deutsche Zeitschrift für europäisches Denken*, 69(5), pp. 86–92.

Bennett, C. J. (2011). In Defence of Privacy: The Concept and the Regime. *Surveillance & Society*, 8(4), pp. 485–496.

Berliner Beauftragte für den Datenschutz (n.d.). *Selbstdatenschutz*. Available at: https://datenschutz-berlin.de//content/service/selbstdatenschutz. [Accessed 15 August 2017].

Berlinghoff, M. (2013). 'Totalerfassung' im 'Computerstaat' – Computer und Privatheit in den 1970er und 1980er Jahren. In: U. Ackermann, ed., *Im Sog des Internets. Privatheit und Öffentlichkeit im digitalen Zeitalter*. Frankfurt/M.: Humanities Online, pp. 93–110.

Bernold, M. (2012). Cypherpunk goes Mainstream. Der Bernold. Available at: http://der-bernold.com/2012/12/04/cypherpunk-goes-mainstream/. [Accessed 15 August].

Beuth, P. (2013). Überwachung – Mein digitaler Schutzschild. *ZEIT ONLINE*. Available at: www.zeit.de/digital/datenschutz/2013-01/serie-mein-digitaler-schutzschild-einleitung. [Accessed 15 August 2017].

BfDI (n.d.). Der Bundesbeauftragter für den Datenschutz und die Informationsfreiheit: Datenschutz ist … [booklet].

BITKOM (2011). *Datenschutz im Internet. Eine repräsentative Untersuchung zum Thema Daten im Internet aus Nutzersicht*. Berlin: BITKOM. [pdf] Available at: www.bitkom.org/noindex/Publikationen/2011/Studie/Studie-Datenschutz-im-Internet/BITKOM-Publikation-Datenschutz-im-Internet.pdf. [Accessed 15 August 2017].

BITKOM (2013a). NSA-Affäre bringt Verschlüsselung in Mode. BITKOM-Website. Available at: www.bitkom.org/de/markt_statistik/64026_78217.aspx. [Accessed 15 August 2017].

BITKOM (2013b). *Bundesverband Informationswirtschaft, Telekommunikation und neue Medien e.V.: Positionspapier zu Abhörmaßnahmen der Geheimdienste und Sicherheitsbehörden, Datenschutz und Datensicherheit*. Berlin: BITKOM. [pdf] Available at: www.bitkom.org/noindex/Publikationen/2013/Positionen/Positionspapier-zu-Abhoermassnahmen/BITKOM-Positionspapier-Abhoermassnahmen.pdf. [Accessed 15 August 2017].

Bourdieu, P. (1979). *Entwurf einer Theorie der Praxis auf der ethnologischen Grundlage der kabylischen Gesellschaft*. Frankfurt/M.: Suhrkamp.

boyd, d. (2010). Privacy and Publicity in the Context of Big Data. Available at: www.danah.org/papers/talks/2010/WWW2010.html. [Accessed 15 August 2017].

boyd, d. (2012). Networked Privacy. *Surveillance & Society*, 10(3/4), pp. 348–350.

boyd, d. and Crawford, K. (2011). *Six Provocations for Big Data.* Available at: http://papers.ssrn.com/sol3/papers.cfm?abstract_id=1926431. [Accessed 16 August 2017].

Bündnis 90/Die Grünen (2013). *Zeit für den grünen Wandel: Teilhaben. Einmischen. Zukunft schaffen. Bundestagswahlprogramm 2013 von BÜNDNIS 90/DIE GRÜNEN.* Berlin: Bündnis 90/die Grünen. [pdf] Available at: www.gruene.de/fileadmin/user_upload/Dokumente/Wahlprogramm/Wahlprogramm-barrierefrei.pdf. [Accessed 15 August 2017].

BVDW (2013). *Goslarer Programm. Medien- und netzpolitisches Grundsatzpapier des Bundesverband Digitale Wirtschaft (BVDW) e.V.* Düsseldorf: BVDW. [pdf] Available at: www.bvdw.org/medien/bvdw-veroeffentlicht-aktuelles-medien-und-netzpolitisches-grundsatzpapier?media=3081. [Accessed 15 August 2017].

BVerfG (1983). *Bundesverfassungsgericht: Volkszählungsurteil.* Karlsruhe: Bundesver-fassungsgericht. [pdf] Available at: https://web.archive.org/web/20101116085553/http://zensus2011.de/fileadmin/material/pdf/gesetze/volkszaehlungsurteil_1983.pdf. [Accessed 26 March 2015].

CDU/CSU (2013a). *Gemeinsam erfolgreich für Deutschland. Regierungsprogramm 2013–2017.* Berlin: CDU-Bundesgeschäftsstelle. [pdf] Available at: www.cdu.de/sites/default/files/media/dokumente/regierungsprogramm-2013-2017-langfassung-20130911.pdf. [Accessed 31 December 2017].

CDU/CSU (2013b). *Antworten der Christlich Demokratischen Union Deutschlands (CDU) und der Christlich-Sozialen Union in Bayern (CSU) auf die Fragen des Bundesverbandes Digitale Wirtschaft (BVDW) e.V.* [booklet].

CDU/CSU and SPD (2013). *Deutschlands Zukunft gestalten: Koalitionsvertrag zwischen CDU, CSU und SPD.* Rheinbach: Union Betr9iebs-GmbH. [pdf] Available at: www.bundesregierung.de/Content/DE/_Anlagen/2013/2013-12-17-koalitionsvertrag.pdf?__blob=publicationFile&v=2. [Accessed 15 August 2017].

ccc.de/de/club (n.d.). *Chaos Computer Club's Official Website: Self-Description.* Available at: http://ccc.de/de/club. [Accessed 15 August 2017].

ccc.de/de/hackerethik (n.d.). *Chaos Computer Club's Official Website: Hackerethik.* Available at: http://ccc.de/de/hackerethik. [Accessed 15 August 2017].

Clarke, A. (1991). Social Worlds/Arenas Theory as Organizational Theory. In: D. R. Maines, ed., *Social Organization and Social Process. Essays in Honor of Anselm Strauss*, 1st edn. New York: Transaction Publishers, pp. 119–157.

Clarke, A. (2012). *Situationsanalyse: Grounded Theory nach dem Postmodern Turn.* Wiesbaden: Springer VS.

Der Spiegel (2014). Interview with Alex Pentland: Can We Use Big Data to Make Society Better? *Spiegel Online.* Available at: www.spiegel.de/international/zeitgeist/scientist-alex-pentland-argues-big-data-can-be-used-to-improve-society-a-970443-2.html. [Accessed 15 August 2017].

Deutsche Vereinigung für Datenschutz (n.d.). *Datenschutz im Internet.* Available at: www.datenschutzverein.de/themen/datenschutz-im-internet/. [Accessed 15 August 2017].

Deutscher Bundestag (2017). *Beschlussfassung und Bericht des 1. Untersuchung-sausschusses nach Artikel 44 des Grundgesetzes (Drucksache 18/12850).* [pdf] Available at: http://dip21.bundestag.de/dip21/btd/18/128/1812850.pdf. [Accessed 15 August 2017].

Die Linke (2013). *100% sozial: Wahlprogramm zu Bundestagswahl 2013*. Berlin: Die Linke. [pdf] Available at: www.mehr-demokratie.de/fileadmin/pdf/DIE_LINKE-Wahlprogramm_2013.pdf. [Accessed 15 August 2017].

Dienlin, T. and Trepte, S. (2015). Is the privacy paradox a relic of the past? An in-depth analysis of privacy attitudes and privacy behaviors. *European Journal of Social Psychology*, 45, pp. 285–297.

Digital Courage (n.d.). *Datenschutz und Bürgerrechte*. Available at: http://digitalcourage. de/themen/datenschutz-und-buergerrechte. [Accessed 15 August 2017].

Dourish, P. and Anderson, K. (2006). Collective Information Practice: Exploring Privacy and Security as Social and Cultural Phenomena. *Human–Computer Interaction*, 21(3), pp. 319–342.

Flade, F. (2016). So lassen Islamisten Terrorfahnder ins Leere laufen. *DIE WELT*. Available at: www.welt.de/politik/deutschland/article154518365/So-lassen-Islamisten-Terrorfahnder-ins-Leere-laufen.html. [Accessed 15 August 2017].

Foucault, M. (2000). Die Gouvernementalität. In: U. Bröckling, S. Krasmann, and T. Lemke, eds., *Gouvernementalität der Gegenwart. Studien zur Ökonomisierung des Sozialen*. Frankfurt/M.: Suhrkamp, pp. 41–67.

Frohman, L. (2013). Rethinking Privacy in the Age of the Mainframe: Integrated Information Systems, the Changing Logic of Privacy, and the Problem of Democratic Politics in Surveillance Societies. In: U. Ackermann, ed., *Im Sog des Internets. Privatheit und Öffentlichkeit im digitalen Wandel*, 1st edn. Frankfurt/M.: Humanities Online, pp. 71–92.

Garfinkel, H. (1984). *Studies in Ethnomethodology*. Cambridge: Polity Press.

Giddens, A. (1984). *The Constitution of Society. Outline of a Theory of Structuration*. Cambridge: Polity Press.

Grimm, R. (2015). Big Data aus Informatiksicht und die Wirkung von Verschlüsselung. In: P. Richter, ed., *Privatheit, Öffentlichkeit und demokratische Willensbildung in Zeiten von Big Data*, 1st edn. Baden-Baden: Nomos, pp. 127–150.

Gruber, A. (2013). 'Verschlüsselung ist Bürgerpflicht': Interview mit Phil Zimmermann. *Die Zeit*. Available at: www.zeit.de/digital/datenschutz/2013-09/verschluesselung-interview-phil-zimmermann. [Accessed 15 August 2017].

Haggerty, K. D. and Ericson, R. V. (2000). The Surveillant Assemblage. *The British Journal of Sociology*, 51(4), pp. 605–622.

Hamburgischer Datenschutzbeauftragter (2011). *'Meine Daten kriegt ihr nicht!' – Projekt tritt in 2. Phase ein*. Available at: www.datenschutz-hamburg.de/news/detail/article/meine-daten-kriegt-ihr-nicht-projekt-tritt-in-2-phase-ein.html. [Accessed 15 August 2017].

Heuzeroth, T. (2014). GfK-Umfrage: Deutsche unterschätzen den Wert persönlicher Daten. *DIE WELT*. Available at: www.welt.de/wirtschaft/article126882276/Deutsche-unterschaetzen-den-Wert-persoenlicher-Daten.html. [Accessed 15 August 2017].

Hughes, E. (1993). *A Cypherpunk's Manifesto*. Available at: http://activism.net/cypherpunk/manifesto.html. [Accessed 15 August 2017].

Konferenz der Datenschutzbeauftragten des Bundes und der Länder (2010). *Ein modernes Datenschutzrecht für das 21. Jahrhundert*. Available at: www.bfdi.bund.de/Shared Docs/Publikationen/Allgemein/79DSKEckpunktepapierBroschuere.pdf?__blob=publicationFile. [Accessed 15 August 2017].

Konferenz der Datenschutzbeauftragten des Bundes und der Länder (2013). *Entschließung der Konferenz der Datenschutzbeauftragten des Bundes und der Länder vom 13. März 2013 Europa muss den Datenschutz stärken*. Available at: https://datenschutz-berlin. de/content/deutschland/konferenz. [Accessed 15 August 2017].

Latour, B. (1986). The Powers of Association. In: J. Law, ed., *Power, Action, and Belief. A New Sociology of Knowledge?* 1st edn. London: Routledge & Kegan Paul, pp. 264–280.

Latour, B. (1999). *Pandora's Hope: Essays on the Reality of Science Studies.* Cambridge, MA and London: Harvard University Press.

Lechtenbörger, J. (2017). *Informationelle Selbstbestimmung für mehr Privatsphäre im Internet mit Firefox, NoScript, Werbe-Blockern, Tor und GnuPG/PGP.* Available at: www.informationelle-selbstbestimmung-im-internet.de/. [Accessed 15 August 2017].

Lee, M. (2015). *Edward Snowden Explains how to Reclaim Your Privacy.* In: *The Intercept.* Available at: https://theintercept.com/2015/11/12/edward-snowden-explains-how-to-reclaim-your-privacy/. [Accessed 15 August 2017].

Leigh Star, S. (1999). The Ethnography of Infrastructure. *American Behavioral Scientist,* 43(3), pp. 377–391.

Lemke, T., Krasmann, S., and Bröckling, U. (2000). Gouvernementalität, Neoliberalismus und Selbsttechnologien. Eine Einleitung. In: U. Bröckling, S. Krasmann, and T. Lemke, eds., *Gouvernementalität der Gegenwart. Studien zur Ökonomisierung des Sozialen,* 1st edn. Frankfurt/M.: Suhrkamp, pp. 7–40.

Maas, H. (2014). *Rede zum Safer Internet Day 2014.* Available at: www.bmjv.de/SharedDocs/Reden/DE/2014/02112014_Rede_Safer_Internet_Day.html?nn=6704226. [Accessed 15 August 2017].

Ochs, C. (2015). Die Kontrolle ist tot – lang lebe die Kontrolle! Plädoyer für ein nachbürgerliches Privatheitsverständnis. *Mediale Kontrolle unter Beobachtung* 4/1 (2015). Available at: www.medialekontrolle.de/wp-content/uploads/2015/11/Ochs-Carsten-2015-04-01.pdf. [Accessed 15 August 2017].

Ochs, C. (2018). Privacies in Practice. In: U. Bergermann, M. Dommann, E. Schüttpelz, and J. Stolow, eds., *Connect & Divide: The Practice Turn in Media Studies. 3rd Media Studies Symposion of the German Research Foundation 2015.* Diaphanes: Zürich.

Ochs, C. and Lamla, J. (2017). Demokratische Privacy by Design: Kriterien soziotechnischer Gestaltung von Privatheit. *Forschungsjournal Soziale Bewegungen,* 30(2), pp. 189–199.

Peikert, D. (2013). Crypto-Party: Anleitung zur digitalen Selbstverteidigung. In: *FAZ.* Available at: www.faz.net/aktuell/rhein-main/crypto-party-anleitung-zur-digitalen-selbstverteidigung-12309561.html. [Accessed 10 June 2014].

Pew Research Center (2014). *Public Perceptions of Privacy and Security in the Post-Snowden Era.* [pdf] Available at: http://assets.pewresearch.org/wp-content/uploads/sites/14/2014/11/PI_PublicPerceptionsofPrivacy_111214.pdf. [Accessed 15 August 2017].

Pfitzmann, A. and Waidner, M. (1986). Networks without user observability – design options. In: F. Pichler, ed., *Advances in Cryptology – EUROCRYPT '85. Proceedings of a Workshop on the Theory and Application of Cryptographic Techniques.* Berlin/Heidelberg: Springer, pp. 245–253.

Pfitzmann, A., Pfitzmann, B. and Waidner, M. (1988). Datenschutz garantierende offene Kommunikationsnetze. *Informatik Spektrum,* 11(3), pp. 118–142.

Prantl, H. (2017). Der Staatstrojaner ist ein Einbruch ins Grundrecht. *Süddeutsche Zeitung.* Available at: www.sueddeutsche.de/digital/ueberwachung-der-staatstrojaner-ist-ein-einbruch-ins-grundgesetz-1.3555917. [Accessed 15 August 2017].

Preibusch, S. (2015). Privacy Behaviors After Snowden. *Communications of the ACM,* 58(5), 48–55. Available at: DOI: 10.1145/2663341. [Accessed 15 August 2017].

Privacy International/Amnesty International (2015). *Two Years After Snowden: Protecting Human Rights in an Age of Mass Surveillance.* Available at: www.privacy international.org/sites/default/files/Two%20Years%20After%20Snowden_Final%20 Report_EN.pdf. [Accessed 15 August 2017].

Rabhansl, C. (2013). Spionageabwehr ist keine Privatsache: Vom Umgang der deutschen Politik mit der NSA-Affäre. *Deutschlandfunk Kultur.* Available at: www.deutschland radiokultur.de/spionageabwehr-ist-keine-privatsache.996.de.html?dram:article_id= 254644. [Accessed 15 August 2017].

Reißmann, O. (2012). Cyptoparty-Bewegung: Verschlüsseln, verschleiern, verstecken. *Der Spiegel.* Available at: www.spiegel.de/netzwelt/netzpolitik/cryptoparty-bewegung-die-cypherpunks-sind-zurueck-a-859473.html. [Accessed 15 August 2017].

Rössler, B. (2001). *Der Wert des Privaten.* Frankfurt/M.: Suhrkamp.

Rössler, B. and Mokrosinska, D. (eds.) (2015). *Social Dimensions of Privacy: Interdisciplinary Perspectives.* Cambridge: Cambridge University Press.

Sächsischer Datenschutzbeauftragter (2014). *Selbstdatenschutz – Was ist Selbstdatenschutz?* Available at: www.saechsdsb.de/datenschutz-fuer-buerger/112-selbstdatenschutz. [Accessed 15 August 2017].

Scherschel, F. A. (2016). *Test: Hinter den Kulissen der WhatsApp-Verschlüsselung,* heise security. Available at: www.heise.de/security/artikel/Test-Hinter-den-Kulissen-der-WhatsApp-Verschluesselung-3165567.html. [Accessed 15 August 2017].

Scholz, K.-A. (2014). Wie ist die Privatsphäre zu retten? *Deutsche Welle.* Available at: www.dw.com/de/wie-ist-die-privatsph%C3%A4re-zu-retten/a-17425091. [Accessed 15 August 2017].

selbstdatenschutz.info (n.d.). *Selbstdatenschutz und digitale Selbstverteidigung.* Available at: www.selbstdatenschutz.info/. [Accessed 15 August 2017].

Shelton, M., Rainie, L., and Madden, M. (2015). *Pew Research Center: Americans' Privacy Strategies Post-Snowden.* [pdf] Available at: www.pewinternet.org/2015/03/16/ Americans-Privacy-Strategies-Post-Snowden/. [Accessed 15 August 2017].

Simo, H. (2015). Big Data: Opportunities and Privacy Challenges. In: P. Richter, ed., *Privatheit, Öffentlichkeit und demokratische Willensbildung in Zeiten von Big Data,* 1st edn. Baden-Baden: Nomos, pp. 13–44.

SPD (2013). *Das Wir entscheidet. Das Regierungsprogramm 2013–2017.* Available at: www.spd.de/fileadmin/Dokumente/Beschluesse/Bundesparteitag/20130415_regierungs programm_2013_2017.pdf. [Accessed 15 August 2017].

Steinmüller, W. (1988). Vorwort des Herausgebers. In: W. Steinmüller, ed., *Verdatet und vernetzt. Sozialökologische Handlungsspielräume in der Informationsgesellschaft,* 1st edn. Frankfurt/M.: Fischer, pp. 12–14.

Strauss, A. (1978). A Social World Perspective. *Studies in Symbolic Interaction,* 1, pp. 119–128.

Strauss, A. and Corbin, J. (1996). *Grounded Theory: Grundlagen Qualitativer Sozialforschung.* Weinheim: Beltz.

SurPRISE (2014). *Citizen Summits on Privacy, Security and Surveillance: Country report Germany.* [pdf] Available at: http://surprise-project.eu/wp-content/uploads/2014/10/ D6.3_Country_report_Germany_final_30.9.pdf. [Accessed 15 August 2017].

Tarde, G. (1903). *The Laws of Imitation.* New York: Henry Holt and Company.

Thüringer Datenschutzbeauftragter (n.d.). *Sicherheit mit Kryptographischen Verfahren.* Available at: www.tlfdi.de/tlfdi/datenschutz/technischer-und-organisatorischer-daten schutz/sicherheit/. [Accessed 15 August 2017].

Unknown Author (n.d.). *The Cyphernomicon.* Available at: http://groups.csail.mit.edu/mac/classes/6.805/articles/crypto/cypherpunks/cyphernomicon/CP-FAQ. [Accessed 15 August 2017].

Voßhoff, A. (2014). Globales Netz braucht globalen Datenschutz (Interview). *Deutsche Welle.* Available at: www.dw.com/de/globales-netz-braucht-globalen-datenschutz/a-17421683. [Accessed 15 August 2017].

Whitten, A. and Tygar, J. D. (1999). Why Johnny Can't Encrypt: A Usability Evaluation of PGP 5.0, In: SSYM'99 Proceedings of the 8th conference on USENIX Security Symposium. Washington, DC: USENIX Association, pp. 4–14. Available at: www.gaudior.net/alma/johnny.pdf. [Accessed 10 June 2014].

Winkel, O. (2000). Netzwerksicherheit – (k)ein Thema für Sozialwissenschaftler. *Rubin,* 2, pp. 6–12.

Wittgenstein, L. (1958). *Philosophical Investigations.* Oxford: Basil Blackwell.

Woolgar, S. (1991). *Configuring the User: The Case of Usability Trials.* In: J. Law, ed., *A Sociology of Monsters: Essays on Power, Technology and Domination,* 1st edn. London: Routledge, pp. 57–99.

14 Understanding the 'open' in making research data open

Policy rhetoric and research practice

Merel Noorman, Bridgette Wessels,
Thordis Sveinsdottir, and Sally Wyatt

Introduction

Big Data is part of a wider trend of data-driven approaches within the commercial and public sectors. The increased digitisation of data, both born digital and later digitised, in many social and technical processes has resulted in more and more data being available in potentially transferable, collated, cross-referenced and relational forms. This easy availability is combined with a general assumption that having more data will result in more accurate analysis, improved decision-making, innovation, economic growth and so on. The growing call for open data is part of this wider trend of turning to data-driven processes and is underpinned by a socially progressive and morally informed belief that everyone should benefit from data (Wessels *et al.* 2017). There is a particularly strong drive for open data in academic and publicly funded research. This chapter discusses the meaning of 'open' in science, social science and humanities research. In so doing it highlights technological, organisational and moral issues in assessing the policy push for open and Big Data-driven practices within the private, public and research sectors.

Open access (OA) to research data has become increasingly popular amongst research policymakers since the turn of the millennium. Sharing data without restrictions has been on the agenda of funders and scientific and scholarly organisations for some time, but has received even more attention in recent years. As far back as 1997, the United States (US) National Research Council argued for making research data freely available in its report *Bits of Power: Issues in Global Access to Scientific Data*. Open access to research data was also part of the Berlin Declaration, published by the Max Planck Institute in 2003. Since these early examples, various other international groups and organisations, including funding agencies, umbrella organisations and learned societies, have published their own reports arguing for open access to research data and providing visions of what open research data should entail (see, for example, League of European Research Universities 2013; Research Data Alliance 2014). Like all things 'open', these organisations regard open access to research data in general as beneficial for research, for industry, for policy and for the public.

Various value judgements and assumptions underlie the call to make research data open, based on particular ideas about what good science is and how scientific and scholarly practices should be organised. Yet, claims about the benefits of openness are contested and the concept has acquired multiple meanings over time and within different disciplinary practices (Levin *et al.* 2016). The push for open access to research data goes beyond recent developments in open access to publications because of the focus on data rather than the published results of data analysis. Publications typically reflect the interpretations of the researchers who collected or generated the data. Open access to research data would allow other researchers to evaluate, reuse, recombine, and reinterpret data, including but not limited to uses in Big Data analytics. Open data, thus, challenges established scientific and scholarly processes in which data and their interpretation are the responsibility of authors who gain recognition for the work.

In this chapter, we argue that in the current policy push for open research data the complexity and diversity of both research practices and 'openness' are obscured and overlooked (see also Borgman 2015). It is not surprising, then, that despite an increasing emphasis on open research data and the growing use of Open Access mandates by research funders, many researchers do not make their data open (Nelson 2009; Kuipers and van der Hoeven 2009; Kennan and Markauskaite 2015). We show that by paying close attention to the differences in conceptions of 'openness' in policy documents and in practice, we can develop an understanding of openness that is better suited for the diversity of ways of producing knowledge.

In the next section, we discuss the methodology of the research project on which this chapter is based. In order to analyse the different conceptions of openness, we then distinguish between three dimensions along which the concept can be elaborated: *technological*, *organisational* and *moral*. We discuss these dimensions of openness and give some background to visions of open access to research. We subsequently explore conceptions of openness in three key policy documents arguing for open research data, along the same dimensions. Finally, we critically analyse how these conceptions relate to, and sometimes conflict with, what openness means in different scientific and scholarly practices. For this analysis, we draw on research we have done as part of a European project in order to provide illustrative examples from different disciplines (Sveinsdottir *et al.* 2013). On the basis of this analysis we conclude that the three dimensions of openness provide a basis for more practice-sensitive policy development.

Methodology

This chapter is based on research undertaken in a project, funded by the European Commission 7th Framework Programme, between 2013 and 2015. The project adopted a mixed methods approach of policy reviews, web surveys, interviews with stakeholders, and validation workshops.[1] The structure of the systematic reviews of policy literature was based on general policy visions followed by reviews of key focus points of that policy: research practice, technology and infrastructure, ethical and legal issues, and organisational issues. Inclusion criteria were then set based on dates (2007 to policy published during the project 2013–2015) and key policy focus points (Sveinsdottir *et al.* 2013). The literature review was followed up with semi-structured interviews with researchers and other stakeholders, including librarians, archivists, policymakers, research funders and data managers. Interviews were subsequently transcribed and then analysed thematically, to identify key issues, motivations and barriers for different stakeholders. An in-depth stakeholder analysis was conducted, resulting in a stakeholder taxonomy, which outlined the key roles and functions of stakeholders in the research ecosystem. Interviewees were selected on the basis of the taxonomy, their role in a research ecosystem and their expertise. In total we interviewed 29 researchers and 33 other stakeholders. The results of the policy review and the interviews were then discussed in five validation work-shops, attended by expert stakeholders in the field of scholarly research, open access, research policy and data management.

Using the material collected in the research project, we analyse what 'open' means in different contexts when it comes to open research data and why the push for more open research data is problematic in many fields of research. More specifically we look at the different conceptions of openness in policy docu-ments, on the one hand, and in various scientific and scholarly practices, on the other. Based on this analysis we examine how a better understanding of these differences can inform policymaking on open research data.

Conceptualising openness and open research data

Various conceptions of openness can be found in the myriad policy documents and reports presenting visions of open access to research data. In arguing for open research data these documents and reports outline what an open research ecosystem should be, why it is desirable and what technology-enabled revolu-tionary changes it will bring to the scientific and scholarly landscape. As such, they are reminiscent of other guiding visions or *leitbilder* of science and techno-logy and they have comparable advantages and problems (Borup *et al.* 2006).

Guiding visions about science and technology, such as visions about the future of eHealth or nanotechnologies, are important tools in policymaking to provide structure and legitimation, attract interest and foster investments. 'They give definition to roles, clarify duties, offer some shared shape of what to expect and how to prepare for opportunities and risks' (Borup *et al.* 2006: 286). They have a performative function in mobilising stakeholders to take action to achieve the future developments that these visions promise (Van de Poel 2003). They are intended to enrol and mobilise allies to realise the technological promises.

Such guiding visions, however, also tend to be abstractions with a distinctly utopian character that obscure the risks, problematic aspects and excluded others of the proposed developments (De Wilde 2000). Moreover, disappointment seems to be built into the hyperbolic expectations that constitute these visions (Brown *et al.* 2003). An initial overinflation of future promises is required to gain attention and resources. Such promises do not take into account the com-plexities of existing practices, the conflicting interests of relevant stakeholders, competing technologies, and other obstacles and barriers. As Borup *et al.* point out:

> Early technological expectations are in many cases technologically deterministic, downplaying the many organizational and cultural factors on which a technology's future may depend. [...] Here it is likely that roles will be ambiguous, lacking form or agreement; regulatory aspects like those of standards and quality control are unlikely to have been developed; market players will experience acute levels of uncertainty in judging appropriate levels of investment; it will probably be the case that numerous competing innovation futures are also being promoted; contestation and conflict may be very high, etc.
>
> (Borup *et al.* 2006: 290)

Policy documents about open access to research data present guiding visions and promises that are likely to be similarly inflated. As we argue in this chapter, their promises build on idealised and narrow conceptions of science and scholarly practices to support abstract and sometimes contradictory and problematic notions of openness.

In order to understand how policy documents conceptualise openness we need to situate the concept in its historical context. The current call for open access to research data is part of a broader societal trend that has openness and sharing of knowledge and information as core values. It builds on various initiatives and movements that call for, inter alia, open operating systems, open source software, open access to publications, open science, open government data and open knowledge (Suber 2012; Molloy 2011; Lathrop and Ruma 2010; Kelty 2009). Openness has acquired different meanings and interpretations that reflect the interests and ambitions of those who pursue openness in different contexts.

We distinguish between three interrelated dimensions along which the concept has been developed: *technological*, *organisational* and *moral*. Although each dimension has its own particular characteristics, they interact with each other in the development of open access to data. Openness has a particular *technological* interpretation when it is used to refer to the interoperability of software, computer networks and operating systems. Advocates of open systems and open source software have used the concept of openness to argue for particular types of computer technologies that allow software and systems to be seamlessly linked (Kelty 2009). They argue that openness is a solution to the problem of information and data being locked into widely varying special purpose and proprietary computers and software.

Along the *organisational* dimension, openness has been tied to ideas about how knowledge-sharing and software development are or should be organised between the various stakeholders involved. It is used to refer to different ways of organising system and software development, sharing information, collaborating and communicating. In the open source software community, 'open' was chosen to emphasise the pragmatic business case of having an engaged community of software developers to create and improve source code collaboratively (Kelty 2009). This is in contrast to more hierarchical types of organisations.

Openness also has what can be termed a '*moral*' dimension. Along this dimension openness is conceptualised as a moral value and is used in reference to morally normative ideas about how software, source code, knowledge, information and data – especially when public or publicly funded – should be free to study, share, modify and use. Here 'free' tends to be used in the sense of 'free speech' and not 'free beer' (Stallman 2002). Openness as a moral value is also at the heart of the ideal of science, as reflected in the influential Mertonian norms of science, which suggests that all knowledge claims, and the data on which they are based, should be open to scrutiny and refutation (Merton 1973). The open access (to publications and data) movement takes the long-established perspective that scientific knowledge is a common good that is often funded by public resources. This brings a moral imperative to the normative ideals of science that the results of publicly funded research, including data, publications, and inventions should be accessible by all (Borgman 2015; Molloy 2011). In the context of the call for open government data, the concept is also strongly associated with other democratic values such as transparency and accountability.

The distinction between the three dimensions of openness is an analytical one to help make sense of the various notions of openness as they appear in the discussions about open access to research data. It is not intended as a basis for an all-encompassing taxonomy of what openness can mean. Rather, the three dimensions highlight aspects of the various ways that openness has been used in the past and how it is currently used in policy documents about open access to research data. In addition, it enables us to map out how it is conceptualised and enacted in different scientific and scholarly practices. As such, the analytical distinction provides insights into the dynamics of developing open access to research data and sheds light on the distinctive character of the relationship between policy and practice in the field of open access to research data, which we discuss in more detail in the conclusion.

Openness in three policy reports

To illustrate how conceptions of openness in policy documents on open research data may conflict with current scientific and scholarly practices, we examine three documents that promote or support open access to research data. During our research we found that several policy documents had an influential role in setting the agenda and driving the open data movement, particularly in policy circles and within institutions. These were repeatedly invoked by interviewees and stakeholders. We have selected three documents that address the issues of open research data for a broad range of disciplines: two from intergovernmental bodies, and one from a learned society. Each document provides a different perspective on and approach to the issue. The three documents, in chronological order, are:

1   *OECD Guidelines and Principles on Research Data from Public Funding* (the OECD document) (2007). The document was attached to an OECD Recommendation and endorsed by the OECD Council in 2006. This Recommendation states that OECD member countries should take into consideration the guidelines and principles provided in the OECD document when preparing national policy. The document counts as a milestone because 30 members of the OECD committed to this early policy document on research data (rather than publications), which explicitly argues for openness. It gave impetus to the open research data movement, putting the issue on the agenda of the governments of these 30 member states.

2   *Riding the Wave*, produced by the EU High Level Expert Group on Scientific Data (the HLEG document) (2010). This document set the stage for the policy development on open access to research data in Horizon2020, the research agenda of the European Commission for the period 2014–2020. It provided a vision for the further development of (funding) policies for open access to research data. As such, it has had an important influence on the advancement of open research data.

3   *Science as an Open Enterprise* (the RS document) (2012). This influential report from the Royal Society was authored by a committee, made up of Royal Society members and was primarily directed at the STEM disciplines (science, technology, engineering, medicine), such as genomics, astronomy and chemistry. Research institutions and policymakers have often taken their cue from this report and, as such, it has given shape to policies on open access in the UK and beyond.

The three documents were written for different purposes and audiences, and each provides a different definition of open access to research data. For the OECD, openness is the first principle and is defined as follows:

> [A]ccess on equal terms for the international research community at the lowest possible cost, preferably at no more than the marginal cost of dissemination. Open access to research data from public funding should be easy, timely, user-friendly and preferably Internet-based.
>
> (OECD 2007: 15)

The emphasis is on costs, but the definition underlines that data should be easily available and comprehensible.

The RS document provides a more elaborate definition of 'open', introducing the concept of 'intelligent openness': data should be assessable, intelligible, usable and accessible (Royal Society (RS) 2012: 7). Data should thus not only be made available, but different audiences also need to be able to find, understand, evaluate and use any such data. The RS document hereby underlines that making research data open entails more than just putting a spreadsheet on a website; openness requires considerable work. In addition, it points out that intelligent openness 'is a response to the varying demands on different sorts of data from diverse research communities and interest groups' (RS 2012: 15).

Finally, the HLEG document does not focus on open access to research data, but presents a vision for the development of a European e-Infrastructure. Open access is a key element and outcome of such an infrastructure. 'Our vision is a scientific e-Infrastructure that supports seamless access, use, re-use and trust of data' (High Level Expert Group (HLEG) 2010: 4). As data are not the main focus, the report does not provide an explicit definition of open research data, but it does state that the vision of the HLEG is that by 2030,

> [R]esearchers and practitioners from any discipline are able to find, access and process the data they need. They can be confident in their ability to use and understand data, and they can evaluate the degree to which that can be trusted.
>
> (HLEG 2010: 4)

Moreover, the HLEG envisions that the public will not only have access to the data, but will also be able to make creative use of, and contribute to, the available scientific data. As such, the HLEG draws attention to what is required for accessing and reusing data, namely the ability to understand and evaluate the data.

These definitions are rather general and abstract, so we now analyse how the reports conceptualise 'openness' of data along the *technical, organisational* and *moral* dimensions, in order to make explicit the underlying assumptions in these visions and to elucidate some of their problematic aspects.

Technological

All three documents assume that open research data are part of revolutionary changes in the scholarly and scientific landscape, driven by technological advances in data production, analysis and communication (OECD 2007: 9; RS 2012: 7; HLEG 2010: 7). The reports share a belief in the technological imperative: inevitable technological progress necessitates immediate action from institutions and individuals (Wyatt 2008). One of the key changes is the exponential growth of data, sometimes referred to in the reports as the 'data deluge' (RS 2012: 16). As the Royal Society notes:

> Modern computers permit massive datasets to be assembled and explored in ways that reveal inherent but unsuspected relationships. This data-led science is a promising new source of knowledge. [...] The emergence of linked data technologies creates new information through deeper integration of data across different datasets with the potential to greatly enhance automated approaches to data analysis. Communication technologies have the potential to create novel social dynamics in science.[2]
>
> (RS 2012: 7)

In order 'to grasp the opportunities' (HLEG 2010: 7) created by these changes, new e-infrastructures, data management practices and data sharing are required immediately. 'Failure will undermine Europe's competitiveness and endanger social progress', warns the HLEG (2010: 7). The HLEG also notes,

> We are on the verge of a great new leap in scientific capability, fuelled by data. We have a vision of how Europe could benefit rather than suffer, lead rather than follow. But we urge speed. We must learn to ride the data wave.
>
> (HLEG 2010: 9)

The documents characterise the current use of technology and of data in science as deficient or at least in need of improvement. The scientific data infrastructure is fragmented or lacking; data are isolated, stored on local hard disks in idiosyncratic formats that cannot be read by other researchers or machines (RS 2012: 65–66; OECD 2007: 15). International metadata standards are absent in many disciplines, as are the incentives to develop standards. Moreover, the tools to process the ever-increasing volumes of data have yet to be developed:

> Given the volume and complexity of modern digital databases, filing, sorting and extracting data have become demanding technical tasks that require sophisticated software tools if they are to be carried out efficiently and effectively. [...] A lot of research and development is still needed from computer scientists if the full potential of the digital revolution is to be realised.
>
> (RS 2012: 64)

Although the technology exists, the documents suggest, it is neither applied sufficiently nor used effectively.

In all three documents, openness of data in a technological sense is an important part of the solution to the problem of disparate data locked in scientific silos. Openness presents an alternative to fragmented infrastructures, as it places the focus on standardisation, interoperability, reusability, and automation of data production and management (HLEG 2010: 18; OECD 2007: 15, 19; RS 2012: 14). The concept of intelligent openness developed in the RS document underlines that data need to be accompanied by the appropriate metadata and presented in standardised formats in order to be assessable, intelligible and usable. In order to be accessible, data and metadata have to be machine readable and part of a larger infrastructure. For the OECD, interoperability is one of the key principles: 'Incompatibility of technical and procedural standards can be the most serious barrier to multiple uses of data sets' (2007: 19). The HLEG also identifies interoperability as one of the main challenges to overcome (2010: 21). Standardisation and interoperability would make data easier to find, share and reuse and they would enable the automation of many processes of the data lifecycle, such as ingestion, quality control and even analysis.

Each document links open research data to the development of global digital infrastructures, which should bring together a network of heterogeneous technologies and data resources that can be instantaneously accessed by anyone, anywhere in the world (HLEG 2010: 4, 18; OECD 2007: 11; RS 2010: chapter 1). Indeed, the HLEG document centres on its vision for a scientific e-Infrastructure 'that supports seamless access, use and re-use, and trust of data' (2010: 4), making open research data possible. As the group points out, diversity is a characteristic of scientific information and in order to tackle that challenge a 'leap forward in interoperability' is required (2010: 19). The OECD also considers such an infrastructure a prerequisite: 'Access to research data, and their optimum exploitation, requires appropriately designed technological infrastructure, broad international agreement on interoperability, and effective data quality controls' (2007: 11). The envisioned global infrastructures are presented as seamless patchworks of interoperable heterogeneous instruments, tools and data, constructed and made interoperable through global collaborative efforts.

Organisational

The technological conceptions of openness in the documents are interlinked with particular assumptions about changes in the way that science and its institutions are organised and how researchers work. The RS document argues that new digital tools enable

> ways of working that some believe have propelled us to the verge of a second open science revolution, every bit as great as that triggered by the invention of scientific journals. Open data, data sharing and collaboration lie at the heart of these opportunities.
>
> (RS 2012: 24)

Both the RS and HGL documents place these kinds of changes in the context of what has been called the *fourth paradigm of science* (RS 2012: 31). The HLEG document describes this paradigm as moving 'beyond observation, theory and simulation, and into a new realm of exploration driven by mining new insights from vast diverse data sets' (2010: 8). Central to this perceived paradigm shift is the expectation that researchers will develop new collaborative practices organised around ever-growing volumes of digital data. All three documents point to examples in bioinformatics and genomics to illustrate new ways of doing 'data-driven' science and the success that they have brought (e.g. OECD 2007: 9). These assumptions about changes in science give shape to the conceptions of openness along the organisational dimension.

The RS and HLEG documents, and to a lesser extent the OECD document, observe a shift from individual, national and disciplinary research projects that yield inaccessible data sets towards large-scale, global, interdisciplinary collaborations organised around open data sharing. In other words, they recognise the importance of 'big science' as both an ideal and in practice (Nowotny *et al.* 2001; Leydesdorff and Etzkowitz 1998). The RS document observes, 'the geography and sociology of research is changing' (2012: 37). Computational and communication technologies have stimulated new ways of doing science, which are increasingly collective, collaborative, interdisciplinary and international. Similarly, the HLEG document notes a shift towards collective ways of doing science and draws a comparison with economic models in food, transport and finance. 'The same path from individual control to international exchange must be trodden by data – indeed, it's already happening' (2010: 21). The conception of open data is intimately tied, in these documents, to collective, collaborative and international research practices.

In order to stay abreast of the changes, researchers and institutions have to adapt, according to the documents, and openness is heralded as the way to do that. They have to collaborate and share data across disciplinary and national boundaries. The HLEG report warns:

> International collaboration is essential; there is no such thing as a purely local or national network anymore. We must collaborate in global architectures and governance for e-infrastructure, and we must share the costs and technologies for archiving, networking and managing data across the globe.
>
> (HLEG 2010: 30)

Opening research data is a prerequisite. The risk of not opening research data, according to the HLEG, is 'a world of fragmented data sources – in fact, a world much like today' (2010: 26). The OECD argues that sharing and open access to publicly funded research will maximise the research potential of new digital technologies and networks and provide greater returns from the public investment in research (2007: 10).

All three documents place the responsibility for making research data open with institutions. The growing collaborations and expanding volumes of data require more coordinated approaches in which institutions play a key role. The RS document, for instance, states, 'Scientists need to take action to make their data available but it is up to supporting institutions to clear barriers and facilitate this process, by offering incentives and infrastructure' (2012: 10). Similarly, the OECD lists 'formal responsibility' as one of its principles, which it interprets as being mostly relevant to institutions: 'Access arrangements should promote explicit, formal institutional practices, such as the development of rules and regulations, regarding the responsibilities of various parties involved in data-related activities' (2007: 17). Moreover, through this principle the OECD assigns responsibility for ensuring the preservation, management and accessibility of research data to research institutions and government organisations. The HLEG directs its recommendations to EU institutions and sees a role for these institutions in almost every area, ranging from funding for infrastructure to developing a framework for a Collaborative Data Infrastructure and to creating international audit certification processes (2010: 5).

Funders are given an important role in all three documents, as they are perceived to have significant leverage in enabling change through funding, development of professional expertise and evaluation instruments (OECD 2007: 18;

RS 2012: 74). Data centres and libraries also feature prominently in the reports and are assigned a range of responsibilities, including data stewardship and curation, education and the establishment of standards (OECD 2007: 19; RS 2012: 72). They also have a responsibility in advocating open data and creating awareness. The documents position all these institutions as actors with central coordinating and leadership roles in constructing and maintaining access arrangements that enable widespread data sharing.

Compared to institutions, researchers play a minor role in the documents. They feature primarily as stakeholders who need to be consulted about data quality, standards, incentives and values, but not as initiators or driving forces behind open research data. The RS report argues for responsiveness to research needs, behaviours and technologies (2012: 62). Likewise, the OECD states, '[s]tandards should be developed in consultation with researchers to ensure that the level of quality and precision meets the needs of various disciplines' (2007: 20). It even assigns research communities the responsibility to perform a number of tasks as part of their research practices, including assisting in establishing agreements on standards for cataloguing data and negotiating the terms of data sharing at the earliest possible stage of a collaborative research project (2007: 15). Yet it remains unclear what responsiveness and consultation mean and to what extent researchers are allowed to determine what data can be released and under what conditions.

Openness in an organisational sense in these reports is, thus, linked to the idea of science as constituted by collaborative and cross-disciplinary global infrastructures, in which institutions gain a more prominent coordinating role. This idea of open science is juxtaposed with the idea of science conducted by autonomous individual scientists working in isolation, an idea that the reports characterise as outdated and deficient.

Moral

The conceptions of openness as a value, present in the three documents, are based on particular ideas about what is right and wrong behaviour in dealing with data. Each report builds in some way on Mertonian-inspired norms about what science should be, that is, open to all, open to scrutiny, communal, and its results should be a common good (Merton 1973). At the same time, they connect openness with other values usually predominant in business-oriented discourses, such as efficiency and effectiveness. Open research data should accelerate the rate of scientific practices, at a lower cost, while contributing to economic growth and innovation. In addition, openness in the reports is presented as enabling democratic values such as equality and citizen empowerment.

Mertonian-inspired norms are more prevalent in the RS document than in the other two. For the RS, openness is already a core tenant of science, inextricably linked to scientific rigour and reproducibility, but recent technological and social developments require new approaches to openness (RS 2012: 13). Openness enables scientific rigour through enabling others to question and verify results and where possible attempt to reproduce the results. However, new data technologies, the RS argues, 'challenge the principle that science is a self-correcting enterprise' (RS 2012: 26). The volumes of data have grown to such an extent that it has become impossible for scientists to publish their arguments and the evidence in a single place, in accordance with traditional scientific communication. 'This represents a serious data-gap that is inimical to the rigorous scrutiny to which scientific conclusions should be subject' (RS 2012: 26). The RS, therefore, concludes that openness as a scientific principle needs to be re-established through making intelligent open access to digital data an integral part of research practices.

The OECD recognises openness and the free exchange of ideas, information and knowledge as key principles underlying 'the public science systems of OECD member countries' (OECD 2007: 9), although it does not link them explicitly to norms such as scientific rigour and reproducibility. The HLEG hardly mentions scientific rigour and reproducibility, but instead focuses on trust. It argues that the right data infrastructure is required to address various trust issues, including the (re-)establishment of confidence in the quality of data and public trust in science (HLEG 2010: 17).

In contrast to the RS document, the HLEG and OECD reports emphasise strongly the economic benefits that open research data would yield, and associate openness with values such as efficiency and effectiveness of scientific research. The OECD goes so far as to state that the ultimate goal of its principles and guidelines is to 'improve the efficiency and effectiveness of the global science system' (2007: 13). The HLEG envisions that as a result of the to-be-developed scientific e-Infrastructure through which open data can be shared, return on investments will increase: 'Public funding rises, because funding bodies have confidence that their investments in research are paying back extra dividends to society, through increased use and re-use of publicly generated data' (2010: 5). It suggests, '[s]cientists' efficiency and productivity will rise because they know they can access, use, reuse and trust the data they find' (2010: 25). In terms of progress, the report notes that through data sharing and the cross-fertilisation of ideas and disciplines, grand challenges can be solved. In addition, 'the innovative power of industry and enterprise is harnessed by clear and efficient arrangements for exchange of data between private and public sectors, allowing appropriate returns on both' (2010: 5). In the preface, the then Vice-President of the European Commission, Neelie Kroes underlines this focus on progress and efficiency:

> My vision is a scientific community that does not waste resources on recreating data that have already been produced, in particular if public money had helped to collect those data in the first place. Scientists should be able to concentrate on the best ways to make use of the data. Data become an infrastructure that scientists can use on their way to new frontiers.
>
> (Kroes cited in HLEG 2010: 2)

The RS and HLEG documents also link openness to various democratic values such as equality and citizen empowerment. The RS document considers the availability of publicly funded data to citizens to be a necessary step in ongoing changes in the technological, social and political environment. 'Recent decades have seen an increased demand from citizens, civic groups and non-governmental organisations for greater scrutiny of the evidence that underpins scientific conclusions, particularly where these have the potential for major impacts on individuals and society' (RS 2012: 22). Openness will enable citizens to verify and discuss scientific claims, the RS maintains, while the available scientific data will also support them in holding authorities to account. The HLEG remarks in this regard, 'Citizens can share and contribute to the scientific process. They understand the benefits and risks of technologies better, and more rational political decisions emerge' (2010: 27). At the same time, open access to research data should enable citizens to participate in scientific practices, according to both the RS and HLEG documents.

> Access to data that fulfils the requirements of accessibility, intelligibility, assessability and usability is important for citizens' involvement in science and their pursuit of scholarship through data which, after all, for publicly funded science they have paid for through their taxes.
>
> (RS 2012: 39)

In establishing the moral dimension of openness, the three documents make their case that openness is not only a necessary outcome of autonomous social and technological developments, it is also a core value to which the scientific community should aspire. More open research data would lead to better and more efficient science, would empower citizens, and would boost innovation and economic growth.

The three documents, nevertheless, qualify openness and recognise that not all data can or should be open. In some contexts, other values, such as privacy, security, and safety, outweigh openness. The RS writes,

> Opening up scientific data is not an unqualified good. There are legitimate boundaries of openness, which must be maintained in order to protect commercial value, privacy, safety and security [...] this report recommends a balanced and proportionate approach rather than a blanket prohibition.
>
> (RS 2012: 9)

Similarly, the HLEG argues, 'the data must be available to whomever, whenever and wherever needed, yet still be protected if necessary by a range of constraints including by-attribution licenses, commercial license, time embargos or institutional affiliation' (2010: 18).

Each of the three documents presents scenarios for open access to research data, and they share common elements that outline a particular narrative about open research data and revolutionary changes in science. Openness in this narrative is a prerequisite for new ways of doing data-driven science and its supporting infrastructure. It is about the seamless exchange of heterogeneous digital data in large-scale, technology-enabled, cross-disciplinary and international networks of collaborating researchers and institutions. In these networks, it is a moral norm to share data in order to achieve fast-paced scientific progress and innovation, while empowering citizens and boosting economic growth. Access to and use of digital data should be easy and instantaneous. This narrative, however, paints a rather abstracted and monolithic view of research data in scientific and scholarly practices.

Openness in practice

The discussions in the previous two sections show how visions of open data point to potential benefits in making data open in scientific research and what that would look like, broadly defined. In this section, we critically reflect on the narrative outlined in the three documents, by discussing how scientific practice informs what openness means, at the conceptual and practical levels. We consider what it entails to acknowledge diversity and be sensitive to the needs of particular disciplines (Noorman *et al.* 2014). To do this, we draw on examples from five disciplines that we examined as part of the research project described earlier: archaeology, environmental sciences, particle physics and particle astrophysics, health and clinical research, and bioengineering (Sveinsdottir *et al.* 2013). These disciplines present different ways in which open data can be conceptualised in technical, organisational and moral dimensions.

In this section we demonstrate that the technological, organisational and moral aspects of open data are embedded and enacted differently in different practices. By research practice we mean the discipline-specific knowledge bases, technical tools, research teams, labs and culture, as well as ethics and moral positions. Studies in science and technology have shown that knowledge is produced through the work of particular scientific communities that form particular epistemic cultures (Knorr Cetina 1999). Knorr Cetina defines epistemic cultures as 'those amalgams of arrangements and mechanisms – bonded through affinity, necessity, and historical coincidence – which, in a given field, make up how we know what we know' (1999: 1). She highlights the distinctiveness of particular disciplines in the sciences and the range of epistemic cultures in order to demonstrate that science is not one tightly coherent whole. She argues that the enterprise of science has 'a geography of its own. In fact it is not one enterprise but many, a whole landscape – or market – of independent epistemic monopolies producing vastly different products' (1999: 4). The way data are produced is shaped by the values and norms of research practice within different disciplines (Leonelli 2014). Following from established research practice, each discipline or sub-discipline has its own epistemic culture from which it develops open data norms and practices.

During our research project, we encountered various differences in data-sharing practices (Sveinsdottir *et al.* 2013). Archaeology has relatively limited experience of sharing data and open data, whereas bioengineering is very open in terms of sharing models and methods but not raw data. Health and clinical studies share data within specific trusted collaborations, but they have strict ethical frameworks that prevent making patient and sensitive data open. The particle physics community has a longer history in sharing data within large-scale collaborations, often based on the collective use of large-scale research equipment, for example, telescopes and large hadron colliders. Its experience in making research data open to people and organisations within a wider collaboration is based on the need to share the costs and use of expensive equipment. Furthermore, the knowledge required to understand and analyse the data is both vast and varied, hence the need to draw on experts from around the world who may not have been part of a particular project. Environmental sciences, due to their broad focus, encapsulating climate, forestry, maritime, and other types of data, also have a longer history in making data open. For this community the key challenge is the integration and interoperability of different data sources and formats.

The focus on research practice provides insights into how data sharing and open research data are constituted and constructed within different scientific disciplines. Swidler (2001) argues that practices produce and reproduce the way knowledge is understood and how that knowledge is shared within epistemic communities. Practices serve to reproduce the 'rules' of each domain by 'people acting strategically in a world that presumes those rules' (Swidler 2001: 91). Practices are therefore located within their specific contexts and epistemic cultures and in that sense practices are anchored in knowledge domains. In practical terms the ways in which research disciplines create and develop practice is seen in the work done in projects, in research handbooks, in the methods sections of journal articles, and in the training of doctoral students.

By addressing the ways in which research practice shapes the way data are produced we can assess some of the limitations of the policy documents regarding open access to research data along the technological, organisational and moral dimensions. First, the documents seem to assume that data can travel, and be understood, relatively easily between contexts, once the right technology is in place. Second, they seem to suggest that large-scale collaborations are the preferred organisational form for scientific endeavours. Third, the documents prioritise a too-limited set of values and overlook the conflicts that may occur between values present within different research practices and domains. In the sets of practices that make up the broad church of 'research', we show that openness means different things and it will be practised in a variety of ways. It is thus through the practices of research that openness is negotiated.

Technological dimension: data as commodity

In order for the visions presented in the policy documents of open data seamlessly travelling across data infrastructures to materialise, data need to be interoperable and standardised. In elaborating this technological dimension of openness, the documents build on a narrow conception of data that obscures complexities of research data in particular scientific disciplines.

Making data interoperable, standardised, using non-proprietary formats, turns out to be more difficult than the visions in the documents suggest; not only in the humanities and the social sciences, but also in the natural and life sciences (Borgman 2015; Edwards *et al.* 2011). 'Research data are complex sociotechnical objects that exist within communities, not simply commodities that can be traded in a public market' (Borgman 2015: 213). Research data acquire meaning and value within particular contexts and data standards may differ between and even within scientific disciplines. Researchers from different disciplines in a collaborative research project may have very different conceptions of what data are significant and how they need to be stored (see also Edwards *et al.* 2011; Leonelli 2009). These complexities are mostly overlooked in the reports. The reports acknowledge the multifaceted character of data, introducing data pyramids and other categorisations of data. They also stress the importance of metadata. Nevertheless, they treat data as objects that can be easily extracted from their context, packaged and transported across various cultural, disciplinary and technological boundaries.

Even in disciplines in which sharing data has an obvious importance, it can be difficult to establish commonly shared standards. This is a considerable challenge in archaeology, for example. The richness of archaeology datasets means that categorisation and attendant information needs to be provided for each dataset (Hantman and Most 2006). 'Research data does not stand alone and in order for it to be meaningful for any potential user, standardisation of language, clarity of annotation, models, methods, metadata and context will need to be supplied' (Sveinsdottir *et al.* 2013: 75). Yet few general standards exist in this discipline and interoperability is problematic (see also Borgman 2015). This is the result of particular research practices within the discipline and its sub-disciplines.

> We have faced more challenges … within archaeology, people who collect and analyse ceramics – I think it may be because bone data is so standardised in so many ways that it is easier for people to see the benefits of sharing it and using other people's data but perhaps there are other areas, like ceramics, where it is more idiosyncratic – you have your own method and your own way of describing them.
>
> (Senior researcher, Archaeology)

Archaeology involves some overarching principles, but research practice and data collection need to be adapted to the context within which the research takes place. The discovery, collection and understanding of the data are anchored both within practice as well as in a physical environment. They need not only to be discovered and categorised, they also need to be interpreted and contextualised. Archaeological work on-site excavations yields data in different formats, for example, field diaries, artefacts, spatial data, images and measurement data. The (re-)use of these data requires background information (metadata) for handwritten excavation diaries, spreadsheets that may not be uniform given the richness of the data, or contain site-specific abbreviations that may need further explanation from the authors. The researchers to whom we spoke feel that archaeology is a very personal undertaking because they work on a site for a long period of time, inductively explore the site, and adapt their research practices to the site. Sharing and opening data, thus, require approaches that are sensitive to these considerations and data specificities in order to capture the richness of the data. It requires specialised tools and particular collaborations (e.g. information management), which can design research and data collection plans for each particular site, on the basis of its history and context.

Another complexity regarding data that the policy documents overlook is that interoperability and standardisation do not necessarily allow for reuse and interpretation by others. Our research within particle physics shows that sometimes data are neither comprehensible nor meaningful outside of the context in which they are generated, even if they are highly standardised and interoperable (Sveinsdottir *et al.* 2013). Particle physics data are produced in vast quantities, they are numerical, computer-generated and analysed using complex and custom-made equipment, hardware and software, which are built and programmed by scientists. Much of the research data are generated by particle physics detectors, in which the tracking and measuring of particles is undertaken. The data analysis requires a grid approach, which requires the power of thousands of interconnected machines around the world. Therefore, highly standardised data and interoperability are an integral part of particle physics experiments.

Yet, open access, in the case of particle physics, is not only about the data but involves technical, theoretical and organisational capacity, as one researcher expressed:

> If you were to try to make the raw data available to outsiders you would have to make available the raw data, the reconstruction programs, the simulation and its database, the programs that handle the simulation and you would need to ensure there was access to the physics generators which are usually written by theorists and not the experimenters who wrote the experimental simulation and it just gets too complicated.
>
> (Senior Researcher, Particle Physics)

There is an established culture of sharing in this research community; however, the move to making data more open has proven to be difficult due to its volume and complexity. In the few instances that data have been made open, the researchers found that those trying to understand the data had to speak to the physicist who had carried out the experiment, in order to clarify the context within which the experiment was conducted. Although access was straightforward, the data were neither usable nor intelligible without an explanation.

> The data was public but you needed an insider's viewpoint to use it so it was not very public. (...) It was just the problem of knowing the data well,

then some things are obvious to you, they are not necessarily obvious to someone who does not know the experiment. It is like trying to write an instruction manual for something you do all the time.

(Senior Researcher, Particle Physics)

This example demonstrates that data cannot be easily reused outside their context of production, even if the technology is available and standards are in place.

The official reports sketch scenarios of research data moving seamlessly from one context to the next as a result of standardisation and interoperability as well as technological infrastructure. However, a closer look at research practices reveals that data may be difficult to standardise, and considerable time, effort and expertise are needed to make data open in this way. Not all data can be standardised or made interoperable because of disagreements about what data are or the difficulties in making them accessible and reusable. Moreover, data cannot be easily extracted from the context in which they were generated, for reuse. Disciplines will need to find their own tools and (technological) solutions for data sharing and openness.

Organisational dimension: large-scale collaboration

Research data and technologies that support their generation, dissemination, use and interpretations exist within variously organised and governed networks of researchers and institutions. The assumption underlying the organisational dimension of openness in the three documents, that scientific practices will necessarily become more international and collaborative with a bigger role for institutions, is problematic because it conflates a range of different scientific practices and histories. It prioritises a particular normative idea about what scientific collaboration should look like: large scale and data-driven, rather than small scale and hypothesis- or theory-driven projects. Moreover, the three documents suggest that open research data would stimulate researchers and institutions to work together, but in some cases it might undermine collaborative projects. A closer look at research practices shows that collaboration takes varying forms that produce different conceptions of open research data.

The way in which research is organised varies by (sub-)discipline. There is a range of configurations that combine different levels of scale. For instance, a bioengineering project such as the Virtual Physiological Human project requires large-scale collaboration because the scale of the problem is too big for any single research group (2015). Yet it takes the form of individual groups working on their own part of the jigsaw, as well as collaborative projects, which include several research groups. The approach is far from monolithic, and much of the collaboration takes the form of the research community developing standards, making tools available, and sharing models. Other research fields require smaller scale or even individual exploration. In the STEM fields, this is particularly the case for the underpinning mathematics, which is often the result of individual work. It is understood by few people, and may take decades before it becomes an important part of scientific research and technological innovations.

Collaboration may even lead to exclusion or limit the availability of data in some research practices. The organisation of research in particle physics tends to be large-scale collaborative research with tens or even hundreds of international partners working together. For example, the European Organisation for Nuclear Research (known by its French abbreviation, CERN) has 21 member states and over 2400 staff members. More than 600 universities and research institutions around the world make use of CERN's facilities (CERN 2015). However, only those in the global CERN community involved in particular experiments can access data produced by particle accelerators and detectors. Access to the data is the incentive for participating in an experiment at CERN for years without immediate results:

> Now, clearly, there is a mood amongst governments and funding agencies that takes a more open view of the data and we're not unaware of that, but what we can't do is an immediate transition that says, 'We take the data and then anybody that likes can suddenly analyse this stuff' because that would completely undermine the vast amounts of effort that are required by the people who analyse the data to collect the data and to maintain the detector and to upgrade the detector. [...] There is a reward system that is built in.
> (Physicist member of the ATLAS experiment at CERN, particle physics)

The privilege to be the first to analyse the data is part of how most of the experiments in CERN are organised. Making the data more open would diminish one important incentive for researchers and member countries to invest time and money in these large-scale experiments.

In disciplines where large-scale collaborations are more common, collaborations often consist of multiple partners with different disciplinary backgrounds and interests. The way that these collaborations make research data open is the result of ongoing negotiations between partners with their particular interests and ambitions. These interests may include ownership of data. The environmental sciences provide an illustrative example here. The organisation of environmental research varies from that at the level of a university department to large-scale developments, such as pan-European institutions and initiatives. As a field, environmental research is multidisciplinary, and addresses complex grand challenges (e.g. climate change), and thus requires the integration of diverse data from different scientific fields (e.g. biology, agricultural research, meteorology and forestry) as well as from commercial and public administrative partners. A key motivation for making data available through open access is the prospect of integrating datasets from the different disciplines, time periods and geographical locations to produce new environmental knowledge. Nevertheless, open data in the environmental sciences is not a free market nor a space without responsibility; rather the openness of data and the collaborations they enable are achieved through agreed and shared governance principles (Finn *et al.* 2014).

The consensus about the need for open data is fostering developments in both legal and technical areas to support openness. These areas present significant barriers especially when dealing with different interests and data in different formats and from different sources (e.g. governments, research institutions etc.).

The Global Earth Observation System of Systems (GEOSS) is one initiative that has made progress in the area of governance of open data (Group on Earth Observation 2015). In seeking to link environmental data, GEOSS found that a priority was to put in place governance agreements on how data should be shared. These agreements then shaped the way in which decisions could be made about data formats, interoperability and data reuse (Noorman *et al.* 2014). In particular, it established GEOSS Data-CORE principles in 2010, which were extended in 2014. These cover a range of open data principles including that data are free of restrictions on reuse, that user registration or login to access or use the data is permitted, that attribution of the data provider is permitted as a condition of use, and marginal cost recovery charges (i.e. not greater than the cost of reproduction and distribution) are permitted (Doldirina *et al.* 2014: 19–22). The principles also state that any waiver or licence should be valid under the laws of as many different jurisdictions as possible and should be available in different languages, at a minimum in the language(s) of the country/organisation making the data available, as well as in English. These guidelines have been established collaboratively through GEOSS and are based on the idea of governance that highlights the collective responsibility of scientists and scholars working within their epistemic culture.

A closer look at research practices thus shows that open research data are no guarantee for larger-scale international collaborations, nor are they the inevitable and necessary outcome. Large-scale international collaboration is one possible outcome, but for many research topics individual and small-scale projects are preferable. Moreover, collaborations often involve heterogeneous partners with their own interests and legal constraints. Access to data is thus the result of negotiations between particular partners that come up with governance principles, dependent on the characteristics of the field and the data. Especially in cases of commercial ownership such negotiations can take years.

Moral dimensions: conflicting values and norms

Data, technologies and the organisational structures in which they are embedded shape and are shaped by the moral values of research communities. The policy documents sketch enticing and morally persuasive scenarios of future scientific practices: open research data will result in better science to the benefit of society, while at the same time yielding higher returns on investment and maximising productivity. In sketching this scenario the reports prioritise particular values, such as reproducibility, quality, efficiency and effectiveness. Yet these values are ambiguous and may conflict in practice. In bioengineering, for example, the work of making research data open was seen as not contributing to efficiency. Sharing models and software code is an integral part of research practices in this discipline, but the researchers we interviewed agreed that access to raw data is much less developed (Sveinsdottir *et al.* 2013). One reason for this is that it requires significant extra work to annotate and prepare data for reuse, while the benefits and rewards for those who did were unclear. There would also be considerable work included in gaining ethical approval and informed consent for those researchers working with patient data. Researchers expressed concern that the data would not be meaningful to anyone outside of the field, as a potential user would need in-depth knowledge, expertise and specialised software in order to understand and work with the patient data. Making data open would thus impede efficiency and possibly the rate of scientific progress; and in such cases it makes more sense to share models and code than to share data. Such conflicts and how to deal with them receive little attention in the sweeping generalisations that the reports present.

Different values, norms and principles affect and shape scientific practices of data sharing and the level of openness of these data. Indeed, the policy documents recognise that openness is not without limits as it may conflict with concerns about privacy, security, safety or commercial value. Such concerns may warrant access control, according to the documents. For example, making research data open in health and clinical research raises ethical concerns about the involvement of human and vulnerable subjects. Such concerns have inspired researchers and institutions to develop sociotechnical access arrangements that allow for various levels of access control. Access to research data might require an application process or a more informal email request. The concerns have also led to initiatives to develop research practices that rely on new kinds of consent from research participants (see, for example, Lunshof *et al.* 2008). Such arrangements can be found in various disciplines and they are usually shaped by the practices in which they are embedded.

Negotiations about the conflicts between various values prevalent in particular disciplines or fields give rise to different kinds of access arrangements and governance structures. Although the three documents identify privacy, security, and safety as values that set bounds on openness, they leave unexplored other values that shape research practices and the way researchers engage with and share their data. For example, the autonomy of researchers and the originality of research significantly influence data-sharing practices in some disciplines (Borgman 2015). Standards and interoperability requirements can present substantial methodological constraints in such disciplines. They may facilitate the availability of data, but they can also limit the flexibility researchers have to determine their research design and data management. When researchers have to fit their data to standardised formats, in order to make them better accessible and reusable, the quality of their data may be significantly affected. Sometimes, as one of the repository managers in archaeology whom we interviewed notes, it is preferable to let the autonomy of researchers prevail over efficiency:

> I'm very much in favour of different stakeholder communities maintaining their own information systems and repositories where the communities have

more direct control over governance issues. It's more expensive, less efficient to be sure, since it means many more systems that need to be maintained and standards will be harder to implement. But the key point is [...] trying to maximise autonomy and ethical approaches toward data management, and that's not necessarily going to be the cheapest or most efficient approach.

(Repository manager, Archaeology)

The responsibility of researchers towards their research participants or those affected by their research is another key value that has a significant influence on data sharing (Mauthner and Parry 2013). Concerns about unintended secondary uses or misinterpretation can motivate researchers or research communities to establish governance structures for data sharing. Data that are used in ways that researchers did not intend can potentially damage identities, reputations and relationships between individuals, and may even endanger research subjects or sites. For instance, misinterpretations of publicly available medical health data can put patients at risk. To evaluate and interpret such research data generally requires considerable knowledge and expertise, especially when they are used to decide on medical diagnosis and treatment (see, for example, McGuire *et al.* 2008). Unintended use of personal data about research participants' ethnic or racial origins, political opinions, sexuality, religious beliefs, criminal background, or physical or mental health may result in stigmatisation, discrimination or other kinds of harm (see Schneider, Chapter 8 in this volume). In addition, research participants may feel wronged or betrayed when their expectations about the use of their information do not match the intentions and practices of new studies. Another concern is that unanticipated or unintended uses may harm the reputation of researchers and public trust in science or social institutions (Finn *et al.* 2014).

Research communities have established governance structures that help monitor and mitigate the risks of data sharing and making research data open. In archaeology, for instance, researcher communities have instituted review and editorial boards that include local communities or local governments to review requests for data (Finn *et al.* 2014: 54). In another field, a physician and policymaker whom we interviewed described how the public release of data about hospital performance led to problematic claims about the ranking of different hospitals in the media, despite the fact that the observed differences were not statistically significant. The interviewee pointed out that as a result researchers had to learn how to communicate about their data to a wider audience:

It took a long time to sort that out and to make people understand that you cannot draw conclusions like that. So it is very important that if you present to people who are not in science or journalists or other people that they don't over-interpret data. So we have to be very humble about what you see.

(Physician and policymaker, Health)

The responsibility of researchers may thus lead to access arrangements that not only control the level of access, but also embed the data within communication strategies, protocols, legal licences and other methods to influence what happens to the data. It is, thus, another important value that may compete with and shape openness.

In this section, we have shown that scientific practices are characterised by their heterogeneity and this heterogeneity gives rise to different conceptions of openness and various ways of dealing with and sharing data. Although the three policy documents acknowledge the heterogeneity of scientific practices, the implications remain unexplored. They present a narrow and abstracted conception of the technological, organisational and moral dimensions of openness that do not match well with actual research practices in different fields. It is important that in furthering open data, the concept of openness and what that means in practice, for different disciplines, be differentiated in order to create appropriate access arrangements and governance structures.

There are strong similarities between the issues facing openness with regard to research data and Big Data discourses more generally. Heterogeneity of practices also plays an important role in conceptualising Big Data in the public and private sectors along the technological, organisational and moral dimensions. Organisations may, for example, vary in their technical capacity (equipment and skills) to process large volumes of heterogeneous data, make them open, or use and interpret them appropriately. Many large corporations may have vast data sets, which are only used internally, while smaller and medium-sized companies may struggle to access data sets from which to draw value. Looking at the organisational aspects, for example, may help to shed light on the gap between Big Data promises and how sharing data between different governmental departments, or between government and commercial companies, works out in practice. Along the moral dimension, conceptions of Big Data and its relevance may vary as a result of the values that organisations or companies prioritise, such as the conflict between data accuracy and efficiency or privacy and cost-reduction. The three dimensions can, thus, also help to bring into view the disparities between different Big Data practices.

Conclusion

In this chapter, we have examined three influential policy documents that promote open research data, focusing on how they conceptualise openness along three dimensions: technological, organisational and moral. These documents share a similar narrative, in which open access to research data is the necessary and inevitable outcome of current developments. Openness will enable large-scale and global collaborations supported by technological data infrastructures that will help to solve grand societal challenges, accelerate scientific progress, and open up new avenues for scientific research. Data will be shared seamlessly across national and interdisciplinary boundaries. In these visionary narratives, open access to research data is not only an outcome but also a moral duty that can only be trumped by justified concerns for privacy, security, safety or commercial value. These utopian narratives echo similar Big Data promises discussed elsewhere in this volume.

The overarching policy drive reflected in the documents we have analysed seeks to support the ways in which research data might be used in new ways to benefit wider society and for it to have commercial value. The policy drive is to extend and enhance the role of academic research beyond its current role by changing the processes through which research outputs and findings can be exploited. In particular it seeks to facilitate the use of data for a wide range of societal stakeholders.

However, as our discussion shows, policy visions about open research data can, and often do, conflict with existing practices and conceptions of openness, as they are based on abstracted notions of research and prioritise certain values over others. Policy visions tend to draw upon a few examples of good practice and extrapolate them to other areas of research, thus ignoring the heterogeneity of scientific and scholarly practices. They also overlook the diversity of access arrangements and governance structures that have already emerged in various fields and that give new meaning to openness and what data sharing is intended to accomplish. Many different research communities have already developed their own standards, sharing practices, validation methods and incentives. They construct their own conceptions of openness, which manifest in different configurations of the technological, organisational and moral dimensions of open research data.

We suggest that open access to research data has the potential to be beneficial for science, industry and society, but only if openness is allowed to be defined and take shape within different epistemic communities with their own research practices and processes. The policy documents suggest that established practices will have to change. Moreover, to ensure data quality and responsible use of data beyond the individual researchers or groups involved in the data production we have to move beyond changing very individual and local research practices towards changes at the institutional level. Translating such visions of change into policy decisions, regarding, for example, funding or institutional structures, requires that these decisions take account of and allow for the heterogeneity of research practices and conceptions of openness. Not doing so runs the risk of constraining creativity and the richness of research. Moreover, it can affect the quality and validity of data and may even lead to harm, for both research subjects and researchers.

Although openness is a value held by many researchers, they are nonetheless also aware of the moral responsibility of practising science and developing data. Research practice in all its variations seeks to reduce the possibility of harm by reviewing and checking the validity of the data and its interpretation as well seeking to consider the limits of claims made by members of the science community. This, of course, is an imperfect process, as the history of science shows, but it remains important. In encouraging and developing open access to research data, it is therefore crucial that institutions not only consult but also collaborate with research communities to develop policies that are sensitive to the needs of a particular field of research.

The technological, organisational and moral dimensions of open access can help to structure the explorations and negotiations about what openness can and should mean in a particular field. These interlinked dimensions provide an analytical tool that helps to better understand the different practices and conceptions of openness. The technological dimension directs attention to the different ways in which openness can be conceived in terms of the technologies that support data sharing in particular contexts. The organisational dimension places the focus on the various informal and institutionalised relations between the different stakeholders involved in making research data open. The moral dimension in turn highlights the various values and how they may conflict or be balanced. Examining how these three dimensions work together provides insight into what is required to change particular practices in order to facilitate the sharing of high-quality data in a responsible way with a broader range of stakeholders. In a similar way, these three dimensions can elucidate the heterogeneity of Big Data practices throughout the public and private sectors.

Acknowledgements

This chapter is based on research done as part of the project Policy Recommendations for Open Access to Research Data in Europe (RECODE) funded by the European Union's Seventh Framework Programme for research, technological development and demonstration under grant agreement no. 285593.

Notes

1 See the project website for all deliverables and further information about the project: http://recodeproject.eu/ (accessed 22 July 2017).
2 This echoes several of the Big Data promises of creating new kinds of knowledge and practices.

References

Borgman, C. (2015). *Big Data, Little Data, No Data. Scholarship in the Networked World.* Cambridge, MA: MIT Press.
Borup, M., Brown, N., Konrad, K. and Van Lente, H. (2006). The Sociology of Expectations in Science and Technology. *Technology Analysis and Strategic Management,* 18(3/4), pp. 285–298.
Brown, N., Rip, A. and Van Lente, H. (2003). Expectation in and about Science and Technology. *Expectations in Science and Technology, 13th–14th June 2003* Utrecht, The Netherlands. Available at: www.york.ac.uk/satsu/expectations/Utrecht%202003/Backgroundpaper%20version%2014May03.pdf. [Accessed 22 July 2017].
CERN (2015). About CERN. *CERN Website.* Available at: http://home.web.cern.ch/about. [Accessed 25 September 2015].
De Wilde, R. (2000). *De Voorspellers: Een Kritiek op de Toekomstindustrie.* Amsterdam: De Balie.
Doldirina, C., Eisenstadt, A., Onsrud, H. and Uhlir, P. (2014). *White Paper: Mechanisms to Share Data as Part of GEOSS Data-CORE.* Available at: www.earthobservations. org/documents/dswg/Annex%20VI%20-%20%20Mechanisms%20to%20share%20 data%20as%20part%20of%20GEOSS%20Data_CORE.pdf. [Accessed 20 June 2016].

Edwards, P., Mayerik, M., Batcheller, A., Bowker, G. and Borgman, C. (2011). Science Friction: Data, Metadata, and Collaboration. *Social Studies of Science*, 41(5), pp. 667–690.

Finn, R., Wadhwa, K., Taylor, M., Sveinsdottir, T., Noorman, M. and Sondervan, J. (2014). Legal and ethical issues in open access to research data, RECODE D3.1, April 2014. Available at: http://recodeproject.eu/wpcontent/uploads/2014/05/D3.1-legal-and-ethical-issues-FINAL.pdf. [Accessed 22 July 2017].

Group on Earth Observation (2015). Available at: www.earthobservations.org/geoss.php. [Accessed 23 September 2015].

Hantman, J. and Most, R. (eds) (2006). *Managing Archaeological Data: Essays in Honor of Sylvia W. Gaines.* Anthropological Research Paper No. 57, Tempe, AZ: Arizona State University.

High Level Expert Group (2010). *Riding the Wave: How Europe can Gain from the Rising Tide of Scientific Data.* Final report of the High Level Expert Group on Scientific Data, October 2010. Available at: http://ec.europa.eu/information_society/news room/cf/document.cfm?action=display&doc_id=707. [Accessed 20 June 2016].

Kelty, C. (2009). Conceiving Open Systems. *Washington University Journal of Law & Policy*, 30(1), pp. 139–177.

Kennan, M. and Markauskaite, L. (2015). Research Data Management Practices: A Snapshot in Time. *The International Journal of Digital Curation*, 10(2). Available at: www.ijdc.net/index.php/ijdc/article/view/329. [Accessed 21 July 2017].

Knorr Cetina, K. (1999). *Epistemic Cultures. How the Sciences make Knowledge.* Cambridge, MA: Harvard University Press.

Kuipers, T. and Van der Hoeven, J. (2009). PARSE.Insight: Insight into Digital Preservation of Research Output in Europe: Survey Report. Retrieved from www.parse-insight.eu/downloads/PARSE-Insight_D3-4_SurveyReport_final_hq.pdf.

Lathrop, D. and Ruma, L. (2010). *Open Government: Collaboration, Transparency, and Participation in Practice.* Sebastopol, CA: O'Reilly Media.

League of European Research Universities (2013). *Roadmap for Research Data, Advice Paper*, No. 14. Available at: www.fosteropenscience.eu/content/leru-roadmap-research-data. [Accessed 22 July 2017].

Leonelli, S. (2009). On the Locality of Data and Claims about Phenomena. *Philosophy of Science*, 76, pp. 737–749.

Leonelli, S. (2014). Data Interpretation in the Digital Age. *Perspectives on Science*, 22(3), pp. 397–417.

Levin, N., Leonelli, S., Weckowska, D., Castle, D. and Dupré, J. (2016). How Do Scientists Define Openness? Exploring the Relationship between Open Science Policies and Research Practice. *Bulletin of Science, Technology & Society*, 36(2), pp. 128–141.

Leydesdorff, L. and Etzkowtiz, H. (1998). The Triple Helix as a Model for Innovation Studies. *Science & Public Policy*, 25(3), pp. 195–203.

Lunshof, J., Chadwick, R., Vorhaus, D. and Church, G. (2008). From Genetic Privacy to Open Consent. *Nature*, 9, pp. 406–411.

Mauthner, N. and Parry, O. (2013). Open Access Digital Data Sharing: Principles, Policies and Practices. *Social Epistemology: A Journal of Knowledge, Culture and Policy*, 27(1), pp. 47–67.

McGuire, A., Caulfield, T. and Cho, M. (2008). Research Ethics and the Challenge of Whole-Genome Sequencing. *Nature*, 9, pp. 152–156.

Merton, R.K. (1973). The Normative Structure of Science. In Merton R.K. (ed.) *The Sociology of Science: Theoretical and Empirical Investigations.* Chicago, IL: University of Chicago Press.

Molloy, J. (2011). The Open Knowledge Foundation: Open Data Means Better Science. *PLoS Biology*, 9(12).

Nelson, B. (2009). Empty Archives. *Nature*, 461, pp. 160–163.

Noorman, M., Kalaitzi, V., Angelaki, M., Tsoukala, V., Linde, P., Sveinsdottir, T., Price, L. and Wessels, B. Institutional barriers and good practice solutions, RECODE D4.1, September 2014. http://recodeproject.eu/wpcontent/uploads/2014/09/RECODE-D4.1-Institutional-barriers-FINAL.pdf. [Accessed 22 July 2017].

Nowotny, H., Scott, P. and Gibbons, M. (2001). *Re-thinking Science: Knowledge and the Public in an Age of Uncertainty*. Cambridge: Polity.

Organization for Economic Cooperation and Development (OECD) (2007). *OECD Principles and Guidelines for Access to Research Data from Public Funding*. Available at: www.oecd.org/sti/sci-tech/oecdprinciplesandguidelinesforaccesstoresearchdata-frompublicfunding.htm. [Accessed 15 November 2017].

Research Data Alliance (2014). *The Data Harvest. How Sharing Research Data Can Yield Knowledge, Jobs and Growth*. A special report by RDA Europe, December 2014. Available at: https://europe.rd-alliance.org/sites/default/files/report/TheDataHarvest Report_%20Final.pdf. [Accessed 20 June 2016].

Royal Society (2012). *Science as an Open Enterprise*. The Royal Society Science Policy Centre report 02/12, June 2012. Available at: https://royalsociety.org/~/media/royal_society_content/policy/projects/sape/2012-06-20-saoe.pdf. [Accessed 20 June 2016].

Stallman, R. (2002). *Free Software, Free Society: Selected Essays of Richard M. Stallman*. Boston, MA: Free Software Foundation.

Suber, P. (2012). *Open Access*. Cambridge, MA: MIT Press.

Sveinsdottir, T., Wessels, B., Smallwood, R., Linde, P., Kala, V., Tsoukala, V. and Sondervan, J. (2013). Stakeholder values and relationships within open access and data dissemination and preservation ecosystems, RECODE D1, September 2013. Available at: http://recodeproject.eu/wp-content/uploads/2013/10/RECODE_D1-Stakeholder-values-and-ecosystems_Sept2013.pdf. [Accessed 22 July 2017].

Swidler, A. (2001). What Anchors Social Practices? In Schatzki, T., Knorr Cetina, K. and Savigny, E. (eds) *The Practice Turn in Contemporary Theory*, 1st edn. London: Routledge, pp. 74–92.

Van de Poel, I. (2003). The Transformation of Technological Regimes. *Research Policy*, 32, pp. 49–68.

Virtual Physiological Human (2015). VPH Institute: Building the Physiological Virtual Human. Available at: www.vph-institute.org/documents.html. [Accessed 23 September 2015].

Wessels, B., Finn, R., Sveinsdottir, T. and Wadhwa, K. (2017). *Open Data and the Knowledge Society*. Amsterdam: Amsterdam University Press.

Wyatt, S. (2008). Technological Determinism is Dead; Long Live Technological Determinism. In Hackett, E., Amsterdamska, O., Lynch, M. and Wajcman, J. (eds) *Handbook of Science and Technology Studies*, 1st edn. Cambridge, MA: MIT Press, pp. 165–180.

Part IV

Postscript

15 Big Data's methodological challenges

Nicola Green

Introduction

In Chapter 1 of this volume, we attempted to map some of the challenges, tensions and contradictions in the definitions and characterisations of Big Data circulating both within and beyond research institutions, and as they are situated in wider social and cultural debates. The central questions raised in that chapter have certainly been considered before across social science research on Big Data: What is 'it'? Where do we look to find 'it'? What kinds of research approaches can adequately and effectively develop critical understandings of Big Data that can account for the complexities of human/technology/data relationships and interactions in Big Datascapes?

In that introductory chapter, and considering the development of arguments in the chapters throughout this volume, we have a number of – albeit necessarily partial and provisional – critical responses to some of those questions (although, of course, themselves dependent on the process of ongoing research). Considering the what, how, when, where and whom of Big Data in each grounded and situated case leads us through the complexities of principles, policies and practices in respect of Big Data (and the interaction between them). Furthermore, however, those questions also necessarily lead us to focus on our own research practices – as well as those of others – to consider the claims that can reasonably be made about Big Data, on the basis of the research questions that can be asked, those that are considered important, and how they might be articulated in research practice.

We began our consideration of Big Data by noting a (relatively) simple aphorism – that technologies and human societies are mutually shaping via constant processes of *intra-action*, and that the implications and effects of any such shaping and reshaping processes are unevenly distributed (Barad 2007; Sætnan *et al.*, Chapter 1, this volume). In the corpus of work on Big Data developed over the past few years, however, there is sometimes a tendency to treat Big Data as a noun, as a singular (technologically-based) object that acts in the world in a linear fashion. This is perhaps not surprising if we consider that one dimension of Big Data is its discursive framing across social domains concerned with the construction and outcomes of digitised networks and the accompanying complexities of ambient and ubiquitous computing. As was remarked in Chapter 1, under such conditions 'Big Data' at the very least serves as 'a socio-technical imaginary ... a meta-narrative to capture the present and future' (Sætnan *et al.*, Chapter 1, this volume). What nevertheless adds even more complexity to the investigation of Big Data is that – rather than being as singular as a meta-narrative might suggest – we stress the fact that *data* is plural, thereby implying multiple and layered objects, processes and practices. Big Data is articulated, enacted and embodied across a number of social and political dimensions simultaneously. As we argued, 'Big Data is constituted by a nexus of technologies – data-processing hardware and software and a myriad of digitised apparatuses and processes networked through a constant data flow, each element embedded into the varied ecologies of current society' (Sætnan *et al.*, Chapter 1, this volume).

It is therefore no coincidence that in Chapter 1 we stress processes rather than products – processes of *datafication* and *digitisation* – Big Data as a verb rather than a noun. Research methodologies towards analysis therefore need to account for specific identifiable processes (or sets of processes), located across bits and bytes, people and things, discourses and practices (Callon 1986; Latour 1987; Akrich 1992; Akrich and Latour 1992). As we also suggested in Chapter 1, these configurations locate Big Data politically with respect to research as much as any other domain of social enterprise: Big Data is a process (or sets of processes and practices) in much the same way that research itself is a process (or sets of processes and practices) – and each is therefore also and always mutually shaping.

The following arguments therefore review the contributions made to this volume in respect of Big Data's principles, policies and practices – and the politics thereby identified – with the specific aim of exploring the relationship between Big Data and the challenges those processes present for social research methodologies. Particular attention is therefore paid to issues in *in/visibilities*, *scales*, *locations* and *approaches* as crucial considerations to be accounted for in the design of research, and therefore in the politics of research.

The processes and politics of research

As has been emphasised throughout this collection, interdisciplinary researchers have variously engaged with social science, STS and Surveillance Studies approaches to critically evaluate the principles, policies and practices of Big Data across numerous social and cultural domains. The very articulation of these aims, however, serves to immediately engage in an epistemological politics that frames the very research questions we are able to ask of Big Data, with fundamental implications for the design of research on or with Big Data more broadly.

Research questions

As has already been noted, Big Data currently serves as a powerful cultural imaginary, a discourse that serves to 'scientise' a complex nexus of technological and social processes (boyd and Crawford 2012: 663). Such a mythology (Barthes 1972[1957]) promises the semblance of absolute knowledge via data: objectively generated authority by virtue of unlimited quantification in multiple directions. Its status as a mythology therefore necessarily produces its own *visibilities* and *invisibilities* – what phenomena can be intellectually perceived, critically interrogated and thereby investigated. The degree to which we accept the essential premises of these discourses fundamentally influences and shapes the politics of social research practice. In particular, our research practices are framed by the social and political configurations of Big Data that situate, contextualise and frame the very research questions we are able to ask.

A number of contributors throughout the volume have engaged with the critical epistemological politics that frame the possible research questions to be asked of Big Data. In his initial contribution to the volume, for example, Matzner (Chapter 3) goes to the very heart of critical issues with respect to the largely unquestioned logic of unparalleled quantification itself. Matzner's arguments raise a number of issues of *scale* in respect of epistemological questions. On the one hand, Matzner focuses on what might arguably be characterised as the 'smallest' of the activities and relationships that might be identified as constituting 'data' – the bits and bytes that comprise the process of computation itself. On the other hand, his analysis simultaneously emphasises the ways in which such small-scale phenomena are brought together via specific politically inflected technological and human processes – the formulation and deployment of algorithms – to underpin an entire algorithmic logic of Big Data at a macro-social and political scale. Matzner goes on to raise a series of critical questions about the transparency of data itself (questions related to data *in/visibilities*), but importantly with respect to the possibilities of, or claims towards, the 'objectivity' of Big Data in the context of its social and economic settings. Matzner argues that bias (and 'prediction' and its generalisation as operationalised bias) is inevitable when based on contextually defined relationships between human and non-human actants (Latour 1987; Matzner, Chapter 3 in this volume) in the form of algorithms, and that these relationships therefore have unevenly distributed implications in the form of social power and its attendant ethical relationships.

These arguments have inevitable consequences for the types of research question that can be asked or applied. If we accept Matzner's critical arguments that bias in Big Data is inevitable and consequential, the question that therefore remains in research practice pertains to where we then direct the research gaze, at any particular scale. At the 'smallest' scale of data, the relevant issues therefore refer to the degree to which social researchers are even able to identify (or indeed trace) the configurations of machine/human interactions that might introduce such biases in iterative data processing – such that we can pose meaningful research questions that will critically interrogate those relationships. At the 'biggest' scale, those questions pertain to the processes (and degrees) through which, in our research questions as posed, we are able to connect those 'smaller' material processes with wider concerns about social organisations and their concomitant politics in an algorithmic logic.

Sætnan (Chapter 2, this volume) echoes and extends a number of Matzner's points of critique, particularly with respect to the epistemic logics of Big Data. Specifically, Sætnan engages with these politics of knowledge with respect to the particular case of 'securitisation', and the potential for errors that contribute to resulting biases that feed into public debates about security and threat. What the particular case of securitisation illustrates with respect to the formulation of questions for research is the specific organisational configurations within which such logics are embedded, and which therefore impact any investigation that might be possible. Both Sætnan and Matzner's contributions reinforce the conclusion that while an algorithmic logic might provide a starting point to ask questions about large-scale populations, a deconstruction of such logic – as it is enacted in particular social contexts – demonstrates the ways that technological configurations such as those entailed in Big Data are shaped by pre-existing assumptions, as much as they shape 'new' forms of knowledge (however dubious they might be).

The epistemological insights derived from such detailed critical analyses of Big Data can be further deployed to reflexively consider the structure of our own research practices, and the methodological principles on which that research is based. Such insights caution researchers to carefully interrogate the epistemic foundations upon which their research questions are based. As we argued in Chapter 1, any attempt to define or categorise Big Data simultaneously enacts a normative existence or shape for Big Data, at the same time as potentially disrupting the ways that the social and technological processes concerned are defined and reproduced. As we also argued in Chapter 1, the several 'Vs' of Big Data as identified by Kitchin (2014) – volume, velocity, variety (and IBM's addition of a largely unquestioned 'veracity' – Sætnan *et al.*, Chapter 1, this volume) – each produce their own *in/visibilities* with respect to knowledge and the ways that it is shaped, as do considerations of scope, scale and relationality. Such framings are not, of course, unique to the case of Big Data – but in the face of extensive empirical complexity, such circumstances remind us that the research questions posed by social and political scientists need to pay detailed critical attention to the underlying assumptions built into their research approaches, and direct reflexive scrutiny at each stage of research to the epistemic politics underpinning the directions of their research endeavours.

Research design

The interrogation of the very premises of Big Data's claims to knowledge, and conceptual critiques directed at the definitions and characterisations of Big Data, both lead researchers to (re)evaluate the theoretical frameworks through which they approach their investigations, and on the basis of which any empirical research might be designed. As many contributors to this volume argue, any critical interventions with respect to Big Data need to account for theoretical or conceptual formulations we might already have available to understand not only what Big Data is, but also how it comes to be (re)created that way in processes of technological and social co-construction (including through our own research questions).

Strauß (Chapter 4), for example, elaborates the theme of 'securitisation' as touched on by Sætnan, including the themes of uncertainty and *in*security that constitute its corollaries. Strauß deconstructs 'security' with respect to both its status as a concept in discourse, and simultaneously as a set of power-laden techno-social processes that are currently intertwined with the enactment of Big Data. In doing so, he not only directs critique towards the limitations of algorithmic analytics' predictive powers (based on a number of empirical case studies), but also joins with Matzner's second contribution (Chapter 5) in both using and evaluating the notion of 'Surveillance' as a means of understanding the ways that Big Data is constructed and performed. Indeed, both Strauß, and Matzner in this latter piece, argue for a thoroughgoing interrogation of the limits of any current conceptual apparatus such as 'Surveillance' in an environment characterised by the complexities of Big Data. For all these contributors, epistemic deconstructions of (potentially dubious) knowledge production only go so far.

Examples of theoretical development can also be found elsewhere extensively throughout the collection: Simões and Jerónimo (Chapter 9) not only join Strauß and Matzner in exploring the conceptual limits of 'Surveillance', but also interrogate the notions of 'transparency' (of both citizen and data) and 'autonomy' (in the sense of political engagement) in respect of the role of Big Data in the potentially surveillant knowledge regimes of nation-states. In doing so, they mirror Rieder's (Chapter 6) concern to question linkages between the roles of transparency and autonomy in respect of 'the surveillant state', and contemporary formulations of 'democracy'. Both Pasquale (Chapter 7) and Schneider (Chapter 8) further link contemporary conceptualisations of 'democracy' in the context of Big Data to competing definitions of the 'public' or 'public sphere', especially with respect to the discourses and practices of extant regulatory regimes. Ochs (Chapter 13) takes these considerations even further when critically examining the notion of 'privacy' as a collective endeavour and social good. In the context of contemporary democratic political landscapes, Ochs deconstructs the tensions underlying privacy practices in an era of Big Data, and demonstrates the limits of individualised understandings of privacy under conditions of large-scale and ubiquitous data processing. In some ways Ochs's arguments serve to summarise a more widespread critical concern amongst all these contributors in their theoretical development to identify, understand and critique the potential social harms posed by Big Data analytics in the face of discourses of social goods so dominant in Big Data metanarratives.

In all of these contributions to theoretical development, conceptual evaluation is part and parcel of a wider concern to empirically ground any such discursive constructions in specific cases that are both demonstrable and verifiable. The theoretical frameworks and conceptual development on which our research is based inevitably have implications not only for the research questions we might ask, but also for the design of any empirical research that we might thereafter undertake. While theoretical development is one means through which we can explore what Big Data is – how it is constructed, and how it is enacted – where we ask questions that imply an empirical dimension, disciplinary (and/or inter-disciplinary) questions on method inevitably come to the fore.

One of the most enduring of those questions is the set of tools available within our research repertoires to apprehend and comprehend the complexities Big Data poses not only as an 'object' of investigation, but also for the practices and processes of socio-cultural research itself. There are, for example, degrees to which social and political scientists may themselves employ the analytic tech-niques implied in the logics of Big Data processing. In the current collection, Noorman *et al.* (Chapter 14) address exactly this point when they explore the conditions under which the 'products' of social research are considered as large (Big?) datasets that may (or may not) be widely accessible to researchers or publics of various sorts – depending on the ways in which they are generated, accessed and circulated amongst diverse epistemic communities (and their bodies of regulation and/or governance). The social benefits to accrue from such social science deployments of these data logics have yet to be fully evaluated, recognised, or perhaps appreciated – but nevertheless remain open to such questions.

However the case of 'Big' social science data in open contexts might play out, a decade ago Savage and Burrows (2007) pointed to a 'coming crisis in empirical sociology', both presaging the proliferation of Big Data logics (includ-ing within social science disciplines themselves), as well as highlighting the ways that the privatisation of data generation and its analysis dislodges the (for-merly) relatively privileged position of political and social scientists to access and interpret social data. What Savage and Burrows (2007) draw attention to here is particularly the reconfiguration of the role of (Big) Data in the newly data-driven economies of the early twenty-first century. Indeed, in their further contemplation of such issues, they remark (2009) that after the initial publication of their arguments, various representatives of both professional associations and public (including funding) bodies were in contact as to how, when and where social scientists might avail themselves of the relevant privately generated data sources.

The privatised generation and analysis of large datasets refers to what Thrift (2005) termed 'knowing capitalism', a configuration of social relations in which comprehensive and unparalleled processes of social and cultural digitisation underpin a radical reconfiguration – via data – of the relationships between capital, the state and citizens. Indeed, several chapters in this volume document these shifting relationships. Schneider (Chapter 8), for example, underpins her analysis of EU nation-state and supranational regulation of (privatised) Big Data practices with reference to the oligopolising tendencies of emerging platform and application-based data capital, and the power relations between states, busi-nesses and citizens that are thereby suggested (including the potential for social sorting in such relationships). Pasquale (Chapter 7) reinforces such an analysis with his consideration of the ways in which the public sphere itself becomes automated within what he characterises as 'communicative capitalism', and within which citizen-subjects become more generally subject to knowledge regimes.

The *location* of data – where it is held, whether it is private or public, whether it is propietary or open – is therefore paramount in any interrogation of Big Data: who has access, to what kinds of data, in any specific time, place and context. The privatisation of data in 'knowing capitalism' (Thrift 2005) therefore sets the scene for issues beyond simply 'research design', but what kinds of data collection might be possible, in any given context, at what times, places and locales within the context of the research questions we might ask of Big Data. Such questions furthermore raise issues with respect to the *locations* of *researchers*, and the kinds of questions any particular researchers might have in relation to the data concerned.

Data collection

Asking questions about the *locations* of both data and researchers leads us naturally to asking questions about how we as researchers would go about collecting relevant 'data' about 'Big Data' should we be in a position to do so. The *location* of data is of paramount concern here – that is, the degree to which any particular data are, as we comment in Chapter 1 of this volume, (another V) aVailable – whether or not social researchers are able to access any dataset, for any particular purposes. One question here might be about whether 'Big Datasets' are available to us as social researchers above and beyond their already politically inflected original usages (whether publicly or privately generated). Even beyond these questions, however, is the degree to which we might investigate Big Data in respect of its instanciation as a multiple and layered social phenomenon above and beyond its material and symbolic representation in datasets as such. That is, how do we investigate Big Data beyond the constraints presented by the structured parameters enacted by Big Datasets themselves?

The contributions to this volume present rich and varied empirical responses to such a question. Noorman *et al.* (Chapter 14) base their analysis of the 'openness' of large-scale data on the premise that the social and political sciences have always had their quantitative dimensions, albeit predicated on the fact that any such data are always theoretically derived, and are also open to contextually derived interpretation. Where the relevant research questions demand qualitative rather than quantitative empirical verification, a range of options is available to underpin any investigation. In this volume, for example, Tøndel and Sætnan (Chapter 10), in their analysis of popular media responses to the Snowden affair, demonstrate the nuance of understanding that might be derived from an in-depth treatment of textual sources in analyses that are sensitised to the layers of multiple discursive understandings available from such materials. Similarly, the analysis of policy and regulation in the domains of Big Data entail the thoroughgoing deconstruction of documentary evidence derived from publicly available documents with respect to governance and government, at a number of different and layered scales (see Schneider – Chapter 8, Pasquale – Chapter 7 and Rieder

– Chapter 6 in this volume). Textual analysis is, of course, not limited to written documentary texts. Bellanova and González Fuster (Chapter 11), for example, explore both popular cultural content on Netflix, as well as the means through which users' engagement with that content is monitored and assessed. The analysis of popular cultural 'texts' here, therefore, refer as extensively to audiovisual texts as the written word.

By way of contrast to a textually based analysis, Fleischhack's contribution (Chapter 12) on the enactment of digital political sovereignty amongst young people – and their popular education by 'hackers' – demonstrates the role that primary qualitative data collection in the form of ethnographic approaches might have in contributing towards our understandings of Big Data. Both Fleischhack's ethnographic contribution, as well as that of Bellanova and González Fuster, emphasise the ways in which researcher's own engagement with their data self-referentially positions them in multiple critical (and layered) ways with respect to the 'objects' of their research. Researchers are themselves members of the social groups to be interpellated with and by Big Data – whether that data takes the form of large-scale numbers that aggregate populations, or the form of bits of personal information and bytes about actions and activities, or the form of writing about the regulation of Big Data, or the form of popular cultural representations of Big Data and its social implications and effects. In different ways, all of these different 'embodiments' of Big Data position the researcher both as researcher, but also simultaneously as social subject. In doing so they thereby challenge social and political scientists to identify and self-reflexively position themselves in critical relationships with and to the very objects that they study.

Conclusions

Research is a collective enterprise, and as such this Postscript is an invitation for researchers and critics to collectively reflect upon how the methodological choices we make while investigating Big Data both shape, and are shaped by the very objects of our research and our orientations towards them. It is also an invitation for researchers to reflect upon how we go about building communities of research practice with respect to Big Data. The dimensions of in/visibilities, of scale, location and approach with respect to Big Data all draw our reflexive attention to the multiple ways in which we are positioned with respect to multiple objects and subjects of research, and hint at how our theoretical understandings might be enriched and enhanced via thoroughgoing and grounded empirical analyses.

The epistemic questions raised earlier in the volume prompt methodological considerations with respect to how researchers go about framing Big Data processes and politics as both objects and subjects of study. Upon reaching a characterisation of Big Data in Chapter 1 that attempted to encompass some of the multiple dimensions of Big Data available via social science and STS approaches, we noted that much of the data either generated or analysed in Big Datasets is 'personal' data – and that in Big Data, the personal is political.

The political inflections of the methodological choices we make therefore include the ways that we characterise the configuration of data and the ways in which they are enacted or embodied via things, people, actions, organisations and discourses. Necessarily, the location of the researcher and their relationship to the objects of their study in the design of methodological frameworks (and any related data collection) is therefore a similarly political process.

In Chapter 1, we identified the issue of scale as a fundamental in the definition and characterisation of Big Data: What sorts of digitisation processes culminate in Data that is 'Big'? How Big is Big? And what scales have implications and impacts for our data collection processes in research practice? A number of different ways to empirically address such questions have emerged throughout the volume. At the level of the algorithm, as Matzner (Chapter 3 in this volume) suggests, there are insights to be gained in amongst the 'deep infrastructures' of bits, bytes and the multiple layers of machine language through which they are organised. Similarly, some (at least partial) understandings might be gleaned from attention paid to the hybrid machine/human interactions that frame, produce and enact an underlying algorithmic logic. The organisational processes – whether public or private – that embody the principles, goals and outcomes of Big Data's algorithmic outputs (and the interpretation of them) are also potentially rich sites of social investigation. Similarly, the multiple layers of policy and regulation upon which algorithmic processes are based are also deserving of research attention, as are the extensive discursive formulations in different social settings that frame what Big Data is and what it does.

Finally, the politics of Big Data research are inevitably framed via the enactment of a final 'V' – how Value is performed and invested via Big Data processes. On the one hand, as we commented in Chapter 1, 'Data available to a given Big Data operator *may* be freely and openly available, but much is privately held, proprietary, confidential, even classified as secret. This of course entails that data now have commercial value…' (Sætnan *et al.* Chapter 1, this volume). If we can recognise and critically interrogate the politics of the *commercial* value of Big Data, we can similarly recognise and critically interrogate the *social* value of our own research. In doing so, we not only build Big Data research communities, but also recognise social and cultural research practice as a social good within a broader Politics of Big Data.

References

Akrich, M. (1992). The De-Scription of Technical Objects. In Bijker, W.E. and Law, J. (eds.) *Shaping Technology/Building Society*. Cambridge, MA: MIT Press: 205–224.

Akrich, M. and Latour, B. (1992). A Summary of a Convenient Vocabulary for the Semiotics of Human and Nonhuman Assemblies. In Bijker, W.E. and Law, J. (eds.) *Shaping Technology/Building Society*. Cambridge, MA: MIT Press: 259–264.

Barad, K. (2007). *Meeting the Universe Halfway: Quantum Physics and the Entanglement of Matter and Meaning*. Durham, NC and London: Duke University Press.

Barthes, R. (1972[1957]). *Mythologies*. London: Paladin.

boyd, d. and Crawford, K. (2012). Critical Questions for Big Data. *Information, Communication & Society*, 15(5): 662–679.

Callon, M. (1986). Some Elements of a Sociology of Translation: Domestication of the Scallops and the Fishermen of St Brieuc Bay. In Law, J. (ed.) *Power, Action and Belief: A New Sociology of Knowledge?* London: Routledge: 196–223.

Kitchin, R. (2014). Big Data, New Epistemologies and Paradigm Shifts. *Big Data & Society*, 1(1). Available at: http://journals.sagepub.com/doi/abs/10.1177/2053951714 528481. [Accessed 31 October 2017].

Latour, B. (1987). *Science in Action: How to Follow Scientists and Engineers through Society*. Cambridge, MA: Harvard University Press.

Savage, M. and Burrows, R. (2007). The Coming Crisis of Empirical Sociology. *Sociology*, 41(5): 885–899.

Savage, M. and Burrows, R. (2009). Some Further Reflections on the Coming Crisis of Empirical Sociology. *Sociology*, 43(4): 762–772.

Thrift, N. (2005). *Knowing Capitalism*. London: Sage.

Index

Page numbers in **bold** denote tables, those in *italics* denote figures.